CHEVY CAVALIER
BUICK SKYHAWK
CADILLAC CIMARRON
PONTIAC 2000 AND SUNBIRD
OLDS FIRENZA
1982-92

CHILTON'S

Covers all U.S. and Canadian models of Cadillac Cimarron, Chevrolet Cavalier, Buick Skyhawk, Oldsmobile Firenza and Pontiac 2000/Sunbird

by **Anthony Tortorici,** A.S.E., S.A.E.

CHILTON *Automotive Books*

PUBLISHED BY **HAYNES NORTH AMERICA, Inc.**

AUTOMOTIVE PARTS & ACCESSORIES ASSOCIATION MEMBER

Manufactured in USA
© 1992 Haynes North America, Inc.
ISBN 0-8019-8366-5 pbk
Library of Congress Catalog
0123456789 9876543

Haynes Publishing Group
Sparkford Nr Yeovil
Somerset BA22 7JJ England

Haynes North America, Inc
861 Lawrence Drive
Newbury Park
California 91320 USA

ABCDE
FGHIJ
KLMNO
PQRST

D0891090

CONTENTS

GENERAL INFORMATION and MAINTENANCE

ENGINE PERFORMANCE and TUNE-UP

ENGINE and ENGINE OVERHAUL

EMISSION CONTROLS

FUEL SYSTEM

CHASSIS ELECTRICAL

DRIVE TRAIN

SUSPENSION and STEERING

BRAKES

BODY

MECHANIC'S DATA

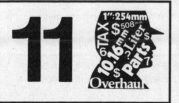

SAFETY NOTICE

Proper service and repair procedures are vital to the safe, reliable operation of all motor vehicles, as well as the safety of those performing repairs. This book outlines procedures for servicing and repairing vehicles using safe effective methods. The procedures contain many NOTES, CAUTIONS and WARNINGS which should be followed along with standard safety procedures to eliminate the possibility of personal injury or improper service which could damage the vehicle or compromise its safety.

It is important to note that repair procedures and techniques, tools and parts for servicing motor vehicles, as well as the skill and experience of the individual performing the work vary widely. It is not possible to anticipate all of the conceivable ways or conditions under which vehicles may be serviced, or to provide cautions as to all of the possible hazards that may result. Standard and accepted safety precautions and equipment should be used during cutting, grinding, chiseling, prying, or any other process that can cause material removal or projectiles.

Some procedures require the use of tools specially designed for a specific purpose. Before substituting another tool or procedure, you must be completely satisfied that neither your personal safety, nor the performance of the vehicle will be endangered.

Although the information in this guide is based on industry sources and is as complete as possible at the time of publication, the possibility exists that some car manufacturers made later changes which could not be included here. While striving for total accuracy, the authors or publishers cannot assume responsibility for any errors, changes or omissions that may occur in the compilation of this data.

PART NUMBERS

Part numbers listed in the reference are not recommendations by Haynes North America, Inc. for any product brand name. They are references that can be used with interchange manuals and aftermarket supplier catalogs to locate each brand supplier's discrete part number.

SPECIAL TOOLS

Special tools are recommended by the vehicle manufacturer to perform their specific job. Use has been kept to a minimum, but where absolutely necessary, they are referred to in the text by the part number of the tool manufacturer. These tools can be purchased, under the appropiate part number, from the Owatonna Tool Company, Owatonna, MN 55060 or an equivalent tool can be purchased locally from a tool supplier or parts outlet. Before substituting any tool for the one recommended, read the SAFETY NOTICE at the top of this page.

ACKNOWLEDGEMENTS

The publisher expresses appreciation to the Ford Motor Company for the technical information and pictures contained within this manual.

General Information and Maintenance

HOW TO USE THIS BOOK

Chilton's Repair Manual for the Chevrolet Cavalier, Buick Skyhawk, Cadillac Cimarron, Pontiac 2000 and Sunbird, and the Oldsmobile Firenza is intended to help you learn more about the inner workings of your vehicle and save you money on its upkeep and operation.

The first two Chapters will be the most used, since they contain maintenance and tune-up information and procedures. Studies have shown that a properly tuned and maintained car can get at least 10% better gas mileage than an out-of-tune car. The other Chapters deal with the more complex systems of your car. Operating systems from engine through brakes are covered to the extent that the do-it-yourselfer becomes mechanically involved. It will give you detailed instructions to help you change your own brake pads and shoes, replace spark plugs, and do many more jobs that will save you money, give you personal satisfaction, and help you avoid expensive problems.

A secondary purpose of this book is a reference for owners who want to understand their car and/or their mechanics better. In this case, no tools at all are required.

Before removing any bolts, read through the entire procedure. This will give you the overall view of what tools and supplies will be required. There is nothing more frustrating than having to walk to the bus stop on Monday morning because you were short one bolt on Sunday afternoon. So read ahead and plan ahead. Each operation should be approached logically and all procedures thoroughly understood before attempting any work.

All Chapters contain adjustments, maintenance, removal and installation procedures, and repair or overhaul procedures. When repair is not considered practical, we tell you how to remove the part and then how to install the new or rebuilt replacement. In this way, you at least save the labor costs.

Two basic mechanic's rules should be mentioned here. One, whenever the left side of the car or engine is referred to, it is meant to specify the driver's side of the car. Conversely, the right side of the car means the passenger's side. Secondly, most screws and bolts are removed by turning counterclockwise, and tightened by turning clockwise.

Safety is always the most important rule. Constantly be aware of the dangers involved in working on an automobile and take the proper precautions. See the section in Servicing Your Vehicle Safely and the SAFETY NOTICE on the acknowledgment page.

Pay attention to the instructions provided. There are 3 common mistakes in mechanical work:

1. Incorrect order of assembly, disassembly or adjustment. When taking something apart or putting it together, doing things in the wrong order usually justs cost you extra time; however, it CAN break something. Read the entire procedure before beginning disassembly. Do everything in the order in which the instructions say you should do it, even if you can't immediately see a reason for it. When you're taking apart something that is very intricate (for example, a carburetor), you might want to draw a picture of how it looks when assembled at one point in order to make sure you get everything back in its proper position. (We will supply exploded view whenever possible). When making adjustments, especially tune-up adjustments, do them in order; often, one adjustment affects another, and you cannot expect even satisfactory results unless each adjustment is made only when it cannot be changed by any order.

2. Overtorquing (or undertorquing). While it is more common for over-torquing to cause damage, undertorquing can cause a fastener to

vibrate loose causing serious damage. Especially when dealing with aluminum parts, pay attention to torque specifications and utilize a torque wrench in assembly. If a torque figure is not available, remember that if you are using the right tool to do the job, you will probably not have to strain yourself to get a fastener tight enough. The pitch of most threads is so slight that the tension you put on the wrench will be multiplied many, many times in actual force on what you are tightening. A good example of how critical torque is can be seen in the case of spark plug installation, especially where you are putting the plug into an aluminum cylinder head. Too little torque can fail to crush the gasket, causing leakage of combustion gases and consequent overheating of the plug and engine parts. Too much torque can damage the threads, or distort the plug which changes the spark gap.

There are many commercial products available for ensuring that fasteners won't come loose, even if they are not torqued just right (a very common brand is Loctite®). If you're worried about getting something together tight enough to hold, but loose enough to avoid mechanical damage during assembly, one of these products might offer substantial insurance. Read the label on the package and make sure the products is compatible with the materials, fluids, etc. involved before choosing one.

3. Crossthreading. This occurs when a part such as a bolt is screwed into a nut or casting at the wrong angle and forced. Cross threading is more likely to occur if access is difficult. It helps to clean and lubricate fasteners, and to start threading with the part to be installed going straight in. Then, start the bolt, spark plug, etc. with your fingers. If you encounter resistance, unscrew the part and start over again at a different angle until it can be inserted and turned several turns without much effort. Keep in mind that many parts, especially spark plugs, used tapered threads so that gentle turning will automatically bring the part you're treading to the proper angle if you don't force it or resist a change in angle. Don't put a wrench on the part until its's been turned a couple of turns by hand. If you suddenly encounter resistance, and the part has not seated fully, don't force it. Pull it back out and make sure it's clean and threading properly.

Always take your time and be patient; once you have some experience, working on your car will become an enjoyable hobby.

TOOLS AND EQUIPMENT

Naturally, without the proper tools and equipment it is impossible to properly service

you vehicle. It would be impossible to catalog each tool that you would need to perform each or any operation in this book. It would also be unwise for the amateur to rush out and buy an expensive set of tool on the theory that he may need on or more of them at sometime.

The best approach is to proceed slowly gathering together a good quality set of those tools that are used most frequently. Don't be misled by the low cost of bargain tools. It is far better to spend a little more for better quality. Forged wrenches, 6- or 12-point sockets and fine tooth ratchets are by far preferable to their less expensive counterparts. As any good mechanic can tell you, there are few worse experiences than trying to work on a car with bad tools. Your monetary savings will be far outweighed by frustration and mangled knuckles.

Begin accumulating those tools that are used most frequently; those associated with routine maintenance and tune-up.

In addition to the normal assortment of screwdrivers and pliers you should have the following tools for routine maintenance jobs:

1. SAE (or Metric) or SAE/Metric wrenches-sockets and combination open end-box end wrenches in sizes from $\frac{1}{8}$ in. (3 mm) to $\frac{3}{4}$ in. (19 mm) and a spark plug socket ($\frac{13}{16}$ in. or $\frac{5}{8}$ in. depending on plug type).

If possible, buy various length socket drive extensions. One break in this department is that the metric sockets available in the U.S. will all fit the ratchet handles and extensions you may already have ($\frac{1}{4}$ in., $\frac{3}{8}$ in., and $\frac{1}{2}$ in. drive).

2. Jackstands for support.
3. Oil filter wrench.
4. Oil filler spout for pouring oil.
5. Grease gun for chassis lubrication.
6. Hydrometer for checking the battery.
7. A container for draining oil.
8. Many rags for wiping up the inevitable mess.

In addition to the above items there are several others that are not absolutely necessary, but handy to have around. these include oil dry, a transmission funnel and the usual supply of lubricants, antifreeze and fluids, although these can be purchased as needed. This is a basic list for routine maintenance, but only your personal needs and desire can accurately determine you list of tools.

The second list of tools is for tune-ups. While the tools involved here are slightly more sophisticated, they need not be outrageously expensive. There are several inexpensive tach/dwell meters on the market that are every bit as good for the average mechanic as an expensive professional model. Just be sure that it goes to a least 1,200-1,500 rpm on the tach scale and that it works on 4, 6, 8 cylinder engines. (A special

You need only a basic assortment of hand tools for most maintenance and repair jobs tach is needed for diesel engines). A basic list of tune-up equipment could include:

1. Tach/dwell meter.
2. Spark plug wrench.
3. Timing light (a DC light that works from the car's battery is best, although an AC light that plugs into 110V house current will suffice at some sacrifice in brightness).
4. Wire spark plug gauge/adjusting tools.
5. Set of feeler blades.

Here again, be guided by your own needs. A feeler blade will set the points as easily as a dwell meter will read well, but slightly less accurately. And since you will need a tachometer anyway. . . well, make your own decision.

In addition to these basic tools, there are several other tools and gauges you may find useful. These include:

1. A compression gauge. The screw-in type is slower to use, but eliminates the possibility of a faulty reading due to escaping pressure.
2. A manifold vacuum gauge.
3. A test light.

As a final note, you will probably find a torque wrench necessary for all but the most basic work. The beam type models are perfectly adequate, although the newer click type are more precise.

Special Tools

Normally, the use of special factory tools is avoided for repair procedures, since these are not readily available for the do-it-yourself mechanic. When it is possible to preform the job with more commonly available tools, it will be pointed out, but occasionally, a special tool was designed to perform a specific function and should be used. Before substituting another tool, you should be convinced that neither your safety nor the performance of the vehicle will be compromised.

• A hydraulic floor jack of at least 1½ ton capacity. If you are serious about maintaining your own car, then a floor jack is as necessary as a spark plug socket. The greatly increased utility, strength, and safety of a hydraulic floor jack makes it pay for itself many times over through the years.

• A compression gauge. The screw-in type is slower to use but it eliminates the possibility of a faulty reading due to escaping pressure.

• A manifold vacuum gauge, very useful in troubleshooting ignition and emissions problems.

• A drop light, to light up the work area (make sure yours is Underwriter's approved, and has a shielded bulb).

• A volt/ohm meter, used for determining whether or not there is current in a wire. These are handy for use if a wire is broken somewhere and are especially necessary for working on today's electronics-laden vehicles.

As a final note, a torque wrench is necessary for all but the most basic work. It should even be used when installing spark plugs. The more common beam-type models are perfectly adequate and are usually much less expensive than the more precise click type on which you pre-set the torque and the wrench clicks when that setting arrives on the fastener you are torquing).

NOTE: *Special tools are occasionally necessary to perform a specific job or are recommended to make a job easier. Their use has been kept to a minimum. When a special tool is indicated, it will be referred to by a manufacturer's part number. and, where possible, an illustration of the tool will be provided so that an equivalent tool may be used. The tool manufacturer and address is: Service Tool Division Kent-Moore 29784 Little Mack Roseville, MI 48066-2298*

SERVICING YOUR CAR SAFELY

It is virtually impossible to anticipate all of the hazards involved with automotive maintenance and service, but care and common sense will prevent most accidents.

The rules of safety for mechanics range from "don't smoke around gasoline," to "use the proper tool for the job." The trick to avoiding injuries is to develop safe work habits and take every possible precaution.

Dos

• Do keep a fire extinguisher and first aid kit within easy reach.

• Do wear safety glasses or goggles when cutting, drilling, grinding or prying, even if you have 20-20 vision. If you wear glasses for the sake of vision, they should be made of hardened glass that can serve also as safety glasses, or wear safety goggles over your regular glasses.

• Do shield your eyes whenever you work around the battery. Batteries contain sulphuric acid. In case of contact with the eyes or skin, flush the area with water or a mixture of water and baking soda and get medical attention immediately.

• Do use safety stands for any undercar service. Jacks are for raising vehicles; safety stands are for making sure the vehicle stays raised until you want it to come down. Whenever the car is raised, block the wheels remaining on the ground and set the parking brake.

• Do use adequate ventilation when working with any chemicals or hazardous materials. Like carbon monoxide, the asbestos dust resulting from brake lining wear can be poisonous in sufficient quantities.

• Do disconnect the negative battery cable when working on the electrical system. The secondary ignition system can contain up to 40,000 volts.

• Do follow manufacturer's directions whenever working with potentially hazardous materials. Both brake fluid and antifreeze are poisonous if taken internally.

• Do properly maintain your tools. Loose hammerheads, mushroomed punches and chisels, frayed or poorly grounded electrical cords, excessively worn screwdrivers, spread wrenches (open end), cracked sockets, slipping ratchets, or faulty droplight sockets can cause accidents.

• Likewise, keep your tools clean; a greasy wrench can slip off a bolt head, ruining the bolt and often ruining your knuckles in the process.

• Do use the proper size and type of tool for the job being done.

• Do when possible, pull on a wrench handle rather than push on it, and adjust you stance to prevent a fall.

• Do be sure that adjustable wrenches are tightly closed on the nut or bolt and pulled so that the face is on the side of the fixed jaw.

• Do select a wrench or socket that fits the nut or bolt. The wrench or socket should sit straight, not cocked.

• Do strike squarely with a hammer; avoid glancing blows.

• Do set the parking brake and block the drive wheels if the work requires the engine running.

Don'ts

• Don't run the engine in a garage or anywhere else without proper ventilation-EVER!' Carbon monoxide is poisonous; it takes a long time to leave the human body and you can build up a deadly supply of it in your system by simply breathing in a little every day. You may not realize you are slowly poisoning yourself. Always use power vents, windows, fans or open the garage doors.

• Don't work around moving parts while wearing a necktie or other loose clothing. Short sleeves are much safer than long, loose sleeves; hard-toed shoes with neoprene soles protect your toes and give a better grip on slippery surfaces. Jewelry such as watches, fancy belt buckles, beads or body adornment of any kind is not safe working around a car. Long hair should be tied back under a hat or cap.

• Don't use pockets for toolboxes. A fall or bump can drive a screwdriver deep into your body. Even a wiping cloth hanging from the back pocket can wrap around a spinning shaft or fan.

• Don't smoke when working around gasoline, cleaning solvent or other flammable material.

• Don't smoke when working around the battery. When the battery is being charged, it gives off explosive hydrogen gas.

• Don't use gasoline to wash your hands; there are excellent soaps available. Gasoline may contain lead, and lead can enter the body through a cut, accumulating in the body until you are very ill. Gasoline also remove all the natural oils from the skin so that bone dry hands will such up oil and grease.

• Don't service the air conditioning system unless you are equipped with the necessary tools and training. The refrigerant, R-12, is extremely cold when compressed, and when released into the air will instantly freeze any surface it contacts, including your eyes. Although the refrigerant is normally non-toxic, R-12 becomes a deadly poisonous gas in the presence of an open flame. One good whiff of the vapors from burning refrigerant can be fatal.

• Don't use screwdrivers for anything other than driving screws! A screwdriver used as an prying tool can snap when you least expect it, causing injuries. At the very least, you'll ruin a good screwdriver.

• Don't use a bumper jack (that little ratchet, scissors, or pantograph jack supplied with the car) for anything other than chaining a flat! These jacks are only intended for emergency use out on the road; they are NOT designed as a maintenance tool. If you are serious about maintaining your car yourself, invest in a hydraulic floor jack of a least 1½ ton capacity, and at least two sturdy jackstands.

SERIAL NUMBER IDENTIFICATION

Vehicle

The vehicle identification number is a seventeen place sequence stamped on a plate at-

Always support the car on jackstands when working underneath it

The body identification plate looks like this

tached to the left front of the instrument panel, visible through the windshield.

Body

The body style identification plate is located on the front bar, just behind the right headlamp.

Engine

The engine VIN code is stamped on a pad at various locations on the cylinder block.

Explanation of a typical Vehicle Identification Number (VIN)

Engine serial number location—1.8L OHV

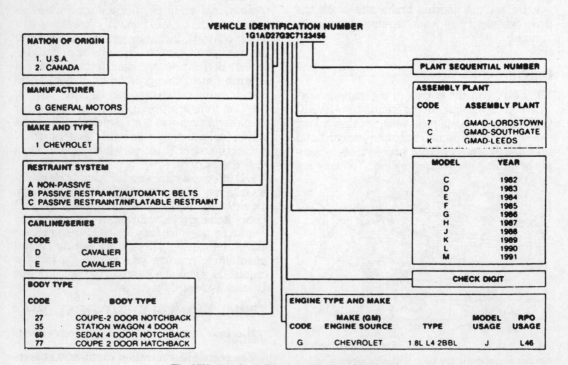

The VIN plate is visible through the windshield

Engine serial number locations—1982–86 2.0L OHV

1. VIN location   2. Engine code location

Engine serial number locations—1987–92 2.0L and 2.2L OHV

Engine serial number locations—1.8L, 2.0 OHC

1. Engine identification label locations
2. Verification label
3. Optional ID label

Engine label locations—1988–92 2.8L and 3.1L V6

1. VIN location   2. Engine code location

Engine serial number locations—1985–87 2.8L V6

1. VIN location   2. Engine code location

Engine serial number locations—1988–92 2.8L and 3.1L V6

VEHICLE IDENTIFICATION CHART

It is important for servicing and ordering parts to be certain of the vehicle and engine identification. The VIN (vehicle identification number) is a 17 digit number visible through the windshield on the driver's side of the dash and contains the vehicle and engine identification codes. The tenth digit indicates model year and the eighth digit indicates engine code. It can be interpreted as follows:

Engine Code						Model Year	
Code	Liters	Cu. In. (cc)	Cyl.	Fuel Sys.	Eng. Mfg.	Code	Year
G (1982)	1.8	110 (OHV)	4	2 bbl	Chevrolet	B	1981
O	1.8	110 (OHC)	4	TBI	Pontiac	C	1982
J	1.8	110 (OHC)	4	MFI Turbo	Pontiac	D	1983
B	2.0	121 (OHV)	4	①	Chevrolet	E	1984
P	2.0	121 (OHV)	4	TBI	Chevrolet	F	1985
M	2.0	121 (OHC)	4	MFI Turbo	GM-Brazil	G	1986
1	2.0	121 (OHV)	4	TBI HO	Chevrolet	H	1987
K	2.0	121 (OHC)	4	TBI	GM-Brazil	J	1988
H	2.0	121 (OHC)	4	MFI	GM-Brazil	K	1989
W	2.8	173	V6	MFI	Chevrolet	L	1990
G (1990–91)	2.2	134 (OHV)	4	TBI	Chevrolet	M	1991
T	3.1	192 (OHV)	V6	MFI	Chevrolet (U.S.A. and Canada)	N	1992
4	2.2	134 (OHV)	4	MFI	U.S.A.		

NOTE: Some 1983–85 Canadian models with the 2.0 Liter engine use a 2 bbl carburetor

The seventeen digit Vehicle Identification Number can be used to determine engine identification and model year. The tenth digit indicates model year, and the fourth digit indicates engine code.

HO—High Output
OHV—Overhead Valve engine
OHC—Overhead Cam engine
TBI—Throttle Body Injection
MFI—Multi-Port Fuel Injection
① 1982: 2 bbl carb.
   1983 and later: TBI

Transaxle

The manual transaxle identification number is stamped on a pad on the forward side of the transaxle case, between the upper and middle transaxle-to-engine mounting bolts. The automatic transaxle identification number is stamped on the oil flange pad to the right of the oil dipstick, at the rear of the transaxle. The automatic transaxle model code tag is on top of the case, next to the shift lever.

ROUTINE MAINTENANCE

Routine maintenance is the self-explanatory term used to describe the sort of periodic work necessary to keep a car in safe and reliable working order. A regular program aimed at monitoring essential systems ensures that the car's components are functioning correctly (and will continue to do so until the next inspection, one hopes), and can prevent small problems from developing into major headaches.

Routine maintenance also pays off big dividends in keeping major repair costs at a minimum, extending the life of the car, and enhancing resale value, should you ever desire to part with your new J-car.

The J-cars require less in the way of routine maintenance than any cars in recent memory. However, a very definite maintenance schedule is provided by General Motors, and must be followed not only to keep the new car warranty in effect, but also to keep the car working properly. The Maintenance Intervals chart in this Chapter outlines the routine maintenance which must be performed according to intervals based on either accumulated mileage or time. Your J-car also came with a maintenance schedule provided by G.M. Adherence to these schedules will result in a longer life for your car, and will, over the long run, save you money and time.

The checks and adjustments in the following Chapters generally require only a few minutes of attention every few weeks; the services to be performed can be easily accomplished in a morning. The most important part of any maintenance program is regularity. The few minutes

Manual transaxle serial number locations—1982–86 76mm (Muncle) 4 speed

Manual transaxle serial number locations—1983–87 76mm (Isuzu) 5 speed

Manual transaxle serial number locations—1988–89 Code MG1/MG2, (Model HM-282) 5 speed

or occasional morning spent on these seemingly trivial tasks will forestall or eliminate major problems later.

Air Cleaner

All the dust present in the air is kept out of the engine by means of the air cleaner filter element. Proper maintenance is vital, as a clogged element not only restricts the air-flow, and thus the power, but may also cause premature engine wear.

The filter element should be checked and cleaned at least every 15,000 miles and replaced every 50,000 miles; more often if the car is driven in dry, dusty areas. The condition of the element should be checked periodically; if it appears to be overly dirty or clogged, shake it, if this does not help, the element should be replaced.

NOTE: *The paper element should never be cleaned or soaked with gasoline, cleaning solvent or oil.*

CLEANING OR REPLACING THE FILTER ELEMENT

On most engines the air cleaner is located in the center of the engine compartment, directly over the carburetor or throttle body. On some

1. VIN location   2. Optional VIN location

Manual transaxle serial number locations—1987 (Getrag) 5 speed

1. VIN location   2. Optional VIN location

Manual transaxle serial number locations—1988–92 Code MK7/MT2 (Isuzu) 5 speed

Manual transaxle serial number locations—1990–92 Code M27/MG2/MU1 (Model 5T40) 5 speed

Automatic transaxle serial number locations—1982–92 model 125C and model H-M 3T40

1987 and later 4-cyl. engines the air cleaner is more conveniently located toward the front of the engine compartment with an air duct connected to the throttle body.

1. Unscrew the wing nut on top of the air cleaner and then lift off the housing lid.

2. Lift out the filter element and shake the dirt out of it. If it remains clogged, replace it with a new one.

3. Before reinstalling the filter element, wipe out the housing with a damp cloth. Check the lid gasket to ensure that it has a tight seal.

4. Position the filter element, replace the lid and tighten the wing nut.

The part of the air cleaner assembly, containing the air filter element, is off to one side of the engine compartment on 1987–89 2.0L OHV engines

Fuel Filter

REPLACEMENT

Carbureted Engines

CAUTION: *Never smoke when working around gasoline! Avoid all sources of sparks*

1. Air cleaner
2. Wing nuts
3. Air filter element
4. Intake air temperature tube
5. Vent hose
6. Air cleaner gasket

Air cleaner element location shown on the 1990–91 2.2L OHV engines. All 1983–86 models equipped with the 2.0L engine use a similar design

1. Duct clamp
2. Vent tube
3. Duct assembly
4. Air cleaner assembly
5. Duct clamp
6. Air cleaner assembly base bracket
7. Transaxle mount
8. Battery tray bracket

Air induction assembly on the 3.1L engine. The air cleaner assembly containing the filter element is off to one side

The fuel filter is located behind the large inlet nut on the carburetor

or ignition. Gasoline vapors are EXTREMELY volatile!

All models have a fuel filter located within the carburetor body. The fuel filter has a check valve to prevent fuel spillage in the event of an accident. When the filter is replaced, make sure the new one is of the same type. All filters are of the paper element type. Replace the filter every 15,000 miles.

1. Place a few absorbent rags underneath the fuel line where it joins the carburetor.

2. Disconnect the fuel line connection at the fuel inlet nut.

3. Unscrew the fuel inlet nut from the carburetor. As the nut is removed, the filter will be pushed part way out by spring pressure.

4. Remove the filter and spring.

5. Install the new spring and filter. The hole in the filter faces the nut.

6. Install a new gasket on the inlet nut and install the nut into the carburetor. Tighten securely.

7. Install the fuel line. Tighten the connector to 18 ft. lbs. (24 Nm.) while holding the inlet nut with a wrench.

8. Start the engine and check for leaks.

Fuel Injected Engines

CAUTION: *Never smoke when working around gasoline! Avoid all sources of sparks or ignition. Gasoline vapors are EXTREMELY volatile!*

An inline filter can be found in the fuel feed line attached to the rear crossmember of the vehicle.

1. Release the fuel system pressure.

2. Place absorbent rags under the connections and disconnect the fuel lines.

NOTE: *Always use a back-up wrench anytime the fuel filter is removed or installed.*

3. Remove the fuel filter from the retainer or mounting bolt.

4. When installing, always use a good O-ring at the coupling locations and torque the fittings at 22 ft. lbs. Start the engine and check for leaks.

NOTE: *The filter has an arrow (fuel flow direction) on the side of the case, be sure to install it correctly in the system, the with arrow facing away from the fuel tank.*

Fuel Pressure Release

CAUTION: *To reduce the risk of fire or personal injury, it is necessary to relieve the fuel system pressure before servicing the fuel system.*

The fuel filter assembly on injected engines is located under the vehicle attached to the rear crossmember or frame rail

Carbureted Engines

To release the fuel pressure on the carbureted system, remove and replace the fuel tank cap.

Throttle Body Injection (TBI)

1983-91 1.8L and 2.0L (OHC)
1983-84 2.0L (OHV)

1. Remove the fuel pump fuse from the fuse block.
2. Crank the engine. The engine will run until it runs out of fuel. Crank the engine again for 3 seconds making sure it is out of fuel.
3. Turn the ignition off and replace the fuse.

1985-86 2.0L (OHV)
1989 2.0L (OHV)
1990–91 2.2L (OHV)

The TBI injection systems used on these engines contain a constant bleed feature in the pressure regulator that relieves pressure any time the engine is turned off. Therefore, no special relieve procedure is required, however, a small amount of fuel may be released when the fuel line is disconnected.

CAUTION: *To reduce the chance of personal injury, cover the fuel line with cloth to collect the fuel and then place the cloth in an approved container.*

Never smoke when working around gasoline! Avoid all sources of sparks or ignition. Gasoline vapors are EXTREMELY volatile!

1987-88 2.0L (OHV)

The TBI Model 700 used on these engines contains no constant bleed feature to relieve pressure as the 1985-86 models therefore, the following procedure must be followed:

1. Place the transmission selector in Park (Neutral on manual transmissions), set the parking brake and block the drive wheels.
2. Disconnect the fuel pump at the rear body connector.

CAUTION: *A small amount of fuel may be released after the fuel line is disconnected. To reduce the chance of personal injury, cover the fuel line with cloth to collect the fuel and then place the cloth in an approved container.*

Never smoke when working around gasoline! Avoid all sources of sparks or ignition. Gasoline vapors are EXTREMELY volatile!

3. Start the engine and allow it to run a few seconds until it stops for lack of fuel.
4. Engage the starter for three seconds to dissipate fuel pressure in the lines. The fuel connections are now safe for servicing.
5. When pressure is relieved and servicing is complete, reconnect the fuel pump at the rear body connector.

Port Fuel Injection (PFI)

2.0L VIN CODE M (OHC)
2.8L, 3.IL V6

1. Connect a J-34730-1 fuel gage or equivalent to the fuel pressure valve. Wrap a shop towel around the fitting while connecting the gage to avoid spillage.
2. Install a bleed hose into an approved container and open the valve to bleed the system pressure.

CAUTION: *Never smoke when working around gasoline! Avoid all sources of sparks or ignition. Gasoline vapors are EXTREMELY volatile!*

1992 2.2L VIN CODE 4 (OHV)
1992 2.0L VIN CODE H (OHC)

1. Loosen fuel filter cap to relieve tank pressure (do not tighten at this time).
2. Raise the vehicle.
3. Disconnect fuel pump electrical connector.
4. Lower the vehicle.
5. Start engine and run until fuel supply remaining in fuel pipes is consumed. Engage starter for 3 seconds to assure relief of any remaining pressure.
6. Raise vehicle.
7. Connect fuel pump electrical connector.
8. Lower vehicle.
9. Disconnect negative battery cable. Perform the necessary service work.

PCV Valve

REMOVAL AND INSTALLATION

The Positive Crankcase Ventilation (PCV) valve regulates crankcase ventilation during various engine running conditions. At high vacuum (idle speed and partial load range) it will open slightly and at low vacuum (full throttle) it will open fully. This causes vapors to be drawn from the crankcase by engine vacuum and then sucked into the combustion chamber where they are dissipated.

The PCV valve must be replaced every 30,000

PCV valve location—1982 2.0L OHV engine

1. PCV valve
2. PCV hose
3. PCV tube

PCV valve location—1983–86 2.0L OHV engine

miles. Details on the PCV system, including system tests, are given in Chapter 4.

The valve is located in a rubber grommet in the valve cover, connected to the air cleaner housing by a large diameter rubber hose. To replace the valve:

1. Pull the valve (with the hose attached) from the rubber grommet in the valve cover.

2. Remove the valve from the hose.

3. Install a new valve into the hose.

4. Press the valve back into the rubber grommet in the valve cover.

PCV Filter

Some models have a PCV filter, located in the air cleaner housing. This filter must be replaced at every 50,000 miles, or sooner, upon inspection.

1. Remove the air cleaner housing lid.

1. PCV valve

PCV valve location—1987–91 2.0L OHV engine

1. PCV valve
2. Intake manifold
3. Boot
4. Camshaft support cover

PCV valve location—2.0L OHC (CODE M) engine

1. PCV valve

PCV valve location—2.0L OHC (CODE K) engine

2. Slide back the filter retaining clip and remove the old filter.

3. Install the new filter, replace the retaining clip and replace the housing lid.

Evaporative Emissions System

Check the evaporative emission control system every 15,000 miles. Check the fuel vapor lines and the vacuum hoses for proper connections and correct routing, as well as condition. Replace clogged, damaged or deteriorated parts as necessary.

For more details on the evaporative emissions system, please refer to Chapter 4.

Battery

GENERAL MAINTENANCE

The J-cars have a maintenance free battery as standard equipment, eliminating the need for fluid level checks and the possibility of specific gravity tests. On top of the battery is a built-in temperature compensated hydrometer. When observing the hydrometer, make sure that the battery has a clean top. A light may be required in some poorly lit areas. Although claimed to be maintenance free, the battery does require some attention.

Once a year, the battery terminals and the cable clamps should be cleaned. Remove the side terminal bolts and the cables and the battery terminals with a wire brush until all corrosion, grease, etc. is removed and the metal is shiny. It is especially important to clean the inside of the clamp thoroughly, since a small deposit of foreign material or oxidation there will prevent a sound electrical connection and inhibit either starting or charging. Special tools are available for cleaning the side terminal clamps and terminals.

1. PCV tube
2. PCV valve
3. Manifold pipe
4. Air vent tube assembly

PCV valve location—1985–89 2.8L engine

1. PCV valve hose
2. PCV valve
3. Rocker cover
4. Plenum
5. Inlet manifold

PCV valve location—1990–92 3.1L engine

1	HOSE	**4**	SEALS - (O-RINGS)
2	INSTALL HOSE SO THAT ARROW IS POINTING TOWARD COVER	**5**	CRANKCASE VENT VALVE (PCV)
3	COVER - TORQUE TO 10 N·m (89 lb. ft.)	**6**	PUSH AIR INTAKE DUCT (NOT SHOWN) ON TO FITTING UNTIL FULLY SEATED

PCV valve location—1992 2.2L (CODE 4) engine

Before installing the cables, loosen the battery hold-down clamp, remove the battery, and check the battery tray. Clear it of any debris and check it for soundness. Rust should be wire brushed away, and the metal given a coat of anti-rust paint. Replace the battery and tighten the hold-down clamp securely, but be careful not to overtighten, which will crack the battery case.

After the clamps and terminals are clean, re-install the cables, negative cables last. Give the clamps and terminals a thin external coat of grease after installation, to retard corrosion.

Check the cables at the same time that the terminals are cleaned. If the cable insulation is cracked or broken, or if the ends are frayed, the cable should be replaced with a new cable of the same length and gauge.

CAUTION: *Keep flame or sparks away from the battery; it gives off explosive hydrogen gas. Battery electrolyte contains sulphuric acid. If you should get any on your skin or in your eyes, flush the affected areas with plenty* *of clear water; if it lands in your eyes, get medical help immediately.*

REPLACEMENT

Refer to the necessary Removal and Installation service procedures in Chapter 3.

BUILT-IN HYDROMETER

Original equipment maintenance free battery

JUMP STARTING A DEAD BATTERY

The chemical reaction in a battery produces explosive hydrogen gas. This is the safe way to jump start a dead battery, reducing the chances of an accidental spark that could cause an explosion.

Jump Starting Precautions

1. Be sure both batteries are of the same voltage.
2. Be sure both batteries are of the same polarity (have the same grounded terminal).
3. Be sure the vehicles are not touching.
4. Be sure the vent cap holes are not obstructed.
5. Do not smoke or allow sparks around the battery.
6. In cold weather, check for frozen electrolyte in the battery.
7. Do not allow electrolyte on your skin or clothing.
8. Be sure the electrolyte is not frozen.

Jump Starting Procedure

1. Determine voltages of the two batteries; they must be the same.
2. Bring the starting vehicle close (they must not touch) so that the batteries can be reached easily.
3. Turn off all accessories and both engines. Put both cars in Neutral or Park and set the handbrake.
4. Cover the cell caps with a rag—do not cover terminals.
5. If the terminals on the run-down battery are heavily corroded, clean them.
6. Identify the positive and negative posts on both batteries and connect the cables in the order shown.
7. Start the engine of the starting vehicle and run it at fast idle. Try to start the car with the dead battery. Crank it for no more than 10 seconds at a time and let it cool off for 20 seconds in between tries.
8. If it doesn't start in 3 tries, there is something else wrong.
9. Disconnect the cables in the reverse order.
10. Replace the cell covers and dispose of the rags.

Side terminal batteries occasionally pose a problem when connecting jumper cables. There frequently isn't enough room to clamp the cables without touching sheet metal. Side terminal adaptors are available to alleviate this problem and should be removed after use.

TO STARTER SWITCH   JUMPER CABLE   TO STARTER SWITCH

STARTING VEHICLE BATTERY   DISCHARGED (DEAD) BATTERY

JUMPER CABLE

TO GROUND   TO GROUND   ENGINE BLOCK OR FRAME

Make certain vehicles do not touch

This hook-up for negative ground cars only

Built-in hydrometer

ESTIMATED TEMPERATURE	MINIMUM VOLTAGE
70° F. (21° C.)	9.6
50° F. (10° C.)	9.4
30° F. (0° C.)	9.1
15° F. (−10° C.)	8.8
0° F. (−18° C.)	8.5
0° F. (BELOW: −18° C.)	8.0

Battery temperature vs voltage drop

A special tool is available for cleaning the side terminals and clamps

Standard Drive Belts

BELT TENSION

Every 12 months or 15,000 miles, check the water pump, alternator, power steering pump (if so equipped), and air conditioning compressor (if so equipped) drive belts for proper tension. Also look for signs of wear, fraying, separation, glazing and so on, and replace the belts as required.

Belt tension should be checked with a gauge made for the purpose. If a gauge is not available, tension can be checked with moderate thumb pressure applied to the belt at its longest span midway between pulleys. If the belt has a free span less than twelve inches, it should deflect approximately ⅛-¼ in. If the span is longer than twelve inches, deflection can range between ⅛-⅜ in.

1. Loosen the driven accessory's pivot and adjustment bolts. The pivot bolts are the bolts that enable the accessory to move in the either direction for adjustment. The adjustment bolts are the bolts in the slotted brackets.

2. Move the accessory toward or away from the engine until the tension is correct. You can use a wooden hammer handle or a broomstick as a lever, but do not use anything metallic.

3. Tighten the bolts and recheck the tension. If new belts have been installed, run the engine for a few minutes, then recheck and readjust as necessary.

It is better to have belts too loose than too tight, because overtight belts will lead to bearing failure, particularly in the water pump and alternator. However, loose belts place an extremely high impact load on the driven component due to the whipping action of the belt.

Serpentine Belts

Models equipped with the V6 engine and most 1987 and later engines use a single (serpentine belt) to drive all engine accessories. The serpentine belt driven accessories are rigidly mounted with belt tension maintained by a spring loaded tensioner assembly. The belt tensioner has the ability to control belt tension over a fairly broad range of belt lengths. However, there are limits to the tensioner's ability to compensate for varying lengths of belts. Poor tension control and/or damage to the tensioner could result with the tensioner operating outside of its range.

INSPECTION

1. If fraying of the belt is noticed, check to make sure both the belt and the tensioner assembly are properly aligned and that the belt edges are not in contact with the flanges of the tensioner pulley.

2. If, while adjusting belt tension, tensioner runs out of travel, the belt is stretched beyond adjustment and should be replaced.

3. If a whining is heard around the tensioner

Drive belts and pulleys—1.8L, 2.0L (OHV) engines

Drive belt adjustment points—1.8L, 2.0L (OHV) engines

or idler assemblies, check for possible bearing failure.

NOTE: *Routine inspection of the belt may reveal cracks in the belt ribs. These cracks will not impair belt performance and therefore should not be considered a problem requiring belt replacement. However, the belt should be replaced if belt slip occurs or if sections of the belt ribs are missing.*

REPLACEMENT

To replace the belt push (rotate) the the belt tensioner and remove the belt. Use a 15mm socket on the 4-cyl. engines and a ¾ in. open end wrench on the V6 engines.

Hoses

Upper and lower radiator hoses and all heater hoses should be checked for deterioration, leaks and loose hose clamps every 15,000 miles. To remove the hoses:

1. Drain the radiator as detailed later in this Chapter.

2. Loosen the hose clamps at each end of the hose to be removed.

1. Generator
2. P/S pump
3. Tensioner
4. Crankshaft
5. Water pump
6. A/C

Serpentine belt routing 2.0L, 2.2L (OHV) engines

1. Generator
2. P/S pump
3. Tensioner
4. Crankshaft
5. Water pump
6. Idler
7. A/C

A/C

Serpentine belt routing 2.8L, 3.1L (V6) engines

1. Generator
2. Serpentine drive belt
3. Power steering pump
4. Serpentine tensioner
5. Crankshaft pulley
6. A/C tensioner
7. A/C compressor
8. A/C "V" belt

FRT

Serpentine belt routing 1989–91 2.0L (OHC) engines

Serpentine belt tensioner 2.8L, 3.1L (V6) engines

1. Tensioner
2. 30–35 ft. lbs.
3. 14–22 ft. lbs.

Serpentine belt tensioner 2.0L, 2.2L (OHV) engines

3. Working the hose back and forth, slide it off its connection and then install the new hose.

NOTE: *If the hose is stuck, use a suitable razor cutting tool or knife, and carefully slit the hose enough to split it open along the connecting neck.*

4. Position the hose clamps at least ¼ in. from the end of the new hose and tighten them.

NOTE: *Always make sure that the hose clamps are beyond the bead and placed in the center of the clamping surface before tightening them.*

Air Conditioning

GENERAL SERVICING PROCEDURES

Antifreeze

In order to prevent heater core freeze-up during A/C operation, it is necessary to maintain permanent type antifreeze protection of +15°F, or lower. A reading of –15°F is ideal since this protection also supplies sufficient corrosion inhibitors for the protection of the engine cooling system.

NOTE: *The same antifreeze should not be used longer than the manufacturer specifies.*

Radiator Cap

For efficient operation of an air conditioned car's cooling system, the radiator cap should have a holding pressure which meets manufacturer's specifications. A cap which fails to hold these pressures should be replaced.

Condenser

Any obstruction of or damage to the condenser configuration will restrict the air flow which is essential to its efficient operation. It is there-

HOW TO SPOT WORN V-BELTS

V-Belts are vital to efficient engine operation—they drive the fan, water pump and other accessories. They require little maintenance (occasional tightening) but they will not last forever. Slipping or failure of the V-belt will lead to overheating. If your V-belt looks like any of these, it should be replaced.

Cracking or weathering

This belt has deep cracks, which cause it to flex. Too much flexing leads to heat build-up and premature failure. These cracks can be caused by using the belt on a pulley that is too small. Notched belts are available for small diameter pulleys.

Softening (grease and oil)

Oil and grease on a belt can cause the belt's rubber compounds to soften and separate from the reinforcing cords that hold the belt together. The belt will first slip, then finally fail altogether.

Glazing

Glazing is caused by a belt that is slipping. A slipping belt can cause a run-down battery, erratic power steering, overheating or poor accessory performance. The more the belt slips, the more glazing will be built up on the surface of the belt. The more the belt is glazed, the more it will slip. If the glazing is light, tighten the belt.

Worn cover

The cover of this belt is worn off and is peeling away. The reinforcing cords will begin to wear and the belt will shortly break. When the belt cover wears in spots or has a rough jagged appearance, check the pulley grooves for roughness.

Separation

This belt is on the verge of breaking and leaving you stranded. The layers of the belt are separating and the reinforcing cords are exposed. It's just a matter of time before it breaks completely.

HOW TO SPOT BAD HOSES

Both the upper and lower radiator hoses are called upon to perform difficult jobs in an inhospitable environment. They are subject to nearly 18 psi at under hood temperatures often over 280°F., and must circulate nearly 7500 gallons of coolant an hour—3 good reasons to have good hoses.

A good test for any hose is to feel it for soft or spongy spots. Frequently these will appear as swollen areas of the hose. The most likely cause is oil soaking. This hose could burst at any time, when hot or under pressure.

Swollen hose

Cracked hoses can usually be seen but feel the hoses to be sure they have not hardened; a prime cause of cracking. This hose has cracked down to the reinforcing cords and could split at any of the cracks.

Cracked hose

Weakened clamps frequently are the cause of hose and cooling system failure. The connection between the pipe and hose has deteriorated enough to allow coolant to escape when the engine is hot.

Frayed hose end (due to weak clamp)

Debris, rust and scale in the cooling system can cause the inside of a hose to weaken. This can usually be felt on the outside of the hose as soft or thinner areas.

Debris in cooling system

fore a good rule to keep this unit clean and in proper physical shape.

NOTE: *Bug screens are regarded as obstructions.*

Condensation Drain Tube

This single molded drain tube expels the condensation, which accumulates on the bottom of the evaporator housing, into the engine compartment. If this tube is obstructed, the air conditioning performance can be restricted and condensation buildup can spill over onto the vehicle's floor.

SAFETY PRECAUTIONS

Avoid contact with a charged refrigeration system, even when working on another part of the air conditioning system or vehicle. If a heavy tool comes into contact with a section of copper tubing or a heat exchanger, it can easily cause the relatively soft material to rupture.

All refrigerant should be discharged in a Enviromental Protection Agency (E.P.A.) approved container.

Always have the system completely discharged professionally before painting the vehicle (if the paint is to be baked on), or before welding anywhere near refrigerant lines.

SYSTEM CHECKS

1. Run the engine until it reaches normal operating temperature.
2. Open the hood and all doors.
3. Turn the air conditioning on, move the temperature selector to the first detent to the right of COLD (outside air) and then turn the blower on HI.
4. Idle the engine at 1,000 rpm.
5. Feel the temperature of the evaporator inlet and the accumulator outlet with the compressor clutch engaged.
6. Both lines should be cold. If the inlet pipe is colder than the outlet pipe, the system is low on charge.

Windshield Wipers

For maximum effectiveness and longest element lift, the windshield and wiper blades should be kept clean. Dirt, tree sap, road tar and so on will cause streaking, smearing and blade deterioration if left on the glass. It is advisable to wash the windshield carefully with a commercial glass cleaner at least once a month. Wipe off the rubber blades with the wet rag afterwards. Do not attempt to move the wipers back and forth by hand; damage to the motor and drive mechanism will result.

If the blades are found to be cracked, broken or torn, they should be replaced immediately. Replacement intervals will vary with usage, al-

though ozone deterioration usually limits blade life to about one year. If the wiper pattern is smeared or streaked, or if the blade chatters across the glass, the blades should be replaced. It is easiest and most sensible to replace them in pairs.

There are basically three different types of wiper blade refills, which differ in their method of replacement. Your J-Car could come originally equipped with either one of the first two types, Anco® or Trico®. The first type (Anco®) has two release buttons, approximately ⅓ of the way up from the ends of the blade frame. Pushing the buttons down releases a lock and allows the rubber blade to be removed from the frame. The new blade slides back into the frame and locks in place.

The second type (Trico®), has two metal tabs which are unlocked by squeezing them together. The rubber blade can then be withdrawn from the frame jaws. A new one is installed by inserting it into the front frame jaws and sliding it rearward to engage the remaining frame jaws. There are usually four jaws; be certain when installing that the refill is engaged in all of them. At the end of its travel, the tabs will lock into place on the front jaws of the wiper blade frame.

The third type is a refill made from polycarbonate. The refill has a simple locking device at one end which flexes downward out of the groove into which the jaws of the holder fit, allowing easy release. By sliding the new refill through all the jaws and pushing through the slight resistance when it reaches the end of its travel, the refill will lock into position.

Regardless of the type of refill used, make sure that all the frame jaws are engaged as the refill is pushed into place and locked. The metal blade holder and frame will scratch the glass if allowed to touch it.

Tires and Wheels

INFLATION

Tires should be checked weekly for proper air pressure. A chart, located either in the glove compartment or on the driver's or passenger's door, gives the recommended inflation pressures. Maximum fuel economy and tire life will result if the pressure is maintained at the highest figure given on the chart. Pressures should be checked before driving since pressure can increase as much as six pounds per square inch (psi) due to heat buildup. It is a good idea to have you own accurate pressure gauge, because not all gauges on service station air pumps can be trusted. When checking pressures, do not neglect the spare tire. Note that some spare tires

TRICO

BLADE FRAME LEVER

RUBBER BLADE ELEMENT ASSY.

SQUEEZE SIDES OF RETAINER

LEVER JAWS

LATCH LOCK RELEASE

METAL BACKING IS WIDER

HOLD FRAME FROM TWISTING

METAL BACKING STRIP

RETAINING TABS

METAL BACKING STRIP

FRAME

INSERT SCREWDRIVER BEHIND TAB AND PUSH HANDLE DOWN

ANCO

LATCH-PIN

YOKE JAWS

RUBBER BLADE ELEMENT ASSY.

YOKE JAWS

The rubber element can be changed without replacing the entire blade assembly; your J-car may have either one of these types of blades

Typical tire identification

METRIC TIRE SIZES

P   205 /   75   R   15   86H

TIRE TYPE		ASPECT RATIO		RIM DIAMETER	
P - PASSENGER		(SECTION HEIGHT)		(INCHES)	
T - TEMPORARY		(SECTION WIDTH)		13	
LT - LIGHT TRUCK		70		14	
		75		15	
		80			

SECTION WIDTH
(MILLIMETERS)
185
195
205
ETC

CONSTRUCTION TYPE
R - RADIAL
B - BIAS BELTED
D - DIAGONAL (BIAS)

LOAD INDEX

SPEED SYMBOL
SERVICE
DESCRIPTION

SECTION WIDTH

SECTION HEIGHT

Metric tire size format

require pressures considerably higher than those used in the other tires.

While you are about the task of checking air pressure, inspect the tire treads for cuts, bruises and other damage. Check the air valves to be sure that they are tight. Replace any missing valve caps.

PROPERLY INFLATED   IMPROPERLY INFLATED

RADIAL TIRE

Don't judge a radial tire's pressure by its appearance. An improperly inflated radial tire looks similar to a properly inflated one

Inexpensive gauges are also available for measurement of tread wear

Tread wear indicators will appear as bands across the tread when the tire is due for replacement.

You can use a penny for tread wear checks; if the top of Lincoln's head is visible in two adjacent grooves, the tire should be replaced

Check the tires for uneven wear that might indicate the need for front end alignment or tire rotation. Tires should be replaced when a tread wear indicator appears as a solid band across the tread.

TIRE DESIGN

When buying new tires, give some thought to the following points, especially if you are considering a switch to larger tires or a different profile series:

1. All four tires must be of the same construction type. This rule cannot be violated, Radial, bias, and bias-belted tires must not be mixed.

2. The wheels should be the correct width for the tire. Tire dealers have charts of tire and rim compatibility. A mis-match will cause sloppy handling and rapid tire wear. The tread width should match the rim width (inside bead to inside bead) within an inch. For radial tires, the rim should be 80% or less of the tire (not tread) width.

3. The height (mounted diameter) of the new tires can change speedometer accuracy, engine speed at a given road speed, fuel mileage, acceleration, and ground clearance. Tire manufacturers furnish full measurement specifications.

4. The spare tire should be usable, at least for short distance and low speed operation, with the new tires.

5. There shouldn't be any body interference when loaded, on bumps, or in turns.

TIRE ROTATION

Tire rotation is recommended every 6,000 miles or so, to obtain maximum tire wear. The pattern shown does not include the "temporary use only" sparee. Due to their design, radial tires tend to wear faster in the shoulder area particualrly in front positions. Radial tires in non-drive locations may develop an irregular wear pattern that can increase tire noise if not rotated. This makes regular rotation especially necessary. Snow tires sometimes have directional arrows molded into the side of the carcass; the arrow shows the direction of rotation. They will wear very rapidly if the rotation is reversed. Studded tires will lose their studs if their rotational direction is reversed.

NOTE: *Mark the wheel position or direction or rotation on radial tires or studded snow tires before removing them.*

CAUTION: *Tighten the lug nuts to 100 ft. lbs., in the pattern indicated. Avoid overtightening the lug nuts to prevent damage to the brake disc or drum. Alloy wheels can also be cracked by overtightening. Use of a torque wrench is highly recommended.*

STORAGE

Store the tires at the proper inflation pressure if they are mounted on wheels. Keep them in a cool dry place, laid on their sides. If the tires are stored in the garage or basement, do not let them stand on a concrete floor; set them on strips of wood.

Tire rotation

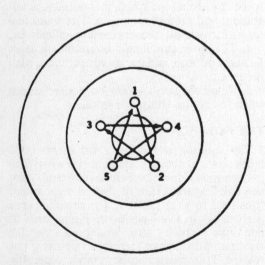

Five hole wheel nut tightening sequence

CARE OF ALUMINUM WHEELS

Normal appearance maintenance of aluminum wheels includes frequent washing and waxing. However, you must be careful to avoid the use of abrasive cleaners. Failure to heed this warning will cause the protective coating to be damaged.

The special coating may also be abraded by repeated washing of the car in an automatic car wash using certain types of brushes. Once the finish abrades, it will provide less protection; then, even normal exposure to either caustic cleaners or road salt will cause the process to continue. If the wheel reaches this point it will require refinishing.

FLUIDS AND LUBRICANTS

Fuel and Engine Oil Recommendations

Oil

The SAE (Society of Automotive Engineers) grade number indicates the viscosity of the engine oil, and thus its ability to lubricate at a given temperature. The lower the SAE grade number, the lighter the oil; the lower the viscosity, the easier it is to crank the engine in cold weather.

The API (American Petroleum Institute) designation indicates the classification of engine oil for use under given operating conditions. Only oils designated for use Service SG should be used. Oils of the SG type perform a variety of functions inside the engine in addition to the basic function as a lubricant. Through a balanced system of metallic detergents and polymeric dispersants, the oil prevents the formation of high and low temperature deposits, and also keeps sludge and dirt particles in suspension. Acids, particularly sulfuric acid, as well as other by products of combustion, are neutralized. Both the SAE grade number and the API designation can be found on the top of the oil can.

NOTE: *Non-detergent or straight mineral oils must never be used. Oil viscosities should be chosen from those oils recommended for the lowest anticipated temperatures during the oil change interval.*

Multi-viscosity oils offer the important advantage of being adaptable to temperature extremes. They allow easy starting at low temperatures, yet give good protection at high speeds and engine temperatures. This is a decided advantage in changeable climates or in long distance touring.

USE THESE SAE VISCOSITY GRADES

NOTICE: DO NOT USE SAE 5W-20 OILS FOR CONTINUOUS HIGH-SPEED DRIVING. 5W-30 OILS MAY BE USED UP TO 100°F (38°C)

Oil viscosity chart; multi-viscosity oils offer greater temperature latitude

Fuel

All G.M. J-cars must use unleaded fuel. The use of leaded fuel will plug the catalyst rendering it inoperative, and will increase the exhaust back pressure to the point where engine output will be severely reduced. The minimum octane for all engines is 91 RON. All unleaded fuels sold in the U.S. are required to meet this minimum octane rating.

Use of a fuel too low in octane (a measurement of anti-knock quality) will result in spark knock. Since many factors affect operating efficiency, such as altitude, terrain, and air temperature and humidity, knocking may result even though the recommended fuel is being used. If persistent knocking occurs, it may be necessary to switch to a slightly higher grade of unleaded gasoline. Continuous or heavy knocking may result in serious engine damage, for which the manufacturer is not responsible.

NOTE: *Your car's engine fuel requirement can change with time, due to carbon buildup, which changes the compression ratio. If your car's engine knocks, pings, or runs on, switch to a higher grade of fuel, if possible, and check the ignition timing. Sometimes changing brands of gasoline will cure the problem.*

Engine
OIL LEVEL CHECK

The engine oil level should be checked at every fuel stop, or once a week, whichever occurs more regularly. The best time to check is when the engine is warm, although checking immediately after the engine has been shut off will result in an inaccurate reading, since it takes a few minutes for all of the oil to drain back down into the crankcase. If the engine is cold, the en-

gine should not be run before the level is checked. The oil level is checked by means of a dipstick, located at the front of the engine compartment:

1. If the engine is warm, it should be allowed to sit for a few minutes after being shut off to allow the oil to drain down into the oil pan. The car should be parked on a level surface.

2. Pull the dipstick out from its holder, wipe it clean with a rag, and reinsert it firmly. Be sure it is pushed all the way home, or the reading you're about to take will be incorrect.

3. Pull the dipstick again and hold it horizontally to prevent the oil from running. The dipstick is marked with Add and Full lines. The oil level should be above the Add line.

4. Reinstall the dipstick.

If oil is needed, it is added through the capped opening in the cylinder head cover. One quart of oil will raise the level from Add to Full. Only oils labeled SF should be used; select a viscosity that will be compatible with the temperatures expected until the next drain interval. See the Oil and Fuel Recommendations section later in this Chapter if you are not sure what type of oil to use. Check the oil level again after any additions. Be careful not to overfill, which will lead to leakage and seal damage.

OIL AND FILTER CHANGE

CAUTION: *The EPA warns that prolonged contact with used engine oil may cause a number of skin disorders, including cancer! You should make every effort to minimize your exposure to used engine oil. Protective gloves should be worn when changing the oil. Wash your hands and any other exposed skin areas as soon as possible after exposure to used engine oil. Soap and water, or waterless hand cleaner should be used.*

If you purchased your J-car new, the engine oil and filter should be changed at the first 7,500 miles or 12 months (whichever comes first), and every 7,500 miles or 12 months thereafter. You should make it a practice to

The oil drain plug is located at the lowest point of the oil pan

Use an oil filter strap wrench to remove the oil filter; install the new filter by hand

Apply a thin film of clean oil to the new gasket to prevent it from tearing upon installation

change the oil filter at every oil change; otherwise, a approximately a pint of dirty oil remains in the engine every other time the oil is changed. The change interval should be halved when the car is driven under severe conditions, such as in extremely dusty weather, or when the car is used for trailer towing, prolonged high speed driving, or repeated short trips in freezing weather.

1. Drive the car until the engine is at normal operating temperature. A run to the parts store for oil and a filter should accomplish this. If the engine is not hot when the oil is changed, most of the acids and contaminants will remain inside the engine.

2. Shut off the engine, and slide a pan of at least 6 quarts capacity under the oil pan.

NOTE: *Six quart plastic drain pan/containers are available, which can be capped, and taken later to a recycling station to dispose of the dirty oil. Do not pour on the ground.*

3. Remove the drain plug from the engine oil pan, after wiping the plug area clean. The drain plug is the bolt inserted at an angle into the lowest point of the oil pan.

4. The oil from the engine will be HOT. It will probably not be possible to hold onto the drain plug. You may have to let it fall into the pan and fish it out later. Allow all the oil to drain completely. This will take a few minutes.

5. Wipe off the drain plug, removing any traces of metal particles. Pay particular atten-

tion to the threads. Replace it, and tighten it snugly.

6. The oil filter is at the back of the engine. It is impossible to reach from above, and almost as inaccessible from below, because of the location of the fender skirt. It may be easiest to remove the right front wheel and reach through the fender opening to get at the four cylinder oil filter. Use an oil filter strap wrench, or a wrench that fits like a cap over the oil filter, along with a rachet wrench, to loosen the oil filter; these are available at auto parts stores. Place the drain pan on the ground, under the filter. Unscrew and discard the old filter. It will be VERY HOT, so be careful.

7. If the oil filter is on so tightly that it collapses under pressure from the wrench, drive a long punch or a nail through it, across the diameter and as close to the base as possible, and use this as a lever to unscrew it. Make sure you are turning it counterclockwise.

8. Clean off the oil filter mounting surface with a rag. Apply a thin film of clean engine oil to the filter gasket.

9. Screw the filter on by hand until the gasket makes contact. Then tighten it by hand an additional ½-¾ turn. Do not overtighten.

10. Remove the filler cap on the rocker (valve) cover, after wiping the area clean.

11. Add the correct number of quarts of oil specified in the Capacities chart. If you don't have an oil can spout, you will need a funnel. Be certain you do not overfill the engine, which can cause serious damage. Replace the cap.

12. Check the oil level on the dipstick. It is normal for the level to be a bit above the full mark. Start the engine and allow it to idle for a few minutes.

CAUTION: *Do not run the engine above idle speed until it has built up oil pressure, indicated when the oil light goes out.*

Check around the filter and drain plug for any leaks.

13. Shut off the engine, allow the oil to drain for a minute, and check the oil level.

After completing this job, you will have several quarts of filthy oil to dispose of. If you didn't use a drain pan/container as noted earlier, the best thing to do with it is to funnel it into old plastic milk or detergent containers. Then, you can pour it into the recycling container at a gas station or service center.

Manual Transaxle

FLUID RECOMMENDATION AND LEVEL CHECK

The fluid level in the manual transaxle should be checked every 12 months or 7,500 miles, whichever comes first.

1. Park the car on a level surface. The transaxle should be cool to the touch. If it is hot, check the level later, when it has cooled.

2. Remove the dipstick from the left side of the transaxle.

3. If lubricant is needed, add it through the filler tube until the level is correct. All 4-speeds use DEXRON®II transmission fluid. All 5-speeds through 1986 use 5W-30 engine oil. All 5-speeds from 1988–92 use GM part number 12345349 transaxle oil. When the level is correct, reinstall the dipstick firmly.

DRAIN AND REFILL

The fluid in the manual transaxle normally does not require changing, however you may want to change it if the car is used under severe conditions.

1. The fluid should be hot before it is drained. If the car is driven until the engine is at normal operating temperature, the fluid should be hot enough.

2. Remove the filler plug (or dipstick) from the left side of the transaxle to provide a vent.

Most models use a dipstick and tube like this to check the level of the manual transaxle lubricant

3. The drain plug is located on the bottom of the transaxle case. Place a pan under the drain plug and remove it.

CAUTION: *The fluid will be HOT. Push up against the threads as you unscrew the plug to prevent leakage.*

4. Allow the fluid to drain completely. Check the condition of the plug gasket and replace it if necessary. Clean off the plug and replace, tightening it until snug.

5. Fill the transaxle with fluid through the fill or dipstick tube. You will need the aid of a long neck funnel or a funnel and a hose to pour through.

6. Use the dipstick to gauge the level of the fluid.

7. Replace the filler plug or dipstick and dispose of the old fluid in the same manner as you would old engine oil.

8. Take a drive in the car, stop on a level surface, and check the oil level.

Automatic Transaxle

FLUID RECOMMENDATION AND LEVEL CHECK

The fluid level in the automatic transaxle should be checked every 12 months or 7,500 miles, whichever comes first. The transaxle has a dipstick for fluid level checks.

1. Drive the car until it is at normal operating temperature. The level should not be checked immediately after the car has been driven for a long time at high speed, or in city traffic in hot weather; in those cases, the transaxle should be given a half hour to cool down.

2. Stop the car, apply the parking brake, then shift slowly through all gear positions, ending in Park. Let the engine idle for about

1. Transaxle
2. Fluid level indicator

Some earlier models use a dipstick and plug such as this to check the level of the manual transaxle lubricant five minutes with the selector in Park. The car should be on a level surface.

3. With the engine still running, remove the dipstick, wipe it clean, then reinsert it, pushing it fully home.

4. Pull the dipstick again and, holding it horizontally, read the fluid level.

5. Cautiously feel the end of the dipstick to determine the temperature. Note that on the J-cars the cool and warm level dimples are above the hot level area. If the fluid level is not in the correct area, more will have to be added.

6. Fluid is added through the dipstick tube. You will probably need the aid of a spout or a long-necked funnel. Be sure that whatever you pour through is perfectly clean and dry. Use an automatic transmission fluid marked DEXRON®II. Add fluid slowly, and in small amounts, checking the level frequently between additions. Do not overfill, which will cause foaming, fluid loss, slippage, and possible transaxle damage. It takes only one pint to raise the level from Add to Full when the transaxle is hot.

DRAIN AND REFILL

The fluid should be changed according to the schedule in the Maintenance Intervals chart. If the car is normally used in severe service, such as stop and start driving, trailer towing, or the like, the interval should be halved. If the car is driven under especially nasty conditions, such as in heavy city traffic where the temperature normally reaches 90°F, or in very hilly or mountainous areas, or in police, taxi, or delivery ser-

Automatic transaxle dipstick markings

Loosen the pan bolts and allow one corner of the pan to tilt slightly to drain the fluid

Clean the pan thoroughly with solvent and allow it to air dry completely

Install a new pan gasket

Fill the transaxle with the required amount of fluid. Do not overfill. Check the fluid level and add fluid if necessary

vice, the fluid should be changed every 15,000 miles (24,000 km.).

The fluid must be hot before it is drained; a 20 minute drive should accomplish this.

1. There is no drain plug; the fluid pan must be removed. Place a drain pan underneath the transaxle pan and remove the pan attaching bolts at the front and sides of the pan.

2. Loosen the rear pan attaching bolts approximately four turns each.

3. Very carefully pry the pan loose. You can use a small prybar for this if you work CARE-FULLY. Do not distort the pan flange, or score the mating surface of the transaxle case. You'll be very sorry later if you do. As the pan is pried

1. Apply thread lock to this bolt

Apply thread locker to this automatic transaxle oil pan bolt

loose, all of the fluid is going to come pouring out.

4. Remove the remaining bolts and remove the pan and gasket. Throw away the gasket.

5. Clean the pan with solvent and allow it to air dry. If you use a rag to wipe out the pan, you risk leaving bits of lint behind, which will clog the dinky hydraulic passages in the transaxle.

6. Remove and discard the filter and the O-ring seal.

7. Install a new filter and O-ring, locating the filter against the dipstick stop.

8. Install a new gasket on the pan and install the pan. Tighten the bolts evenly and in rotation to 8 ft. lbs. (11 Nm.). Do not overtighten.

9. Add approximately 4 qts. (3.8 L) of DEXRON®II automatic transmission fluid to the transaxle through the dipstick tube. You will need a long necked funnel, or a funnel and tube to do this.

10. With the transaxle in Park, put on the parking brake, block the front wheels, start the engine and let it idle. DO NOT RACE THE ENGINE. DO NOT MOVE THE LEVER THROUGH ITS RANGES.

11. With the lever in Park, check the fluid level. If it's OK, take the car out for a short drive, park on a level surface, and check the level again, as outlined earlier in this Chapter. Add more fluid if necessary. Be careful not to overfill, which will cause foaming and fluid loss.

NOTE: *If the drained fluid is discolored (brown or black), thick, or smells burnt, serious transmission troubles, probably due to overheating, should be suspected. Your car's transaxle should be inspected by a reliable transmission specialist to determine the problem.*

Cooling System

FLUID RECOMMENDATION AND LEVEL CHECK

CAUTION: *Never remove the radiator cap under any conditions while the engine is running! Failure to follow these instructions could result in damage to the cooling system or engine and/or personal injury. To avoid having scalding hot coolant or steam blow out of the radiator, use extreme care when removing the radiator cap from a hot radiator. Wait until the engine has cooled, then wrap a thick cloth around the radiator cap and turn it slowly to the first stop. Step back while the pressure is released from the cooling system. When you are sure the pressure has been released, press down on the radiator cap (still have the cloth in position) turn and remove the radiator cap.*

Dealing with the cooling system can be dangerous matter unless the proper precautions are observed. It is best to check the coolant level in the radiator when the engine is cold. The cooling system has, as one of its components, a coolant recovery tank. If the coolant level is at or near the FULL COLD line (engine cold) or the FULL HOT line (engine hot), the level is satisfactory. Always be certain that the filler caps on both the radiator and the recovery tank are closed tightly.

In the event that the coolant level must be checked when the engine is hot on engines without a coolant recovery tank, place a thick rag over the radiator cap and slowly turn the cap counterclockwise until it reaches the first detent. Allow all hot steam to escape. This will allow the pressure in the system to drop gradually, preventing an explosion of hot coolant. When the hissing noise stops, remove the cap the rest of the way.

The coolant recovery tank is at the right front of the engine compartment

If the coolant level is found to be low, add a 50/50 mixture of ethylene glycol-based anti-freeze and clean water. On older models, coolant must be added through the radiator filler neck. On newer models with the recovery tank, coolant may be added either through the filler neck on the radiator or directly into the recovery tank.

CAUTION: *Never add coolant to a hot engine unless it is running. If it is not running you run the risk of cracking the engine block.*

If the coolant level is chronically low or rusty, refer to Cooling System Troubleshooting Chart at the end of this Chapter.

At least once every 2 years, the engine cooling system should be inspected, flushed, and refilled with fresh coolant. If the coolant is left in the system too long, it loses its ability to prevent rust and corrosion. If the coolant has too much water, it won't protect against freezing.

The pressure cap should be looked at for signs of age or deterioration. Fan belt and other drive belts should be inspected and adjusted to the proper tension. (See checking belt tension).

Hose clamps should be tightened, and soft or cracked hoses replaced. Damp spots, or accumulations of rust or dye near hoses, water pump or other areas, indicate possible leakage, which must be corrected before filling the system with fresh coolant.

CHECK THE RADIATOR CAP

While you are checking the coolant level, check the radiator cap for a worn or cracked gasket. It the cap doesn't seal properly, fluid will be lost and the engine will overheat.

Worn caps should be replaced with a new one.

Check the condition of the radiator cap gasket

Clean the front of the radiator of any bugs, leaves or other debris at every yearly coolant change

CLEAN RADIATOR OF DEBRIS

Periodically clean any debris — leaves, paper, insects, etc. — from the radiator fins. Pick the large pieces off by hand. The smaller pieces can be washed away with water pressure from a hose.

Carefully straighten any bent radiator fins with a pair of needle nose pliers. Be careful — the fins are very soft. Don't wiggle the fins back and forth too much. Straighten them once and try not to move them again.

DRAIN AND REFILL

Completely draining and refilling the cooling system every two years at least will remove accumulated rust, scale and other deposits. Coolant in late model cars is a 50/50 mixture of ethylene glycol and water for year round use. Use a good quality antifreeze with water pump lubricants, rust inhibitors and other corrosion inhibitors along with acid neutralizers.

1. Drain the existing antifreeze and coolant. Open the radiator and engine drain petcocks, or

You can use an inexpensive tester to check the antifreeze protection

disconnect the bottom radiator hose, at the radiator outlet.

CAUTION: *When draining the coolant, keep in mind that cats and dogs are attracted by the ethylene glycol antifreeze, and are quite likely to drink any that is left in an uncovered container or in puddles on the ground. This will prove fatal in sufficient quantity. Always drain the coolant into a sealable container. Coolant should be reused unless it is contaminated or several years old.*

2. Close the petcock or reconnect the lower hose and fill the system with water.

3. Add a can of quality radiator flush.

4. Idle the engine until the upper radiator hose gets hot.

5. Drain the system again.

6. Repeat this process until the drained water is clear and free of scale.

7. Close all petcocks and connect all the hoses.

8. If equipped with a coolant recovery system, flush the reservoir with water and leave empty.

9. Determine the capacity of your coolant system (see capacities specifications). Add a 50/50 mix of quality antifreeze (ethylene glycol) and water to provide the desired protection.

10. Run the engine to operating temperature.

11. Stop the engine and check the coolant level.

12. Check the level of protection with an antifreeze tester, replace the cap and check for leaks.

Master Cylinder

FLUID RECOMMENDATION AND LEVEL CHECK

Once a month, the fluid level in the brake master cylinder should be checked.

1. Park the car on a level surface.

2. Clean off the master cylinder cover before removal.

3. The early models without a filler cap the cover simply snaps onto the master cylinder body. Use your thumbs to press up on the two tabs on the side of the cover to unsnap it. Remove the cover or cap, being careful not to drop or tear the rubber diaphragm underneath. Be careful also not to drip any brake fluid on painted surfaces; the stuff eats paint.

NOTE: *Brake fluid absorbs moisture from the air, which reduces effectiveness, and will corrode brake parts once in the system. Never leave the master cylinder or the brake fluid container uncovered for any longer than necessary.*

4. The fluid level should be about ¼ in. below the lip of the master cylinder well on early

models or the full mark on the inside on later models.

5. If fluid addition is necessary, use only extra heavy duty disc brake fluid meeting DOT 3 specifications. The fluid should be reasonably fresh because brake fluid deteriorates with age.

6. Replace the cover or cap, making sure that the diaphragm is correctly seated.

If the brake fluid level is constantly low, the system should be checked for leaks. However, it is normal for the fluid level to fall gradually as the disc brake pads wear; expect the fluid level to drop not more than ⅛ in. for every 10,000 miles of wear.

Steering Gear

The rack and pinion steering gear used on the J-cars is a sealed unit; no fluid level checks or additions are ever necessary.

Use thumb pressure to remove the brake master cylinder cover on models through 1987

The proper brake fluid level is approximately ¼ in. below the lip of the master cylinder on models through 1987

The fluid level full mark is located on the inside of the reservoir on 1988–92 models

Power Steering Pump

The power steering hydraulic fluid reservoir is attached to the firewall at the back of the engine compartment. It is a translucent plastic container with fluid level markings on the outside. Check the fluid level every 12 months or 7,500 miles, whichever comes first. If the level is low, add power steering fluid until it is correct. Be careful not to overfill as this will cause fluid loss and seal damage.

Windshield Washer Fluid

Check the fluid level in the windshield washer tank at every oil level check. The fluid can be mixed in a 50% solution with water, if desired, as long as temperatures remain above freezing. Below freezing, the fluid should be used full strength. Never add engine coolant antifreeze to the washer fluid, because it will damage the car's paint.

The power steering pump reservoir is located at the back of the engine compartment

Chassis Greasing

There are only two areas which require regular chassis greasing: the front suspension components and the steering linkage. These parts should be greased every 12 months or 7,500 miles (12,000 Km.) with an EP grease meeting G.M. specification 6031M.

If you choose to do this job yourself, you will need to purchase a hand operated grease gun, if you do not own one already, and a long flexible extension hose to reach the various grease fittings. You will also need a cartridge of the appropriate grease.

Press the fitting on the grease gun hose onto the grease fitting on the suspension or steering linkage component. Pump a few shots of grease into the fitting, until the rubber boot on the joint begins to expand, indicating that the joint is full. Remove the gun from the fitting. Be careful not to overfill the joints, which will rupture the rubber boots, allowing the entry of dirt. You can keep the grease fittings clean by covering them with a small square of tin foil.

NOTE: *This is a good opportunity, while under the vehicle, to check for any tears or holes in the axle CV-joint boots, which may cause loss of or contamination of the axle grease. Damaged boots must be replaced as soon as possible or joint failure could result.*

Chassis Lubrication

Every 12 months or 7,500 miles (12,000 km.), the various linkages and hinges on the chassis and body should be lubricated, as follows:

TRANSAXLE SHIFT LINKAGE

Lubricate the manual transaxle shift linkage contact points with the EP grease used for chassis greasing, which should meet G.M. specification 6031M. The automatic transaxle linkage should be lubricated with clean engine oil.

HOOD LATCH AND HINGES

Clean the latch surfaces and apply clean engine oil to the latch pilot bolts and the spring anchor. Use the engine oil to lubricate the hood hinges as well. Use a chassis grease to lubricate all the pivot points in the latch release mechanism.

DOOR HINGES

The gas tank filler door, car door, and rear hatch or trunk lid hinges should be wiped clean and lubricated with clean engine oil. Silicone spray also works well on these parts, but must be applied more often. Use engine oil to lubricate the trunk or hatch lock mechanism and the

STEERING AND SUSPENSION

4 BALL JOINTS TOTAL (2 EACH SIDE)

BALL JOINT FRONT LOWER CONTROL ARM

BALL JOINT

BALL JOINT TIE ROD END-TO-STRUT

STRUT

Lubrication points

lock bolt and striker. The door lock cylinders can be lubricated easily with a shot of silicone spray or one of the may dry penetrating lubricants commercially available.

PARKING BRAKE LINKAGE

Use chassis grease on the parking brake cable where it contacts the guides, links, levers, and pulleys. The grease should be a water resistant one for durability under the car.

ACCELERATOR LINKAGE

Lubricate the carburetor stud, carburetor lever, and the accelerator pedal lever at the support inside the car with clean engine oil.

Throttle Body Mounting Torque

Check torque of mounting bolts and or nuts of the throttle body assembly. Refer to Chapter 5 for specifications.

TRAILER TOWING

General Recommendations

Your car was primarily designed to carry passengers and cargo. It is important to remember that towing a trailer will place additional loads on your vehicle's engine, drive train, steering, braking and other systems. However, if you find it necessary to tow a trailer, using the proper equipment is a must.

Local laws may require specific equipment such as trailer brakes or fender mounted mirrors. Check your local laws.

WARNING: *Some early models equipped with the V6 engines were not recommended for trailer towing because of insuffcient cooling system capacity. These vehicles could overheat. Check your owners manual or local GM dealer for any trailer towing warnings.*

Trailer Weight

The weight of the trailer is the most important factor. A good weight-to-horsepower ratio is about 35:1, 35 lbs. of GCW (Gross Combined Weight) for every horsepower your engine develops. Multiply the engine's rated horsepower by 35 and subtract the weight of the car passengers and luggage. The result is the approximate ideal maximum weight you should tow, although a a numerically higher axle ratio can help compensate for heavier weight.

Hitch Weight

Figure the hitch weight to select a proper hitch. Hitch weight is usually 9-11% of the trailer gross weight and should be measured with the trailer loaded. Hitches fall into three types: those that mount on the frame and rear bumper or the bolt-on or weld-on distribution type used for larger trailers. Axle mounted or clamp-on bumper hitches should never be used.

Check the gross weight rating of your trailer.

Tongue weight is usually figured as 10% of gross trailer weight. Therefore, a trailer with a maximum gross weight of 2,000 lb. will have a maximum tongue weight of 200 lb. Class I trailers fall into this category. Class II trailers are those with a gross weight rating of 2,000-3,500 lb., while Class III trailers fall into the 3,500-6,000 lb. category. Class IV trailers are those over 6,000 lb. and are for use with fifth wheel trucks, only.

When you've determined the hitch that you'll need, follow the manufacturer's installation instructions, exactly, especially when it comes to fastener torques. The hitch will subjected to a lot of stress and good hitches come with hardened bolts. Never substitute an inferior bolt for a hardened bolt.

Cooling
ENGINE

One of the most common, if not THE most common, problems associated with trailer towing is engine overheating.

If you have a standard cooling system, without an expansion tank, you'll definitely need to get an aftermarket expansion tank kit, preferably one with at least a 2 quart capacity. These kits are easily installed on the radiator's overflow hose, and come with a pressure cap designed for expansion tanks.

Another helpful accessory is a Flex Fan. These fan are large diameter units are designed to provide more airflow at low speeds, with blades that have deeply cupped surfaces. The blades then flex, or flatten out, at high speed, when less cooling air is needed. These fans are far lighter in weight than stock fans, requiring less horsepower to drive them. Also, they are far quieter than stock fans.

If you do decide to replace your stock fan with a flex fan, note that if your car has a fan clutch, a spacer between the flex fan and water pump hub will be needed.

Aftermarket engine oil coolers are helpful for prolonging engine oil life and reducing overall engine temperatures. Both of these factors increase engine life.

While not absolutely necessary in towing Class I and some Class II trailers, they are recommended for heavier Class II and all Class III towing.

Engine oil cooler systems consist of an adapter, screwed on in place of the oil filter, a remote filter mounting and a multi-tube, finned heat exchanger, which is mounted in front of the radiator or air conditioning condenser.

TRANSMISSION

An automatic transmission is usually recommended for trailer towing. Modern automatics have proven reliable and, of course, easy to operate, in trailer towing.

The increased load of a trailer, however, causes an increase in the temperature of the automatic transmission fluid. Heat is the worst enemy of an automatic transmission. As the temperature of the fluid increases, the life of the fluid decreases.

It is essential, therefore, that you install an automatic transmission cooler.

The cooler, which consists of a multi-tube, finned heat exchanger, is usually installed in front of the radiator or air conditioning compressor, and hooked inline with the transmission cooler tank inlet line. Follow the cooler manufacturer's installation instructions.

Select a cooler of at least adequate capacity, based upon the combined gross weights of the car and trailer.

Cooler manufacturers recommend that you use an aftermarket cooler in addition to, and not instead of, the present cooling tank in your radiator. If you do want to use it in place of the radiator cooling tank, get a cooler at least two sizes larger than normally necessary.

NOTE: *A transmission cooler can, sometimes, cause slow or harsh shifting in the transmission during cold weather, until the fluid has a chance to come up to normal operating temperature. Some coolers can be purchased with or retrofitted with a temperature bypass valve which will allow fluid flow through the cooler only when the fluid has reached operating temperature, or above.*

Handling A Trailer

Towing a trailer with ease and safety requires a certain amount of experience. It's a good idea to learn the feel of a trailer by practicing turning, stopping and backing in an open area such as an empty parking lot.

PUSHING AND TOWING

The J-cars may not be pushed or towed to start, because doing so may cause the catalytic converter to explode. If the battery is weak, the engine may be jump started, using the procedure outlined in the following section.

Your J-car may be towed on all four wheels at speeds less than 35 mph (60 km/h) for distances up to 50 miles (80 km). The driveline and steering must be normally operable. If either one is damaged, the car may not be flat-towed. If the car is flat-towed (on all four wheels), the steering must be unlocked, the transaxle shifted to Neutral, and the parking brake released. Towing attachment must be made to the main

Check the appearance of the charge indicator on the top of the battery before attempting a jump start; if its not green or dark, do not jump start the car

JACKING AND HOISTING

The J-cars are supplied with a scissors jack for changing tires. This jack engages in notches behind the front wheel and forward of the rear wheel under the rocker flange. This jack is satisfactory for its intended purpose; it is not meant to support the car while you go crawling around underneath it. Never crawl under the car when it is supported by only the scissorsjack.

The car may also be jacked at the rear axle between the spring seats, or at the front end at the engine cradle crossbar or lower control arm. The car must never be lifted by the rear lower control arms.

The car can be raised on a four point hoist which contacts the chassis at points just behind the front wheels and just ahead of the rear wheels, as shown in the accompanying diagram. Be certain that the lift pads do not contact the catalytic converter.

It is imperative that strict safety precautions be observed both while raising the car and in the subsequent support after the car is raised. If a jack is used to raise the car, the transaxle should be shifted to Park (automatic) or First (manual), the parking brake should be set, and the opposite wheel should be blocked. Jacking should only be attempted on a hard level surface.

structural members of the chassis, not to the bumpers or sheetmetal.

The car may be towed on its rear wheels by a wrecker; make sure that safety chains are used. J-cars with manual transaxles may be towed on their front wheels, for short distances and at low speeds. Be sure the transaxle is in Neutral. Cars with automatic transaxles should not be towed on their front wheels; transaxle damage may result. If it is impossible to tow the car on its rear wheels, place the front wheels on a dolly.

CAPACITIES

Year	Model	Engine VIN	No. Cylinder Displacement cu. in. (liter)	Engine Crankcase with Filter	Transmission (pts.) 4-Spd	5-Spd	Auto. ⑥	Fuel Tank (gal.)	Cooling System (qts.)
1982	All	G	4-110 (1.8)	4.0	5.9	—	10.5	14	8.0
	All	B	4-121 (2.0)	4.0	5.9	—	10.5	14	8.3
1983	All	O, J	4-110 (1.8)	①	—	5.0	10.5	14	7.9
	All	P	4-121 (2.0)	4.0	5.9	—	10.5	14	8.3
1984	All	O, J	4-110 (1.8)	①	—	5.0	10.5	14	7.9
	All	P	4-121 (2.0)	4.0	5.9	—	10.5	14	8.3
1985	All	O, J	4-110 (1.8)	①	—	5.0	10.5	14	7.9
	All	P	4-121 (2.0)	4.0	5.9	—	10.5	14	8.3
	All	W	6-173 (2.8)	4.0	6.0	—	8.0	14③	12.4
1986	All	O, J	4-110 (1.8)	①	5.9	5.3	8.0	14	7.9
	All	P	4-121 (2.0)	4.0	5.9	—	8.0	14	8.3
	All	W	6-173 (2.8)	4.0	6.0	—	8.0	14	12.4
1987	All	M, 1, K	4-121 (2.0)	4.0	6.0	④	8.0	13.6	8.8
	All	W	6-173 (2.8)	4.0	5.36	—	8.0	14③	11.4
1988	All	M, 1, K	4-121 (2.0)	4.0⑦	—	⑤	8.0	13.6	9.7⑥
	All	W	6-173 (2.8)	4.0⑦	—	⑤	8.0	13.6	11.0
1989	All	M, 1, K	4-121 (2.0)	4.0⑦	—	4.0	8.0	13.6	9.7⑥
	All	W	6-173 (2.8)	4.0⑦	—	4.0	8.0	13.6	11.0

CAPACITIES

Year	Model	Engine VIN	No. Cylinder Displacement cu. in. (liter)	Engine Crankcase with Filter	Transmission (pts.)			Fuel Tank (gal.)	Cooling System (qts.)
					4-Spd	5-Spd	Auto. ⑥		
1990	All	M, K	4-121 (2.0)	4.0⑦	—	4.0	8.0	13.6	8.5
	All	G	4-134 (2.2)	4.0⑦	—	4.0	8.0	13.6	8.5
	All	T	6-192 (3.1)	4.0⑦	—	4.0	8.0	13.6	11.0
1991	All	K	4-121 (2.0)	4.0⑦	—	4.0	8.0	13.6	11.7
	All	G	4-134 (2.2)	4.0⑦	—	4.0	8.0	13.6	11.7
	All	T	6-192 (3.1)	4.0⑦	—	4.0	8.0	13.6	14.2
1992	All	H	4-121 (2.0)	4.0⑦	—	4.0	8.0	15.2	11.7
	All	4	4-134 (2.2)	4.0⑦	—	4.0	8.0	15.2	9.2
	All	T	6-192 (3.1)	4.0⑦	—	4.0	8.0	15.2	13.1

① Add 3 quarts, check oil level at dipstick and add as necessary
② Cimarron 8.0 pints
③ Cimarron 16.0 gallons
④ Isuzu: 5.3
   Muncie: 4.1
⑤ Transaxle Model No. MK7 or MT2—5.4 pts., No. MG1 and MG2—4.0 pts.
⑥ Engine VIN code M or K—8.5 qts.
⑦ Check oil level at dipstick and add as necessary

MAINTENANCE INTERVALS CHART

Intervals are for number of months or thousands of miles, whichever comes first.

Maintenance	Service Intervals
Air cleaner (Replace)	30,000 mi. (48,000 km.)
PCV filter element (Replace)	50,000 mi. (48,000 km.)
PCV valve (Replace)	30,000 mi. (48,000 km.)
Power steering (Check)	12 mo./7,500 mi. (12,000 km.)
Belt tension (Adjust)	12 mo./15,000 mi. (24,000 km.)
Engine oil and filter (Change)	12 mo./7,500 mi. (12,000 km.)
Fuel filter (Change)	15,000 mi. (24,000 km.)
Manual transaxle Check Change	 12 mo./7,500 mi. (12,000 km.) 100,000 mi (160,000 km.)
Automatic transaxle Check Change	 12 mo./7,500 mi. (12,000 km.) 100,000 mi (160,000 km.)
Engine coolant Check Change	 Weekly 24 mo./30,000 mi. (24,000 km.)
Chassis lubrication	12 mo./7,500 mi. (12,000 km.)
Rotate tires	7,500 (12,000 km.)
Brake fluid (Check)	12 mo./7,500 mi. (12,000 km.)
Spark plugs and wires, ignition timing, idle speed	30,000 mi. (48,000 km.)
Torque throttle body mounting bolts	6,000 mi. (10,000 km.)

NOTE: Heavy-duty operation (trailer towing, prolonged idling, severe stop and start driving) should be accompanied by a 50% increase in maintenance. Cut the interval in half for these conditions.

FRAME CONTACT HOIST   FLOOR JACK   SUSPENSION CONTACT HOIST

Jacking and hoisting locations

Engine Performance and Tune-Up

2

TUNE-UP PROCEDURES

In order to extract the full measure of performance and economy from your car's engine it is essential that it be properly tuned at regular intervals. Although the tune-up intervals have been stretched to limits which would have been thought impossible a few years ago, periodic maintenance is still required. A regularly scheduled tune-up will keep your car's engine running smoothly and will prevent the annoying minor breakdowns and poor performance associated with an untuned engine.

A complete tune-up should be performed at the interval specified in the Maintenance Intervals chart in Chapter 1. This interval should be halved if the car is operated under severe conditions, such as trailer towing, prolonged idling, continual stop-and-start driving, or if starting and running problems are noticed. It is assumed that the routine maintenance described in the first section has been kept up, as this will have a decided effect on the results of a tune-up. All of the applicable steps should be followed in order, as the result is a cumulative one.

If the specifications on the tune-up label in the engine compartment of your vehicle disagree with the Tune-Up Specifications chart in this Chapter, the figures on the sticker must be used. The label often reflects changes made during the production run.

Spark Plugs

Spark plugs ignite the air and fuel mixture in the cylinder as the piston reaches the top of the compression stroke. The controlled explosion that results forces the piston down, turning the crankshaft and the rest of the drive train.

The average life of a spark plug in your vehicle is 30,000 miles. Part of the reason for this extraordinarily long life is the exclusive use of unleaded fuel, which reduces the amount of deposits within the combustion chamber and on the spark plug electrodes themselves, compared with the deposits left by the leaded gasoline used in the past. An additional contribution to long life is made by the HEI (High Energy Ignition) System, which fires the spark plugs with over 35,000 volts of electricity. The high voltage serves to keep the electrodes clear, and because it is a cleaner blast of electricity than that produced by conventional breaker-points ignitions, the electrodes suffer less pitting and wear.

Nevertheless, the life of a spark plug is dependent on a number of factors, including the mechanical condition of the engine, driving conditions, and the driver's habits.

When you remove the plugs, check the condition of the electrodes; they are a good indicator of the internal state of the engine. Since the spark plug wires should be checked every 15,000 miles, the spark plugs can be removed and examined at the same time. This will allow you to keep an eye on the mechanical status of the engine.

A small deposit of light tan or rust-red material on a spark plug that has been used for any period of time is to be considered normal. Any other color, or abnormal amounts of wear or deposits, indicates that there is something amiss in the engine.

The gap between the center electrode and the side or ground electrode can be expected to increase not more than 0.001 in. every 1,000 miles under normal conditions.

When a spark plug is functioning normally or, more accurately, when the plug is installed in an engine that is functioning properly, the plugs can be taken out, cleaned, regapped, and reinstalled in the engine without doing the engine any harm.

When, and if, a plug fouls and begins to misfire, you will have to investigate, correct the cause of the fouling, and either clean or replace the plug.

TUNE-UP SPECIFICATIONS

Year	VIN	No. Cylinder Displacement cu. in. (liter)	Spark Plugs Gap (in.)	Ignition Timing (deg.) MT	AT	Com- pression Pressure (psi)	Fuel Pump (psi)	Idle Speed (rpm) MT	AT	Valve Clearance In.	Ex.
1982	G	4-110 (1.8)	0.045①	12B	12B	NA	4.5–6.0	②	②	Hyd.	Hyd.
	B	4-122 (2.0)	②	②	②	NA	4.5–6.0	②	②	Hyd.	Hyd.
1983	O	4-110 (1.8)	0.060	8B	8B	NA	9–13	②	②	Hyd.	Hyd.
	J	4-110 (1.8)	0.035	②	②	NA	30–40	②	②	Hyd.	Hyd.
	P	4-121 (2.0)	0.035	②	②	NA	12	②	②	Hyd.	Hyd.
	B	4-121 (2.0)	0.035	—	12B	NA	12	②	②	Hyd.	Hyd.
1984	O	4-110 (1.8)	0.060	8B	8B	NA	9–13	②	②	Hyd.	Hyd.
	J	4-110 (1.8)	0.035	②	②	NA	30–40	②	②	Hyd.	Hyd.
	P	4-121 (2.0)	0.035	②	②	NA	12	②	②	Hyd.	Hyd.
1985	O	4-110 (1.8)	0.060	8B	8B	NA	9–13	②	②	Hyd.	Hyd.
	J	4-110 (1.8)	0.035	②	②	NA	30–40	②	②	Hyd.	Hyd.
	P	4-121 (2.0)	0.035	②	②	NA	12	②	②	Hyd.	Hyd.
	W	6-173 (2.8)	0.045	②	②	NA	40.5–47	②	②	Hyd.	Hyd.
1986	O	4-110 (1.8)	0.060	8B	8B	NA	9–13	②	②	Hyd.	Hyd.
	J	4-110 (1.8)	0.035	②	②	NA	30–40	②	②	Hyd.	Hyd.
	P	4-121 (2.0)	0.035	②	②	NA	12	②	②	Hyd.	Hyd.
	W	6-173 (2.8)	0.045	②	②	NA	40.5–47	②	②	Hyd.	Hyd.
1987	M	4-121 (2.0)	0.060	②	②	NA	35–38	②	②	Hyd.	Hyd.
	1	4-121 (2.0)	0.035	②	②	NA	10–12	②	②	Hyd.	Hyd.
	K	4-121 (2.0)	0.060	②	②	NA	10	②	②	Hyd.	Hyd.
	W	6-173 (2.8)	0.045	②	②	NA	40.5–47	②	②	Hyd.	Hyd.
1988	M	4-121 (2.0)	0.035	②	②	NA	35–38	②	②	Hyd.	Hyd.
	1	4-121 (2.0)	0.035	②	②	NA	9–13	②	②	Hyd.	Hyd.
	K	4-121 (2.0)	0.060	②	②	NA	9–13	②	②	Hyd.	Hyd.
	W	6-173 (2.8)	0.045	②	②	NA	40.5–47	②	②	Hyd.	Hyd.
1989	M	4-121 (2.0)	0.035	②	②	NA	35–38	②	②	Hyd.	Hyd.
	1	4-121 (2.0)	0.035	②	②	NA	9–13	②	②	Hyd.	Hyd.
	K	4-121 (2.0)	0.060	②	②	NA	9–13	②	②	Hyd.	Hyd.
	W	6-173 (2.8)	0.045	②	②	NA	40.5–47	②	②	Hyd.	Hyd.
1990	K	4-121 (2.0)	0.045	②	②	NA	9–13	②	②	Hyd.	Hyd.
	M	4-121 (2.0)	0.035	②	②	NA	35–38	②	②	Hyd.	Hyd.
	G	4-134 (2.2)	0.035	②	②	NA	9–13	②	②	Hyd.	Hyd.
	T	6-192 (3.1)	0.045	②	②	NA	40.5–47	②	②	Hyd.	Hyd.
1991	K	4-121 (2.0)	0.045	②	②	NA	9–13	②	②	Hyd.	Hyd.
	G	4-134 (2.2)	0.035	②	②	NA	9–13	②	②	Hyd.	Hyd.
	T	6-192 (3.1)	0.045	②	②	NA	40.5–47	②	②	Hyd.	Hyd.
1992	H	4-121 (2.0)	0.045	②	②	NA	41–47	②	②	Hyd.	Hyd.
	4	4-134 (2.2)	0.045	②	②	NA	40.5–47	②	②	Hyd.	Hyd.
	T	6-192 (3.1)	0.045	②	②	NA	40.5–47	②	②	Hyd.	Hyd.

NOTE: The underhood specifications sticker often reflects tune-up specification changes in production. Sticker figures must be used if they disagree with those in this chart.

Part numbers in this chart are not recommendations by Chilton for any product by brand name

B—Before top dead center

NA—Not available

① Certain models may use 0.035 in. gap. See underhood specifications sticker to be sure

② See underhood specifications sticker

There are several reasons why a spark plug will foul and you can learn which is at fault by just looking at the plug. A few of the most common reasons for plug fouling, and a description of the fouled plug's appearance, are shown in the Color Insert section.

Spark plugs suitable for use in your car's engine are offered in a number of different heat ranges. The amount of heat which the plug absorbs is determined by the length of the lower insulator. The longer the insulator, the hotter the plug will operate; the shorter the insulator, the cooler it will operate. A spark plug that absorbs (or retains) little heat and remains too cool will accumulate deposits of oil and carbon, because it is not hot enough to burn them off. This leads to fouling and consequent misfiring. A spark plug that absorbs too much heat will have no deposits, but the electrodes will burn away quickly and, in some cases, pre-ignition may result. Pre-ignition occurs when the spark plug tips get so hot that they ignite the fuel/mixture before the actual spark fires. This premature ignition will usually cause a pinging sound under conditions of low speed and heavy load. In severe cases, the heat may become high enough to start the fuel/air mixture burning throughout the combustion chamber rather than just to the front of the plug. In this case, the resultant explosion (detonation) will be strong enough to damage pistons, rings, and valves.

In most cases the factory recommended heat range is correct; it is chosen to perform well under a wide range of operating conditions. However, if most of your driving is long distance, high speed travel, you may want to install a spark plug one step colder than standard. If most of your driving is of the short trip variety, when the engine may not always reach operating temperature, a hotter plug may help burn off the deposits normally accumulated under those conditions.

REMOVAL

1. Number the wires with pieces of adhesive tape so that you won't cross them when you replace them.

2. The spark plug boots have large grips to aid in removal. Grasp the wire by the rubber boot and twist the boot ½ turn in either direction to break the tight seal between the boot and the plug. Then twist and pull on the boot to remove the wire from the spark plug. DO NOT PULL ON THE SPARK PLUG WIRE ITSELF OR YOU WILL DAMAGE THE CARBON CORD CONDUCTOR.

3. Use a ⅝ in. spark plug socket to loosen all of the plugs about two turns. A universal joint installed at the socket end of the extension will ease the process.

If removal of the plugs is difficult, apply a few drops of penetrating oil or silicone spray to the area around the base of the plug, and allow it a few minutes to work.

4. If compressed air is available, apply it to the area around the spark plug holes. Otherwise, use a rag or a brush to clean the area. Be careful not to allow any foreign material to drop into the spark plug holes.

5. Remove the plugs by unscrewing them the rest of the way.

INSPECTION

Check the plugs for deposits and wear. If they are not going to be replaced, clean the plugs thoroughly. Remember that any kind of deposit will decrease the efficiency of the plug. Plugs can be cleaned on a spark plug cleaning machine, which can sometimes be found in service stations, or you can do an acceptable job of cleaning with a stiff brush. If the plugs are cleaned, the electrodes must be filed flat. use an ignition points file, not an emery board or the like, which will leave deposits. The electrodes must be filed perfectly flat with sharp edges; rounded edges reduce the spark plug voltage by as much as 50%.

Check spark plug gap before installation. The ground electrode (the L-shaped one connected to the body of the plug) must be parallel to the center electrode and the specified size wire gauge (see Tune-Up Specifications) should pass through the gap with a slight drag. Always check the gap on new plugs, too; they are not always set correctly at the factory. Do not use a flat feeler gauge when measuring the gap, because the reading will be inaccurate. Wire gapping tools usually have a bending tool attached. Use that to adjust the side electrode until the proper distance is obtained. Absolutely never bend the center electrode. Also, be careful not to bend the side electrode too far or too often; it may weaken and break off within the engine, requiring removal of the cylinder head to retrieve it.

INSTALLATION

1. Lubricate the threads of the spark plugs with a drop of oil or a shot of silicone spray. ALWAYS INSTALL THE SPARK PLUGS AND TIGHTEN THEM HAND TIGHT FIRST. Take care not to cross-thread them.

2. Tighten the spark plugs with the socket. Do not apply the same amount of force you would use for a bolt; just snug them in. These spark plugs do nut use gaskets, and over-tightening will make future removal difficult. If a

torque wrench is available, tighten to 7-15 ft. lbs.

NOTE: *While over-tightening the spark plug is to be avoided, under-tightening is just as bad. If combustion gases leak past the threads, the spark plug will overheat and rapid electrode wear will result.*

3. Install the wires on their respective plugs. Make sure the wires are firmly connected. You will be able to feel them click into place.

CHECKING AND REPLACING SPARK PLUG WIRES

Every 15,000 miles, inspect the spark plug wires for burns, cuts, or breaks in the insulation. Check the boots and the nipples on the distributor cap. Replace any damaged wiring.

Every 45,000 miles or so, the resistance of the wires should be checked with an ohmmeter. Wires with excessive resistance will cause misfiring, and may make the engine difficult to start in damp weather. Generally, the useful life of the cables is 45,000-60,000 miles.

To check resistance, remove the distributor cap, leaving the wires in place. Connect one lead of an ohmmeter to an electrode within the cap; connect the other lead to the corresponding spark plug terminal (remove it from the spark plug for this test). Replace any wire which shows a resistance over 30,000Ω. The following chart gives resistance values as a function of length. Generally speaking, however, resis-

THE SHORTER THE PATH, THE FASTER THE HEAT IS DISSIPATED AND THE COOLER THE PLUG

HEAVY LOADS, HIGH SPEEDS

SHORT Insulator Tip
Fast Heat Transfer
LOWER Heat Range
COLD PLUG

THE LONGER THE PATH, THE SLOWER THE HEAT IS DISSIPATED AND THE HOTTER THE PLUG

SHORT TRIP STOP-AND-GO

LONG Insulator Tip
Slow Heat Transfer
HIGHER Heat Range
HOT PLUG

Spark plug heat range

Twist and pull on the rubber boot to remove the spark plug wires; never pull on the wire itself

SPARK PLUG IDENTIFICATION CHART

PREFIX
F=FINE LINE
(14 MM 5/8" HEX)
R-RESISTOR

THREAD SIZE
4 = 14 MM
(NOT USED WITH "FINE LINE")

R 4 6 T S

HEAT RANGE
0-1-2-3-4-5-6-7-8-9

COLD ———▶ HOT
The higher the digit, the "hotter" the plug. The lower the digit, the "cooler" the plug.

SUFFIX
C = Copper Core
E = Special Design Electrode, Extended Tip
K = Special Design
L = Long Reach
M = Special Design Electrode
S = Extended Tip
T = Tapered Seat Shell Design
TS = Tapered Seat With Extended Tip
X = Wide Gap
Z = Special Gap (Usually Denotes Wide Gap)
6 = .060 (1.5mm)
8 = .080 (2.0mm)

Suffixes are combined to form such designations as: SX, CTS, LS6 etc.

Spark plug identification diagram

Plugs that are in good condition can be filed and reused

INSERT SCREWDRIVER TO UNLOCK

RETAINER

DO NOT PULL ON WIRE WITH RETAINER LOCKED

Unlock the plastic retainers to replace the spark plug wires

Always use a wire gauge to check the electrode gap

Adjust the electrode gap by bending the side electrode

tance should not be considered the outer limit of acceptability.
- 0-15 in.: 3,000-10,000Ω
- 15-25 in.: 4,000-15,000Ω
- 25-35 in.: 6,000-20,000Ω
- Over 35 in.: 25,000Ω

It should be remembered that resistance is also a function of length; the longer the wire, the greater the resistance. Thus, if the wires on your car are longer than the factory originals, resistance will be higher, quite possible outside these limits.

WHEN INSTALLING NEW WIRES, REPLACE THEM ONE AT A TIME TO AVOID MIXUPS. START BY REPLACING THE LONGEST ONE FIRST.

Install the boot firmly over the spark plug. Route the wire over the same path as the original. Insert the nipple firmly onto the tower on the distributor cap, then install the cap cover and latches to secure the wires.

FRONT

1.8L, 110 cu. in. (VIN CODE G), 1982
2.0L, 122 cu. in. (VIN CODE B & P), 1983–86
4-cylinder, overhead valve engine
Firing order: 1–3–4–2
Distributor rotation: clockwise

2.0L, 122 cu. in. (VIN CODE 1), 1987–89
2.2L, 134 cu. in. (VIN CODE G and 4), 1990–92
4-cylinder, overhead valve engine
Firing order: 1–3–4–2
Distributorless

2.8L, 173 cu. in. (VIN CODE W) 1987–89
3.1L, 192 cu. in. (VIN CODE T) 1990–92
V6 overhead valve engine
Firing order: 1–2–3–4–5–6
Distributorless

2.8L, 173 cu. in. (VIN CODE W) 1985–86
V6 overhead valve engine
Firing order: 1–2–3–4–5–6
Distributor rotation: clockwise

1 1.8L, 110 cu. in. (VIN CODE O & J), 1983–86
2.0L, 122 cu. in. (VIN CODE M & K), 1987–91
4-cylinder, overhead cam engine
Firing order: 1–3–4–2
Distributor rotation: counterclockwise

FIRING ORDERS

To avoid confusion, replace the spark plug wires one at a time.

GM DELCO-REMY HIGH ENERGY IGNITION (HEI)

General Information

The High Energy Ignition distributor is used on all engines. The ignition coil is either mounted to the top of the distributor cap or is externally mounted on the engine, having a secondary circuit high tension wire connecting the coil to the distributor cap and interconnecting primary wiring as part of the engine harness.

HEI SYSTEM PRECAUTIONS

Timing Light Use

Inductive pick-up timing lights are the best kind of use with HEI. Timing light which connect between the spark plug and the spark plug wire occasionally (not always) give false readings.

Spark Plug Wires

The plug wires used with HEI systems are of a different construction than conventional wires. When replacing them, make sure you get the correct wires, since conventional wires won't carry the voltage. Also, handle them carefully to avoid cracking or splitting them and never pierce them.

Tachometer Use

Not all tachometers will operate or indicate correctly when used on a HEI system. While some tachometers may give a reading, this does not necessarily mean the reading is correct. In addition, some tachometers hook up differently from others. If you can't figure out whether or not your tachometer will work on your car, check with the tachometer manufacturer. Dwell readings, or course, have no significance at all.

HEI System Testers

Instruments designed specifically for testing HEI systems are available from several tool manufacturers. Some of these will even test the module itself.

Troubleshooting

NOTE: *An accurate diagnosis is the first step to problem solution and repair. For several of the following steps, a HEI spark tester, tool ST 125, which has a spring clip to attach it to ground. Use of this tool is recommended, as there is more control of the high energy spark and less chance of being shocked. If a tachometer is connected to the TACH terminal on the distributor, disconnect it before proceeding with this test.*

SECONDARY CIRCUIT

Testing

SECONDARY SPARK

1. Check for spark at the spark plugs by attaching the HEI spark tester, tool ST 125, to one of the plug wires, grounding the HEI spark tester on the engine and cranking the starter.

2. If no spark occurs on one wire, check a second. If spark is present, the HEI system is good.

3. Check fuel system, plug wires, and spark plugs.

4. If no spark occurs from EST distributor, disconnect the 4 terminal EST connector and recheck for spark. If spark is present, EST system service check should be performed.

NOTE: *Before making any circuit checks with test meters, be sure that all primary circuit connectors are properly installed and that spark plug cables are secure at the distributor and at the plugs.*

Distributor Component Testing

DISTRIBUTOR WITH SEPARATE COIL TYPE ONE

NOTE: *This type distributor has no vacuum or centrifugal advance mechanism and has the pick-up coil mounted above the module. This distributor is used with the EST system.*

Testing

IGNITION COIL

1. Disconnect the primary wiring connectors and secondary coil wire from the ignition coil.

2. Using an ohmmeter on the high scale, connect one lead to a grounding screw and the second lead to one of the primary coil terminals.

3. The reading should be infinite. If not, replace the ignition coil.

4. Using the low scale, place the ohmmeter leads on both the primary coil terminals.

5. The reading should be very low or zero. If not, replace the ignition coil.

HEI/EST distributor—type one distributor

Testing the ignition coil—type one distributor

6. Using the high scale, place one ohmmeter lead on the high tension output terminal and the other lead on a primary coil terminal.

7. The reading should NOT be infinite. If it is, replace the ignition coil.

Testing

PICK-UP COIL

1. Remove the rotor and pick-up coil leads from the module.

2. Using an ohmmeter, attach one lead to the distributor base and the second lead to one of the pick-up coil terminals of the connector.

3. The reading should be infinite at all times.

4. Position both leads of the ohmmeter to the pick-up terminal ends of the connector.

5. The reading should be a steady value between 500-1500Ω.

6. If not within the specification value, the pick-up coil is defective.

NOTE: *While testing, flex the leads to determine if wire breaks are present under the wiring insulation.*

IGNITION MODULE

Because of the complexity of the internal circuitry of the HEI/EST module, it is recommended the module be tested with an accurate module tester.

It is imperative that silicone lubricant be used under the module when it is installed, to prevent module failure due to overheating.

NOTE: *The module and the Hall Effect switch (if used) can be removed from the distributor without disassembly. To remove the pick-up coil, the distributor shaft must be removed to expose a waved retaining ring (C-washer) holding the pick-up coil in place.*

HALL EFFECT SWITCH

The Hall Effect Switch, when used, is installed in the HEI distributor. The purpose of the switch is to sense engine speed and send the information to the Electronic Control Module (ECM). To remove the Hall Effect Switch, the distributor shaft must be removed from the distributor.

Testing

1. Remove the switch connectors from the switch.

2. Connect a 12 volt battery and voltmeter to the switch. Note and follow the polarity markings.

3. With a knife blade inserted straight down and against the magnet, the voltmeter should

Testing the Hall Effect Switch—type one distributor

Testing the pick-up coil—type one distributor

HEI/EST distributor—type two distributor

read within 0.5 volts of battery voltage. If not, the switch is defective.

4. Without the knife blade inserted against the magnet, the voltmeter should read less than 0.5 volts. If not, the switch is defective.

DISTRIBUTOR WITH SEPARATE COIL TYPE TWO

NOTE: *This type distributor has no vacuum or centrifugal advance mechanisms and the module has two outside terminal connections for the wiring harness. This distributor is used with the EST system.*

Testing

IGNITION COIL

1. Using an ohmmeter set on the high scale, place one lead on a ground of the ignition coil.
2. Place the second lead into one of the rearward terminals of the ignition coil primary connector.
3. The ohmmeter scale should read infinite. If not, replace the ignition coil.
4. Using the low scale, place the ohmmeter leads into each of the outer terminals of the coil connector.
5. The reading should be zero or very low. If not, replace the ignition coil.
6. Using the high scale, place one ohmmeter lead on the coil secondary terminal and the second lead into the rearward terminal of the ignition coil primary connector.
7. The reading should not be infinite. If so, replace the ignition coil.

Testing

PICK-UP COIL

1. Remove the rotor and pick-up leads from the module.

2. Using an ohmmeter, connect one of the leads to the distributor base.
3. Connect the second lead to one of the pick-up coil lead terminals
4. The reading should be infinite. If not, the pick-up coil is defective.
NOTE: *During the ohmmeter tests, flex the leads by hand to check for intermediate opens in the wiring.*
5. Connect both ohmmeter lead to the pick-up coil terminals at the connector.
6. The reading should be of one steady value, 500-1500Ω.
7. If the reading is not within specifications, the pick-up coil must is defective.

Testing

IGNITION MODULE

Because of the complexity of the internal circuitry of the HEI/EST module, it is recommended the module be tested with an accurate module tester.

It is imperative that silicone lubricant be

Testing the pick-up coil—type two distributor

Pick-up coil removal—type two distributor

Testing the ignition coil—type two distributor

Module replacement—type two distributor

used under the module when it is installed, to prevent module failure due to overheating.

NOTE: *The module can be removed without distributor disassembly. To remove the pick-up coil, the distributor shaft must be removed. A retainer can then be removed from the top of the pole piece and the pick-up coil removed.*

DISTRIBUTOR WITH SEPARATE COIL TYPE THREE W/TANG DRIVE

NOTE: *This distributor is used with the EST system. The unit is mounted horizontally to the valve cover housing and is driven by the camshaft, through a tang on the distributor shaft.*

Testing

IGNITION COIL

1. Using an ohmmeter set on the high scale, place one lead on a ground of the ignition coil.

2. Place the second lead into one of the rearward terminals of the ignition coil primary connector.

3. The ohmmeter scale should read infinite. If not, replace the ignition coil.

4. Using the low scale, place the ohmmeter leads into each of the outer terminals of the coil connector.

5. The reading should be zero or very low. If not, replace the ignition coil.

6. Using the high scale, place one ohmmeter lead on the coil secondary terminal and the second lead into the rearward terminal of the ignition coil primary connector.

7. The reading should not be infinite. If so, replace the ignition coil.

Testing

PICK-UP COIL

1. Remove the rotor and pick-up leads from the module.

2. Using an ohmmeter, connect one of the leads to the distributor base.

3. Connect the second lead to one of the pick-up coil lead terminals

4. The reading should be infinite. If not, the pick-up coil is defective.

NOTE: *During the ohmmeter tests, flex the leads by hand to check for intermediate opens in the wiring.*

5. Connect both ohmmeter lead to the pick-up coil terminals at the connector.

6. The reading should be of one steady value, 500-1500Ω.

HEI/EST distributor—type three (tang drive) distributor

Testing the ignition coil—type three (tang drive) distributor

7. If the reading is not within specifications, the pick-up coil must is defective.

Testing

IGNITION MODULE

Because of the complexity of the internal circuitry of the HEI/EST module, it is recommended the module be tested with an accurate module tester.

It is imperative that silicone lubricant be used under the module when it is installed, to prevent module failure due to overheating.

NOTE: *The module can be removed without distributor disassembly. The distributor shaft and C-clip must be removed before the pick-up coil can be removed. Before removing*

Module replacement—type three (tang drive) distributor

Testing the pick-up coil—type three (tang drive) distributor

Pick-up coil removal—type three (tang drive) distributor

the roll pin from the distributor tang drive to shaft, a spring must first be removed.

GENERAL MOTORS DIRECT IGNITION SYSTEM (DIS) ELECTRONIC SPARK TIMING (EST)

General Information

The Direct Ignition System (DIS) is used on the 1987–92 2.0L (VIN 1), 2.2L (VIN G and 4) and all V6 engines.

The Direct Ignition System (DIS) does not use the conventional distributor and ignition coil. The system consists of ignition module, crankshaft sensor or combination sensor, along with the related connecting wires and Electronic Spark Timing (EST) portion of the Electronic Control Module (ECM).

The DIS system uses a "waste spark" method of spark distribution. Companion cylinders are paired and the spark occurs simultaneously in the cylinder with the piston coming up on the compression stroke and in the companion cylinder with the piston coming up on the exhaust stroke.

Example of firing order and companion cylinders:

- 1-2-3-4-5-6; 1/4, 2/5, 3/6
- 1-6-5-4-3-2; 1/4, 6/3, 5/2
- 1-3-4-2; 1/4, 2/3

NOTE: *Notice the companion cylinders in the V6 engine firing order remain the same, but the cylinder firing order sequence differs.*

The cylinder on the exhaust stroke requires very little of the available voltage to arc, so the remaining high voltage is used by the cylinder in the firing position (TDC compression). This same process is repeated when the companion cylinders reverse roles.

It is possible in an engine no-load condition, for one plug to fire, even though the spark plug lead from the same coil is disconnected from the other spark plug. The disconnected spark plug lead acts as one plate of a capacitor, with the engine being the other plate. These two capacitors plates are charged as a current surge (spark) jumps across the gap of the connected spark plug.

These plates are then discharged as the secondary energy is dissipated in an oscillating current across the gap of the spark plug still connected. Because of the direction of current flow in the primary windings and thus in the secondary windings, one spark plug will fire from the center electrode to the side electrode, while the other will fire from the side electrode to the center electrode.

These systems utilize the EST signal from the ECM, as do the convention distributor type ignition systems equipped with the EST system to control timing.

In the Direct Ignition system and while under 400 rpm, the DIS ignition module controls the spark timing through a module timing mode. Over 400 rpm, the ECM controls the spark timing through the EST mode. In the Direct Ignition system, to properly control the ignition timing, the ECM relies on the the following information from the various sensors.

1. Engine load (manifold pressure or vacuum).
2. Atmospheric (barometric) pressure.
3. Engine temperature.
4. Manifold air temperature.
5. Crankshaft position.
6. Engine speed (rpm).

Direct Ignition System Components

NOTE: *The Direct Ignition System/EST is used with TBI and Ported fuel injection systems.*

CRANKSHAFT SENSOR

A magnetic crankshaft sensor (Hall Effect switch) is used and is remotely mounted on the opposite side of the engine from the DIS module. The sensor protrudes in to the engine block, within 0.050 in. (1.27mm) of the crankshaft reluctor.

The reluctor is a special wheel cast into the crankshaft with seven slots machined into it, six of them being evenly spaced at 60° apart. A seventh slot is spaced 10° from one of the other slots and serves as a generator of a "sync-pulse". As the reluctor rotates as part of the crankshaft, the slots change the magnetic field of the sensor, creating an induced voltage pulse. Based on the crankshaft sensor pulses, the

DIS module sends reference signals to the ECM, which are used to indicate crankshaft position and engine speed. The DIS module will continue to send these reference pulses to the ECM at a rate of one per each 120° of crankshaft rotation. The ECM actvates the fuel injectors, based on the recognition of every other reference pulse, beginning at a crankshaft position 120° after piston top dead center (TDC). By comparing the time between the pulses, the DIS module can recognize the pulse representing the seventh slot (sync-pulse) which starts the calculation of ignition coil sequencing. The second crankshaft pulse following the sync-pulse signals the DIS module to fire the No.2-5 ignition coil, the fourth crankshaft pulse signals the module to fire No.3-6 ignition coil and the sixth crankshaft pulse signals the module to fire the 1-4 ignition coil.

1. Crankshaft reluctor
2. Crankshaft sensor
3. Dis-assembly

Sensor to crank reluctor relationship—V6 engine

1. Crankshaft relucter
2. Crankshaft sensor
3. DIS assembly

Sensor to crank reluctor relationship—4 cylinder engine

IGNITION COILS

There are two separate coils for the four cylinder engines and three separate coils for the V6 engines, mounted to the coil/module assembly. Spark distribution is synchronized by a signal from the crankshaft sensor which the ignition module uses to trigger each coil at the proper time. Each coil provides the spark for two spark plugs.

Two types of ignition coil assemblies are used, Type I and Type II During the diagnosis of the systems, the correct type of ignition coil assembly must be identified and the diagnosis directed to that system.

Type I module/coil assembly has three twin tower ignition coils, combined into a single coil pack unit. This unit is mounted to the DIS module. ALL THREE COILS MUST BE REPLACED AS A UNIT. A separate current source through a fused circuit to the module terminal **P** is used to power the ignition coils.

Type II coil/module assembly has three separate coils that are mounted to the DIS module. EACH COIL CAN BE REPLACED SEPARATELY. A fused low current source to the module terminal **M**, provides power for the sensors, ignition coils and internal module circuitry.

DIS MODULE

The DIS module monitors the crankshaft sensor signal and based on these signals, sends a reference signal to the ECM so that correct spark and fuel injector control can be maintained during all driving conditions. During cranking, the DIS module monitors the syncpulse to begin the ignition firing sequence. Below 400 rpm, the module controls the spark advance by triggering each of the ignition coils at a predetermined interval, based on engine speed only. Above 400 rpm, the ECM controls the spark timing (EST) and compensates for all

driving conditions. The DIS module must receive a sync-pulse and then a crank signal, in that order, to enable the engine to start.

The DIS module is not repairable. When a module is replaced, the remaining DIS components must be transferred to the new module.

DIRECT IGNITION ELECTRONIC SPARK TIMING (EST) CIRCUITS

This system uses the same EST to ECM circuits that the distributor type systems with EST use. The following is a brief description for the EST circuits.

DIS REFERENCE, CIRCUIT 430

The crankshaft sensor generates a signal to the ignition module, which results in a reference pulse being sent to the ECM. The ECM uses this signal to calculate crankshaft position and engine speed for injector pulse width.

NOTE: *The crankshaft sensor is mounted to the base of the DIS module on the 2.5L four cylinder engines and is mounted directly into the side of the engine block.*

REFERENCE GROUND CIRCUIT 453

This wire is grounded through the module and insures that the ground circuit has no voltage drop between the ignition module and the ECM, which can affect performance.

BY-PASS, CIRCUIT 424

At approximately 400 rpm, the ECM applies 5 volts to this circuit to switch spark timing control from the DIS module to the ECM. An open or grounded by pass circuit will set a code 42 and result in the engine operating in a back-up ignition timing mode (module timing) at a calculated timing value. This may cause poor performance and reduced fuel economy.

ELECTRONIC SPARK TIMING (EST), CIRCUIT 423

The DIS module sends a reference signal to the ECM when the engine is cranking. While the engine is under 400 rpm, the DIS module controls the ignition timing. When the engine speed exceeds 400 rpm, the ECM applies 5 volts to the By-pass line to switch the timing to the ECM control (EST).

An open or ground in the EST circuit will result in the engine continuing to run, but in a back-up ignition timing mode (module timing mode) at a calculated timing value and the SERVICE ENGINE SOON light will not be on. If the EST fault is still present, the next time the engine is restarted, a code 42 will be set and the engine will operate in the module timing mode. This may cause poor performance and reduced fuel economy.

1. Bracket
2. Module
3. Shield
4. 1–4 coil
5. 6–3 coil
6. 5–2 coil
7. Screws (6)
   4.5 N·m (40 lbs. in.)

Exploded view of the DIS assembly—V6 engine

Diagnosis

DIRECT IGNITION SYSTEM

NOTE: *The following diagnostic aids are quick checks. Should more in-depth diagnosis of the system be needed, refer to Chilton's Electronic Engine Control Manual.*

The ECM uses information from the MAP and Coolant sensors, in addition to rpm to calculate spark advance as follows;

1. Low MAP output voltage = More spark advance.
2. Cold engine = More spark advance.
3. High MAP output voltage = Less spark advance.
4. Hot engine = Less spark advance.

Therefore, detonation could be caused by low MAP output or high resistance in the coolant sensor circuit.

Poor performance could be caused by high MAP output or low resistance in the coolant sensor circuit.

If the engine cranks but will not operate, or starts, then immediately stalls, diagnosis must be accomplished to determine if the failure is in the DIS system or the fuel system.

CHECKING EST PERFORMANCE

The ECM will set timing at a specified value when the diagnostic **TEST** terminal in the ALDL connector is grounded. To check for EST operation, run the engine at 1500 rpm with the terminal ungrounded. Then ground the **TEST** terminal. If the EST is operating, there should be a noticeable engine rpm change. A fault in the EST system will set a trouble code 42.

CODE 12

Code 12 is used during the diagnostic circuit check procedure to test the diagnostic and code display ability of the ECM. This code indicates that the ECM is not receiving the engine rpm (reference) signal. This occurs with the ignition key in the ON position and the engine not operating.

SETTING IGNITION TIMING

Because the reluctor wheel is an integral part of the crankshaft and the crankshaft sensor is mounted in a fixed position, timing adjustment is not possible.

DIS Assembly

REMOVAL AND INSTALLATION

1. Disconnect the negative battery cable.
2. Disconnect the electrical wires from the DIS assembly.
3. Mark the location of the spark plug wires on the DIS assembly and remove the wires.

4. Remove the DIS assembly mounting bolts and remove the assembly from the block.

NOTE: *With the coil pack removed, the coils can each be removed and the ignition module can be removed as well.*

To install:

5. Install the DIS assembly on the block.
6. Reconnect the plug wires to their original location.
7. Connect the DIS assembly wiring.
8. Connect the negative battery cable.
9. If equipped with the 3.1L engine, perform the idle learn procedure to allow the ECM memory to be updated with the correct IAC valve pintle position and provide for a stable idle speed.

   a. Install a Tech 1 scan tool.
   b. Turn the ignition to the **ON** position, engine not running.
   c. Select **IAC SYSTEM**, then **IDLE LEARN** in the **MISC TEST** mode.
   d. Proceed with idle learn as directed by the scan tool.

Crankshaft Sensor

REMOVAL AND INSTALLATION

1. Disconnect the negative battery cable.
2. Disconnect the sensor harness plug.

Crankshaft sensor installation—V6 engine

1. 2–3 coil
2. 1–4 coil
3. Module
4. Crank sensor assembly
5. Bolt 71 inch lbs. (8 Nm)

Ignition coils, module and sensor—4 cylinder engines

3. Remove the sensor-to-block bolt and remove the sensor from the engine.

4. To install the sensor, position the sensor in the block and install the sensor bolt. Torque the sensor bolt to 71 inch lbs.

5. Reconnect the sensor harness plug.

GENERAL MOTORS CORPORATION ELECTRONIC SPARK TIMING (EST) SYSTEM

GENERAL DESCRIPTION

The High Energy Ignition (HEI) system controls fuel combustion by providing the spark to ignite the compressed air/fuel mixture, in the combustion chamber, at the correct time. To provide improved engine performance, fuel economy and control of the exhaust emissions, the ECM controls distributor spark advance (timing) with the Electronic Spark Timing (EST) system.

The standard High Energy Ignition (HEI) system has a modified distributor module which is used in conjunction with the EST system. The module has seven terminals instead of the four used without EST. Two different terminal arrangements are used, depending upon the distributor used with a particular engine application.

To properly control ignition/combustion timing, the ECM needs to know the following information:

1. Crankshaft position.
2. Engine speed (rpm).
3. Engine load (manifold pressure or vacuum).
4. Atmospheric (barometric) pressure.
5. Engine temperature.
6. Transmission gear position (certain models)

The EST system consists of the distributor module, ECM and its connecting wires. The distributor has four wires from the HEI module connected to a four terminal connector, which mates with a four wire connector from the ECM.

These circuits perform the following functions:

1. Distributor reference at terminal **B**. This provides the ECM with rpm and crankshaft position information.

2. Reference ground at terminal **D**. This wire is grounded in the distributor and makes sure the ground circuit has no voltage drop, which could affect performance. If this circusit is open, it could cause poor performance.

3. By-pass at terminal **C**. At approximately 400 rpm, the ECM applies 5 volts to this circuit to switch the spark timing control from the HEI module to the ECM. An open or grounded bypass circuit will set a Code 42 and the engine will run at base timing, plus a small amount of advance built into the HEI module.

4. EST at terminal **A**. This triggers the HEI module. The ECM does not know what the acrtual timing is, but it does know when it gets its reference signal. It then advances or retards the spark timing from that point. Therefore, if the base timing is set incorrectly, the entire spark curve will be incorrect.

An open circuit in the EST circuit will set a Code 42 and cause the engine to run on the HEI module timing. This will cause poor performance and poor fuel economy. A ground may set a Code 42, but the engine will not run.

The ECM uses information from the MAP or VAC and coolant sensors, in addition to rpm, in order to calculate spark advance as follows:

1. Low MAP output voltage (high VAC sensor output voltage) would require MORE spark advance.

2. Cold engine would require MORE spark advance.

3. High MAP output voltage (low VAC sensor output voltage) would require LESS spark advance.

4. Hot engine would require LESS spark advance.

RESULTS OF INCORRECT EST OPERATION

Detonation could be caused by low MAP output (high VAC sensor output), or high resistance in the coolant sensor circuit.

Poor performance could be caused by high MAP output (low VAC sensor output) or low resistance in the coolant sensor circuit.

HOW CODE 42 IS DETERMINED

When the systems is operating on the HEI module with no voltage in the by-pass line, the HEI module grounds the EST signal. The ECM expects to sense no voltage on the EST line during this condition. If it senses voltage, it sets Code 42 and will not go into the EST mode.

When the rpm for EST is reached (approximately 400 rpm), the ECM applies 5 volts to the by-pass line and the EST should no longer be grounded in the HEI module, so the EST voltage should be varying.

If the by-pass line is open, the HEI module will not switch to the EST mode, so the EST voltage will be low and Code 42 will be set.

If the EST line is grounded, the HEI module will switch to the EST, but because the line is grounded, there will be no EST signal and the engine will not operate. A Code 42 may or may not be set.

GENERAL MOTORS CORPORATION ELECTRONIC SPARK CONTROL (ESC) SYSTEM

GENERAL DESCRIPTION

The Electronic Spark Control (ESC) operates in conjunction with the Electronic Spark Timing (EST) system and modifies (retards) the spark advance when detonation occurs. The retard mode is held for approximately 20 seconds after which the spark control will again revert to the Electronic Spark Timing (EST) system. There are three basic components of the Electronic Spark Control (ESC) system.

SENSOR

The Electronic Spark Control (ESC) sensor detects the presence (or absence) and intensity of the detonation by the vibration characteristics of the engine. The output is an electrical signal that goes to the controller. A sensor failure would allow no spark retard.

DISTRIBUTOR

The distributor is an HEI/EST unit with an electronic module, modified so it can respond to the ESC controller signal. This command is delayed when detonation is occurring, thus providing the level of spark retard required. The amount of spark retard is a function of the degree of detonation.

CONTROLLER

The Electronic Spark Control (ESC) controller processes the sensor signal into a command signal to the distributor, to adjust the spark timing. The process is continuous, so that the presence of detonation is monitored and controlled. The controller is a hard wired signal processor and amplifier which operates from 6-16 volts. Controller failure would be no ignition, no retard or full retard. The controller has no memory storage.

CODE 43

Should a Code 43 be set in the ECM memory, it would indicate that the ESC system retard signal has been sensed by the ECM for too long a period of time. When voltage at terminal L of the ECM is low, spark timing is retarded. Normal voltage in the non-retarded mode is approximately 7.5 volts or more.

BASIC IGNITION TIMING

NOTE: *Late model vehicles, both 4 cylinder and 6 cylinder engines, have distributorless ignition systems (DIS). Because the reluctor wheel is an integral part of the crankshaft, and the crankshaft sensor is mounted in a fixed position, timing adjustment is not possible.*

Basic ignition timing is critical to the proper operation of the ESC system. ALWAYS FOLLOW THE VEHICLE EMISSION CONTROL INFORMATION LABEL PROCEDURES WHEN ADJUSTING IGNITION TIMING.

Some engines will incorporate a magnetic timing probe hole for use with special electronic timing equipment. Consult the manufacturer's instructions for the use of this electronic timing equipment.

Ignition timing is the measurement, in degrees of crankshaft rotation, of the point at which the spark plugs fire in each of the cylinders. It is measured in degrees before or after Top Dead Center (TDC) of the compression stroke.

Because it takes a fraction of a second for the spark plug to ignite the mixture in the cylinder, the spark plug must fire a little before the piston reaches TDC. Otherwise, the mixture will not completely ignited as the piston passes TDC and the full power of the explosion will not be used by the engine.

The timing measurement is given in degrees of crankshaft rotation before the piston reaches TDC (BTDC). If the setting for the ignition timing is 5° BTDC, the spark plug must fire 5° before each piston reaches TDC. This only holds true, however, when the engine is at idle speed.

As the engine speed increases, the pistons go faster. The spark plugs have to ignite the fuel even sooner if it is to be completely ignited when the piston reaches TDC.

If the ignition is set too far advanced (BTDC), the ignition and expansion of the fuel in the cylinder will occur too soon and tend to force the piston down while it is still traveling up. This causes engine ping. If the ignition spark is set too far retarded, after TDC (ATDC), the piston will have already passed TDC and started on its way down when the fuel is ignited. This will cause the piston to be forced down for only a portion of its travel. This will result in poor engine performance and lack of power.

Ignition timing for this engine should be accomplished using the averaging method in which the timing of each cylinder can be brought into closer agreement with the base timing specification.

The averaging method involves the use of a double notched crankshaft pulley. When timing the engine, the coil wire, instead of the Number 1 plug wire, should be used to trigger the timing light. The notch for the No. 1 cylinder is scribed across all three edges of the double sheave pulley. Another notch located 180° away from the No. 1 cylinder notch is scribed only across the center section of the pulley to make it distinguishable from the No. 1 cylinder notch.

Since the trigger signal for the timing light is picked up at the coil wire, each spark firing results in a flash from the timing light. A slight jiggling of the timing notch may be apparent since each cylinder firing is being displayed. Optimum timing of all cylinders is accomplished by centering the total apparent notch width about the correct timing specification.

There are three basic types of timing light available. The first is a simple neon bulb with two wire connections (one for the spark plug and one for the plug wire, connecting the light in series). This type of light is quite dim, and must be held closely to the marks to be seen, but it is quite inexpensive. The second type of light operates from the car's battery. Two alligator clips connect to the battery terminals, while a third wire connects to the spark plug with an adapter. This type of light is more expensive, but the xenon bulb provides a nice bright flash which can even be seen in sunlight. The third type replaces the battery source with 110 volt house current. Some timing lights have other functions built into them, such as dwell meters, tachometers, or remote starting switches. These are convenient, in that they reduce the tangle of wires under the hood, but may duplicate the functions of tools you already have.

Because your car has electronic ignition, you should use a timing light with an inductive pickup. This pickup simply clamps around the Number 1 spark plug wire (in this case, the coil wire), eliminating the adapter. It is not susceptible to crossfiring or false triggering, which may occur with a conventional light due to the greater voltages produced by HEI.

Ignition Timing

ADJUSTMENT

1.8L, 2.0L OHV engine

1982-86

1. REFER TO THE INSTRUCTIONS ON THE EMISSION CONTROL STICKER INSIDE THE ENGINE COMPARTMENT. FOLLOW ALL INSTRUCTIONS ON THE LABEL.

2. Locate the timing marks on the crankshaft pulley and the front of the engine.

3. Clean off the marks so that you can see them. Chalk or white paint will help to make them more visible.

4. Attach a tachometer to the engine as detailed previously.

5. Disconnect the 4-terminal EST connector at the distributor so that the engine will switch to the bypass timing mode (please refer to Chapter 4 for more information).

6. Attach a timing light as per the manufacturer's instructions. Clamp the inductive pickup around the HIGH TENSION COIL WIRE (not the No. 1 spark plug wire) at the distributor. Before installing the pick-up on the wire, it

Ignition timing using the averaging method

will be necessary to peel back the protective plastic cover which encases the wire.

7. Loosen the distributor clamp bolt slightly so that the distributor may be rotated as necessary to adjust timing.

8. Check that all wires are clear of the fan and then start the engine. Allow the engine to reach normal operating temperature.

9. Aim the timing light at the marks. A slight jiggling of the notch on the pulley may appear due to the fact that each cylinder is being displayed as it fires. The apparent notch width cannot be reduced by a timing adjustment.

10. Center the total apparent notch width about the correct timing mark on the indicator by rotating the distributor housing. This will insure that the average cylinder timing is as close to specifications as possible. Once again, the apparent notch width cannot be reduced by timing adjustment.

11. Turn off the engine and tighten the distributor lock bolt. Start the engine and recheck the timing. Sometimes the distributor will move a little during the tightening process. If the ignition timing is within 1° of the correct setting, that is close enough; a tolerance of up to 2° is permitted by the manufacturer.

12. Turn off the engine and disconnect the timing light and the tachometer. Reconnect the 4-terminal EST connector.

2.0L (VIN 1) 2.2L, 2.8L AND 3.1L Engines
1987–92

The ignition timing on engines with distributorless ignitions, is controlled by the Electronic Control Module (ECM). No adjustments are possible.

2.0L (VIN K AND M) Engines
AVERAGING METHOD

1. REFER TO THE UNDERHOOD EMISSION CONTROL LABEL AND FOLLOW ALL OF THE TIMING INSTRUCTIONS IF THEY DIFFER FROM BELOW.

2. Warm the engine to normal operating temperature.

3. Place the transmission in **N** or **P**. Apply the parking brake and block wheels.

4. Air conditioning, cooling fan and choke must be **OFF**. Do not remove the air cleaner, except as noted.

5. Ground the ALCL connector under the dash by installing a jumper wire between the **A** and **B** terminals. The Check Engine light should begin flashing.

6. Connect an inductive timing light to the No. 1 spark plug wire lead and record timing.

7. Connect an inductive timing light to the No. 4 spark plug wire lead and record timing.

8. Add the 2 timing numbers and divide by 2 to obtain "average timing".

For example: No. 1 timing = 4 degrees and No. 4 timing = 8 degrees; 4 + 8 = 12 ÷ 2 = 6 degrees average timing. If a change is necessary, subtract the average timing from the timing specification to determine the amount of timing change to No. 1 cylinder. For example: if the timing specification is 8 degrees and the average timing is 6 degrees, advance the No. 1 cylinder 2 degrees to set the timing.

Tachometer hookup connections on the 4 cylinder OHV engines through 1986

9. To correct the timing, loosen the distributor hold-down clamp, adjust the distributor and retighten the hold-down bolt.

10. Once the timing is properly set, remove the jumper wire from the ALCL connector.

11. If necessary to clear the ECM memory, disconnect the ECM harness from the positive battery pigtail for 10 seconds with the key in the **OFF** position.

Tachometer Hook-up

OHV Engines

1982–86

Due to the relative inaccessibility of the ignition coil, a separate tachometer hookup has been provided. It is taped to the main wiring harness in the back of the engine compartment, near the firewall. Connect one tachometer lead to this terminal and the other lead to a suitable ground. On some tachometers, the leads must be connected to the terminal and then to the positive battery terminal.

CAUTION: *Never ground the TACH terminal; serious module and ignition coil damage will result. If there is any doubt as to the correct tachometer hookup, check with the tachometer manufacturer.*

OHC Engines

There is a terminal marked TACH on the distributor cap. Connect one tachometer lead to this terminal and the other lead to a ground. On some tachometer, the leads must be connected

THERMO TIME SWITCH

DISTRIBUTOR COIL LEAD

TACH LEAD

COIL

E.V.R.V SOLENOID

COOLANT TEMPERATURE SENSOR

Tachometer hookup connection on the V6 engine through 1986

to the TACH terminal and to the battery positive terminal.

CAUTION: *Never ground the TACH terminal; If there is any doubt as to the correct tachometer hookup, check with the tachometer manufacturer.*

Valve Adjustment

All models utilize an hydraulic valve lifter system to obtain zero lash. No adjustment is necessary. An initial adjustment is required anytime that the lifters are removed or the valve train is disturbed, this procedure is covered in Chapter 3.

Idle Speed and Mixture Adjustment

Carbureted Engines

All carbureted vehicles are equipped with an Idle Speed Control (ISC) motor which is in turn controlled by the Electronic Control Module (ECM). All idle speeds are programmed into the ECM's memory and then relayed to the ISC motor as any given situation requires. Curb idle is pre-set at the factory and not routinely adjustable. Although curb idle is not to be adjusted under normal conditions, it can be adjusted, but only upon replacement of the ISC (for further details, refer to Chapter 5).

The idle mixture screws are concealed under staked-in plugs. Idle mixture is not considered to be a normal tune-up procedure, because of the sensitivity of emission control adjustments. Mixture adjustment requires not only the special tools with which to remove the concealing plugs, but also the addition of an artificial enrichment substance (generally propane) which must be introduced into the carburetor by means of a finely calibrated metering valve. These tools are not generally available and require a certain amount of expertise to use, therefore, mixture adjustments are purposely not covered in this book. If you suspect that your car's carburetor requires a mixture adjustment, we strongly recommend that the job be referred to a qualified service technician.

Fuel Injected Engines

The fuel injected vehicles are controlled by a computer which supplies the correct amount of fuel during all engine operating conditions; no adjustment is necessary.

ENGINE ELECTRICAL

Ignition Coil

The High Energy Ignition distributor is used on all engines. The ignition coil is either mounted to the top of the distributor cap or is externally mounted on the engine, having a secondary circuit high tension wire connecting the coil to the distributor cap and interconnecting primary wiring as part of the engine harness.

The Direct Ignition System (DIS) does not use the conventional distributor and ignition coil. The system consists of ignition module, crankshaft sensor or combination sensor, along with the related connecting wires and Electronic Spark Timing (EST) portion of the Electronic Control Module (ECM).

TESTING

Distributor With Separate Coil
Type One

1. Disconnect the primary wiring connectors and secondary coil wire from the ignition coil.
2. Using an ohmmeter on the high scale, connect one lead to a grounding screw and the second lead to one of the primary coil terminals.
3. The reading should be infinite. If not, replace the ignition coil.
4. Using the low scale, place the ohmmeter leads on both the primary coil terminals.
5. The reading should be very low or zero. If not, replace the ignition coil.
6. Using the high scale, place one ohmmeter lead on the high tension output terminal and the other lead on a primary coil terminal.
7. The reading should NOT be infinite. If it is, replace the ignition coil.

Distributor With Separate Coil
Type Two

1. Using an ohmmeter set on the high scale, place one lead on a ground of the ignition coil.

2. Place the second lead into one of the rearward terminals of the ignition coil primary connector.
3. The ohmmeter scale should read infinite. If not, replace the ignition coil.
4. Using the low scale, place the ohmmeter leads into each of the outer terminals of the coil connector.
5. The reading should be zero or very low. If not, replace the ignition coil.
6. Using the high scale, place one ohmmeter lead on the coil secondary terminal and the second lead into the rearward terminal of the ignition coil primary connector.
7. The reading should not be infinite. If so, replace the ignition coil.

Distributor With Separate Coil
Type Three w/Tang Drive

1. Using an ohmmeter set on the high scale, place one lead on a ground of the ignition coil.
2. Place the second lead into one of the rearward terminals of the ignition coil primary connector.
3. The ohmmeter scale should read infinite. If not, replace the ignition coil.
4. Using the low scale, place the ohmmeter leads into each of the outer terminals of the coil connector.
5. The reading should be zero or very low. If not, replace the ignition coil.
6. Using the high scale, place one ohmmeter lead on the coil secondary terminal and the second lead into the rearward terminal of the ignition coil primary connector.
7. The reading should not be infinite. If so, replace the ignition coil.

Direct Ignition System (DIS)

There are two separate coils for the 4-cylinder engines and three separate coils for the V6 engines, mounted to the coil/module assembly. Spark distribution is synchronized by a signal from the crankshaft sensor which the ignition module uses to trigger each coil at the proper time. Each coil provides the spark for two spark plugs.

Two types of ignition coil assemblies are used, Type I and Type II During the diagnosis of the systems, the correct type of ignition coil assembly must be identified and the diagnosis directed to that system.

Type I module/coil assembly has three twin tower ignition coils, combined into a single coil pack unit. This unit is mounted to the DIS module. ALL THREE COILS MUST BE REPLACED AS A UNIT. A separate current source through a fused circuit to the module terminal **P** is used to power the ignition coils.

Type II coil/module assembly has three separate coils that are mounted to the DIS module. EACH COIL CAN BE REPLACED SEPARATELY. A fused low current source to the module terminal **M**, provides power for the sensors, ignition coils and internal module circuitry.

Ignition Module
DISTRIBUTOR WITH SEPARATE COIL TYPE ONE

NOTE: *This type distributor has no vacuum or centrifugal advance mechanism and has the pickup coil mounted above the module. This distributor is used with the EST system.*

Because of the complexity of the internal circuitry of the HEI/EST module, it is recommended the module be tested with an accurate module tester.

It is imperative that silicone lubricant be used under the module when it is installed, to prevent module failure due to overheating.

NOTE: *The module and the Hall Effect switch (if used) can be removed from the distributor without disassembly. To remove the pickup coil, the distributor shaft must be removed to expose a waved retaining ring (C-washer) holding the pickup coil in place.*

DISTRIBUTOR WITH SEPARATE COIL TYPE TWO

NOTE: *This type distributor has no vacuum or centrifugal advance mechanisms and the module has two outside terminal connections for the wiring harness. This distributor is used with the EST system.*

Because of the complexity of the internal circuitry of the HEI/EST module, it is recommended the module be tested with an accurate module tester.

It is imperative that silicone lubricant be used under the module when it is installed, to prevent module failure due to overheating.

NOTE: *The module can be removed without distributor disassembly. To remove the pickup coil, the distributor shaft must be removed. A retainer can then be removed from the top of the pole piece and the pickup coil removed.*

DISTRIBUTOR WITH SEPARATE COIL TYPE THREE W/TANG DRIVE

NOTE: *This distributor is used with the EST system. The unit is mounted horizontally to the valve cover housing and is driven by the camshaft, through a tang on the distributor shaft.*

Because of the complexity of the internal circuitry of the HEI/EST module, it is recommended the module be tested with an accurate module tester.

It is imperative that silicone lubricant be used under the module when it is installed, to prevent module failure due to overheating.

NOTE: *The module can be removed without distributor disassembly. The distributor shaft and C-clip must be removed before the pickup coil can be removed. Before removing the roll pin from the distributor tang drive to shaft, a spring must first be removed.*

Distributor
REMOVAL AND INSTALLATION
1.8L and 2.0L OHV Engines

NOTE: *On Chevrolet V6 models the distributor body is involved in the engine lubricating system. The lubricating circuit to the right bank valve train can be interrupted by misalignment of the distributor body. See Firing Order illustrations for correct distributor positioning.*

The 1987–92 Chevrolet built 4-cylinder 2.0L and V6 2.8L engines do not have a distributor. For an explanation of this type of ignition system refer to (DIS) Ignition System in Chapter 2.

1. Disconnect the negative battery cable.
2. Tag and disconnect all wires leading from the distributor cap.
3. Remove the air cleaner housing as previously detailed.
4. Remove the distributor cap.
5. Disconnect the AIR pipe-to-exhaust manifold hose at the air management valve.
6. Unscrew the rear engine lift bracket bolt and nut, lift it off the stud and then position the entire assembly out of the way to facilitate better access to the distributor.
7. Mark the position of the distributor, relative to the engine block and then scribe a mark on the distributor body indicating the initial position of the rotor.

8. Remove the holddown nut and clamp from the base of the distributor. Remove the distributor from the engine. The drive gear on the distributor shaft is helical and the shaft will rotate slightly as the distributor is removed. Note and mark the position of the rotor at this second position. Do not crank the engine while the distributor is removed.

9. To install the distributor, rotate the shaft until the rotor aligns with the second mark you made (when the shaft stopped moving). Lubricate the drive gear with clean engine oil and install the distributor into the engine. As the distributor is installed, the rotor should move to the first mark that you made. This will ensure proper timing. If the marks do not align properly, remove the distributor and try again.

10. Install the clamp and holddown nut.

NOTE: *You may wish to use a magnet attached to an extension bar to position the clamp on the stud.*

11. Installation of the remaining components is in the reverse order of removal. Check the ignition timing.

1.8L and 2.0L OHC Engines

1. Disconnect the battery ground.

2. Mark the spark plug wires and remove the wires and coil.

3. Matchmark the position of the rotor, distributor body and cylinder head.

4. Disconnect the wiring from the distributor.

5. Remove the two distributor holddown nuts.

6. Remove the distributor.

7. Installation is the reverse of removal. Torque the holddown nuts to 13 ft. lbs. If the engine was rotated while the distributor was out, refer to the necessary service procedures.

INSTALLATION IF THE ENGINE WAS DISTURBED

IF THE ENGINE WAS CRANKED WHILE THE DISTRIBUTOR WAS REMOVED, YOU WILL HAVE TO PLACE THE ENGINE ON TDC OF THE COMPRESSION STROKE TO OBTAIN PROPER IGNITION TIMING.

1. Remove the No. 1 spark plug.

2. Place your thumb over the spark plug hole. Crank the engine slowly until compression is felt. It will be easier if you have someone rotate the engine by hand, using a wrench on the crankshaft pulley.

3. Align the timing mark on the crankshaft pulley with the 0° mark on the timing scale attached to the front of the engine. This places the engine at TDC of the compression stroke.

4. Turn the distributor shaft until the rotor points to the No. 1 spark plug tower on the cap.

5. Install the distributor into the engine. Be sure to align the distributor-to-engine block mark made earlier.

6. Perform all necessary remaining service steps.

Alternator

Two models of the SI series alternator are used on these cars. The 10 SI and 15 SI are of similar construction; the 15 SI is slightly larger, uses different stator windings, and produces more current.

Removing the 1.8L and 2.0L OHV distributor

1. Stud
2. 20 ± 1.0
3. Nut
4. EST connector
5. Coil Connector
6. Distributor

Distributor mounting on 1.8L and 2.0 OHC engines

ALTERNATOR PRECAUTIONS

1. When installing a battery, make sure that the positive and negative cables are not reversed.

2. When jump-starting the car, be sure that like terminals are connected. This also applies to using a battery charger. Reversed polarity will burn out the alternator and regulator in a matter of seconds.

3. Never operate the alternator with the battery disconnected or on an otherwise uncontrolled open circuit.

4. Do not short across or ground any alternator or regulator terminals.

5. Do not try to polarize the alternator.

6. Do not apply full battery voltage to the field (brown) connector.

7. Always disconnect the battery ground cable before disconnecting the alternator lead.

8. Always disconnect the battery (negative cable first) when charging it.

9. Never subject the alternator to excessive heat or dampness. If you are steam cleaning the engine, cover the alternator.

10. Never use arc-welding equipment on the car with the alternator connected.

CHARGING SYSTEM TROUBLESHOOTING

There are many possible ways in which the charging system can malfunction. Often the source of a problem is difficult to diagnose, requiring special equipment and a good deal of experience. This is usually not the case, however, where the charging system fails completely and causes the dash board warning light to come on or the battery to become dead. To troubleshoot a complete system failure only two pieces of equipment are needed: a test light, to determine that current is reaching a certain point; and a current indicator (ammeter), to determine the direction of the current flow and its measurement in amps.

This test works under three assumptions:

1. The battery is known to be good and fully charged.

2. The alternator belt is in good condition and adjusted to the proper tension.

3. All connections in the system are clean and tight.

NOTE: *In order for the current indicator to give a valid reading, the car must be equipped with battery cables which are of the same gauge size and quality as original equipment battery cables.*

1. Turn off all electrical components on the car. Make sure the doors of the car are closed. If the car is equipped with a clock, disconnect the clock by removing the lead wire from the rear of the clock. Disconnect the positive battery cable from the battery and connect the ground wire on a test light to the disconnected positive battery cable. Touch the probe end of the test light to the positive battery post. The test light should not light. If the test light does light, there is a short or open circuit on the car.

2. Disconnect the voltage regulator wiring harness connector at the voltage regulator. Turn on the ignition key. Connect the wire on a test light to a good ground (engine bolt). Touch the probe end of a test light to the ignition wire connector into the voltage regulator wiring connector. This wire corresponds to the **I** terminal on the regulator. If the test light goes on, the charging system warning light circuit is complete. If the test light does not come on and the warning light on the instrument panel is on, either the resistor wire, which is parallel with the warning light, or the wiring to the voltage regulator, is defective. If the test light does not come on and the warning light is not on, either the bulb is defective or the power supply wire form the battery through the ignition switch to the bulb has an open circuit. Connect the wiring harness to the regulator.

3. Examine the fuse link wire in the wiring harness from the starter relay to the alternator. If the insulation on the wire is cracked or split, the fuse link may be melted. Connect a test light to the fuse link by attaching the ground wire on the test light to an engine bolt and touching the probe end of the light to the bottom of the fuse link wire where it splices into the alternator output wire. If the bulb in the test light does not light, the fuse link is melted.

4. Start the engine and place a current indicator on the positive battery cable. Turn off all electrical accessories and make sure the doors are closed. If the charging system is working properly, the gauge will show a draw of less than 5 amps. If the system is not working properly, the gauge will show a draw of more than 5 amps. A charge moves the needle toward the battery, a draw moves the needle away from the battery. Turn the engine off.

5. Disconnect the wiring harness from the voltage regulator at the regulator at the regulator connector. Connect a male spade terminal (solderless connector) to each end of a jumper wire. Insert one end of the wire into the wiring harness connector which corresponds to the **A** terminal on the regulator. Insert the other end of the wire into the wiring harness connector which corresponds to the **F** terminal on the regulator. Position the connector with the jumper wire installed so that it cannot contact any metal surface under the hood. Position a current indicator gauge on the positive battery cable. Have an assistant start the engine. Observe the

reading on the current indicator. Have your assistant slowly raise the speed of the engine to about 2,000 rpm or until the current indicator needle stops moving, whichever comes first. Do not run the engine for more than a short period of time in this condition. If the wiring harness connector or jumper wire becomes excessively hot during this test, turn off the engine and check for a grounded wire in the regulator wiring harness. If the current indicator shows a charge of about three amps less than the output of the alternator, the alternator is working properly. If the previous tests showed a draw, the voltage regulator is defective. If the gauge does not show the proper charging rate, the alternator is defective.

REMOVAL AND INSTALLATION

1. Disconnect the negative battery cable at the battery.

CAUTION: *Failure to disconnect the negative cable may result in injury from the positive battery lead at the alternator, and may short the alternator and regulator during the removal process.*

2. Disconnect and label the two terminal plug and the battery leads from the rear of the alternator.
3. Loosen the mounting bolts. Push the alternator inwards and slip the drive belt off the pulley.
4. Remove the mounting bolts and remove the alternator.

To install:

5. Place the alternator in its brackets and install the mounting bolts. Do not tighten them yet.
6. Slip the belt back over the pulley. Pull outwards on the unit and adjust the belt tension (see Chapter 1). Tighten the mounting and adjusting bolts.
7. Install the electrical leads.
8. Install the negative battery cable.

Regulator

A solid state regulator is mounted within the alternator. All regulator components are enclosed in a solid mold. The regulator is non-adjustable and requires no maintenance.

Starter

REMOVAL AND INSTALLATION

1. Disconnect the negative battery cable at the battery.
2. Label and disconnect the solenoid wires and battery cable.
3. Remove the rear motor support bracket. Remove the air conditioning compressor support rod (if so equipped).
4. Working under the car, remove the two starter-to-engine bolts, and allow the starter to drop down. Note the location and number of any shims. Remove the starter.
5. Installation is the reverse. Tighten the mounting bolts to 25–35 ft. lbs. Check system for proper operation.

Alternator installation details—1982–86 1.8L and 2.0L OHV engines

MANUAL STEERING

POWER STEERING

1. Alternator
2. Spacer
3. Bracket
4. Bracket (front)
5. 45 N·m (34 lbs. ft.)
6. Bracket (rear)
7. 28 N·m (21 lbs. ft.)
8. 35 N·m (26 lbs. ft.)
9. 50 N·m (37 lbs. ft.)
10. Power steering pump

Alternator installation details—1.8L and 2.0L OHC except turbo engines

1. Alternator
2. Bracket, generator
3. Bolt—33 Nm (24 lbs. ft.)
4. Belt
5. Bolt—27 N·m (19 lbs. ft.)
6. Bolt—50 N·m (37 lbs. ft.)
7. Tensioner asm.
8. Bolt—50 N·m (37 lbs. ft.)
9. Support, generator front
10. Intake manifold
11. Nut—20 N·m (14 lbs. ft.)
12. Stud
13. Bracket
14. Bracket, rear

Alternator installation details—2.0L OHC turbo engines

1. 21 N·m (20 lb. ft.)
2. Alternator bracket (rear)
3. 50 N·m (38 lb. ft.)
4. 33 N·m (26 lb. ft.)
5. Generator bracket
6. Power steering pump
7. 27 N·m (20 lb. ft.)
8. 50 N·m (38 lb. ft.)
9. Generator assembly
10. Generator bracket
11. 10 N·m (7 lb. ft.)
12. Retainer clip

Alternator installation details—1.8L OHC turbo engines

1. 30 N·m (22 lbs. ft.)
2. Brace
3. 3.3 N·m (29 lbs. in.)
4. W/K99
5. Nut
6. 45 N·m (22 lbs. ft.)
7. Bracket
8. Alternator

Alternator installation details—1987–92 2.0L and 2.2L OHV engines

1. Alternator
2. Through bolt
3. Bolt
4. Nut

Alternator installation details—1985–86 2.8L V6 engines

1. Alternator
2. 25 N·m (18 lbs. ft.)
3. Bracket
4. 50 N·m (37 lbs. ft.)
5. Brace

Alternator installation details—1987–92 2.8L and 3.1L V6 engines

Battery

Refer to Chapter 1 for details on battery maintenance.

REMOVAL AND INSTALLATION

1. Disconnect the negative (ground) cable first, then the positive cable. The side terminal cables are retained only by the center bolt.

CAUTION: *To avoid sparks, always disconnect the negative cable first, and connect it last.*

2. Remove the battery holddown clamp.
3. Remove the battery.
4. Before installing the battery, clean the battery terminals and the cables thoroughly.
5. Check the battery tray to be sure it is clear of any debris. If it is rusty, it should be wire-

1. BRACKET
2. WASHER
3. STARTER MOTOR

Starter mounting—1.8L and 2.0L OHC engines

1. Shim, starter motor
2. Starter motor
3. Bolt—43 N·m (32 lbs. ft.)

Starter mounting—2.8L and 3.1L V6 engines

1. Shim, starter asm.
2. Starter asm.
3. Bolt—43 N.m (32 lbs. ft.)
4. Bolt—12 N.m (9 lbs. ft.)
5. Bracket, starter asm.
6. Washer
7. Nut—32 N.m (24 lbs. ft.)

Starter mounting—1.8L and 2.0L OHV engines

brushed clean and given a coat of anti-rust paint, or replaced.

6. Install the battery in the tray, being sure it is centered in the lip.

7. Install the holddown clamp. Tighten to 6 ft. lbs., which is tight enough to hold the battery in place, but loose enough to prevent the case from cracking.

8. Connect the positive, then the negative battery cables. Installation torque for the ca-

bles is 9 ft. lbs. Give the terminals a light external coat of grease after installation to retard corrosion.

NOTE: *Make absolutely sure that the battery is connected properly before you turn on the ignition switch. Reversed polarity can burn out the alternator and regulator in a matter of seconds.*

ENGINE MECHANICAL

These cars use 5 different 4-cylinder engines. Three are built by Chevrolet: a 1835.5cc (1.8L) 112 cid, a 1986.8cc (2.0L) 121 cid, and a 2196.3cc (2.2L) 134 cid. All of these Chevrolet-built engines are of the overhead valve configuration (OHV). That means that the camshaft is in the block and the rest of the valve train is on top of the head. The two other engines are Pontiac (Brazil) built. The 1797.9cc (1.8L) 110 cid and the (2.0) 122 overhead cam engines (OHC). This means that the camshaft and valve components are all located in the engine head. The 3 Chevrolet-built engines are virtually identical in all aspects except displacement.

The Pontiac-built engines are quite different in most respects.

In the 1985 Model year, a 2838.4cc (2.8L) 173 cid V6 engine was introduced. This engine is a high output version of the Chevy-built V6, using MFI (multi-port fuel injection). In 1990 the 3148.8cc (3.1L) 192 cid engine replaced the 2.8L engine. Both V6 engines are basically identical except for the cubic inch displacement.

Engine Overhaul Tips

Most engine overhaul procedures are fairly standard. In addition to specific parts replacement procedures and complete specifications for your individual engine, this section also is a guide to accept rebuilding procedures. Examples of standard rebuilding practice are shown and should be used along with specific details concerning your particular engine.

Competent and accurate machine shop services will ensure maximum performance, reliability and engine life.

In most instances it is more profitable for the do-it-yourself mechanic to remove, clean and inspect the component, buy the necessary parts and deliver these to a shop for actual machine work.

On the other hand, much of the rebuilding work (crankshaft, block, bearings, piston rods, and other components) is well within the scope of the do-it-yourself mechanic.

TOOLS

The tools required for an engine overhaul or parts replacement will depend on the depth of your involvement. With a few exceptions, they will be the tools found in a mechanic's tool kit (see Chapter 1). More in-depth work will require any or all of the following:
- a dial indicator (reading in thousandths) mounted on a universal base
- micrometers and telescope gauges
- jaw and screw-type pullers
- scraper
- valve spring compressor
- ring groove cleaner
- piston ring expander and compressor
- ridge reamer
- cylinder hone or glaze breaker
- Plastigage®
- engine stand

The use of most of these tools is illustrated in this Chapter. Many can be rented for a one-time use from a local parts jobber or tool supply house specializing in automotive work.

Occasionally, the use of special tools is called for. See the information on Special Tools and Safety Notice in the front of this book before substituting another tool.

INSPECTION TECHNIQUES

Procedures and specifications are given in this Chapter for inspecting, cleaning and assessing the wear limits of most major components. Other procedures such as Magnaflux® and Zyglo® can be used to locate material flaws and stress cracks. Magnaflux® is a magnetic process applicable only to ferrous materials. The Zyglo® process coats the material with a fluorescent dye penetrant and can be used on any material Check for suspected surface cracks can be more readily made using spot check dye. The dye is sprayed onto the suspected area, wiped off and the area sprayed with a developer. Cracks will show up brightly.

OVERHAUL TIPS

Aluminum has become extremely popular for use in engines, due to its low weight. Observe the following precautions when handling aluminum parts:
- Never hot tank aluminum parts (the caustic hot tank solution will eat the aluminum.
- Remove all aluminum parts (identification tag, etc.) from engine parts prior to the tanking.
- Always coat threads lightly with engine oil or anti-seize compounds before installation, to prevent seizure.
- Never overtorque bolts or spark plugs especially in aluminum threads.

Stripped threads in any component can be repaired using any of several commercial repair kits (Heli-Coil®, Microdot®, Keenserts®, etc.).

When assembling the engine, any parts that will be frictional contact must be prelubed to provide lubrication at initial start-up. Any product specifically formulated for this purpose can be used, but engine oil is not recommended as a prelube.

When semi-permanent (locked, but removable) installation of bolts or nuts is desired, threads should be cleaned and coated with Loctite® or other similar, commercial non-hardening sealant.

REPAIRING DAMAGED THREADS

Several methods of repairing damaged threads are available. Heli-Coil® (shown here), Keenserts® and Microdot® are among the most widely used. All involve basically the same principle — drilling out stripped threads, tapping the hole and installing a prewound insert —

making welding, plugging and oversize fasteners unnecessary.

Two types of thread repair inserts are usually supplied: a standard type for most Inch Coarse, Inch Fine, Metric Course and Metric Fine thread sizes and a spark lug type to fit most spark plug port sizes. Consult the individual manufacturer's catalog to determine exact applications. Typical thread repair kits will contain a selection of prewound threaded inserts, a tap (corresponding to the outside diameter threads of the insert) and an installation tool. Spark plug inserts usually differ because they require a tap equipped with pilot threads and a combined reamer/tap section. Most manufacturers also supply blister-packed thread repair inserts separately in addition to a master kit containing a variety of taps and inserts plus installation tools.

Before effecting a repair to a threaded hole, remove any snapped, broken or damaged bolts or studs. Penetrating oil can be used to free frozen threads. The offending item can be removed with locking pliers or with a screw or stud extractor. After the hole is clear, the thread can be repaired, as shown in the series of accompanying illustrations.

Drill out the damaged threads with specified drill. Drill completely through the hole or to the bottom of a blind hole

With the tap supplied, tap the hole to receive the thread insert. Keep the tap well oiled and back it out frequently to avoid clogging the threads

Damaged bolt holes can be repaired with thread repair inserts

Screw the threaded insert onto the installation tool until the tang engages the slot. Screw the insert into the tapped hole until it is ¼–½ turn below the top surface. After installation break off the tang with a hammer and punch.

Checking Engine Compression

A noticeable lack of engine power, excessive oil consumption and/or poor fuel mileage measured over an extended period are all indicators of internal engine war. Worn piston rings, scored or worn cylinder bores, blown head gaskets, sticking or burnt valves and worn valve

Standard thread repair insert (left) and spark plug thread insert (right)

seats are all possible culprits here. A check of each cylinder's compression will help you locate the problems.

As mentioned in the Tools and Equipment (Chapter 1), a screw-in type compression gauge is more accurate that the type you simply hold against the spark plug hole, although it takes slightly longer to use. It's worth it to obtain a more accurate reading. Follow the procedures below.

1. Warm up the engine to normal operating temperature.

2. Remove all the spark plugs.

3. Disconnect the **BAT** terminal and if so equipped, the four terminal connector from the HEI distributor. On 1987 and later Cavaliers, disconnect the ECM fuse.

4. Fully open the throttle either by operating the throttle linkage by hand or by having an assistant floor the accelerator pedal.

5. Screw the compression gauge into the no.1 spark plug hole until the fitting is snug.

NOTE: *Be careful not to crossthread the plug hole. On aluminum cylinder heads use extra care, as the threads in these heads are easily ruined.*

6. Ask an assistant to depress the accelerator pedal fully on both carbureted and fuel injected vehicles. Then, while you read the compression gauge, ask the assistant to crank the engine two or three times in short bursts using the ignition switch.

7. Read the compression gauge at the end of each series of cranks, and record the highest of these readings. Repeat this procedure for each of the engine's cylinders. Compare the highest reading of each cylinder to the compression pressure specification in the Tune-Up Specifications chart in Chapter 2. The specs in this chart are maximum values.

A cylinder's compression pressure is usually acceptable if it is not less than 70% of maximum. And no cylinder should be less than 100 lbs.

The screw-in type compression gauge is more accurate

8. If a cylinder is unusually low, pour a tablespoon of clean engine oil into the cylinder through the spark plug hole and repeat the compression test. If the compression comes up after adding the oil, it appears that the cylinder's piston rings or bore are damaged or worn. If the pressure remains low, the valves may not be seating properly (a valve job is needed), or the head gasket may be blown near that cylinder. If compression in any two adjacent cylinders is low, and if the addition of oil doesn't help the compression, there is leakage past the head gasket. Oil and coolant water in the combustion chamber can result from this problem. There may be evidence of water droplets on the engine dipstick when a head gasket has blown.

Engine
REMOVAL AND INSTALLATION

CAUTION: *When draining the coolant, keep in mind that cats and dogs are attracted by the ethylene glycol antifreeze, and are quite likely to drink any that is left in an uncovered container or in puddles on the ground. This will prove fatal in sufficient quantity. Always drain the coolant into a sealable container. Coolant should be reused unless it is contaminated or several years old.*

1.8L, 2.0L and 2.2L OHV Engines
1982–84

NOTE: *This procedure will require the use of a special powertrain alignment tool #M6 × 1 × 65.*

1. Disconnect the battery cables at the battery, negative cable first.

2. Remove the air cleaner. Drain the cooling system.

3. Remove the power steering pump (if so equipped) and position it out of the way. Leave the lines connected. Remove the windshield washer bottle.

4. If the car is equipped with air conditioning, remove the relay bracket at the bulkhead connector. Remove the bulkhead connector and then separate the wiring harness connections.

5. If equipped with cruise control, remove the servo bracket and position it out of the way.

6. Tag and disconnect all vacuum hoses and wires.

7. Remove the master cylinder at the vacuum booster.

8. Remove all heater and radiator hoses and position them out of the way.

9. Remove the fan assembly. Remove the horn.

10. Disconnect the carburetor or TBI body

Standard Torque Specifications and Fastener Markings

In the absence of specific torques, the following chart can be used as a guide to the maximum safe torque of a particular size/grade of fastener.

- There is no torque difference for fine or coarse threads.
- Torque values are based on clean, dry threads. Reduce the value by 10% if threads are oiled prior to assembly.
- The torque required for aluminum components or fasteners is considerably less.

U.S. Bolts

SAE Grade Number	1 or 2			5			6 or 7		
Number of lines always 2 less than the grade number.									
Bolt Size (Inches)—(Thread)	Maximum Torque			Maximum Torque			Maximum Torque		
	Ft./Lbs.	Kgm	Nm	Ft./Lbs.	Kgm	Nm	Ft./Lbs.	Kgm	Nm
¼—20	5	0.7	6.8	8	1.1	10.8	10	1.4	13.5
—28	6	0.8	8.1	10	1.4	13.6			
5/16—18	11	1.5	14.9	17	2.3	23.0	19	2.6	25.8
—24	13	1.8	17.6	19	2.6	25.7			
⅜—16	18	2.5	24.4	31	4.3	42.0	34	4.7	46.0
—24	20	2.75	27.1	35	4.8	47.5			
7/16—14	28	3.8	37.0	49	6.8	66.4	55	7.6	74.5
—20	30	4.2	40.7	55	7.6	74.5			
½—13	39	5.4	52.8	75	10.4	101.7	85	11.75	115.2
—20	41	5.7	55.6	85	11.7	115.2			
9/16—12	51	7.0	69.2	110	15.2	149.1	120	16.6	162.7
—18	55	7.6	74.5	120	16.6	162.7			
⅝—11	83	11.5	112.5	150	20.7	203.3	167	23.0	226.5
—18	95	13.1	128.8	170	23.5	230.5			
¾—10	105	14.5	142.3	270	37.3	366.0	280	38.7	379.6
—16	115	15.9	155.9	295	40.8	400.0			
⅞—9	160	22.1	216.9	395	54.6	535.5	440	60.9	596.5
—14	175	24.2	237.2	435	60.1	589.7			
1—8	236	32.5	318.6	590	81.6	799.9	660	91.3	894.8
—14	250	34.6	338.9	660	91.3	849.8			

Metric Bolts

Relative Strength Marking	4.6, 4.8			8.8		
Bolt Markings						
Bolt Size Thread Size x Pitch (mm)	Maximum Torque			Maximum Torque		
	Ft./Lbs.	Kgm	Nm	Ft./Lbs.	Kgm	Nm
6 x 1.0	2–3	.2–.4	3–4	3–6	.4–.8	5–8
8 x 1.25	6–8	.8–1	8–12	9–14	1.2–1.9	13–19
10 x 1.25	12–17	1.5–2.3	16–23	20–29	2.7–4.0	27–39
12 x 1.25	21–32	2.9–4.4	29–43	35–53	4.8–7.3	47–72
14 x 1.5	35–52	4.8–7.1	48–70	57–85	7.8–11.7	77–110
16 x 1.5	51–77	7.0–10.6	67–100	90–120	12.4–16.5	130–160
18 x 1.5	74–110	10.2–15.1	100–150	130–170	17.9–23.4	180–230
20 x 1.5	110–140	15.1–19.3	150–190	190–240	26.2–46.9	160–320
22 x 1.5	150–190	22.0–26.2	200–260	250–320	34.5–44.1	340–430
24 x 1.5	190–240	26.2–46.9	260–320	310–410	42.7–56.5	420–550

GENERAL ENGINE SPECIFICATIONS

Year	VIN	No. Cylinder Displacement cu. in. (liter)	Fuel System Type	Net Horsepower @ rpm	Net Torque @ rpm (ft. lbs.)	Bore × Stroke (in.)	Compression Ratio	Oil Pressure @ rpm
1982	G	4-110 (1.8)	2 bbl	88 @ 5100	100 @ 2800	3.50 × 2.91	9.0:1	45 @ 2400
	B	4-122 (2.0)	2 bbl	90 @ 5100	111 @ 2800	3.50 × 3.15	9.0:1	45 @ 2400
1983	O	4-110 (1.8)	TBI	84 @ 5200	102 @ 2800	3.34 × 3.13	8.8:1	45 @ 2400
	J	4-110 (1.8)	MFI Turbo	150 @ 5600	150 @ 2800	3.34 × 3.13	8.0:1	65 @ 2500
	P	4-121 (2.0)	TBI	86 @ 4900	100 @ 3000	3.50 × 3.15	9.3:1	68 @ 1200
	B	4-121 (2.0)	TBI	86 @ 4900	110 @ 3000	3.50 × 3.15	9.3:1	45 @ 2400
1984	O	4-110 (1.8)	TBI	84 @ 5200	102 @ 2800	3.34 × 3.13	8.8:1	45 @ 2400
	J	4-110 (1.8)	MFI Turbo	150 @ 5600	150 @ 2800	3.34 × 3.13	8.0:1	65 @ 2500
	P	4-121 (2.0)	TBI	86 @ 4900	100 @ 3000	3.50 × 3.15	9.3:1	68 @ 1200
1985	O	4-110 (1.8)	TBI	84 @ 5200	102 @ 2800	3.34 × 3.13	8.8:1	45 @ 2400
	J	4-110 (1.8)	MFI Turbo	150 @ 5600	150 @ 2800	3.34 × 3.13	8.0:1	65 @ 2500
	P	4-121 (2.0)	TBI	86 @ 4900	100 @ 3000	3.50 × 3.15	9.3:1	68 @ 1200
	W	6-173 (2.8)	MFI	120 @ 4800	155 @ 3600	3.50 × 2.99	8.9:1	50 @ 2400
1986	O	4-110 (1.8)	TBI	84 @ 5200	102 @ 2800	3.34 × 3.13	8.8:1	45 @ 2400
	J	4-110 (1.8)	MFI Turbo	150 @ 5600	150 @ 2800	3.34 × 3.13	8.0:1	65 @ 2500
	P	4-121 (2.0)	TBI	86 @ 4900	100 @ 3000	3.50 × 3.15	9.3:1	68 @ 1200
	W	6-173 (2.8)	MFI	120 @ 4800	155 @ 3600	3.50 × 2.99	8.9:1	50 @ 2400
1987	M	4-121 (2.0)	MFI Turbo	160 @ 5600	160 @ 2800	3.38 × 3.38	8.0:1	65 @ 2500
	1	4-121 (2.0)	TBI (HO)	90 @ 5600	108 @ 3200	3.50 × 3.15	9.0:1	63–77 @ 1200
	K	4-121 (2.0)	TBI	102 @ 5200	130 @ 2800	3.38 × 3.38	8.8:1	45 @ 2000
	W	6-173 (2.8)	MFI	120 @ 4800	155 @ 3600	3.50 × 2.99	8.9:1	50 @ 2400
1988	M	4-121 (2.0)	MFI Turbo	160 @ 5600	160 @ 2800	3.38 × 3.38	8.0:1	65 @ 2500
	1	4-121 (2.0)	TBI (HO)	90 @ 5600	108 @ 3200	3.50 × 3.15	9.0:1	63–77 @ 1200
	K	4-121 (2.0)	TBI	102 @ 5200	130 @ 2800	3.38 × 3.38	8.8:1	45 @ 2000
	W	6-173 (2.8)	MFI	120 @ 4800	155 @ 3600	3.50 × 2.99	8.9:1	50 @ 2400
1989	M	4-121 (2.0)	MFI Turbo	160 @ 5600	160 @ 2800	3.38 × 3.38	8.0:1	65 @ 2500
	1	4-121 (2.0)	TBI	90 @ 5600	108 @ 3200	3.50 × 3.15	9.0:1	63–77 @ 1200
	K	4-121 (2.0)	TBI	102 @ 5200	130 @ 2800	3.38 × 3.38	8.8:1	45 @ 2000
	W	6-173 (2.8)	MFI	120 @ 4800	155 @ 3600	3.50 × 2.99	8.9:1	50 @ 2400
1990	K	4-121 (2.0)	TBI	102 @ 5200	108 @ 3200	3.39 × 3.39	8.8:1	NA
	M	4-121 (2.0)	MFI Turbo	160 @ 5600	160 @ 2800	3.39 × 3.39	8.0:1	NA
	G	4-134 (2.2)	TBI	95 @ 5200	120 @ 3200	3.50 × 3.46	9.0:1	56 @ 3000
	T	6-192 (3.1)	MFI	140 @ 4500	180 @ 3600	3.50 × 3.31	8.8:1	15 @ 1100
1991	K	4-121 (2.0)	TBI	96 @ 4800	118 @ 3600	3.39 × 3.39	8.8:1	NA
	G	4-134 (2.2)	TBI	95 @ 5200	120 @ 3200	3.50 × 3.46	8.85:1	56 @ 3000
	T	6-192 (3.1)	MFI	140 @ 4500	180 @ 3600	3.50 × 3.31	8.8:1	15 @ 1100

GENERAL ENGINE SPECIFICATIONS

Year	VIN	No. Cylinder Displacement cu. in. (liter)	Fuel System Type	Net Horsepower @ rpm	Net Torque @ rpm (ft. lbs.)	Bore × Stroke (in.)	Compression Ratio	Oil Pressure @ rpm
1992	H	4-121 (2.0)	MFI	111 @ 5200	125 @ 3600	3.38 × 3.38	9.2:1	NA
	4	4-134 (2.2)	MFI	110 @ 5200	176 @ 3200	3.50 × 3.46	8.85:1	56 @ 3000
	T	6-192 (3.1)	MFI	140 @ 4200	180 @ 3200	3.50 × 3.31	8.8:1	15 @ 1100

NOTE: Horsepower and torque are SAE net figures. They are measured at the rear of the transmission with all accessories installed and operating. Since the figures vary when a given engine is installed in different models, some are representative rather than exact.

CAMSHAFT SPECIFICATIONS

All measurements given in inches.

Year	VIN	No. Cylinder Displacement cu. in. (liter)	Journal Diameter					Elevation		Bearing Clearance	Camshaft End Play
			1	2	3	4	5	In.	Ex.		
1982	G	4-110 (1.8)	1.8677–1.8696	1.8677–1.8696	1.8677–1.8696	1.8677–1.8696	1.8677–1.8696	0.2625	0.2625	0.0010–0.0039	NA
	B	4-121 (2.0)	1.8677–1.8696	1.8677–1.8696	1.8677–1.8696	1.8677–1.8696	1.8677–1.8696	0.2600	0.2600	0.0010–0.0039	NA
1983	O	4-110 (1.8)	1.6714–1.6720	1.6812–1.6816	1.6911–1.6917	1.7009–1.7015	1.7108–1.7114	0.2409	0.2409	NA	0.0160–0.0640
	J	4-110 (1.8)	1.6714–1.6720	1.6812–1.6816	1.6911–1.6917	1.7009–1.7015	1.7108–1.7114	0.2409	0.2409	NA	0.0160–0.0640
	P	4-121 (2.0)	1.8677–1.8696	1.8677–1.8696	1.8677–1.8696	1.8677–1.8696	1.8677–1.8696	0.2600	0.2600	0.0010–0.0039	NA
	B	4-121 (2.0)	1.8677–1.8696	1.8677–1.8696	1.8677–1.8696	1.8677–1.8696	1.8677–1.8696	0.2600	0.2600	0.0010–0.0039	NA
1984	O	4-110 (1.8)	1.6714–1.6720	1.6812–1.6816	1.6911–1.6917	1.7009–1.7015	1.7108–1.7114	0.2409	0.2409	NA	0.0160–0.0640
	J	4-110 (1.8)	1.6714–1.6720	1.6812–1.6816	1.6911–1.6917	1.7009–1.7015	1.7108–1.7114	0.2409	0.2409	NA	0.0160–0.0640
	P	4-121 (2.0)	1.8677–1.8696	1.8677–1.8696	1.8677–1.8696	1.8677–1.8696	1.8677–1.8696	0.2600	0.2600	0.0010–0.0039	NA
1985	O	4-110 (1.8)	1.6714–1.6720	1.6812–1.6816	1.6911–1.6917	1.7009–1.7015	1.7108–1.7114	0.2409	0.2409	NA	0.0160–0.0640
	J	4-110 (1.8)	1.6714–1.6720	1.6812–1.6816	1.6911–1.6917	1.7009–1.7015	1.7108–1.7114	0.2409	0.2409	NA	0.0160–0.0640
	P	4-121 (2.0)	1.8677–1.8696	1.8677–1.8696	1.8677–1.8696	1.8677–1.8696	1.8677–1.8696	0.2600	0.2600	0.0010–0.0039	NA
	W	6-173 (2.8)	1.8678–1.8815	1.8678–1.8815	1.8678–1.8815	1.8678–1.8815	1.8678–1.8815	0.2626	0.2732	NA	NA
1986	O	4-110 (1.8)	1.6714–1.6720	1.6812–1.6816	1.6911–1.6917	1.7009–1.7015	1.7108–1.7114	0.2409	0.2409	NA	0.0160–0.0640
	J	4-110 (1.8)	1.6714–1.6720	1.6812–1.6816	1.6911–1.6917	1.7009–1.7015	1.7108–1.7114	0.2409	0.2409	NA	0.0160–0.0640
	P	4-121 (2.0)	1.8677–1.8696	1.8677–1.8696	1.8677–1.8696	1.8677–1.8696	1.8677–1.8696	0.2600	0.2600	0.0010–0.0039	NA
	W	6-173 (2.8)	1.8678–1.8815	1.8678–1.8815	1.8678–1.8815	1.8678–1.8815	1.8678–1.8815	0.2626	0.2732	NA	NA

CAMSHAFT SPECIFICATIONS

All measurements given in inches.

Year	VIN	No. Cylinder Displacement cu. in. (liter)	Journal Diameter					Elevation		Bearing Clearance	Camshaft End Play
			1	2	3	4	5	In.	Ex.		
1987	M	4-121 (2.0)	1.6714–1.6720	1.6812–1.6816	1.6911–1.6917	1.7009–1.7015	1.7108–1.7114	0.2409	0.2409	0.0008	0.0160–0.0640
	1	4-121 (2.0)	1.8670–1.8690	1.8670–1.8690	1.8670–1.8690	1.8670–1.8690	1.8670–1.8690	0.2600	0.2600	0.0010–0.0040	NA
	K	4-121 (2.0)	1.6714–1.6720	1.6812–1.6816	1.6911–1.6917	1.7009–1.7015	1.7108–1.7114	0.2409	0.2409	0.0008	0.0160–0.0640
	W	6-173 (2.8)	1.8678–1.8815	1.8678–1.8815	1.8678–1.8815	1.8678–1.8815	1.8678–1.8815	0.2626	0.2732	NA	NA
1988	M	4-121 (2.0)	1.6714–1.6720	1.6812–1.6816	1.6911–1.6917	1.7009–1.7015	1.7108–1.7114	0.2409	0.2409	0.0008	0.0160–0.0640
	1	4-121 (2.0)	1.8670–1.8690	1.8670–1.8690	1.8670–1.8690	1.8670–1.8690	1.8670–1.8690	0.2600	0.2600	0.0010–0.0040	NA
	K	4-121 (2.0)	1.6714–1.6720	1.6812–1.6816	1.6911–1.6917	1.7009–1.7015	1.7108–1.7114	0.2409	0.2409	0.0008	0.0160–0.0640
	W	6-173 (2.8)	1.8678–1.8696	1.8678–1.8696	1.8678–1.8696	1.8678–1.8696	1.8678–1.8696	0.2626	0.2732	0.0010–0.0030	NA
1989	M	4-121 (2.0)	1.6706–1.6712	1.6812–1.6818	1.6911–1.6917	1.7009–1.7015	1.7100–1.7106	0.2625	0.2625	0.0011–0.0035	0.0016–0.0063
	1	4-121 (2.0)	1.8670–1.8690	1.8670–1.8690	1.8670–1.8690	1.8670–1.8690	1.8670–1.8690	0.2600	0.2600	0.0010–0.0040	NA
	K	4-121 (2.0)	1.6706–1.6712	1.6812–1.6818	1.6911–1.6917	1.7009–1.7015	1.7100–1.7106	0.2366	0.2515	0.0011–0.0035	0.0016–0.0063
	W	6-173 (2.8)	1.8678–1.8815	1.8678–1.8815	1.8678–1.8815	1.8678–1.8815	1.8678–1.8815	0.2626	0.2732	0.0010–0.0040	NA
1990	K	4-121 (2.0)	1.6706–1.6712	1.6812–1.6818	1.6911–1.6917	1.7009–1.7015	1.7100–1.7106	0.2366	0.2515	0.0011–0.0035	0.0016–0.0063
	M	4-121 (2.0)	1.6706–1.6717	1.6812–1.6818	1.6911–1.6917	1.7009–1.7015	1.7100–1.7106	0.2625	0.2625	0.0011–0.0035	0.0016–0.0063
	G	4-134 (2.2)	1.8670–1.8690	1.8670–1.8690	1.8670–1.8690	1.8670–1.8690	1.8670–1.8690	0.2590	0.2590	0.0010–0.0040	NA
	T	6-192 (3.1)	1.8678–1.8815	1.8678–1.8815	1.8678–1.8815	1.8678–1.8815	1.8678–1.8815	0.2626	0.2626	0.0010–0.0040	NA
1991	K	4-121 (2.0)	1.6706–1.6712	1.6812–1.6818	1.6911–1.6917	1.7009–1.7015	1.7100–1.7106	0.2366	0.2515	0.0011–0.0035	0.0016–0.0063
	G	4-134 (2.2)	1.8670–1.8690	1.8670–1.8690	1.8670–1.8690	1.8670–1.8690	1.8670–1.8690	0.2590	0.2590	0.0010–0.0040	NA
	T	6-192 (3.1)	1.8677–1.8815	1.8677–1.8815	1.8677–1.8815	1.8677–1.8815	1.8677–1.8815	0.2626	0.2626	0.0010–0.0040	NA
1992	H	4-121 (2.0)	1.6706–1.6712	1.6812–1.6818	1.6911–1.6917	1.7009–1.7015	1.7100–1.7106	0.2626	0.2626	0.0011–0.0035	0.0016–0.0063
	4	4-132 (2.2)	1.8670–1.8690	1.8670–1.8690	1.8670–1.8690	1.8670–1.8690	1.8670–1.8690	0.2590	0.2590	0.0010–0.0040	NA
	T	6-192 (3.1)	1.8677–1.8815	1.8677–1.8815	1.8677–1.8815	1.8677–1.8815	1.8677–1.8815	0.2626	0.2732	0.0010–0.0040	NA

VALVE SPECIFICATIONS

Year	VIN	No. Cylinder Displacement cu. in. (liter)	Seat Angle (deg.)	Face Angle (deg.)	Spring Test Pressure (lbs.)	Spring Installed Height (in.)	Stem-to-Guide Clearance (in.)		Stem Diameter (in.)	
							Intake	Exhaust	Intake	Exhaust
1982	G	4-110 (1.8)	46	45	183 @ 1.33	1.60	0.0011–0.0026	0.0014–0.0031	0.3139–0.3144	0.3129–0.3136
	B	4-121 (2.0)	46	45	183 @ 1.33	1.60	0.0011–0.0026	0.0014–0.0031	0.3139–0.3144	0.3129–0.3136
1983	O	4-110 (1.8)	46	46	NA	NA	0.0006–0.0016	0.0012–0.0024	NA	NA
	J	4-110 (1.8)	46	46	NA	NA	0.0006–0.0016	0.0012–0.0024	NA	NA
	P	4-121 (2.0)	46	45	183 @ 1.33	1.60	0.0011–0.0026	0.0014–0.0031	0.3139–0.3144	0.3129–0.3136
	B	4-121 (2.0)	46	45	183 @ 1.33	1.60	0.0011–0.0026	0.0014–0.0031	0.3139–0.3144	0.3129–0.3136
1984	O	4-110 (1.8)	46	46	NA	NA	0.0006–0.0016	0.0012–0.0024	NA	NA
	J	4-110 (1.8)	46	46	NA	NA	0.0006–0.0016	0.0012–0.0024	NA	NA
	P	4-121 (2.0)	46	45	183 @ 1.33	1.60	0.0011–0.0026	0.0014–0.0031	0.3139–0.3144	0.3129–0.3136
1985	O	4-110 (1.8)	46	46	NA	NA	0.0006–0.0016	0.0012–0.0024	NA	NA
	J	4-110 (1.8)	46	46	NA	NA	0.0006–0.0016	0.0012–0.0024	NA	NA
	P	4-121 (2.0)	46	45	183 @ 1.33	1.60	0.0011–0.0026	0.0014–0.0031	0.3139–0.3144	0.3129–0.3136
	W	6-173 (2.8)	46	45	195 @ 1.18	1.57	0.0010–0.0027	0.0010–0.0027	NA	NA
1986	O	4-110 (1.8)	46	46	NA	NA	0.0006–0.0016	0.0012–0.0024	NA	NA
	J	4-110 (1.8)	46	46	NA	NA	0.0006–0.0016	0.0012–0.0024	NA	NA
	P	4-121 (2.0)	46	45	183 @ 1.33	1.60	0.0011–0.0026	0.0014–0.0031	0.3139–0.3144	0.3129–0.3136
	W	6-173 (2.8)	46	45	195 @ 1.18	1.57	0.0010–0.0027	0.0010–0.0027	NA	NA
1987	M	4-121 (2.0)	45	46	NA	NA	0.0006–0.0020	0.0010–0.0024	NA	NA
	1	4-121 (2.0)	46	45	183 @ 1.33	1.60	0.0011–0.0026	0.0014–0.0030	NA	NA
	K	4-121 (2.0)	45	46	NA	NA	0.0006–0.0020	0.0010–0.0024	NA	NA
	W	6-173 (2.8)	46	45	195 @ 1.18	1.57	0.0010–0.0027	0.0010–0.0027	NA	NA
1988	M	4-121 (2.0)	45	46	NA	NA	0.0006–0.0020	0.0010–0.0024	NA	NA
	1	4-121 (2.0)	46	45	183 @ 1.33	1.60	0.0011–0.0026	0.0014–0.0030	0.0490–0.0560	0.0630–0.0750
	K	4-121 (2.0)	45	46	NA	NA	0.0006–0.0020	0.0010–0.0024	NA	NA
	W	6-173 (2.8)	46	45	195 @ 1.18	1.57	0.0010–0.0027	0.0010–0.0027	0.0610–0.0730	0.0670–0.0790

VALVE SPECIFICATIONS

Year	VIN	No. Cylinder Displacement cu. in. (liter)	Seat Angle (deg.)	Face Angle (deg.)	Spring Test Pressure (lbs.)	Spring Installed Height (in.)	Stem-to-Guide Clearance (in.)		Stem Diameter (in.)	
							Intake	Exhaust	Intake	Exhaust
1989	M	4-121 (2.0)	45	46	165–179 @ 1.043	1.47	0.0006–0.0017	0.0012–0.0024	NA	NA
	1	4-121 (2.0)	46	45	208–222 @ 1.22	1.61	0.0011–0.0026	0.0014–0.0030	NA	NA
	K	4-121 (2.0)	45	46	165–197 @ 1.043	1.47	0.0006–0.0017	0.0012–0.0024	NA	NA
	W	6-173 (2.8)	46	45	215– @ 1.291	1.57	0.0010–0.0027	0.0010–0.0027	NA	NA
1990	K	4-121 (2.0)	45	46	165–197 @ 1.043	1.47	0.0006–0.0017	0.0012–0.0024	0.2755–0.2760	0.2747–0.2753
	M	4-121 (2.0)	45	46	165–179 @ 1.043	1.47	0.0006–0.0017	0.0012–0.0024	0.2755–0.2760	0.2747–0.2753
	G	4-134 (2.2)	46	45	208–222 @ 1.22	1.61	0.0011–0.0026	0.0014–0.0021	NA	NA
	T	6-192 (3.1)	46	45	215– @ 1.291	1.57	0.0010–0.0027	0.0010–0.0027	NA	NA
1991	K	4-121 (2.0)	45	46	165–197 @ 1.043	1.47	0.0006–0.0017	0.0012–0.0024	0.2755–0.2760	0.2747–0.2753
	G	4-134 (2.2)	46	45	208–222 @ 1.22	1.61	0.0011–0.0026	0.0014–0.0031	NA	NA
	T	6-192 (3.1)	46	45	215– @ 1.291	1.57	0.0010–0.0027	0.0010–0.0027	NA	NA
1992	H	4-121 (2.0)	45	46	165–197 @ 1.043	1.47	0.0006–0.0017	0.0012–0.0024	0.2755–0.2760	0.2747–0.2753
	4	4-134 (2.2)	46	45	NA	NA	0.0011–0.0026	0.0014–0.0031	NA	NA
	T	6-192 (3.1)	46	45	215– @ 1.291	1.57	0.0010–0.0027	0.0010–0.0027	NA	NA

CRANKSHAFT AND CONNECTING ROD SPECIFICATIONS

All measurements are given in inches.

Year	VIN	No. Cylinder Displacement cu. in. (liter)	Crankshaft				Connecting Rod		
			Main Brg. Journal Dia.	Main Brg. Oil Clearance	Shaft End-play	Thrust on No.	Journal Diameter	Oil Clearance	Side Clearance
1982	G	4-110 (1.8)	2.4944–2.4954②	0.0006–0.0018③	0.0019–0.0071	4	1.9983–1.9993	0.0009–0.0031	0.0039–0.0240
	B	4-121 (2.0)	2.4944–2.4954②	0.0006–0.0018③	0.0019–0.0071	4	1.9983–1.9993	0.0009–0.0031	0.0039–0.0240
1983	O	4-110 (1.8)	①	0.0006–0.0016	0.0027–0.0118	3	1.9278–1.9286	0.0007–0.0024	0.0027–0.0095
	J	4-110 (1.8)	①	0.0006–0.0016	0.0027–0.0118	3	1.9278–1.9286	0.0007–0.0024	0.0027–0.0095
	P	4-121 (2.0)	2.4944–2.4954②	0.0006–0.0018③	0.0019–0.0071	4	1.9983–1.9993	0.0009–0.0031	0.0039–0.0240
	B	4-121 (2.0)	2.4944–2.4954②	0.0006–0.0018③	0.0019–0.0071	4	1.9983–1.9993	0.0009–0.0031	0.0039–0.0240

CRANKSHAFT AND CONNECTING ROD SPECIFICATIONS

All measurements are given in inches.

Year	VIN	No. Cylinder Displacement cu. in. (liter)	Crankshaft				Connecting Rod		
			Main Brg. Journal Dia.	Main Brg. Oil Clearance	Shaft End-play	Thrust on No.	Journal Diameter	Oil Clearance	Side Clearance
1984	O	4-110 (1.8)	①	0.0006–0.0016	0.0027–0.0118	3	1.9278–1.9286	0.0007–0.0024	0.0027–0.0095
	J	4-110 (1.8)	①	0.0006–0.0016	0.0027–0.0118	3	1.9278–1.9286	0.0007–0.0024	0.0027–0.0095
	P	4-121 (2.0)	2.4944–2.4954②	0.0006–0.0018③	0.0019–0.0071	4	1.9983–1.9993	0.0009–0.0031	0.0039–0.0240
1985	O	4-110 (1.8)	①	0.0006–0.0016	0.0027–0.0118	3	1.9278–1.9286	0.0007–0.0024	0.0027–0.0095
	J	4-110 (1.8)	①	0.0006–0.0016	0.0027–0.0118	3	1.9278–1.9286	0.0007–0.0024	0.0027–0.0095
	P	4-121 (2.0)	2.4944–2.4954②	0.0006–0.0018③	0.0019–0.0071	4	1.9983–1.9993	0.0009–0.0031	0.0039–0.0240
	W	6-173 (2.8)	2.6473–2.6482	0.0016–0.0033	0.0024–0.0083	3	1.9983–1.9994	0.0014–0.0037	0.0063–0.0173
1986	O	4-110 (1.8)	①	0.0006–0.0016	0.0027–0.0118	3	1.9278–1.9286	0.0007–0.0024	0.0027–0.0095
	J	4-110 (1.8)	①	0.0006–0.0016	0.0027–0.0118	3	1.9278–1.9286	0.0007–0.0024	0.0027–0.0095
	P	4-121 (2.0)	2.4944–2.4954②	0.0006–0.0018③	0.0019–0.0071	4	1.9983–1.9993	0.0009–0.0031	0.0039–0.0240
	W	6-173 (2.8)	2.6473–2.6482	0.0016–0.0033	0.0024–0.0083	3	1.9983–1.9994	0.0014–0.0037	0.0063–0.0173
1987	M	4-121 (2.0)	①	0.0006–0.0016	0.0030–0.0120	3	1.9278–1.9286	0.0007–0.0024	0.0027–0.0095
	1	4-121 (2.0)	2.4945–2.4954	0.0006–0.0019	0.0020–0.0080	4	1.9983–1.9994	0.0010–0.0031	0.0040–0.0150
	K	4-121 (2.0)	①	0.0006–0.0016	0.0030–0.0120	3	1.9278–1.9286	0.0007–0.0024	0.0027–0.0095
	W	6-173 (2.8)	2.6473–2.6482	0.0016–0.0033	0.0024–0.0083	3	1.9983–1.9994	0.0014–0.0037	0.0063–0.0173
1988	M	4-121 (2.0)	①	0.0006–0.0016	0.0030–0.0120	3	1.9278–1.9286	0.0007–0.0024	0.0027–0.0095
	1	4-121 (2.0)	2.4945–2.4954	0.0006–0.0019	0.0020–0.0080	4	1.9983–1.9994	0.0010–0.0031	0.0040–0.0150
	K	4-121 (2.0)	①	0.0006–0.0016	0.0030–0.0120	3	1.9278–1.9286	0.0007–0.0024	0.0027–0.0095
	W	6-173 (2.8)	2.6473–2.6482	0.0016–0.0033	0.0024–0.0083	3	1.9983–1.9994	0.0014–0.0037	0.0063–0.0173
1989	M	4-121 (2.0)	①	0.0006–0.0016	0.0030–0.0120	3	1.9278–1.9286	0.0007–0.0024	0.0027–0.0095
	1	4-121 (2.0)	2.4945–2.4954	0.0006–0.0019	0.0020–0.0080	4	1.9983–1.9994	0.0010–0.0031	0.0040–0.0150
	K	4-121 (2.0)	①	0.0006–0.0016	0.0030–0.0120	3	1.9278–1.9286	0.0007–0.0024	0.0027–0.0095
	W	6-173 (2.8)	2.6473–2.6482	0.0016–0.0033	0.0024–0.0083	3	1.9983–1.9994	0.0014–0.0037	0.0063–0.0173

CRANKSHAFT AND CONNECTING ROD SPECIFICATIONS

All measurements are given in inches.

Year	VIN	No. Cylinder Displacement cu. in. (liter)	Crankshaft				Connecting Rod		
			Main Brg. Journal Dia.	Main Brg. Oil Clearance	Shaft End-play	Thrust on No.	Journal Diameter	Oil Clearance	Side Clearance
1990	K	4-121 (2.0)	①	0.0006–0.0016	0.0028–0.0120	3	1.9279–1.9287	0.0007–0.0025	0.0028–0.0095
	M	4-121 (2.0)	①	0.0006–0.0016	0.0028–0.0118	3	1.9279–1.9287	0.0007–0.0025	0.0028–0.0095
	G	4-134 (2.2)	2.4945–2.4954	0.0006–0.0019	0.0020–0.0070	4	1.9983–1.9994	0.00098–0.0031	0.0039–0.0149
	T	6-192 (3.1)	2.6473–2.6483	0.0012–0.0030	0.0024–0.0083	3	1.9983–1.9994	0.0011–0.0034	0.0140–0.0270
1991	K	4-121 (2.0)	2.2828–2.2833	0.0006–0.0016	0.0028–0.0118	3	1.9279–1.9287	0.0007–0.0025	0.0028–0.0095
	G	4-134 (2.2)	2.4945–2.4954	0.0006–0.0019	0.0020–0.0070	4	1.9983–1.9994	0.00098–0.0031	0.0039–0.0149
	T	6-192 (3.1)	2.6473–2.6483	0.0012–0.0030	0.0024–0.0083	3	1.9983–1.9994	0.0011–0.0034	0.0140–0.0270
1992	H	4-121 (2.0)	2.2828–2.2833	0.0006–0.0016	0.0028–0.0118	3	1.9279–1.9287	0.0007–0.0025	0.0028–0.0095
	4	4-134 (2.2)	2.4945–2.4954	0.0006–0.0019	0.0020–0.0070	4	1.9983–1.9994	0.00098–0.0031	0.0039–0.0149
	T	6-192 (3.1)	2.6473–2.6483	0.0012–0.0030	0.0024–0.0083	3	1.9983–1.9994	0.0011–0.0034	0.0140–0.0270

① Bearings are identified by color:
Brown 2.2830–2.2832;
Green 2.2827–2.2830
② No. 5: 2.4936–2.4946
③ No. 5: 0.0014–0.0027

PISTON AND RING SPECIFICATIONS

All measurements are given in inches.

Year	VIN	No. Cylinder Displacement cu. in. (liter)	Piston Clearance	Ring Gap			Ring Side Clearance		
				Top Compression	Bottom Compression	Oil Control	Top Compression	Bottom Compression	Oil Control
1982	G	4-110 (1.8)	0.0008–0.0018	0.0098–0.0197	0.0098–0.0197	Snug	0.0012–0.0027	0.0012–0.0027	0.0078
	B	4-121 (2.0)	0.0008–0.0018	0.0098–0.0197	0.0098–0.0197	Snug	0.0012–0.0027	0.0012–0.0027	0.0078
1983	O	4-110 (1.8)	0.0004–0.0012	0.0010–0.0020	0.0010–0.0020	0.0010–0.0020	0.0020–0.0030	0.0010–0.0024	Snug
	J	4-110 (1.8)	0.0004–0.0012	0.0010–0.0020	0.0010–0.0020	0.0010–0.0020	0.0020–0.0030	0.0010–0.0024	Snug
	P	4-121 (2.0)	0.0008–0.0018	0.0098–0.0197	0.0098–0.0197	Snug	0.0012–0.0027	0.0012–0.0027	0.0078
	B	4-121 (2.0)	0.0008–0.0018	0.0098–0.0197	0.0098–0.0197	Snug	0.0012–0.0027	0.0012–0.0027	0.0078
1984	O	4-110 (1.8)	0.0004–0.0012	0.0010–0.0020	0.0010–0.0020	0.0010–0.0020	0.0020–0.0030	0.0010–0.0024	Snug
	J	4-110 (1.8)	0.0004–0.0012	0.0010–0.0020	0.0010–0.0020	0.0010–0.0020	0.0020–0.0030	0.0010–0.0024	Snug
	P	4-121 (2.0)	0.0007–0.0017	0.0098–0.0197	0.0098–0.0197	Snug	0.0012–0.0027	0.0012–0.0027	0.0078

PISTON AND RING SPECIFICATIONS

All measurements are given in inches.

Year	VIN	No. Cylinder Displacement cu. in. (liter)	Piston Clearance	Ring Gap Top Compression	Ring Gap Bottom Compression	Ring Gap Oil Control	Ring Side Clearance Top Compression	Ring Side Clearance Bottom Compression	Ring Side Clearance Oil Control
1985	O	4-110 (1.8)	0.0004–0.0012	0.0010–0.0020	0.0010–0.0020	0.0010–0.0020	0.0020–0.0030	0.0010–0.0024	Snug
	J	4-110 (1.8)	0.0004–0.0012	0.0010–0.0020	0.0010–0.0020	0.0010–0.0020	0.0020–0.0030	0.0010–0.0024	Snug
	P	4-121 (2.0)	0.0007–0.0017	0.0098–0.0197	0.0098–0.0197	Snug	0.0012–0.0027	0.0012–0.0027	0.0078
	W	6-173 (2.8)	0.0007–0.0017	0.0098–0.0197	0.0098–0.0197	Snug	0.0012–0.0027	0.0012–0.0027	0.0078 Max.
1986	O	4-110 (1.8)	0.0004–0.0012	0.0120–0.0200	0.0120–0.0200	0.0160–0.0550	0.0020–0.0040	0.0010–0.0024	0.0047
	J	4-110 (1.8)	0.0004–0.0012	0.0120–0.0200	0.0120–0.0200	0.0160–0.0550	0.0020–0.0040	0.0010–0.0024	0.0047
	P	4-121 (2.0)	0.0008–0.0018	0.0098–0.0197	0.0098–0.0197	Snug	0.0012–0.0027	0.0012–0.0027	0.0078
	W	6-173 (2.8)	0.0007–0.0017	0.0098–0.0197	0.0098–0.0197	0.0200–0.0550	0.0012–0.0027	0.0016–0.0037	0.0078 Max.
1987	M	4-121 (2.0)	0.0012–0.0020	0.0120–0.0200	0.0120–0.0200	0.0160–0.0550	0.0020–0.0030	0.0010–0.0024	0.0047
	1	4-121 (2.0)	0.0098–0.0220	0.0100–0.0200	0.0100–0.0200	0.0100–0.0500	0.0010–0.0030	0.0010–0.0030	0.0006–0.0090
	K	4-121 (2.0)	0.0012–0.0020	0.0120–0.0200	0.0120–0.0200	0.0160–0.0550	0.0020–0.0030	0.0010–0.0024	0.0047
	W	6-173 (2.8)	0.0020–0.0028	0.0100–0.0200	0.0100–0.0200	0.0200–0.0550	0.0010–0.0030	0.0010–0.0030	0.0078 Max.
1988	M	4-121 (2.0)	0.0012–0.0020	0.0120–0.0200	0.0120–0.0200	0.0160–0.0550	0.0020–0.0030	0.0010–0.0024	0.0047
	1	4-121 (2.0)	0.00098–0.0022	0.0100–0.0200	0.0100–0.0200	0.0100–0.0500	0.0010–0.0030	0.0010–0.0030	0.0006–0.0090
	K	4-121 (2.0)	0.0004–0.0012	0.0120–0.0200	0.0120–0.0200	0.0160–0.0550	0.0020–0.0030	0.0010–0.0024	Snug
	W	6-173 (2.8)	0.0022–0.0028	0.0100–0.0200	0.0100–0.0200	0.0100–0.0500	0.0020–0.0035	0.0020–0.0035	0.0080 Max.
1989	M	4-121 (2.0)	0.0012–0.0020	0.0098–0.0177	0.0118–0.0197	NA 0.0036	0.0024–0.0032	0.0019–	NA
	1	4-121 (2.0)	0.00098–0.0022	0.0100–0.0200	0.0100–0.0200	0.0100–0.0500	0.0019–0.0027	0.0019–0.0027	0.0019–0.0082
	K	4-121 (2.0)	0.0004–0.0012	0.0980–0.1770	0.1180–0.1970	NA	0.0024–0.0036	0.0019–0.0032	NA
	W	6-178 (2.8)	0.00093–0.0022	0.0100–0.0200	0.0100–0.0200	0.0010–0.0030	0.0020–0.0035	0.0020–0.0035	0.0080 Max.
1990	K	4-121 (2.0)	0.0004–0.0012	0.0098–0.0177	0.0118–0.0197	NA	0.0024–0.0036	0.0019–0.0032	NA
	M	4-121 (2.0)	0.0004–0.0012	0.0098–0.0177	0.0118–0.0197	NA	0.0024–0.0036	0.0019–0.0032	NA
	G	4-134 (2.2)	0.0007–0.0017	0.0100–0.0200	0.0100–0.0200	0.0100–0.0500	0.0019–0.0027	0.0019–0.0027	0.0019–0.0082
	T	6-192 (3.1)	0.00093–0.00222	0.0100–0.0200	0.0200–0.0280	0.0010–0.0300	0.0020–0.0350	0.0020–0.0350	0.0080 Max.

Year	VIN	No. Cylinder Displacement cu. in. (liter)	Piston Clearance	Ring Gap			Ring Side Clearance		
				Top Compression	Bottom Compression	Oil Control	Top Compression	Bottom Compression	Oil Control
1991	K	4-121 (2.0)	0.0004–0.0012	0.0098–0.0177	0.0118–0.0197	NA	0.0024–0.0036	0.0019–0.0032	NA
	G	4-134 (2.2)	0.0007–0.0017	0.0100–0.0200	0.0100–0.0200	0.0100–0.0500	0.0019–0.0027	0.0019–0.0027	0.0019–0.0082
	T	6-192 (3.1)	0.00093–0.00222	0.0100–0.0200	0.0200–0.0280	0.0010–0.0300	0.0020–0.0035	0.0020–0.0035	0.0080 Max.
1992	H	4-121 (2.0)	0.0004–0.0012	0.0098–0.0177	0.0118–0.0197	NA	0.0024–0.0036	0.0019–0.0032	NA
	4	4-134 (2.2)	0.0007–0.0017	0.0100–0.0200	0.0100–0.0200	0.0100–0.0050	0.0019–0.0027	0.0019–0.0027	0.0019–0.0082
	T	6-192 (3.1)	0.00093–0.00222	0.0100–0.0200	0.0200–0.0280	0.0100–0.0300	0.0020–0.0035	0.0020–0.0035	0.0080 Max.

TORQUE SPECIFICATIONS
All readings in ft. lbs.

Year	VIN	No. Cylinder Displacement cu. in. (liter)	Cylinder Head Bolts	Main Bearing Bolts	Rod Bearing Bolts	Crankshaft Pulley Bolts	Flywheel Bolts	Manifold		Spark Plugs	Lug Nut
								Intake	Exhaust		
1982	G	4-110 (1.8)	65–75	63–74	34–40	66–84	45–55	20–25	22–28	15	100
	B	4-121 (2.0)	65–75	63–77	34–43	66–89	45–63②	18–25	20–30	15	100
1983	O	4-110 (1.8)	①	57	39	20⑥	45	25	16	15	100
	J	4-110 (1.8)	①	57	39	20⑥	45	25	16	15	100
	P	4-121 (2.0)	65–75	63–77	34–43	68–89	45–63②	18–25	20–30	15	100
	B	4-121 (2.0)	65–75	63–77	34–43	68–89	45–63②	18–25	20–30	15	100
1984	O	4-110 (1.8)	①	57	39	20⑥	45	25	16	15	100
	J	4-110 (1.8)	①	57	39	20⑥	45	25	16	15	100
	P	4-121 (2.0)	65–75	63–77	34–43	68–89	45–63②	18–25	20–30	15	100
1985	O	4-110 (1.8)	①	57	39	20⑥	45	25	16	15	100
	J	4-110 (1.8)	①	57	39	20⑥	45	25	16	15	100
	P	4-121 (2.0)	65–75	63–77	34–43	68–89	45–63②	18–25	34–44	7–20	100
	W	6-173 (2.8)	65–90	70	34–45	75	45	13–25	19–31	15	100
1986	O	4-110 (1.8)	①	57	39	20⑥	45	25	16	15	100
	J	4-110 (1.8)	①	57	39	20⑥	45	25	16	15	100
	P	4-121 (2.0)	73–85	63–77	34–43	68–89	45–63②	18–25	34–44	7–20	100
	W	6-173 (2.8)	65–90	70	34–45	75	45	13–25	19–31	15	100
1987	M	4-121 (2.0)	①	④	⑤	20⑥	48	16	16	7–15	100
	1	4-121 (2.0)	③	63–77	34–43	68–89	45–63②	18–25	16–13	7–20	100
	K	4-121 (2.0)	①	④	⑤	20⑥	48	16	16	7–15	100
	W	6-173 (2.8)	⑧	70	34–45	75	45	25⑪	15–23	10–25	
1988	M	4-121 (2.0)	①	④	⑤	20⑥	⑦	16	16	25	100
	1	4-121 (2.0)	③	63–70	34–43	66–89	47–63②	19–25	6–13	7–20	100
	K	4-121 (2.0)	①	④	⑤	20⑥	⑦	16	16	25	100
	W	6-173 (2.8)	⑧	63–83	34–40	67–85	46	⑪	15–23	10–25	

TORQUE SPECIFICATIONS
All readings in ft. lbs.

Year	VIN	No. Cylinder Displacement cu. in. (liter)	Cylinder Head Bolts	Main Bearing Bolts	Rod Bearing Bolts	Crankshaft Pulley Bolts	Flywheel Bolts	Manifold Intake	Manifold Exhaust	Spark Plugs	Lug Nut
1989	M	4-121 (2.0)	①	④	⑤	⑬	⑦	18	⑭	15	100
	1	4-121 (2.0)	③	63–77	34–43	⑨	47–63②	15–22	6–13	15	100
	K	4-121 (2.0)	①	④	⑤	⑬	⑦	16	⑭	15	100
	W	6-173 (2.8)	⑧	73	39	76	⑩	⑪	18	⑫	
1990	K	4-121 (2.0)	①	④	⑤	⑬	⑦	16	⑭	15	100
	M	4-121 (2.0)	①	④	⑤	⑬	⑦	18	⑭	15	100
	G	4-134 (2.2)	⑯	70	38	85	⑰	18	⑮	11	100
	T	6-192 (3.1)	⑧	73	39	76	⑰	⑪	18	11	100
1991	K	4-121 (2.0)	①	④	⑤	⑬	⑦	16	⑭	15	100
	G	4-134 (2.2)	⑱	70	38	77	⑰	18	⑮	11	100
	T	6-192 (3.1)	⑧	73	39	76	⑰	⑪	18	11	100
1992	H	4-121 (2.0)	①	④	⑤	15	⑦	16	16	11	100
	4	4-134 (2.2)	⑱	70	38	77	55	22	10	11	100
	T	6-192 (3.1)	⑧	73	39	76	⑰	⑪	18	11	100

CAUTION: Verify the correct original equipment engine is in the vehicle by referring to the VIN engine code before torquing any bolts.

① Torque bolts to 18 ft. lbs., then turn each bolt 60°, in sequence, 3 times for a 180° rotation, then run the engine to normal operating temperature and turn each bolt, in sequence, an additional 30°–50°.
② Auto. Trans.: 45–59
③ Long: 73–83
  Short: 62–70
④ 44 ft. lbs. plus a 40° to 50° turn
⑤ 26 ft. lbs. plus a 40° to 45° turn
⑥ Crankshaft pulley to sprocket bolts
⑦ Manual transaxle: 48 ft. lbs. plus 30 degree turn
  Automatic transaxle: 48 ft. lbs.
⑧ Coat threads with sealer, torque to 33 ft. lbs. plus an additional 90 degrees (¼ turn)
⑨ Crankshaft pulley center 66–89 ft. lbs., crankshaft pulley outer 30–40 ft. lbs.
⑩ Automatic transaxle: 46 ft. lbs.
  Manual transaxle: 59 ft. lbs.
⑪ Tighten in sequence to 15 ft. lbs., retighten to 24 ft. lbs.
⑫ Tapered seat plugs: 15 ft. lbs., without tapered seat: 25 ft. lbs.
⑬ Crankshaft pulley to sprocket bolts: 150 inch lbs.
⑭ 115 inch lbs.
⑮ Nuts: 115 inch lbs., studs: 89 inch lbs.
⑯ Step 1—Tighten all bolts initially to 41 ft. lbs.
  Step 2—Tighten all bolts an additional 45 degrees in sequence
  Step 3—Tighten all bolts an additional 45 degrees in sequence
  Step 4—Tighten the long bolts—8, 4, 1, 5 and 9 an additional 20 degrees and tighten the short bolts—7, 3, 2, 6 and 10 an additional 10 degrees.
⑰ Automatic transaxle: 52 ft. lbs., manual transaxle: 55 ft. lbs.
⑱ Tighten bolts in sequence as follows:
  Long bolts 46 ft. lbs.
  Short bolts 43 ft. lbs.
  Tighten all bolts in sequence an additional 90 degrees.

linkage. Raise the front of the car and support it with jackstands.

11. Release the fuel system pressure (see Chapter 1) and disconnect the fuel line at the intake manifold.

12. Remove the air conditioning brace (if so equipped).

13. Remove the exhaust shield. Remove the starter.

14. Disconnect the exhaust pipe at the manifold. Remove the wheels.

15. Disconnect the stabilizer bar from the lower control arms. Remove the ball joints from the steering knuckle.

16. Remove the drive axles at the transaxle and then remove the transaxle strut.

17. If equipped with air conditioning, remove the inner fender shield. Remove the drive belt,

tag and disconnect the wires and then remove the compressor. Do not disconnect any of the refrigerant lines.

18. Remove the rear engine mount nuts and plate.

19. If equipped with an automatic transaxle, remove the oil filter.

20. Disconnect the speedometer cable and lower the vehicle.

21. If equipped with an automatic transaxle, remove the oil cooler at the transaxle.

22. Remove the front engine mount nuts.

23. Disconnect the clutch cable on the manual transaxle. Disconnect the detent cable on the automatic transaxle.

24. Install an engine lifting device, remove the transaxle mount and bracket. Lift the engine out of the car.

To install:

25. Install the engine mount alignment bolt ($M6 \times 1 \times 65$) to ensure proper power train alignment.

26. Lower the engine into the car, leaving the lifting device attached.

27. Install the transaxle bracket. Install the mount to the side frame and secure with NEW mount bolts.

28. With the weight not yet on the mounts, tighten the transaxle bolts. Tighten the right front mount nuts.

29. Lower the engine fully onto the mounts, remove the lifting device and then raise the front of the car.

30. Installation of the remaining components is in the reverse order of removal. Check the powertrain alignment bolt; if excessive force is required to remove the bolt, loosen the transaxle adjusting bolts and realign the powertrain. Adjust the drive belts and the clutch cable (if equipped with manual transaxle).

1985–89

1. Disconnect the battery.
2. Drain the cooling system.
3. Remove the air cleaner.
4. Disconnect the accelerator cable and T.V. cables.
5. Disconnect the ECM harness at the engine.
6. Disconnect and tag all necessary vacuum hoses.
7. Disconnect the radiator hoses at the engine.
8. Disconnect the heater hoses at the engine.
9. Remove the exhaust heat shield.
10. If equipped with air conditioning, remove the adjustment bolt at the motor mount.
11. Disconnect the engine wiring harness at the bulkhead.
12. Remove the windshield washer bottle.

13. Remove the alternator belt or serpentine, if so equipped.

14. Relieve the fuel system pressure as outlined in Chapter 1 and disconnect the fuel hoses.

15. Raise the vehicle.

16. If equipped with air conditioning, remove the air conditioning brace.

17. Remove the inner fender splash shield.

18. If equipped with air conditioning, remove the air conditioning compressor.

19. Remove the flywheel splash shield.

20. Disconnect the starter wires.

21. Remove the front starter brace and starter.

22. Remove the torque converter bolts.

23. Remove the crankshaft pulley using Tool J-24420 or equivalent.

24. Remove the oil filter.

25. Disconnect the engine to transmission support bracket.

26. Disconnect the right rear motor mount.

27. Disconnect the exhaust pipe at the manifold.

28. Disconnect the exhaust pipe at at the center hanger and loosen the muffler hanger.

29. Disconnect the T.V and shift cable bracket.

30. Remove the lower two bell housing bolts.

31. Lower the car.

32. Remove the right front motor mount nuts.

33. Remove the alternator and if necessary, the adjusting brace.

34. Disconnect the master cylinder from the booster, set aside and suitably support.

35. Install a lifting device.

36. Remove the right front motor mount bracket.

37. Remove the remaining upper bellhousing bolts.

38. Remove the power steering pump while lifting the engine.

39. Remove the engine.

To Install

1. Install the engine.

2. Install the power steering pump while lowering the engine.

3. Install the upper bellhousing bolts.

4. Install the right front motor mount bracket.

5. Remove the lifting device.

6. Connect the master cylinder from the booster, set aside and suitably support.

7. Install the alternator and if removed, the adjusting brace.

8. Install the right front motor mount nuts.

9. Raise the car.

10. Install the remaining two bell housing bolts.

11. Connect the T.V and shift cable bracket.

12. Connect the exhaust pipe at at the center hanger and loosen the muffler hanger.

13. Connect the exhaust pipe at the manifold.

14. Connect the right rear motor mount. If the rear engine mount bracket is removed, the following procedure should be used to ensure proper engine mount bracket locations:

    a. Loosely install the engine mount bracket.

    b. Raise the engine and transaxle.

    c. Torque the engine mount nuts and bolts to the specifications shown.

15. Connect the engine to transmission support bracket.

16. Install the oil filter.

17. Install the crankshaft pulley using Tool J 24420 or equivalent.

18. Install the torque converter bolts.

19. Install the front starter brace and starter.

20. Connect the starter wires.

21. Install the flywheel splash shield.

22. If equipped with air conditioning, install the air conditioning compressor.

23. Install the inner fender splash shield.

24. If equipped with air conditioning, install the air conditioning brace.

25. Lower the vehicle.

26. Connect the fuel hoses.

27. Install the alternator belt or serpentine belt, if so equipped.

28. Install the windshield washer bottle.

29. Connect the engine wiring harness at the bulkhead.

30. Install the exhaust heat shield.

31. Connect the heater hoses at the engine.

32. Connect the radiator hoses at the engine.

33. Connect all vacuum hoses.

34. Connect the ECM harness at the engine.

35. Connect the accelerator cable and T.V. cables.

36. Install the air cleaner.

37. Fill the cooling system.

38. Connect the battery.

1990–92

NOTE: *The following procedure is for the engine and transaxle assembly. On the 1992 model year, slight variations may occur due to extra connections, etc., but the basic procedure is the same.*

1. Disconnect the battery.

2. Drain the cooling system.

3. Relieve the fuel system pressure.

4. Disconnect the hood lamp wiring, if so equipped and remove the hood.

5. Disconnect the throttle body intake duct.

6. Remove the rear sight shields.

7. Disconnect the upper radaitor hose.

8. Disconnect the brake booster vacuum hose.

9. Disconnect the alternator top brace and wiring.

10. Disconnect and tag the upper engine harness from the engine.

11. Discharge the A/C system as outlined in Chapter 1.

12. Disconnect the A/C compressor to condensor and accumulator lines.

13. Raise and support the vehicle safely.

14. Remove the left splash shield.

15. Disconnect the exhaust system.

16. Disconnect and tag the lower engine wiring.

17. Remove the flywheel inspection cover.

18. Remove the front wheels.

19. Disconnect the lower radiator hose.

20. Disconnect the heater hoses from the heater core.

21. Remove the brake calipers from the steering knuckle and wire up out of the way as outlined in Chapter 9.

22. Disconnect the tie rods from the struts.

23. Lower the vehicle.

24. Remove the clutch slave cylinder.

25. With the fuel system pressure released, place an abosorbant shop towel around the connections and disconnect the fuel lines.

26. Disconnect the transaxle linkage at the transaxle.

27. Disconnect the accelerator cables from the TBI unit.

28. Disconnect the cruise control cables from the TBI unit.

29. Disconnect the throttle valve cables from the TBI, on vehicles equipped with an automatic transaxle.

30. Disconnect the automatic transaxle cooling lines.

31. Disconnect the power steering hoses from the power steering pump.

32. Remove the center suspension support bolts.

33. Align Engine/Transaxle Frame Handler tool No. J 36295 or equivalent under the suspension supports, engine and transaxle; lower vehicle to dolly and add support under the engine.

34. Safely support the rear of the vehicle.

35. Disconnect the upper transaxle mount.

36. Remove the upper strut bolts and nuts.

37. Disconnect the front engine mount.

38. Disconnect the rear engine mount.

39. Remove the 4 rear suspension support bolts.

40. Remove the 4 front suspension support bolts and wire the bolt holes together to prevent axle separation.

41. Raise the vehicle and remove the engine

and transaxle assembly on tool No. J 36295 or equivalent.

To install:

42. Lower the vehicle and install the engine and transaxle assembly using tool No. J 36295 or equivalent.

43. Install the suspension supports bolts and tighten to 65 ft. lbs. for the front and rear suspension supports and 66 ft. lbs. for the center suspenion support.

44. Install the transaxle mount but do not tighten.

45. Install the rear engine mount but do not tighten.

46. Install the front engine mount but do not tighten.

47. Torque the manual transaxle mounting bolts as follows:

• Front transaxle strut to body bolts to 40 ft. lbs.

• Rear transaxle mount to body bolts to 23 ft. lbs.

48. Torque the automatic transaxle mount bolts to 22 ft. lbs.

49. Torque the front and rear engine mount bolts, please refer to the engine mount illustration.

NOTE: *All engine mount bolts that have been removed must be cleaned and a new thread locking compound applied to the threads before reinstallation.*

50. Install the power steering hoses.

51. Connect the accelerator, cruise control and T.V. cables to the TBI.

52. Connect the transaxle cooling lines to the automatic transaxle.

53. Connect the transaxle linkage.

54. Reconnect the fuel ines.

55. Reconnect the clutch slave cylinder.

56. Raise and support the vehicle safely.

57. Install the tie rods.

58. Install the calipers tyo the steering knuckle.

59. Install the heater hoses to the heater core.

60. Install the lower radiator hose.

61. Install the A/C compressor.

62. Install the flywheel inspection cover.

63. Install the engine splash shield.

64. Install the front wheel and torque the wheel stud nuts to 100 ft. lbs.

65. Lower the vehicle.

66. Install the upper engine wiring.

67. Install the compressor to condensor and accumulator lines.

68. Install the brake booster vacuum hose.

69. Install the upper radiator hose.

70. Raise and support the vehicle safely.

71. Install the lower engine wiring.

72. Reconnect the exhaust system.

73. Lower the vehicle.

74. Connect the TBI wiring.

75. Install the air cleaner assembly.

76. Recharge the A/C system.

77. Check and adjust the wheel alignment.

78. Install the hood and connect the battery.

1.8L, 2.0L OHC Engines

NOTE: *This procedure requires the use of a special tool.*

1. Remove battery cables.
2. Drain cooling system.
3. Remove air cleaner.

Front engine mount—1982 1.8L OHV engine

Front engine mount—1983–84 2.0L OHV engine

VIEW A
& C60

90-110 N·m
(66-81 FT. LBS.)

60-76 N·m
(44-56 FT. LBS.)   **ENGINE MOUNT BRACKET**

VIEW B

48-60 N·m
(35-44 FT. LBS.)

Front engine mount—1985–92 2.0L and 2.2L OHV engines

4. Disconnect engine electrical harness at bulkhead.

5. Disconnect electrical connector at brake cylinder.

6. Remove throttle cable from bracket and E.F.I. assembly.

7. Remove vacuum hoses from E.F.I. assembly.

8. Remove power steering high pressure hose at cut-off switch.

9. Remove vacuum hoses at map sensor and canister.

10. Disconnect air conditioning relay cluster switches.

11. Remove power steering return hose at pump.

12. Disconnect ECM wire connections and feed harness through bulkhead and lay harness over engine.

13. Remove upper and lower radiator hoses from engine.

14. Remove electrical connections from temperature switch at thermostat housing.

15. Disconnect transmission shift cable at transmission.

16. Hoist car.

17. Remove speedometer cable at transmission and bracket.

18. Disconnect exhaust pipe at exhaust manifold.

1. Bolt—69 N·m (51 lb. ft.)
2. Rear engine mount
3. Bolt—68 N·m (50 lb. ft.)
4. Rear engine mount to engine bracket
5. Power steering pump bracket
6. Crankshaft pulley
7. Rear engine mount to body bracket
8. Nut—24 N·m (18 lb. ft.)
9. Reinforcement plate
10. Bolt—68 N·m (50 lb. ft.)
11. Side rail
12. Bolt—68 N·m (50 lb. ft.)

Rear engine mount—1983–92 2.0L and 2.2L OHV engines

19. Remove exhaust pipe from converter.
20. Remove heater hoses from heater core.
21. Remove fuel lines at flex hoses.
22. Remove transmission cooler lines at flex hoses.
23. Remove left and right front wheels.
24. Remove right hand spoiler section and splash shield.
25. Remove right and left brake calipers and support with wire.
26. Remove right and left tie rod ends.
27. Disconnect electrical connections at air conditioning compressor.
28. Remove air conditioning compressor and mounting brackets, support air conditioning compressor with wire in wheel opening.
29. Remove front suspension support attachment bolts (6 bolts each side).
30. Lower car.
31. Support front of vehicle by placing two short jackstands under core support.
32. Position front post hoist to the rear of cowl.
33. Position a 4 in. (102mm) × 4 in. (102mm) × 6 ft. (2m) timber on front post hoist.
34. Raise vehicle enough to remove jackstands.
35. Position a 4-wheel dolly under engine and transaxle assembly.
36. Position three (3) 4 in. (102mm) × 4 in. (102mm) 12 in. (305mm) blocks under engine and transaxle assembly only, letting support rails hang free.
37. Lower vehicle onto 4-wheel dolly slightly.
38. Remove rear transaxle mount attachment bolts (2).
39. Remove left front engine mount attachment bolts (3).
40. Remove two (2) engine support to body attachment bolts behind right-hand inner axle U-joint.
41. Remove one (1) attaching bolt and nut from right-hand chassis side rail to engine mount bracket.
42. Remove six (6) strut attachment nuts.
43. Raise vehicle letting engine, transaxle and suspension resting on 4-wheel dolly.
Reverse the removal procedure for engine installation with the following exceptions.
1. With one man's assistance, position engine and transaxle assembly in chassis.
2. Install transaxle and left front mounts to side rail bolts loosely.
3. Install a M6 × 1 × 65 alignment bolt in left front mount to prevent powertrain misalignment.
4. Torque transaxle mount bolts to 42 ft. lbs. and left front mount bolts to 18 ft. lbs.
5. Install right rear mount to body bolts and torque to 38 ft. lbs.

6. Install right rear mount to chassis side rail bolt and nut torque to 38 ft. lbs.
7. Place a floor jack under control arms, jack struts into position and install retaining nuts.
8. Raise vehicle.
9. Using a transmission jack or suitable lifting equipment, raise control arms and attach tie rod ends.

2.8L and 3.1L V6 Engine

1985–88

1. Disconnect the negative battery cable. Drain the cooling system and remove the air cleaner assembly.
2. Remove the air flow sensor. Remove the exhaust crossover heat shield and remove the crossover pipe.
3. Remove the serpentine belt tensioner and belt.
4. Remove the power steering pump mounting bracket. Disconnect the heater pipe at the power steering pump mounting bracket.
5. Disconnect the radiator hoses from the engine.
6. Disconnect the accelerator and throttle valve cable at the throttle valve.
7. Remove the alternator. Tag and disconnect the wiring harness at the engine.
8. Relieve the fuel pressure (see Chapter 1) and disconnect the fuel hose. Disconnect the coolant bypass and the overflow hoses at the engine.
9. Tag and remove the vacuum hoses to the engine.
10. Raise the vehicle and support it safely.
11. Remove the inner fender splash shield. Remove the harmonic balancer.
12. Remove the flywheel cover. Remove the starter bolts. Tag and disconnect the electrical connections to the starter. Remove the starter.
13. Disconnect the wires at the oil sending unit.
14. Remove the air conditioning compressor and related brackets.
15. Disconnect the exhaust pipe at the rear of the exhaust manifold.
16. Remove the flex plate-to-torque converter bolts.
17. Remove the transaxle-to-engine bolts. Remove the engine-to-rear mount frame nuts.
18. Disconnect the shift cable bracket at the transaxle. Remove the lower bell housing bolts.
19. Lower the vehicle and disconnect the heater hoses at the engine.
20. Install a suitable engine lifting device. While supporting the engine and transaxle, remove the upper bell housing bolts.
21. Remove the front mounting bolts.
22. Remove the master cylinder from the booster.

23. Remove the engine assembly from the vehicle.

To Install

1. Install the engine and remove the engine lifting device.

2. Install the master cylinder to the booster.

3. Install the front mounting bolts.

4. Install the upper bell housing bolts.

5. Connect the heater hoses at the engine.

6. Connect the shift cable bracket at the transaxle. Install the lower bell housing bolts.

7. Install the transaxle-to-engine bolts. Install the engine-to-rear mount frame nuts.

8. Install the flex plate-to-torque converter bolts.

9. Connect the exhaust pipe at the rear of the exhaust manifold.

10. Install the air conditioning compressor and related brackets.

11. Connect the wires at the oil sending unit.

12. Install the flywheel cover. Install the starter bolts. Connect the electrical connections to the starter. Install the starter.

13. Install the inner fender splash shield. Install the harmonic balancer.

14. Lower the vehicle.

15. Install the vacuum hoses to the engine.

16. Connect the fuel hose. Connect the coolant bypass and the overflow hoses at the engine.

17. Install the alternator. Connect the wiring harness at the engine.

18. Connect the accelerator and throttle valve cable at the throttle valve.

19. Connect the radiator hoses to the engine.

20. Install the power steering pump mounting bracket. Connect the heater pipe at the power steering pump mounting bracket.

21. Install the serpentine belt tensioner and belt.

22. Install the air flow sensor. Install the exhaust crossover heat shield and crossover pipe.

23. Connect the negative battery cable. Fill the cooling system and install the air cleaner assembly.

1989–92

1. Disconnect the negative battery cable. Drain the cooling system and remove the air cleaner assembly.

2. Remove the air cleaner and duct assembly.

3. Disconnect the exhaust manifold/crossover assembly.

4. Remove the serpentine belt tensioner and idler, if equipped.

5. Disconnect the radiator hoses from the engine.

6. Disconnect the cables from the bracket at the plenum.

7. Remove the alternator. Tag and disconnect the wiring harness at the engine.

8. Relieve the fuel pressure (see Chapter 1) and disconnect the fuel hose.

9. Disconnect the coolant bypass and the overflow hoses at the engine.

10. Support the engine using J 28467–A engine support fixture or equivalent.

11. Raise and support the vehicle safely.

12. Remove the inner fender splash shield.

13. Remove the flywheel cover.

14. Remove the starter bolts. Tag and disconnect the electrical connections to the starter. Remove the starter.

15. Remove the air conditioning compressor and related brackets.

16. Disconnect the exhaust pipe at the rear of the exhaust manifold.

17. Remove the flywheel-to-torque converter bolts.

18. Disconnect the engine mounts.

19. If equipped with a manual transaxle, disconnect the intermediate shaft bracket to the engine.

20. Disconnect the shift cable bracket at the transaxle. Remove the lower bell housing bolts.

21. Lower the vehicle and disconnect the heater hoses at the engine.

22. Install a suitable engine lifting device. While supporting the engine and transaxle, remove the J 28467–A engine support fixture.

23. Support the transaxle and remove the transaxle bolts.

24. Remove the engine assembly from the vehicle.

To Install

25. Install J 28467–A engine support fixture, or equivalent.

26. Remove the engine lifting device.

27. Support the transaxle and install the transaxle bolts.

28. Connect the heater hoses at the engine.

29. Raise and support the vehicle safely.

30. Install the lower bell housing bolts.

31. Install the shift cable bracket at the transaxle.

32. If equipped with a manual transaxle, connect the intermediate shaft bracket to the engine.

33. Reconnect the engine mounts and torque as follows:

• Front engine mount to bracket bolt to 50 ft. lbs.

• Front engine mount to frame bolt (top) to 54 ft. lbs.

• Front engine mount to frame bolt (bottom) to 61 ft. lbs.

• Engine mount bracket to body lower bolt to 47 ft. lbs.

• Engine mount bracket to body upper bolt to 74 ft. lbs.

• Rear engine mount to engine bolt to 40 ft. lbs.

• Rear engine bracket to body bolt to 45 ft. lbs.

NOTE: *All engine mount bolts that have been removed must be cleaned and a new thread locking compound applied to the threads before reinstallation.*

34. Install the flywheel-to-torque converter bolts.

35. Connect the exhaust pipe at the rear of the exhaust manifold.

36. Install the air conditioning compressor.

37. Install the starter.

38. Install the flywheel cover.

39. Install the inner fender splash shield.

40. Lower the vehicle and remove J 28467–A engine support fixture, or equivalent.

41. Connect the coolant bypass and the overflow hoses at the engine.

42. Reconnect the fuel lines.

43. Reconnect the wiring harness at the engine.

44. Install the alternator.

45. Connect the cables from the bracket at the plenum.

46. Install the radiator hoses.

47. Install the serpentine belt tensioner and idler, if equipped.

48. Refill the cooling system.

49. Install the air cleaner and duct assembly.

50. Connect the battery.

Front engine mount—1987–92 2.8L and 3.1L V6 engines

Front engine mount—1985–86 2.8L V6 engine

Rear engine mount—2.8L V6 engine

1. 61 N·m (45 lb. ft.)
2. R.H. body rail
3. Cowl panel
4. Engine mount bracket (MG2)
5. Engine mount bracket (MD9)
6. 54 N·m (40 lb. ft.)

Rear engine mount—3.1L V6 engine

NOTE: AT TIME OF INSTALLATION, FLANGES MUST BE FREE OF OIL. A ⅛ BEAD OF SEALANT MUST BE APPLIED TO FLANGES AND SEALANT MUST BE WET TO TOUCH WHEN BOLTS ARE TORQUED.

NOTE: AT TIME OF INSTALLATION, FLANGES MUST BE FREE OF OIL. A 2.0-3.0 BEAD OF SEALANT MUST BE APPLIED TO FLANGES AND SEALANT MUST BE WET TO TOUCH WHEN BOLTS ARE TORQUED.

Rocker arm and cover, 1982–83 1.8L and 2.0L OHV engine

Rocker arm and cover, 1984–86 2.0L OHV engine

Rocker Arm Cover
REMOVAL AND INSTALLATION

1.8L, 2.0L and 2.2L OHV Engines
1982–86

1. Disconnect the negative battery cable.
2. Remove the air cleaner.
3. Disconnect the canister purge line and the PCV valve.
4. Disconnect (mark location of spark plug wires for correct installation) the spark plug wires at the spark plugs and pull the wires away from the rocker arm cover.
5. Loosen the accelerator linkage bracket.
6. Remove the rocker arm cover bolts.
7. Remove the rocker arm cover. If the cover adheres to the cylinder head, lightly tap the end of the cover with a rubber mallet. If necessary, carefully pry until loose.
NOTE: *Do not distort the sealing flange.*
8. Clean the sealing surfaces of the head and the cover.
9. Place a ⅛ in. (3mm) wide bead of RTV sealant all around the rocker arm cover sealing surface.
NOTE: *When going aropund the attaching bolt holes, always flow the RTV on the in-board side of the bolt holes.*
10. Install the valve cover and torque the bolts to 8 ft. lbs. EVENLY while the sealant is still wet.
NOTE: *Keep the sealant out of the bolt holes as this could cause a "Hydraulic lock" condition which could damage the head casting.*
11. Install the remaining parts and reconnect the battery cable.

1987–92

1. Disconnect the negative battery cable.
2. Disconnect the AIR hose at the TBI and air cleaner.
3. Remove the hose from the intake to the cover.
4. Remove the rocker arm cover bolts and remove the cover.
5. Clean the sealing surfaces of the head and the cover.
6. Install a new gasket, reposition the cover and torque the bolts EVENLY to 8 ft. lbs.
7. Install all hoses removed and connect the negative battery cable.

V6 Engine
1984–86 LEFT

1. Disconnect the negative battery cable.
2. Remove the coil at the bracket.
3. Disconnect the PCV hose.
4. Disconnect the spark plug wires at the spark plugs and pull the wires away from the rocker arm cover.

1. 6–9 ft. lbs.   2. 11–18 ft. lbs.

Rocker arm and cover, 1987–92 2.0L and 2.2L OHV engine

5. Loosen the accelerator linkage bracket.
6. Remove the rocker arm cover bolts.
7. Remove the rocker arm cover. If the cover adheres to the cylinder head, lightly tap the end of the cover with a rubber mallet. If necessary, carefully pry until loose. Do not distort the sealing flange.
To install:
8. Clean the sealing surfaces of the head and the cover.
9. Place a ⅛ in. (3mm) wide bead of RTV sealant at the intake manifold and the cylinder head split line.
10. Install the valve cover and torque the bolts EVENLY to 90 inch lbs. while the sealant is still wet.
11. Install the remaining parts and reconnect the battery cable.

1984–86 RIGHT

1. Disconnect the negative battery cable.
2. Disconnect the intake runners.
3. Remove the rocker arm cover bolts.
4. Remove the rocker arm cover. If the cover adheres to the cylinder head, lightly tap the end of the cover with a rubber mallet. If necessary, carefully pry until loose. Do not distort the sealing flange.

Rocker arm cover installation, 1985–86 2.8L V6 engine

Rocker arm cover installation, 1987–92 2.8L and 3.1L V6 engines

To install:

5. Clean the sealing surfaces of the head and the cover.

6. Place a 1/8 in. (3mm) wide bead of RTV sealant at the intake manifold and the cylinder head split line.

7. Install the valve cover and torque the bolts EVENLY to 90 inch lbs. while the sealant is still wet.

8. Install the remaining parts and reconnect the battery cable.

1987–92 LEFT

1. Disconnect the negative battery cable.

2. Remove the bracket tube at the cover.

3. Remove the plug wire cover.

4. Disconnect the heater hose at the filler neck.

5. Remove the cover bolts and remove the cover.

6. If the cover adheres to the cylinder head, lightly tap the end of the cover with a soft rubber mallet or palm of the hand. Do not distort or scratch the sealing flange.

To install:

7. Clean the sealing surfaces of the head and the cover.

8. Install a new gasket and make sure it is seated properly in the rocker cover groove.

9. Apply RTV sealant in the notch.

10. Install the rocker cover and tighten the retaining bolts EVENLY to 89 inch lbs.

11. Install the remaining parts and reconnect the battery cable.

1987–92 RIGHT

1. Disconnect the negative battery cable.

2. Disconnect the brake booster vacuum line at the bracket.

3. Disconnect the cable bracket at the plenum.

4. Remove the vacuum line bracket at the cable bracket.

5. Disconnect the lines at the alternator brace stud.

6. Disconnect the rear alternator brace.

7. Remove the serpentine belt.

8. Disconnect the alternator and lay to one side.

9. Remove the PCV valve.

10. Loosen the alternator bracket.

11. Remove the rocker cover bolts, plug wires and rocker cover.

12. If the cover adheres to the cylinder head, lightly tap the end of the cover with a soft rubber mallet or palm of the hand. Do not distort or scratch the sealing flange.

To install:

13. Clean the sealing surfaces of the head and the cover.

14. Install a new gasket and make sure it is seated properly in the rocker cover groove.

15. Apply RTV sealant in the notch.

16. Install the rocker cover and tighten the retaining bolts EVENLY to 89 inch lbs.

17. Install the remaining parts and reconnect the battery cable.

Camshaft Carrier Cover

REMOVAL AND INSTALLATION

OHC Engines

1. Disconnect the negative battery cable. Remove the air cleaner on non-turbo models.

2. Disconnect the breather hoses.

3. Disconnect the induction tube on turbo models.

4. Remove the bolts and remove the cover.

To install:

5. Clean the sealing surfaces on the camshaft carrier and cover.

Rocker arm cover installation, 1.8L and 2.0L OHC engine

6. Reposition the cover with a new gasket and torque the retainer bolts EVENLY to 71 inch lbs.

7. Install the air cleaner and breather hoses.

8. Install the induction tube on turbo models

Rocker Arms and Pushrods

REMOVAL & INSTALLATION

1.8L, 2.0L and 2.1L OHV Engines

1982–86

1. Remove the air cleaner. Remove the rocker arm cover.

2. Remove the rocker arm nut and ball. Lift the rocker arm off the stud. Always keep the rocker arm assemblies together and install them on the same stud. Remove the pushrods.

To install:

3. Coat the bearing surfaces of the rocker arms and the rocker arm balls with Molykote® or its equivalent.

4. Install the pushrods making sure that they seat properly in the lifter.

5. Install the rocker arms, balls and nuts. Tighten the rocker arm nuts until all lash is eliminated.

6. Adjust the valves when the lifter is on the base circle of a camshaft lobe:

a. Crank the engine until the mark on the crankshaft pulley lines up with the **O** mark on the timing tab. Make sure that the engine is in the No. 1 firing position. Place your fingers on the No. 1 rocker arms as the mark on the crank pulley comes near the **O** mark. If the valves are not moving, the engine is in the No. 1 firing position. If the valves move, the engine is in the No. 4 firing position; rotate the engine one complete revolution and it will be in the No. 1 position.

b. When the engine is in the No. 1 firing position, adjust the following valves:

- Exhaust – 1,3
- Intake – 1,2

c. Back the adjusting nut out until lash can be felt at the pushrod, then turn the nut until all lash is removed (this can be determined by rotating the pushrod while turning the adjusting nut). When all lash has been removed, turn the nut in 1½ additional turns, this will center the lifter plunger.

d. Crank the engine one complete revolution until the timing tab and the **O** mark are again in alignment. Now the engine is in the No. 4 firing position. Adjust the following valves:

- Exhaust – 2,4
- Intake – 3,4

7. Installation of the remaining components is the reverse order of removal.

1987–92

1. Remove the air cleaner. Remove the rocker arm cover.

2. Remove the rocker arm nut and ball. Lift the rocker arm off the stud. Always keep the rocker arm assemblies together and install them on the same stud. Remove the pushrods.

To install:

3. Coat the bearing surfaces of the rocker arms and the rocker arm balls with Molykote® or its equivalent.

4. Install the pushrods making sure that they seat properly in the lifter.

5. Install the rocker arms, balls and nuts. Tighten the rocker arm nuts to 22 ft. lbs.

6. Install the rocker cover.

Compressing the valve spring using special tool J 33302 on 1.8L and 2.0L OHC engines

1. Rocker arm
2. Thrust piece
3. Lash adjuster
4. Valve stem lock
5. Valve spring cap
6. Valve spring
7. Valve seal
8. Exhaust roto cap
9. Inlet spring washer

Exploded view of the rocker arm, adjuster and spring on the 2.0L OHC engine

1.8L and 2.0L OHC Engines

NOTE: *A special tool is required for this procedure.*

1. Remove the camshaft carrier cover.

2. Using a valve train compressing fixture, tool J-33302, depress all the lifters at once.

3. Remove the rocker arms, placing them on the workbench in the same order that they were removed.

4. Remove the hydraulic valve lash compensators keeping them in the order in which they were removed.

5. Installation is the reverse of removal. Rocker arms and compensators must be replaced in the exact same position as when they were removed.

2.8L and 3.1L V6 Engines

1985–86

1. Remove the rocker arm covers as outlined earlier.

2. Remove the rocker arm nuts, rocker arm balls, rocker arms and push rods and place in a rack so that they may be reinstalled in the same location.

To install:

3. Coat the bearing surfaces of the rocker arms and the rocker arm balls with Molykote® or its equivalent.

4. Install the pushrods making sure that they seat properly in the lifter.

5. Install the rocker arms, balls and nuts. Tighten the rocker arm nuts until all lash is eliminated.

6. Adjust the valves when the lifter is on the base circle of a camshaft lobe:

a. Crank the engine until the mark on the crankshaft pulley lines up with the **O** mark on the timing tab. Make sure that the engine is in the No. 1 firing position. Place your fingers on the No. 1 rocker arms as the mark on the crank pulley comes near the **O** mark. If the valves are not moving, the engine is in the No. 1 firing position. If the valves move, the engine is in the No. 4 firing position; rotate the engine one complete revolution and it will be in the No. 1 position.

b. When the engine is in the No. 1 firing position, adjust the following valves:

● Exhaust — 1,2,3
● Intake — 1,5,6

c. Back the adjusting nut out until lash can be felt at the pushrod, then turn the nut until all lash is removed (this can be determined by rotating the pushrod while turning the adjusting nut). When all lash has been removed, turn the nut in 1½ additional turns, this will center the lifter plunger.

d. Crank the engine one complete revolution until the timing tab and the **O** mark are again in alignment. Now the engine is in the No. 4 firing position. Adjust the following valves:

● Exhaust — 4,5,6
● Intake — 2,3,4

7. Installation of the remaining components is the reverse order of removal.

Valve mechanism—1985–86 2.8L V6 engine

Adjusting the valve lash—1985–86 2.8L V6 engine

1987–92

1. Remove the rocker arm covers as outlined earlier.

2. Remove the rocker arm nuts, rocker arm balls, rocker arms, push rod guides and push rods and place in a rack so that they may be re-installed in the same location.

NOTE: *Intake pushrods are marked orange and are 6 in. (152.4mm) long. Exhaust push-rods are marked blue and are 6⅜ in. (161.9mm) long.*

3. Coat the bearing surfaces of the rocker arms and the rocker arm balls with Molykote® or its equivalent.

4. Install the pushrods making sure that they seat properly in the lifter.

5. Install the pushrod guides, rocker arms, pivot balls and nuts.

6. Tighten the rocker arm nuts to 14–20 ft. lbs.

Thermostat

REMOVAL AND INSTALLATION

CAUTION: *When draining the coolant, keep in mind that cats and dogs are attracted by the ethylene glycol antifreeze, and are quite likely to drink any that is left in an uncovered container or in puddles on the ground. This will prove fatal in sufficient quantity. Always drain the coolant into a sealable container. Coolant should be reused unless it is contaminated or several years old.*

1.8L, 2.0L and 2.2L OHV Engines

The thermostat is located inside a housing on the back of the cylinder head. It is not necessary to remove the radiator hose from the thermostat housing when removing the thermostat.

1. Disconnect the negative battery cable.

2. Drain the cooling system and remove the air cleaner.

3. On some models it may be necessary to disconnect the A.I.R. pipe at the upper check valve and the bracket at the water outlet.

4. Disconnect the electrical lead.

5. Remove the two retaining bolts from the thermostat housing and lift up the housing with the house attached. Lift out the thermostat.

To install:

6. Insert (correct position) the new thermostat. Apply a thin bead of silicone sealer to the housing mating surface and install the housing while the sealer is still wet. Tighten the housing retaining bolts to 6 ft. lbs.

NOTE: *Poor heater output and slow warmup is often caused by a thermostat stuck in the open position; occasionally one sticks shut causing immediate overheating. Do not attempt to correct a chronic overheating condition by permanently removing the thermostat. Thermostat flow restriction is designed into the system; without it, localized overheating*

1. Rocker arm
2. 20–27 N·m (14–20 ft. lbs.)
3. Ball

Rocker arm installation—1987–92 2.8L and 3.1L V6 engines

THERMOSTAT

THERMOSTAT
HOUSING ADAPTER

Thermostat installation—1982–86 1.8L and 2.0L OHV engines

1. Bolt—10 Nm (8 lbs. ft.)
2. Thermostat and housing
3. Gasket
4. Thermostat
5. Housing
6. Stud—10 Nm (90 lbs. in.)
7. Nut—10 Nm (90 lbs. in.)

Thermostat installation—1987–92 2.0L and 2.2L OHV engines

(due to coolant turbulence) may occur, causing expensive troubles.

7. Installation of the remaining components is in the reverse order of removal.

1.8L, 2.0L OHC Engines

1. Remove the thermostat housing.
2. Grasp the handle of the thermostat and pull it from the housing.
3. Install the thermostat in the housing, pushing it down as far as it will go to make sure it's seated.
4. Install the housing on the engine, using a new gasket coated with sealer.

1. Thermostat housing cap
2. Thermostat
3. Thermostat housing assembly Cylinder head

Thermostat installation—1.8L and 2.0L OHC engines

2.8L and 3.1L V6 Engines

1. Disconnect the negative battery cable.
2. Drain the cooling system.
3. Some models with cruise control have a vacuum modulator attached to the thermostat housing with a bracket. If your vehicle is equipped as such, remove the bracket from the housing.
4. Unbolt the water outlet from the intake manifold, remove the outlet and lift the thermostat out of the manifold.

To install:

5. Clean both of the mating surfaces and run a ⅛ in. (3mm) wide bead of R.T.V. (room temperature vulcanizing) sealer in the groove of the water outlet.
6. Install the thermostat (spring towards engine) and bolt the water outlet into place while the R.T.V. sealer is still wet. Torque the bolts to 18 ft. lbs. The remainder of the installation is the reverse of removal. Check for leaks after the car is started and correct as required.

Intake Manifold

REMOVAL AND INSTALLATION

CAUTION: *When draining the coolant, keep in mind that cats and dogs are attracted by the ethylene glycol antifreeze, and are quite likely to drink any that is left in an uncovered container or in puddles on the ground. This will prove fatal in sufficient quantity. Always drain the coolant into a sealable container. Coolant should be reused unless it is contaminated or several years old.*

1.8, 2.0L and 2.2L OHV Engines

1985–86

1. Disconnect the negative battery cable.
2. Remove the air cleaner. Drain the cooling system.

WATER OUTLET ADAPTER

Thermostat installation—1985–86 2.8L V6 engine

1. Water outlet
2. Thermostat
3. Inlet manifold
4. Bolt/Nut—
   25 N·m (18 lbs. ft.)

Thermostat installation—1987–92 2.8L and 3.1 V6 engine

3. Tag and disconnect all necessary vacuum lines and wires. Remove the idler pulley.

4. Remove the A.I.R. drive belt. If equipped with power steering, remove the drive belt and then remove the pump with the lines attached. Position the pump out of the way.

5. Remove the A.I.R. bracket-to-intake manifold bolt. Remove the air pump pulley.

6. If equipped with power steering, remove the A.I.R. through-bolt and then the power steering adjusting bracket.

7. Loosen the lower bolt on the air pump mounting bracket so that the bracket will rotate.

8. Disconnect the fuel lines at the carburetor or TBI unit. Disconnect the carburetor or TBI linkage and then remove the carburetor or TBI unit.

CAUTION: *The fuel lines are pressurized (especially with fuel injection). Removal may cause fuel spray resulting in personal injury. Do not remove before bleeding the pressure from the fuel system. See Chapter 1 for the procedure.*

9. Lift off the Early Fuel Evaporation (EFE) heater grid.

10. Remove the distributor.

11. Remove the mounting bolts and nuts and remove the intake manifold. Make sure to disconnect the heater hose and condenser from the bottom of the intake manifold before you lift it all the way out.

To install:

12. Using a new gasket, replace the manifold, tightening the nuts and bolts to specification

Intake manifold installation—1982–86 2.0L OHV engine

(working from the center position to the end position).

13. Installation of the remaining components is in the reverse order of removal. Adjust all necessary drive belts and check the ignition timing.

1987–92

1. Disconnect the negative battery cable.

2. Remove the air cleaner. Drain the cooling system.

3. Tag and disconnect all necessary vacuum lines and wires.

4. Disconnect the fuel lines and linkage at the TBI unit and remove the TBI unit.

CAUTION: *The fuel lines are pressurized (especially with fuel injection). Removal may cause fuel spray resulting in personal injury. Do not remove before bleeding the pressure from the fuel system. See Chapter 1 for the procedure.*

5. Disconnect the power steering pump and lay aside.

20-30 N·m (15-22 FT. LBS.)

Intake manifold installation and torque sequence—1987–88 2.0L OHV engine

6. Disconnect the coolant hose to the intake manifold.

7. Raise and support the vehicle safely.

8. Disconnect the accelerator and T.V. cables and cable bracket.

9. Remove the 6 intake manifold lower nuts.

10. Lower the vehicle.

11. Remove the intake manifold upper nuts and remove the intake manifold.

To install:

12. Clean the mating surfaces on the intake manifold and the cylinder head.

13. Install the intake manifold with a new gasket and tighten the manifold nuts in the proper sequence to 18 ft. lbs. (25 Nm).

14. Raise and support the vehicle safely.

15. Connect the coolant hoses and the accelerator and T.V. cables and cable bracket.

16. Lower the vehicle.

17. Install the TBI unit and connect the linkage and fuel lines.

18. Install the vacuum lines and wires.

19. Install the air cleaner assembly.

20. Fill the cooling system and connect the negative battery cable.

1992

1. Disconnect the negative battery cable.

2. Relieve the fuel system pressure.

3. Remove the air intake duct.

4. Drain the cooling system.

5. Tag and disconnect all necessary vacuum lines and wires.

6. Disconnect the throttle linkage.

7. Remove the power steering pump and lay it aside without disconnecting the fluid lines.

8. Disconnect the MAP sensor and EGR solenoid valve.

9. Remove the upper intake manifold assembly.

10. Remove the EGR valve injector.

11. Remove the fuel injector retainer bracket, regulator and injectors.

12. Disconnect the accelerator and T.V. cables and cable bracket.

13. Raise the vehicle and support it safely.

14. Remove the 6 intake manifold lower nuts.

15. Lower the vehicle.

16. Remove the intake manifold upper nuts and remove the manifold.

To install:

17. Clean the gasket mounting surfaces.

18. Install a new gasket and position the lower intake manifold.

19. Install the fuel injectors, regulator and injector retainer bracket and tighten the retaining bolts to 22 inch lbs. (3.5 Nm).

20. Tighten the upper intake manifold nuts in the proper sequence to 22 ft. lbs. 30 Nm).

1	STUD
2	GASKET
3	INTAKE MANIFOLD
4	NUT
5	CLIP

INTAKE MANIFOLD NUT
TIGHTENING SEQUENCE

Intake manifold installation and torque sequence—1992 2.2L (VIN code 4)

21. Connect the accelerator and T.V. cables and cable bracket.

22. Raise the vehicle and support it safely.

23. Tighten the lower intake manifold nuts in the proper sequence to 22 ft. lbs. 30 Nm).

24. Lower the vehicle.

25. Install the EGR valve injector so that the port is facing directly towards the throttle body.

26. Install the upper intake manifold assembly.

27. Connect the MAP sensor and EGR solenoid valve.

28. Connect the vacuum lines and wires.

29. Install the air intake duct.

30. Install the power steering pump.

31. Connect the negative battery cable.

32. Refill the coolant system.

1.8L and 2.0L OHC Engines

1. Release the fuel pressure. Disconnect the negative battery terminal from the battery.

2. Remove induction tube and hoses.

3. Disconnect and tag wiring to throttle body, fuel injectors, M.A.P sensor and wastegate, if so equipped.

4. Disconnect and tag PCV hose and vacuum hoses on throttle body.

5. Remove throttle cable and cruise control cable if so equipped.

6. Remove wiring to ignition coil and remove manifold support bracket.

7. Remove rear bolt from alternator bracket,

P/S adjusting bracket and front alternator adjusting bracket.

8. Remove fuel lines to fuel rail and regulator outlet.

9. Remove retaining nuts and washers and intake manifold.

To install:

10. To install, use new gasket and reverse the removal procedures. Torque intake manifold retaining nuts and washers EVENLY in sequence to 20–25 ft. lbs. for 1982–86 and 16 ft. lbs. for 1987–92.

NOTE: *The rear adjusting bracket must be the last part secured to prevent distorting the accessory drive system this will prevent the belt from coming off.*

2.8L and 3.1L V6 Engines

1985–88

1. Disconnect the negative battery cable. Release the fuel pressure.

2. Disconnect the accelerator cable bracket at the plenum.

3. Disconnect the throttle body and the EGR pipe from the EGR valve. Remove the plenum assembly.

4. Disconnect the fuel line along the fuel rail.

5. Disconnect the serpentine drive belt. Remove the power steering pump mounting bracket.

6. Remove the heater pipe at the power steering pump bracket.

1	BOLT
2	STUD
3	UPPER INTAKE MANIFOLD ASSEMBLY
4	GASKET
5	LOWER INTAKE MANIFOLD
6	EGR VALVE INJECTOR
A	THROTTLE BODY TIGHTENING SEQUENCE

Upper intake manifold installation—1992 2.2L (VIN code 4)

1. Intake manifold
2. Gasket
3. Nut (18 ft. lbs.)

INLET MANIFOLD NUT
TIGHTENING SEQUENCE

Intake manifold installation and torque sequence—1.8L and 2.0L OHC engine with turbocharger

INLET MANIFOLD NUT
TIGHTENING SEQUENCE

Intake manifold installation and torque sequence—1.8L and 2.0L OHC engine without turbocharger

7. Tag and disconnect the wiring at the alternator and remove the alternator.

8. Disconnect the wires from the cold start injector assembly. Remove the injector assembly from the intake manifold.

9. Disconnect the idle air vacuum hose at the throttle body. Disconnect the wires at the injectors.

10. Remove the fuel rail, breather tube and the fuel runners from the engine.

11. Tag and disconnect the coil wires.

12. Remove the rocker arm covers. Drain the cooling system, the disconnect the radiator hose at the thermostat housing. Disconnect the heater hose from the thermostat housing and the thermostat wiring.

13. Remove the distributor.

14. Remove the thermostat assembly housing.

15. Remove the intake manifold bolts and remove the intake manifold from the engine.

To install:

1. The gaskets are marked for right and left side installation; do not interchange them. Clean the sealing surface of the engine block,

and apply a $^3/_{16}$ in. (5mm) wide bead of silicone sealer to each ridge.

2. Install the new gaskets onto the heads. The gaskets will have to be cut slightly to fit past the center pushrods. Do not cut any more material than necessary. Hold the gaskets in place by extending the ridge bead of sealer ¼ in. (6mm) onto the gasket ends.

3. Install the intake manifold. The area between the ridges and the manifold should be completely sealed.

4. Install the retaining bolts and nuts, and tighten in sequence to 23 ft. lbs. Do not overtighten; the manifold is made from aluminum, and can be warped or cracked with excessive force.

5. The rest of installation is the reverse of removal. Adjust the ignition timing after installation, and check the coolant level after the engine has warmed up.

1989–92

1. Disconnect the negative battery cable.

2. Disconnect the cables at the plenum.

3. Disconnect the brake vacuuum pipe at the plenum.

3. Disconnect the throttle body and the EGR pipe from the EGR valve. Remove the plenum assembly.

4. Release the fuel system pressure and disconnect the fuel line along the fuel rail.

5. Disconnect the serpentine drive belt.

6. Remove the alternator and move to one side. Loosen the alternator bracket.

7. Disconnect the power steering pump and move to one side.

8. Disconnect the idle air vacuum hose at the throttle body.

9. Disconnect the the wires at the injectors.

10. Remove the fuel rail, breather tube and the fuel runners from the engine.

11. Tag and disconnect the plug wires at the manifold.

12. Remove the rocker arm covers — refer to the necessary service procedure. Drain the cooling system, the disconnect the radiator hose at the thermostat housing. Disconnect the heater hose from the thermostat housing and tag and disconnect the thermostat wiring.

13. Remove the intake manifold bolts and remove the intake manifold from the engine.

NOTE: *Retain the Belleville washer in the same orientation on the 4 center bolts.*

14. Loosen the rocker arms and remove the pushrods.

NOTE: *Intake pushrods are marked orange and are 6 in. (152.4mm) long. Exhaust pushrods are marked blue and are 6⅜ in. (161.9mm) long.*

15. Remove the intake gasket.

To install:

A [NOTE] APPLY A SMOOTH CONTINUOUS BEAD APPROX. 2.0-3.0 WIDE AND 3.0-5.0 THICK ON BOTH SURFACES. BEAD CONFIGURATION MUST INSURE COMPLETE SEALING OF WATER AND OIL. SURFACE MUST BE FREE OF OIL AND DIRT TO INSURE ADEQUATE SEAL.

TORQUE TO
18 TO 34 N•M
(13-25 FT.LBS.)

INLET MANIFOLD BOLT/SCREW
& NUT TIGHTENING SEQUENCE

Intake manifold installation—1985–86 2.8L V6 engine

VIEW A

1. Intake manifold
2. Gasket
3. 25 N·m (18 lbs. ft.)
4. Sealer

Intake manifold installation—1987–88 2.8L V6 engine

16. Clean the gasket material and grease from the mating surfaces.

17. Place a bead of RTV sealant on each ridge where the front and rear of the intake manifold contact the block.

18. Install the new intake manifold gasket.

19. Install the pushrods and make sure they are seated in the lifter.

NOTE: *Intake pushrods are marked orange and are 6 in. (152.4mm) long. Exhaust pushrods are marked blue and are 6⅜ in. (161.9mm) long.*

20. Install the rocker arm nuts and tighten to 18 ft. lbs.

21. Install the intake manifold and retaining bolts. Torque the bolts to 15 ft. lbs. in the proper sequence shown, then retighten in sequence to 24 ft. lbs.

22. Install the heater pipe to the manifold.

23. Connect the coolant sensor and any other necessary wiring.

24. Install the upper radiator hose.

25. Install the rocker arm covers.

26. Install the breather tube.

27. Install the fuel rail and the wires to the injectors.

28. Connect the idle air vacuum hose at the throttle body.

29. Install the alternator and bracket.

30. Install the power steering gear and pump.

31. Connect the power steering line at the alternator bracket.

32. Install the serpentine drive belt.

33. Connect the fuel lines to the fuel rail and to the bracket.

34. Install the plenum, plug harness and EGR valve.

35. Install the throttle body.

36. Connect cables at the plenum.

37. Connect the negative battery cable and fill the cooling system.

Exhaust Manifold

REMOVAL AND INSTALLATION

1.8L, 2.0L and 2.2L OHV Engines

1. Disconnect the negative terminal from the battery.

2. Disconnect the oxygen sensor wire.

3. Remove the serpentine belt or alternator drive belt.

4. Remove the alternator-to-bracket bolts and support the alternator (with the wires attached) out of the way.

5. If equipped with A.I.R. or Pulsair system (1982–84), disconnect the pipes and hoses.

6. Raise and support the vehicle safely.

7. Disconnect the exhaust pipe-to-exhaust manifold bolts and lower the vehicle.

8. Remove the exhaust manifold-to-cylinder head bolts.

9. Remove the exhaust manifold from the exhaust pipe flange and the manifold from the vehicle.

To install:

10. Using a gasket scraper, clean the gasket mounting surfaces.

11. To install, use new gaskets and reverse the removal procedures. Torque the exhaust manifold-to-cylinder head nuts to 3–12 ft. lbs. and the bolts to 6–13 ft. lbs. Start the engine and check for exhaust leaks.

1. Tighten in proper sequence to 15 ft. lbs. (20Nm), then retighten to 24 ft. lbs. (33Nm)

⑦ ④ ③ ⑥
⑧ ① ② ⑤

2. Intake manifold
3. Gasket
4. Cylinder head
5. Sealer

Intake manifold installation and torque sequence— 1989–92 2.8L and 3.1 V6 engine

Exhaust manifold installation, 1982–84 1.8L and 2.0L OHV engine

Exhaust manifold installation, 1985–86 2.0L OHV engine

1. 5–15 N·m (3–11 ft. lbs.)
2. 8–18 N·m (6–13 ft. lbs.)

Exhaust manifold installation, 1987–89 2.0L OHV engine

1. Stud
2. Gasket
3. Exhaust manifold
4. Nut

Exhaust manifold ...stallation, 1990–92 2.2L OHV engine

2.8L and 3.1L Engine
1985–86
LEFT SIDE

1. Disconnect the negative battery cable.
2. Remove the air cleaner assembly.
3. Remove the air flow sensor. Remove the engine heat shield.
4. Remove the crossover pipe at the manifold.
5. Remove the exhaust manifold bolts.
6. Remove the exhaust manifold.

To install:

7. Clean the surfaces of the cylinder head and manifold.
8. Place the manifold into position, loosely install the manifold bolts, then install the exhaust crossover pipe to the manifold.
9. Tighten the manifold bolts EVENLY to 25 ft. lbs.
10. Install the heat shield and the mass flow sensor.
11. Install the air cleaner and the negative battery cable.

RIGHT SIDE

1. Disconnect the negative battery cable.
2. Remove the air cleaner assembly.
3. Remove the air flow sensor. Remove the engine heat shield.
4. Disconnect the crossover pipe at the manifold.
5. Disconnect the accelerator and throttle valve cable at the throttle lever and the plenum. Move aside to gain working clearance.
6. Disconnect the power steering line at the power steering pump.
7. Remove the EGR valve assembly.
8. Raise the vehicle and support safely.
9. Disconnect the exhaust pipe at the exhaust manifold.
10. Lower the vehicle.
11. Remove the manifold bolts. Remove the exhaust manifold.

To install:

12. Clean the surfaces of the cylinder head and manifold.
13. Place the manifold into position and loosely install the manifold bolts.
14. Raise and support the vehicle safely.
15. Install the exhaust pipe at the manifold.
16. Lower the vehicle.
17. Tighten the manifold bolts EVENLY to 25 ft. lbs.
18. Install the EGR valve and related parts.
19. Connect the power steering line at the power steering pump.
20. Connect the accelerator and throttle valve cable at the throttle lever and the plenum.
21. Connect the crossover pipe at the manifold.

22. Install the engine heat shield.

23. Install the mass air flow sensor.

24. Install the air cleaner assembly and connect the negative battery cable.

1987–92
LEFT SIDE

1. Disconnect the negative battery cable.

2. Remove the air cleaner inlet hose.

3. Remove the mass air flow sensor, on models so equipped.

4. Drain ther coolant and remove the coolant by-pass pipe and engine heat shield.

CAUTION: *When draining the coolant, keep in mind that cats and dogs are attracted by the ethylene glycol antifreeze, and are quite likely to drink any that is left in an uncovered container or in puddles on the ground. This will prove fatal in sufficient quantity. Always drain the coolant into a sealable container. Coolant should be reused unless it is contaminated or several years old.*

5. Disconnect the exhaust crossover pipe at the manifold.

6. Remove the exhaust manifold bolts and remove the exhaust manifold/crossover assembly.

To install:

7. Clean the surfaces of the cylinder head and manifold.

8. Place the manifold into position and loosely install the manifold bolts.

9. Install the exhaust crossover pipe to the manifold.

10. Tighten the exhaust manifold bolts EVENLY to 18 ft. lbs.

11. Install the heat shield and coolant pipe.

12. Fill the cooling system.

13. Install the air cleaner inlet hose.

14. Connect the negative battery cable.

RIGHT SIDE

1. Disconnect the negative battery cable.

2. Raise and support the vehicle safely.

3. Remove the heat shield.

4. Disconnect the exhaust pipe at the crossover.

5. Lower the vehicle.

6. Remove the EGR valve or pipe from.

7. Disconnect the oxygen sensor wire.

8. Disconnect the exhaust pipe at the exhaust manifold.

9. Lower the vehicle.

VIEW **A**

VIEW **B**

Exhaust manifold installation, 1985–86 2.8L V6 engine

10. Remove the exhaust manifold bolts and remove the exhaust manifold.

To install:

11. Clean the surfaces of the cylinder head and manifold.

12. Install the manifold gasket, place the manifold into position and loosely install the manifold bolts.

13. Install the crossover at the manifold.

14. Tighten the manifold bolts EVENLY to 25 ft. lbs.

15. Install the EGR valve or pipe and connect the oxygen sensor wire.

16. Raise and support the vehicle safely.

17. Install the engine heat shield.

18. Install the exhaust pipe to the crossover.

19. Lower the vehicle.

20. Install the negative battery cable. and check for leaks.

1.8L and 2.0L OHC Engines

EXCEPT TURBOCHARGER

1. Remove air cleaner.

2. Remove spark plug wires and retainers.

3. Remove oil dipstick tube and breather assembly.

4. Disconnect oxygen sensor wire.

5. Disconnect exhaust pipe from manifold flange.

1. 20–30 N·m (14–22 ft. lbs.)
2. 30–40 N·m (22–30 ft. lbs.)
3. Gasket

Exhaust manifold installation, 1987–88 2.8L V6 engine

1. 25 N·m (18 lb. ft.)
2. 10 N·m (89 lb. in.)
3. Heat shield
4. Extension
5. Exhaust manifold (left)
6. Exhaust manifold (right)
7. Gasket

Exhaust manifold installation, 1989–92 2.8L and 3.1L V6 engine

Exhaust manifold installation and torque sequence 1.8L and 2.0L OHC engine without turbocharger

NOTE: *Before installing a new gasket on the 1.8L MFI Turbo engine (code J), check for the location of the stamped part number on the surface. This gasket should be installed with this number toward the manifold. The gasket appears to be the same in either direction but it is not. Installing the gasket backwards will result in a leak.*

6. Remove exhaust manifold to cylinder head attaching nuts and remove manifold and gasket.

7. Installation is the reverse of removal. Torque the bolts EVENLY to 16-19 ft. lbs.

WITH TURBOCHARGER

1. Disconnect the negative battery cable. Remove the turbo induction tube.

2. Disconnect (mark for correct installation) the spark plug wires.

3. Remove the bolts and nuts between the turbo and exhaust manifold.

4. Remove the bolts and nuts and remove the manifold and gasket.

To install:

5. Clean the mating surfaces at the cylinder head and manifold.

6. Install the manifold with a new gasket and torque the nuts EVENLY to 16 ft. lbs.

7. Install the turbocharger to the exhaust manifold and torque the nuts EVENLY to 18 ft. lbs.

8. Install the spark plug wires and the turbo induction tube.

Turbocharger

REMOVAL AND INSTALLATION

1. Disconnect the negative battery cable. Raise the car and support it with jackstands.

2. Remove the lower fan retaining screw.

3. Disconnect the exhaust pipe.

4. Remove the rear air conditioning support bracket and loosen the remaining bolts.

5. Remove the turbo support bracket bolt to the engine.

6. Disconnect the oil drain hose at the turbo.

7. Lower the vehicle.

8. Disconnect the coolant recovery pipe and move to one side.

9. Disconnect the induction tube.

10. Disconnect the cooling fan.

11. Disconnect the oxygen sensor.

12. Disconnect the oil feed pipe at the union.

13. Disconnect the air intake duct and vacuum hose at the actuator.

14. Remove the exhaust manifold retaining nuts and remove the exhaust manifold and turbocharger.

To install:

15. Install the exhaust manifold and turbocharger. Torque the bolts EVENLY to 16 ft. lbs.

16. Install the exhaust manifold retaining nuts.

17. Connect the air intake duct and vacuum hose at the actuator.

1. Gasket
2. Expansion joints face outward
3. Manifold asm.
4. Bolt & Lockwasher asm. 27 N·m (20 lb. ft.)
5. Stud bolt & lockwasher asm. 27 N·m (20 lb.ft.)
6. Shield
7. Nut 22 N·m (16 lb. ft.)

Torque no. 2 & 3 manifold runners prior to no. 1 & 4 runners

Exhaust manifold installation 1.8L and 2.0L OHC engine with turbocharger

18. Connect the oil feed pipe at the union.
19. Connect the oxygen sensor.
20. Connect the cooling fan.
21. Connect the induction tube.
22. Connect the coolant recovery pipe and move to one side.
23. Lower the vehicle.
24. Connect the oil drain hose at the turbo.
25. Install the turbo support bracket bolt to the engine.
26. Install the rear air conditioning support bracket.
27. Connect the exhaust pipe.
28. Install the lower fan retaining screw.

Radiator

REMOVAL AND INSTALLATION

1. Disconnect the negative battery cable.
2. Drain the cooling system.
CAUTION: *When draining the coolant, keep in mind that cats and dogs are attracted by*

Turbocharger mounting—1983–86 1.8L OHC engine

the ethylene glycol antifreeze, and are quite likely to drink any that is left in an uncovered container or in puddles on the ground. This will prove fatal in sufficient quantity. Always drain the coolant into a sealable container. Coolant should be reused unless it is contaminated or several years old.

1. Stud
2. Bolt
3. Gasket
4. Nut 25 N·m (18 lbs. ft.)
5. Stud 25 N·m (18 lbs. ft.)
6. Washer
7. Nut 25 N·m (18 lbs. ft.)
8. Support bracket
9. Exhuast outlet elbow
10. Bolt 50 N·m (37 lbs. ft.)
11. Adapter plate

Turbocharger mounting—1987–90 2.0L OHC engine

3. Disconnect the electrical lead at the fan motor.
4. Remove the fan frame-to-radiator support attaching bolts and then remove the fan assembly.
5. Disconnect the upper and lower radiator hoses and the coolant recovery hose from the radiator.
6. Disconnect the transmission oil cooler lines from the radiator and wire them out of the way.
7. If equipped with A/C, remove the 4 radiator to condensor bolts and the radiator tank to refrigerent line clamp bolt.
8. Remove the radiator-to-radiator support attaching bolts and clamps. Remove the radiator.
To install:
9. Place the radiator in the vehicle so that

the bottom is located in the lower mounting pads. Tighten the attaching bolts and clamps.
10. Connect the transmission oil cooler lines and tighten the bolts to 20 ft. lbs.
11. Installation of the remaining components is in the reverse order of removal. Fill the coolant system, check for coolant leaks.

Electric Cooling Fan

REMOVAL AND INSTALLATION

NOTE: *The electric cooling fan can start whether or not the engine is running. After replacing electric coolant fan, verify that the fan is moving the air in the proper direction.*

4-Cylinder Engines

1. Disconnect the negative battery cable.
2. Remove the air cleaner duct.

3. Disconnect the wiring harness from the motor and the fan frame.

4. Remove the fan assembly from the radiator support.

5. Installation is the reverse of the removal procedure. Torque the fan assembly motor-to-fan 29 inch lbs. and fan-to-radiator support bolt 80 inch lbs.

6-Cylinder Engines

1. Disconnect the negative battery cable. Drain engine coolant to level below the upper radiator hose.

CAUTION: *When draining the coolant, keep in mind that cats and dogs are attracted by the ethylene glycol antifreeze, and are quite likely to drink any that is left in an uncovered container or in puddles on the ground. This will prove fatal in sufficient quantity. Always*

1. FAN ASSEMBLY
2. BOLT - 10 N.m (88 LBS. IN)
3. NUT

Coolant fan mounting

1. NUTS
2. BRACKET
3. INSULATOR
4. BOLT/SCREW – FULLY DRIVEN, SEATED AND NOT STRIPPED

Radiator mounting—2.2L (VIN 4) engine code

1. RETAINER
2. INSULATOR
3. RADIATOR ASM.
4. BOLT/SCREW – 5 N·m (44 LBS. IN.)
5. INSULATOR
6. CONDENSOR
7. BOLT/SCREW – 6 N·m (53 LBS. IN.)

Radiator mounting—3.1L (VIN T) engine code

Water pump installation—1985–86 2.0L OHV engine

Water pump installation—1987–92 2.0L and 2.2L OHV engine

1. FAN
2. MOTOR
3. SHROUD
4. BRACKET
5. NUT 3.3 N m
   (29 LBS. IN.)

Electric coolant fan

drain the coolant into a sealable container. Coolant should be reused unless it is contaminated or several years old.

2. Remove the air cleaner duct.

3. Remove the air cleaner assembly.

4. Mark latch position for reassembly, then remove the main hood latch assembly.

5. Disconnect the upper radiator hose and

Water pump installation—1982–84 1.8L and 2.0L OHV engine

position aside. On automatic transaxle equipped vehicles, position transaxle cooler lines aside.

6. Disconnect the electrical wiring harness connector at the coolant fan. Remove the fan assembly from the radiator support.

7. Installation is the reverse of the removal procedure. Torque the fan assembly motor-to-fan 29 inch lbs. and fan-to-radiator support bolt 80 inch lbs.

Water Pump

REMOVAL AND INSTALLATION

CAUTION: *When draining the coolant, keep in mind that cats and dogs are attracted by the ethylene glycol antifreeze, and are quite likely to drink any that is left in an uncovered container or in puddles on the ground. This will prove fatal in sufficient quantity. Always drain the coolant into a sealable container.*

1. Bolt 28 N·m (21 lb. ft.)
2. Water pump
3. Seal ring

Water pump installation—1.8L and 2.0L OHC engine

Coolant should be reused unless it is contaminated or several years old.

1.8L, 2.0L and 2.2L OHV Engines

1. Disconnect the negative battery cable.
2. Drain the cooling system.
3. Remove all accessory drive belts or the serpentine belt.
4. Remove the alternator.
5. Unscrew the water pump pulley mounting bolts and then pull off the pulley.
6. Remove the mounting bolts and remove the water pump.

To install:

7. Place a ⅛ in. (3mm) wide bead of RTV sealant on the water pump sealing surface or install a new gasket, on models so equipped . While the sealer is still wet, install the pump and tighten the bolts to 13–18 ft. lbs.
8. Installation of the remaining components is in the reverse order of removal. Fill the cooling system to the proper level.

1.8L and 2.0L OHC Engines

1. Remove the timing belt as described later.
2. Remove the timing belt rear protective covers.
3. Remove the hose from the pump.
4. Unbolt and remove the pump.
5. Installation is the reverse of removal. Torque the bolts to 19 ft. lbs.

2.8L and 3.1L V6 Engines

1. Disconnect battery negative cable.
2. Drain cooling system.
3. Disconnect the serpentine belt at the water pump pulley.
4. On 1985–86 models, disconnect the wires at the air conditioning pressure cycling switch and remove the cycling switch.
5. Remove the water pump pulley.
6. Remove the pump retaining bolts and remove the water pump.

To install:

7. Clean the gasket surfaces.
8. Install the gasket and water pump and tighten the pump to block bolts to 18 ft. lbs.

Water pump installation—1985–86 2.8L V6 engine

1. Radiator pump
2. Gasket
3. Bolt—10 Nm (90 lbs. in.)
4. Locator (must be vertical)

Water pump installation—1987–92 2.8L and 3.1L V6 engine

9. Install the water pump pulley.

10. Install the air conditioning pressure cycling switch on 1985–86 models.

11. Install the serpentine belt.

12. Fill the cooling system.

13. Reconnect the battery, start the engine and check for leaks.

Cylinder Head

REMOVAL AND INSTALLATION

CAUTION: *When draining the coolant, keep in mind that cats and dogs are attracted by the ethylene glycol antifreeze, and are quite likely to drink any that is left in an uncovered container or in puddles on the ground. This will prove fatal in sufficient quantity. Always drain the coolant into a sealable container. Coolant should be reused unless it is contaminated or several years old.*

1.8L, 2.0L and 2.2L OHV Engines

1982–86

NOTE: *The engine should be overnight cold before removing the cylinder head.*

1. Disconnect the negative battery cable. Release the fuel pressure.

2. Drain the cooling system into a clean container; the coolant can be reused if it is still good.

3. Remove the air cleaner. Raise and support the front of the vehicle.

4. Remove the exhaust shield. Disconnect the exhaust pipe.

5. Remove the heater hose from the intake manifold and then lower the car.

6. Unscrew the mounting bolts and remove the engine lift bracket (includes air management).

7. Remove (mark for correct installation) the distributor. Disconnect the vacuum manifold at the alternator bracket.

8. Tag and disconnect the remaining vacuum lines at the intake manifold and thermostat.

9. Remove the air management pipe at the exhaust check valve.

10. Disconnect the accelerator linkage at the carburetor or T.B.I. unit and then remove the linkage bracket.

11. Tag and disconnect all necessary wires. Remove the upper radiator hose at the thermostat.

12. Remove the bolt attaching the dipstick tube and hot water bracket.

13. Remove the idler pulley. Remove the A.I.R. and power steering pump drive belts.

14. Remove the A.I.R. bracket-to-intake manifold bolt. If equipped with power steering, remove the air pump pulley, the A.I.R. through-bolt and the power steering adjusting bracket.

15. Loosen the A.I.R. mounting bracket lower bolt so that the bracket will rotate.

16. Disconnect and plug the fuel line at the carburetor.

17. Remove the alternator. Remove the alternator brace from the head and then remove the upper mounting bracket.

18. Remove the cylinder head cover. Remove the rocker arms and pushrods.

19. Remove the cylinder head bolts in the order given in the illustration. Remove the cylinder head with the carburetor or T.B.I. unit, intake and exhaust manifolds still attached.

To install:

20. To install, the gasket surfaces on both the head and the block must be clean of any foreign matter and free of any nicks or heavy scratches. Cylinder bolt threads in the block and the bolt must be clean.

21. Place a new cylinder head gasket in position over the dowel pins on the block. Carefully guide the cylinder head into position.

22. Coat the cylinder bolts with sealing compound and install them finger tight.

23. Using a torque wrench, torque as follows:

   a. 1982–85 — gradually tighten the bolts to 65–75 ft. lbs. in the sequence shown in the illustration.

   b. 1986 — gradually tighten the bolts to 73–85 ft. lbs. in the sequence shown in the illustration.

CYLINDER HEAD BOLT TIGHTENING SEQUENCE

Cylinder head installation and torque sequence— 1982–86 1.8L and 2.0L OHV engine

24. Install the rocker arms and pushrods and adjust the valve lash.

25. Install the cylinder head cover.

26. Install the alternator brace on the head. Install the upper mounting bracket.

27. Install the alternator.

28. Connect the fuel line at the carburetor.

29. Install the A.I.R. bracket-to-intake manifold bolt. If equipped with power steering, install the air pump pulley, the A.IR. throughbolt and the power steering adjusting bracket.

30. Install the idler pulley. Install the A.I.R. and power steering pump drive belts.

31. Install the bolt attaching the dipstick tube and hot water bracket.

32. Connect all wires.

33. Install the upper radiator hose at the thermostat.

34. Install the linkage bracket and connect the accelerator linkage at the carburetor or T.B.I.

35. Install the air management pipe at the exhaust check valve.

36. Connect the remaining vacuum lines at the intake manifold and thermostat.

37. Install the distributor.

38. Connect the vacuum manifold at the alternator bracket.

39. Install the engine lift bracket (includes air management).

1. 99–113 N·m (73–83 ft. lbs.)
2. 85–95 N·m (62–70 ft. lbs.)

Cylinder head installation and torque sequence—1987–89 2.0L and 2.2L OHV engine

40. Install the heater hose at the intake manifold.

41. Connect the exhaust pipe.

42. Install the exhaust shield.

43. Install the air cleaner.

44. Fill the cooling system.

45. Connect the negative battery cable.

1987–92

NOTE: *The engine must be cold before removing the cylinder head. Always release the fuel pressure before starting repair.*

1. Disconnect the negative battery cable.

2. Drain the cooling system.

3. Remove the TBI cover. Raise and safely support the vehicle.

4. Remove the exhaust shield. Disconnect the exhaust pipe.

5. Remove the heater hose from the intake manifold. Lower the vehicle.

6. Disconnect the accelerator and TV cable bracket.

7. Lower the vehicle.

8. Tag and disconnect the vacuum lines at the intake manifold and thermostat.

9. Disconnect the accelerator linkage at the TBI unit and remove the linkage bracket.

10. Tag and disconnect all necessary wires. Remove the upper radiator hose at the thermostat.

11. Remove the serpentine belt.

12. Remove the power steering pump and lay aside.

13. Make sure the fuel system pressure is released and disconnect and plug the fuel lines.

14. Remove the alternator. Remove the alternator brace from the head and remove the upper mounting bracket.

15. Remove the cylinder head cover. Remove the rocker arms and pushrods keeping all parts in order for correct installation.

16. Remove the cylinder head bolts. Remove the cylinder head with the TBI unit, intake and exhaust manifolds still attached.

To install:

17. The gasket surfaces on both the head and the block must be clean of any foreign matter and free of any nicks or heavy scratches. Bolt threads in the block and the bolts must be clean.

18. Place a new cylinder head gasket in position over the dowel pins on the block. Carefully guide the cylinder head into position.

19. Coat the cylinder bolts with sealing compound and install them finger tight.

20. Using a torque wrench, torque as follows:

a. 1987–89 — tighten the long bolts to 73–83 ft lbs. in the sequence shown in the illustration and tighten the short bolts to 62–70 ft lbs. in the sequence shown in the illustration.

1. Long bolts
2. Short bolts
3. Stud
4. Numbers on gasket indicate torque sequence

Cylinder head installation and torque sequence—1990–92 2.2 OHV engine

b. 1990 — Tighten in 4 steps as follows:
● Tighten all bolts in sequence to 41 ft. lbs.
● Tighten all bolts an additional 45° in sequence.
● Tighten all bolts an additional 45° in sequence.
● Tighten the long bolts — 8, 4, 1, 1, 5 and 9 an additional 20° and tighten the short bolts — 7, 3, 2, 6 and 10 an additional 10°.

NOTE: *The short bolts, exhaust side, should end up with a total rotation of 100° and the long bolts, intake side, should end up with a total rotation of 110°.*

c. 1991–92 — Tighten in 3 steps as follows:
● Tighten the long bolts in sequence to 46 ft. lbs.
● Tighten the short bolts in sequence to 43 ft. lbs.
● Tighten all bolts in sequence an additional 90°.

21. Reinstall the alternator. Install the power steering pump and brackets.

22. Reconnect the fuel lines and the hoses. Connect the exhaust pipe to the manifold.

23. Install the valve cover and connect the linkage at the TBI unit. Install the air cleaner and fill all the fluids.

24. Run the engine and check for leaks.

1.8L 1nd 2.0L OHC Engines

1. Remove air cleaner or induction tube (turbo engines). Release the fuel pressure.

2. Drain cooling system.

3. Remove alternator and pivot bracket at camshaft carrier housing.

4. Disconnect power steering pump and bracket and lay to one side.

5. Disconnect ignition coil electrical connections and remove coil.

6. Disconnect spark plug wires and distributor cap and remove.

7. Remove throttle cable from bracket at intake manifold.

8. Disconnect throttle cable, downshift cable and T.V. cable from E.F.I. assembly.

9. Disconnect E.C.M. connectors from E.F.I. assembly.

10. Remove vacuum brake hose at filter.

11. Disconnect inlet and return fuel lines at flex joints.

CAUTION: *The fuel lines are pressurized (especially Turbo Engines). Removal may cause fuel spray resulting in personal injury. Do not remove before bleeding the pressure from the fuel system. See Chapter 1 for the procedure.*

12. Remove water pump bypass hose at intake manifold and water pump.

13. Disconnect ECM harness connectors at intake manifold.

14. Disconnect heater hose from intake manifold.

15. Disconnect exhaust pipe at exhaust manifold. On turbo engines, disconnect the exhaust manifold at the turbo connection.

16. Disconnect breather hose at camshaft carrier.

17. Remove upper radiator hose.

18. Disconnect engine electrical harness and wires from thermostat housing.

19. Remove timing cover.

20. Remove timing probe holder.

21. Loosen water pump retaining bolts and remove timing belt.

22. Loosen camshaft carrier and cylinder head attaching bolts a little at a time in sequence shown.

NOTE: *Camshaft carrier and cylinder head bolts should only be removed when engine is cold.*

23. Remove camshaft carrier assembly.

24. Remove cylinder head, intake manifold and exhaust manifold as an assembly.

To install:

25. Install a new cylinder head gasket in position on the block.

26. Apply a continuous bead of sealer to the cam carrier.

27. Install the cylinder head, reassembled with the intake and exhaust manifolds, if removed.

28. Install the camshaft carrier on the cylinder head and tighten the bolts, in following sequence, to the correct torque.

a. Tighten all bolts in sequence to 18 ft. lbs.

b. Tighten all bolts an additional 180° in 3 steps of 60° each.

29. Install timing belt.

30. Install timing probe holder.

31. Install timing cover.

32. Connect engine electrical harness and wires at thermostat housing.

33. Install upper radiator hose.

34. Connect breather hose at camshaft carrier.

35. Connect exhaust pipe at exhaust manifold. On turbo engines, connect the exhaust manifold at the turbo connection.

36. Connect heater hose at intake manifold.

37. Connect ECM harness connectors at intake manifold.

38. Install water pump bypass hose at intake manifold and water pump.

39. Connect inlet and return fuel lines at flex joints.

40. Install vacuum brake hose at filter.

41. Connect E.C.M. connectors at E.F.I. assembly.

42. Connect throttle cable, downshift cable and T.V. cable at E.F.I. assembly.

43. Install throttle cable at bracket on intake manifold.

44. Connect spark plug wires and install the distributor cap.

45. Connect ignition coil electrical connections and install coil.

46. Install power steering pump and bracket.

47. Install alternator and pivot bracket on camshaft carrier housing.

48. Fill cooling system.

49. Install air cleaner or induction tube (turbo engines).

Camshaft carrier and head bolt loosening sequence—1.8L and 2.0L OHC engines

Camshaft carrier and head bolt tightening sequence—1.8L and 2.0L OHC engines

Cylinder head bolt torque degree sequence—1.8L and 2.0L OHC engines

2.8L and 3.1L V6 Engines

1985–86
LEFT SIDE

1. Disconnect the negative battery cable.
2. Drain the coolant from the block and lower the car.
3. Remove the intake manifold.
4. Remove the exhaust crossover at the intake manifold.
5. Remove the air cleaner cover and air cleaner.
6. Disconnect the MAP sensor.
7. Remove the exhaust crossover heat shield.
8. Disconnect the exhaust crossover at the left maniufold.
9. Remove the oil level indicator tube.
10. Disconnect the wiring harness at the left head.
11. Loosen the rocker arm bolts and remove the pushrods.
12. Remove the cylinder head bolts and cylinder head.

To install:

13. Clean all gasket surfaces and bolts.
14. Place the new head gasket in position over the dowel pins with the words "This side Up" facing upward.
15. Coat the cylinder head bolts with sealer and torque to 77 ft. lbs. in the sequence shown.
16. Install the pushrods in the lifter seats and loosely retain with the rocker arms.
17. Install the intake manifold and gaskets.
18. Install the MAP sensor.
19. Install the exhaust manifold.
20. Install the spark plug wires.
21. Fill the cooling system.
22. Install the oil level indicator tube.
23. Install the air cleaner and cover.
24. Adjust the drive belt and the valve lash.

RIGHT SIDE

1. Disconnect the negative battery cable.
2. Drain the cooling system.
3. Remove the intake manifold.
4. Raise and support the vehicle safely.
5. Remove the exhaust crossover at the right manifold.
6. Lower the vehicle.
7. Loosen the rocker arm bolts and remove the pushrods.
8. Remove the air cleaner cover and air cleaner.
9. Remove the MAP sensor.
10. Remove the exhaust crossover heat shield.
11. Disconnect the exhaust crossover at the right maniufold.
12. Disconnect the spark plug wiring harness at the right head.

Cylinder head installation and torque sequence—1985–86 2.8L V6 engine

11. Loosen the rocker arm bolts and remove the pushrods.
12. Remove the cylinder head bolts and cylinder head.

To install:

13. Clean all gasket surfaces and bolts.
14. Place the new head gasket in position over the dowel pins with the words "This side Up" facing upward.
15. Coat the cylinder head bolts with sealer and torque to 77 ft. lbs. in the sequence shown.
16. Install the pushrods in the lifter seats and loosely retain with the rocker arms.
17. Install the intake manifold and gaskets.
18. Install the MAP sensor.
19. Install the exhaust manifold.
20. Install the spark plug wires.
21. Fill the cooling system.
22. Install the oil level indicator tube.
23. Install the air cleaner and cover.
24. Adjust the drive belt and the valve lash.

1987–92
LEFT SIDE

1. Relieve the fuel system pressure and disconnect the negative battery cable. Drain the cooling system. Remove the rocker cover.
2. Remove the intake manifold. Disconnect the exhaust crossover at the right exhaust manifold.
3. Disconnect the oil level indicator tube bracket.
4. Loosen the rocker arms nuts enough to remove the pushrods.
5. Starting with the outer bolts, remove the cylinder head bolts. Remove the cylinder head with the exhaust manifold.
6. Clean and inspect the surfaces of the cylinder head, block and intake manifold. Clean

HEAD TORQUE SEQUENCE

Coat thread with sealer before install-ing. Using a 12" clicker torque wrench torque to 45 N·m (33 Lbs. Ft.). Rotate wrench an additional 90° (1/4 turn).

Cylinder head installation and torque sequence—1987–92 2.8L and 3.1L V6 engine

the threads in the block and the threads on the bolts.

To install:

7. Align the new gasket over the dowels on the block with the note **THIS SIDE UP** facing the cylinder head.

8. Install the cylinder head and exhaust manifold crossover assembly on the engine.

9. Coat the cylinder head bolts with a proper sealer and install the bolts hand tight.

10. Torque the bolts, in the correct sequence, to 33 ft. lbs., then rotate an additional 90° (¼ turn).

11. Install the pushrods in the same order they were removed.

NOTE: *Intake pushrods are marked orange and are 6 in. (152.4mm) long. Exhaust push-rods are marked blue and are 6⅜ in. (161.9mm) long.*

12. Install the rocker arms. The correct rock-er arm torque is 14–20 ft. lbs.

13. Install the intake manifold using a new gasket and following the correct sequence, torque the bolts to the correct specification.

14. The remainder of the installation is the reverse of the removal.

RIGHT SIDE

1. Disconnect the negative battery cable. Drain the cooling system.

2. Raise and safely support the vehicle. Dis-connect the exhaust manifold from the exhaust pipe.

3. Lower the vehicle. Disconnect the exhaust manifold from the cylinder head and remove the manifold.

4. Remove the rocker cover. Remove the in-take manifold.

5. Loosen the rocker arms enough so the pushrods can be removed. Note the position of the pushrods for assembly.

6. Starting with the outer bolts, remove the

cylinder head bolts and remove the cylinder head.

7. Inspect and clean the surfaces of the cylin-der head, engine block and intake manifold.

8. Clean the threads in the engine block and the threads on the cylinder head bolts.

To install:

9. Align the new gasket on the dowels on the engine block with the note **THIS SIDE UP** fac-ing the cylinder head.

10. Install the cylinder head on the engine. Coat the head bolts with a proper sealer. Install and tighten the bolts hand tight.

11. Torque the bolts, in sequence, to 33 ft. lbs., then rotate an additional 90° (¼ turn).

12. Install the pushrods in the same order as they were removed.

NOTE: *Intake pushrods are marked orange and are 6 in. (152.4mm) long. Exhaust push-rods are marked blue and are 6⅜ in. (161.9mm) long.*

13. Install the rocker arms. The correct rock-er arm torque is 14–20 ft. lbs. (1987–88), 18 ft. lbs. (1989–92).

14. Install the intake manifold using a new gasket. Following the correct sequence, torque the bolts to the proper specification.

15. The remainder of the installation is the reverse of the removal.

RESURFACING

Cylinder Head Flatness

When the cylinder head is removed, check the flatness of the cylinder head gasket surfaces.

1. Place a straightedge across the gasket sur-face of the cylinder head. Using feeler gauges, determine the clearance at the center of the straightedge.

2. If warpage exceeds 0.003 in. (0.076mm) in a 6 in. (152mm) span, or 0.006 in. (0.152mm)

12. Push rod guide
13. E.G.R. valve
14. Thermostat outlet
15. Thermostat
16. Adapter
17. Cylinder head
18. Generator bracket
19. Generator
20. Valves
21. Lifter
22. Exhaust manifold
23. Cylinder head gasket

1. Air cleaner
2. TBI unit
3. Coil and coil wire
4. Fuel line
5. Insulator
6. Rocker arm cover
7. Intake manifold & gasket
8. Valve stem key
9. Valve spring
10. Rocker arm
11. Push rod

Disassembled view of the cylinder head and related parts—1982–86 1.8L and 2.0L OHV engine

over the total length, the cylinder head must be resurfaced.

3. If necessary to refinish the cylinder head gasket surface, do not plane or grind off more than 0.254mm (0.010 in.) from the original gasket surface.

NOTE: *When milling the cylinder heads of V6 engines, the intake manifold mounting position is altered, and must be corrected by milling the manifold flange a proportionate amount. Consult an experienced machinist about this service.*

CLEANING AND INSPECTION

1. Clean all carbon from the combustion chambers and valve ports.
2. Thoroughly clean the valve guides.

3. Clean all carbon and sludge from the pushrods, rocker arms and pushrod guides.
4. Clean the valve stems and heads on a buffing wheel.
5. Clean the carbon deposits from the head gasket mating surface.
6. Inspect the cylinder head for cracks in the exhaust ports, combustion chambers or external cracks to the water jacket.
7. Inspect the valves for burned heads, cracked faces or damaged stems.
8. Measure the valve stem clearance as follows:

   a. Clamp a dial indicator on ones side of the cylinder head. Locate the indicator so that movement of the valve stem from side to side (crosswise to the head) will cause direct movement of the indicator stem. The indica-

1. Air cleaner, TBI
2. Screw
3. Washer
4. Duct, air intake front
5. Bolt
6. Support, spark plug wire front
7. Support, spark plug wire rear
8. Bolt
9. Support, ignition wire
10. Bolt, rocket cover
11. Tube, crankcase vent
12. Bolt, rocket cover
13. Cover, rocker arm
14. Gasket, rocker cover
15. Nut, rocker arm
16. Ball, rocker arm
17. Arm, rocker
18. Stud, valve rocker arm ball
19. Guide, push rod
20. Seat, valve spring
21. Control, heater coolant hose
22. Seal, valve stem oil
23. Spring, valve
24. Cap, valve spring
25. Key, valve stem
26. Plug, spark
27. Wire, spark plug
28. Nut
29. Valve, EGR
30. Gasket, EGR valve
31. Plug, water outlet
32. Sensor, coolant temperature
33. Stud, EGR valve
34. Adapter, coolant outlet
35. Thermostat, engine coolant outlet
36. Outlet, coolant
37. Stud
38. Nut
39. Gasket, coolant outlet
40. Nut
41. Bracket, engine lift
42. Stud, cylinder head
43. Stud, exhaust manifold
44. Gasket, exhaust manifold
45. Manifold, exhaust
46. Nut
47. Oxygen sensor
48. Valve, inlet & exhaust
49. Gasket, cylinder head
50. Head, w guide and insert

51. Bolt
52. Bolt, spl
54. Bracket, drive belt tensioner
55. Bolt
56. Stud
57. Bracket, accelerator control cable
58. Stud
59. Nut
60. Stud
61. Stud, intake manifold
62. Stud, intake manifold
63. Gasket, intake manifold
64. Manifold, intake
65. Fitting, vacuum power brake
66. Fitting, inlet manifold vacuum
67. Tube, EGR vacuum & evaporator canister
68. Gasket, TBI
69. Throttle body injection

70. Bolt, TBI
71. Pipe, fuel injection—fuel return
72. Pipe, fuel injection—fuel feed
73. Valve, crankcase vent
74. Seal, crankcase vent valve cap

76. Hose, crankcase vent
77. Cap, crankcase vent valve
78. Seal, crankcase vent valve (top)
79. Seal, crankcase vent valve (bottom)
80. Sensor, manifold air temperature
81. Seal, air intake duct adapter front
82. Clamp, front air intake duct adapter
83. Adapter, air intake duct front
84. Clamp
85. Duct
86. Clamp

Disassembled view of the cylinder head and related parts—1987–89 2.0L OHV engine

1. Air cleaner assembly
2. PCV fresh air vent hose
3. Nut
4. Air cleaner inlet center duct
5. Air cleaner seal
6. Air cleaner inlet front duct
7. Air intake splash shield
8. Nut
9. Air cleaner inlet front duct bracket
10. Bolt
11. PCV hose
12. PCV valve cap
13. PCV cap O-ring
14. PCV valve upper O-ring
15. PCV valve lower O-ring
16. PCV valve lower O-ring
17. Crank case vent tube
18. Rocker cover and gasket
19. Bracket
20. Spark plug
21. Bolt
22. Bracket
23. Bolt
24. Secondary ignition cables
25. Key
26. Valve spring
27. Valve stem oil seal
28. Valve spring seat

29. Rocker arm stud
30. Pushrod guide
31. Coolant outlet gasket
32. Coolant pipe adapter
33. Coolant pipe adapter
34. Stud
35. Valve spring cap
36. Nut
37. EGR valve
38. EGR valve gasket
39. Plug
40. Coolant sensor
41. Thermostat
42. Coolant outlet
43. Nut
44. Stud

45. Nut
46. Nut
47. Oxygen
48. Engine lift bracket
49. Stud
50. Stud
51. Stud
52. Exhaust manifold
53. Exhaust manifold gasket
54. Hose nipple
55. Exhaust valve
56. Intake valve
57. Cylinder head gasket
58. Cylinder head
59. Coolant jacket plug
60. Bolt
61. Bolt
62. Serpentine drive belt tensioner

63. Bolt
64. Stud
65. Accelerator bracket
66. Nut
67. Stud
68. Stud
69. Intake manifold gasket
70. Intake manifold
71. Vacuum fitting
72. Power brake vacuum fitting
73. Vapor canister harness
74. Rocker arm
75. Rocker arm ball
76. Nut
77. Fuel feed pipe
78. O-ring seal
79. Fuel return pipe
80. O-ring seal
81. Throttle body injector
82. Stud

Disassembled view of the cylinder head and related parts—1990–92 2.2L OHV engine

1. Camshaft cover
2. Camshaft carrier
3. Exhaust manifold (VIN code O)
4. Piston
5. Vent tube (VIN code O)
6. Oil dipstick
7. Tube
8. Cylinder block
9. Flywheel
10. Crankshaft

11. Main thrust bearing
12. Main bearings
13. Main bearing caps
14. Oil pump pickup tube
15. Gasket
16. Oil pan
17. Connecting rod cap
18. Connecting rod bearing
19. Oil pump
20. Gasket

21. Front cover
22. Timing belt
23. Rear cover
24. Water pump
25. Head gasket
26. Cylinder head
27. Camshaft sprocket
28. Water crossover
29. Intake manifold (VIN code O)

Disassembled view of the engine assembly—1.8L OHC engine

Disassembled view of the engine assembly—1987–88 2.0L OHC engine

1. Camshaft cover
2. Camshaft cover gasket
3. Camshaft carrier
4. Cylinder head
5. Cylinder head gasket
6. Front cover backing
7. Camshaft sprocket
8. Timing belt
9. Front cover
10. Water pump
11. Crankshaft gear
12. Oil pump gasket
13. Oil pump
14. Oil filter
15. Oil pan gasket
16. Oil scraper
17. Oil pan
18. Crankshaft bearing caps
19. Crankshaft bearings
20. Crankshaft
21. Flywheel
22. Cylinder block
23. Piston
24. Connecting rod
25. Connecting rod bearings
26. Connecting rod cap
27. Oil pump pickup tube
28. Vent tube
29. Tube
30. Oil dipstick

1. Cap, oil fill
2. Bolt
3. Cover, camshaft carrier
4. Screen, oil seperator
5. Deflector, oil seperator
6. Screen, oil seperator
7. Deflector, oil seperator
8. Bolt
9. Gasket, camshaft carrier cover
10. Bracket, engine lift rear
11. Coil, ignition
12. Bolt
13. Distributor, ignition
14. Stud
15. Bolt
16. Stud
17. Nut
18. Bracket, generator
19. Carrier, camshaft
20. Nut
21. Washer
22. Bracket, engine lift front
23. Nut
24. Sealer, camshaft carrier (RTV 200)
25. Bolt
26. Guide, valve
27. Washer, intake valve spring
28. Seal, valve
29. Spring, valve
30. Adjuster, hydraulic valve lash
31. Arm, valve rocker
32. Thrust piece, valve
33. Lock, valve stem
34. Cap, valve spring
35. Roto cap, exhaust valve
36. Bracket, ign wire harn
37. Nut
38. Wire, ignition coil
39. Retainer, spark plug wire
40. Wire asm, spark plug
41. Plug, spark
42. Nut
43. Bracket, ign wire harn
44. Stud, exhaust manifold
45. Nut
46. Manifold, exhaust
47. Gasket, exhaust manifold
48. Head, cylinder
49. Valve, exhaust
50. Valve, intake
51. Gasket, cylinder head
52. Gasket, thermostat housing
53. Stud
54. Bolt
55. Sensor, coolant temp
56. Outlet, cylinder head water
57. Bolt
58. Seal, coolant outlet
59. Housing, thermostat
60. Thermostat, engine coolant
61. Cap, thermostat housing
62. Cover, timing belt rear
63. Belt, timing
64. Cover, timing belt front

65. Bolt
66. Washer, timing gear
67. Gear, cam shaft timing
68. Ball, cam shaft oil pass plug
69. Seal, cam shaft front
70. Pin, dowel
71. Camshaft, engine
72. Gasket, intake manifold
73. Manifold, intake
74. Pipe, radiator outlet
75. Screw
76. Nut
77. Hose, coolant
78. Clamp

79. Pipe, fuel feed
80. Pipe, fuel return
81. Nut
82. Washer
83. Stud
84. Gasket, EGR valve
85. Valve, EGR
86. Bolt
87. Gasket, TBI
88. Tube, throttle bore mixture
89. Throttle body injector
90. Stud
91. Clamp
92. Hose, crank case vent
93. Gasket, air cleaner
94. Bracket & pulley asm
95. Bolt
96. Harness asm, fuel vapor
97. Stud, timing belt front cover

Disassembled view of the upper engine assembly—1989–91 2.0L OHV (VIN Code K) engine

1. Cover, cam shaft carrier
2. Screen, oil seperator
3. Deflector, oil seperator
4. Bolt
5. Deflector, oil seperator
6. Screen, oil seperator
7. Bolt
8. Coil, ignition
9. Nut
10. Gasket, cam shaft carrier
11. Bracket, engine lift rear
12. Stud
13. Bolt
14. Stud
15. Washer
16. Stud, distributor mount
17. Nut
18. Distributor, ignition
19. Wire, ignition coil
20. Nut

21. Bracket, ignition wire harness
22. Wire, spark plug
23. Nut
24. Bracket, ignition wire harness
25. Retainer, spark plug wire
26. Bracket, engine lift front
27. Sealer, silicone (RTV)

28. Carrier, cam shaft
29. Camshaft
30. Seal, cam shaft front
31. Ball, cam shaft
32. Pipe, fuel vapor
33. Hose, fuel vapor
34. Hose, fuel vapor
35. Tube, manifold press sensor
36. Hose, fuel vapor
37. Solenoid, turbo boost control
38. Bracket, generator
39. Nut

40. Sensor, manifold air temp
41. Harness, EGR
42. Gasket, intake manifold
43. Nut
44. Regulator, fuel press
45. Brace, intake manifold
46. Retainer, solenoid EGR
47. Solenoid, EGR valve
48. Manifold, intake
49. Fitting, intake manifold vacuum
50. Cap, vacuum pipe
51. Fitting, intake manifold vacuum
52. Gasket, throttle body
53. Body, throttle
54. Bolt
55. Lever, throttle control
56. Clip, throttle control lever

57. Bracket, T.V. control cable
58. Bracket, throttle control cable
59. Gasket, EGR valve
60. Valve, EGR
61. Bolt
62. Harness, fuel rail
63. Rail, fuel
64. Clip, injector retainer
65. Clamp
66. Injector, fuel
67. Tube, crank case vent
68. Grommet, cam shaft vent tube
69. Hose, vent
70. Valve, vent
71. Boot, vent
73. Cap, oil filter
74. Bolt
75. Washer

Disassembled view of the upper engine assembly—1989–90 2.0L OHC (VIN Code M) engine

1. Cover, timing belt front
2. Bolt
3. Washer, timing gear
4. Gear, cam shaft
5. Cover, timing belt rear
6. Adjuster, hydraulic valve lash
7. Arm, valve rocker
8. Thrust piece, valve
9. Lock, valve stem
10. Cap, valve spring
11. Seal, valve
12. Roto cap, exhaust valve
13. Spring, valve
14. Washer, intake valve spring
15. Guide, valve
16. Plug, spark
17. Clamp
18. Hose, intake duct
19. Tube, turbo induction
20. Stud
21. Bolt
22. Nut
23. Bolt
24. Gasket, exhaust manifold
25. Manifold, exhaust
26. Valve, exhaust
27. Bracket, turbo oil feed pipe support
28. Nut
29. Clip
30. Screw
31. Stud
32. Hose, turbo oil feed
33. Sensor, exhaust oxygen

34. Nut
35. Washer
36. Stud
37. Turbocharger
38. Duct, A/C outlet
39. Cap, thermostat housing
40. Thermostat, coolant
41. Seal
42. Gasket, thermostat housing
43. Housing, thermostat
44. Brace, turbo
45. Adapter, turbo brace
46. Bolt
47. Clamp
48. Elbow, turbo exhaust
49. Bracket, turbo support
50. Fitting, turbo oil drain
51. Hose, turbo oil drain

52. Hose, turbo water return
53. Bracket
54. Clip, turbo oil feed pipe
55. Tubing, turbo coolant return
56. Pipe, turbo coolant feed
57. Bolt
58. Sensor, coolant temp
59. Sealant, (RTV)
60. Outlet, cylinder head water
61. Bolt
62. Pipe, radiator outlet
63. Bolt
64. Clamp
65. Hose, coolant

66. Hose, heater
67. Clamp
68. Pipe, heater
69. Gasket, cylinder head
70. Valve, intake
71. Union, fluid tube
72. Clip, turbo oil feed pipe
73. Fitting, turbo oil feed pipe
74. Clip, turbo feed pipe
75. Tubing (5/16)
76. Belt, timing
77. Head, cylinder
78. Stud, timing belt front cover
79. Tensioner, timing belt

Disassembled view of the upper engine assembly—1989–90 2.0L OHC (VIN Code M) engine (cont.)

Disassembled view of the engine assembly—1987–88 2.0L OHC engine (cont.)

tor stem must contact the side of the valve stem just above the guide.

b. Drop the valve head 1.5mm off the valve seat.

c. Move the stem of the valve from side to side, using light pressure to obtain a clearance reading. If the clearance exceeds specifications, it will be necessary to ream the valve guides for oversize valves. Service valves are available as follows:

• 1.8L and 2.0L (OHV), 2.8L and 3.1L engines – standard, 0.089mm, 0.394mm and 0.775mm O.S. sizes.

• 2.2L (OHV) engine – standard, 0.075mm, 0.150mm and 0.300mm O.S. sizes.

• 1.8L and 2.0L (OHC) engine – standard, 0.075mm, 0.150mm and 0.250mm O.S. sizes.

NOTE: *If valve guides must be reamed this service is available at most machine shops.*

9. Check the valve spring tension with tool J-8056, spring tester. Springs should be compressed to the specified height and checked against the specifications chart. Springs should be replaced if not within (10 lbs. of the specified load (without dampers).

10. Inspect the rocker arms studs for wear or damage.

NOTE: *If a dial indicator is not available to you, take your cylinder head to a qualified machine shop for inspection*

Valve spring compressing tool

Valves and Springs

REMOVAL AND INSTALLATION

1. Block the head on its side, or install a pair of head-holding brackets made especially for valve removal.

2. Use a socket slightly larger than the valve stem and keepers, place the socket over the valve stem and gently hit the socket with a plastic hammer to break loose any varnish buildup.

3. Remove the valve keepers, retainer, spring shield and valve spring using a valve spring compressor (the locking C-clamp type is the easiest kind to use).

4. Put the parts in a separate container numbered for the cylinder being worked on; do not mix them with other parts removed.

5. Remove and discard the valve stem oil seals. A new seal will be used at assembly time.

6. Remove the valves from the cylinder head and place them, in order, through numbered holes punched in a stiff piece of cardboard or wood valve holding stick.

NOTE: *The exhaust valve stems, on some engines, are equipped with small metal caps. Take care not to lose the caps. Make sure to reinstall them at assembly time. Replace any caps that are worn.*

7. Use an electric drill and rotary wire brush to clean the intake and exhaust valve ports, combustion chamber and valve seats. In some cases, the carbon will need to be chipped away. Use a blunt pointed drift for carbon chipping. Be careful around the valve seat areas.

8. Use a wire valve guide cleaning brush and safe solvent to clean the valve guides.

9. Clean the valves with a revolving wires brush. Heavy carbon deposits may be removed with the blunt drift.

NOTE: *When using a wire brush to clean carbon on the valve ports, valves etc., be sure that the deposits are actually removed, rather than burnished.*

10. Wash and clean all valve springs, keepers, retaining caps etc., in safe solvent.

11. Clean the head with a brush and some safe solvent and wipe dry.

12. Check the head for cracks. Cracks in the cylinder head usually start around an exhaust valve seat because it is the hottest part of the combustion chamber. If a crack is suspected but cannot be detected visually have the area checked with dye penetrant or other method by the machine shop.

13. After all cylinder head parts are reasonably clean, check the valve stem-to-guide clearance. If a dial indicator is not on hand, a visual inspection can give you a fairly good idea if the guide, valve stem or both are worn.

14. Insert the valve into the guide until slight away from the valve seat. Wiggle the valve sideways. A small amount of wobble is normal, excessive wobble means a worn guide or valve stem. If a dial indicator is on hand, mount the indicator so that the stem of the valve is at 90° to the valve stem, as close to the valve guide as possible. Move the valve off the seat, and measure the valve guide-to-stem clearance by rocking the stem back and forth to actuate the dial indicator. Measure the valve stem using a micrometer and compare to specifications to determine whether stem or guide wear is causing excessive clearance.

15. The valve guide, if worn, must be repaired before the valve seats can be resurfaced. The machine shop will be able to handle the guide reaming for you. In some cases, if the guide is not too badly worn, knurling may be all that is required.

16. Reface, or have the valves and valve seats refaced. The valve seats should be a true 46° angle (OHV) engines and 46° angle (OHC) engines. Remove only enough material to clean up any pits or grooves. Be sure the valve seat is not too wide or narrow. Use a 60° grinding wheel to remove material from the bottom of the seat for raising and a 30° grinding wheel to remove material from the top of the seat to narrow.

17. After the valves are refaced by machine, hand lap them to the valve seat. Clean the grinding compound off and check the position of face-to-seat contact. Contact should be close to the center of the valve face. If contact is close to the top edge of the valve, narrow the seat; if too close to the bottom edge, raise the seat.

18. Valves should be refaced to a true angle of 45° (OHV) engines and 46° (OHC) engines. Remove only enough metal to clean up the valve face or to correct runout. If the edge of a valve head, after machining, is $1/32$ in. (0.8mm) or less replace the valve. The tip of the valve stem should also be dressed on the valve grinding machine, however, do not remove more than 0.010 in. (0.254mm).

19. After all valve and valve seats have been machined, check the remaining valve train parts (springs, retainers, keepers, etc.) for wear. Check the valve springs for straightness and tension.

20. Install the valves in the cylinder head and metal caps.

21. Install new valve stem oil seals.

22. Install the valve keepers, retainer, spring shield and valve spring using a valve spring compressor (the locking C-clamp type is the easiest kind to use).

23. Check the valve spring installed height, shim or replace as necessary.

CHECKING VALVE SPRINGS

Place the valve spring on a flat surface next to a carpenter's square. Measure the height of the spring, and rotate the spring against the edge of the square to measure distortion. If the spring height varies (by comparison) by more than $1/16$ in. (1.6mm) or if the distortion exceeds $1/16$ in. (1.6mm), replace the spring.

Have the valve springs tested for spring pressure at the installed and compressed (installed height minus valve lift) height using a valve spring tester. Springs should be within one pound, plus or minus each other. Replace springs as necessary.

VALVE SPRING INSTALLED HEIGHT

After installing the valve spring, measure the distance between the spring mounting pad and the lower edge of the spring retainer. Compare the measurement to specifications. If the installed height is incorrect, add shim washers between the spring mounting pad and the spring. Use only washers designed for valve springs, available at most parts houses.

Check the installed height of the valve springs, using a narrow thin scale. On the OHV 4-cylinder engine, measure from the top of the spring seat to the bottom of the cap.

On the V6 engine measure from the top of the spring damper "feet" to the bottom inside of the oil shedder for exhaust and from the top of the spring shim to the bottom of the valve cap for the intake. If this is found to exceed the specified height, install an additional valve spring seat shim approximately 0.7mm thick.

NOTE: *At no time should the valve spring be shimmed to give an installed height under the minimum specified.*

VALVE STEM OIL SEALS

When installing valve stem oil seals, ensure that a small amount of oil is able to pass the seal to lubricate the valve stems and guide walls, otherwise, excessive wear will occur.

On the V6 engine, check each valve stem oil seal by placing the valve stem leak detector tool J-23994, over the end of the valve stem and against the cap. Operate the vacuum pump and make sure no air leaks past the seal.

VALVE SEATS

If the valve seat is damaged or burnt and cannot be serviced by refacing, it may be possible to have the seat machined and an insert installed. Consult an automotive machine shop for their advice.

VALVE GUIDES

Worn valve guides can, in most cases, be reamed to accept a valve with an oversized stem. Valve guides that are not excessively worn or distorted may, in some cases, be knurled rather than reamed. However, if the valve stem is worn reaming for an oversized valve stem is the answer since a new valve would be required.

Knurling is a process in which metal is displaced and raised, thereby reducing clearance. Knurling also produces excellent oil control. The possibility of knurling instead of reaming the valve guides should be discussed with a machinist.

Valve Lifters

REMOVAL AND INSTALLATION

4-Cylinder Engines

1. Disconnect the negative battery cable.
2. Remove the rocker cover.
3. Loosen rocker arm nut and position rocker arm aside. Remove the pushrod — keep all parts in order for correct installation.
4. With a suitable tool remove the lifter assembly form the bore.
5. Installation is the reverse of the removal procedure. Soak engine lifters in clean engine oil before installation.

6-Cylinder Engines

1. Disconnect the negative battery cable. Drain the engine coolant.

CAUTION: *When draining the coolant, keep in mind that cats and dogs are attracted by the ethylene glycol antifreeze, and are quite likely to drink any that is left in an uncovered container or in puddles on the ground. This will prove fatal in sufficient quantity. Always drain the coolant into a sealable container. Coolant should be reused unless it is contaminated or several years old.*

2. Remove the intake manifold assembly — refer to the necessary service procedures in this Chapter.
3. Remove the rocker arm nut, rocker arm and pushrod. Keep all parts in order for correct installation.
4. With a suitable tool remove the lifter assembly form the bore.
5. Installation is the reverse of the removal procedure. Soak engine lifters in clean engine oil before installation.

Oil Pan

REMOVAL AND INSTALLATION

1.8L, 2.0L and 2.2L OHV Engines

1. Disconnect the negative battery cable.
2. Drain the crankcase. Raise and support the front of the vehicle.

CAUTION: *The EPA warns that prolonged*

contact with used engine oil may cause a number of skin disorders, including cancer! You should make every effort to minimize your exposure to used engine oil. Protective gloves should be worn when changing the oil. Wash your hands and any other exposed skin areas as soon as possible after exposure to used engine oil. Soap and water, or waterless hand cleaner should be used.

3. On 1982–86 models ,remove the air conditioning brace at the starter and air conditioning bracket.

4. Remove the exhaust shield and disconnect the exhaust pipe at the manifold.

5. Remove the starter motor and position it out of the way.

6. Remove the flywheel cover.

7. On 1982–90 models, remove the 4 right support bolts. Lower the support slightly to gain clearance for oil pan removal.

8. On cars equipped with automatic transmission, remove the oil filter and extension.

9. Remove the oil pan bolts and remove the oil pan.

To install:

10. Prior to oil pan installation, check that the sealing surfaces on the pan, cylinder block and front cover are clean and free of oil. If installing the old pan, be sure that all old RTV has been removed.

11. Apply a ⅛ in. (3mm) bead of RTV sealant to the oil pan sealing surface. Use a new oil pan rear seal and apply a thin coat of RTV sealant to the ends of the gasket down to the ears and install the pan in place.

12. On 1982–86 models, tighten the front bolts to 7–13 ft. lbs., the rear bolts to 11–18 ft. lbs., the stud to 5–7 ft. lbs., and all others to 4–9 ft. lbs. On 1987–92 models tighten the bolts to 77 inch lbs.

13. On cars equipped with automatic transmission, replace the oil filter adapter seal and replace the oil filter adapter.

14. Install the remaining components is in the reverse order of removal.

1.8L and 2.0L OHC Engines

1. Raise and support the car safely.
2. Remove right front wheel.
3. Remove right hand splash shield.
4. Position jackstands at jacking points.
5. Drain engine oil.

CAUTION: *The EPA warns that prolonged contact with used engine oil may cause a number of skin disorders, including cancer! You should make every effort to minimize your exposure to used engine oil. Protective gloves should be worn when changing the oil. Wash your hands and any other exposed skin areas as soon as possible after exposure to*

Oil pan installation—1982–86 1.8L and 2.0L OHV engine

1. Seal
2. Bolt
3. Nut
4. Oil pan

Oil pan installation—1987–92 2.0L and 2.2L OHV engine

used engine oil. Soap and water, or waterless hand cleaner should be used.

6. If necessary on some models, remove lower air conditioning bracket strut rod attachment bolt and swing aside.

7. Remove exhaust pipe to manifold attachment bolts. On turbo models, disconnect the exhaust pipe at the wastegate.

8. Remove flywheel dust cover.

9. Remove oil pan bolts and remove the oil pan.

10. Clean the sealing surfaces, install the oil

Oil pan installation—1.8L OHC engine

SECTION AA

Oil pan installation—2.0L OHC engine

pan with a new gasket and apply RTV as shown in the illustration. Install the bolts to the oil pan with Loctite® on the threads. Torque the pan bolts to 48 inch lbs.

2.8L and 3.1L Engines

1985–88

1. Disconnect the battery ground.
2. Raise and support the car on jackstands.
3. Drain the oil.

CAUTION: *The EPA warns that prolonged contact with used engine oil may cause a number of skin disorders, including cancer! You should make every effort to minimize your exposure to used engine oil. Protective gloves should be worn when changing the oil. Wash your hands and any other exposed skin areas as soon as possible after exposure to used engine oil. Soap and water, or waterless hand cleaner should be used.*

4. Remove the bellhousing cover.
5. Remove the starter.
6. Remove the oil pan bolts and remove the oil pan.

To install:

7. Intallation is the reverse of removal. On 1985–86 models, the pan is installed using RTV gasket material in place of a gasket. Make sure that the sealing surfaces are free of old RTV material. Use a ⅛ in. (3mm) bead of RTV material on the pan sealing flange. On 1987–88 models the pan is installed using a gasket. Torque the M8 × 1.25 × 14.0 pan bolts to 15–30 ft. lbs. and the M6 × 1 × 16.0 pan bolts to 6–15 ft. lbs.

1989–92

1. Disconnect the negative battery cable.
2. Remove the serpentine belt and the tensioner.
3. Support the engine with tool J–28467 or equivalent.
4. Raise and safely support the vehicle. Drain the engine oil.
5. Remove the starter shield and the flywheel cover. Remove the starter.
6. Remove the engine to frame mount retaining nuts.
7. Lower the vehicle.
8. Support the engine using tool J–28467–A or equivalent, then raise and support the vehicle safely.
9. Remove the right tire and wheel assembly. Remove the right inner fender splash shield.
10. Remove the oil pan retaining bolts and nuts and remove the oil pan.

To install:

11. Clean the gasket mating surfaces.
12. Install a new gasket on the oil pan. Apply silicon sealer to the portion of the pan that contacts the rear of the block.
13. Install the oil pan retaining nuts. Tighten the nuts to 89 inch lbs.
14. Install the oil pan retaining bolts. Tighten the rear bolts to 18 inch lbs. and the remaining bolts to 89 inch lbs.
15. Install the right inner fender splash shield.
16. Lower the vehicle and remove the engine support tool.
17. Raise and support the vehicle safely.
18. Install the engine to frame mounting nuts.
19. Install the starter and splash shield. Install the flywheel shield.
20. Lower the vehicle and fill the crankcase with oil, install the belt tensioner and belt and connect the negative battery cable. Run the engine to normal operating temperature and check for leaks.

Oil pan and pump installation—1985–86 2.8L V6 engine

1. 25 N·m (18 lb. ft.)
2. 17 N·m (13 lb. ft.) all others 10 N·m (89 lb. in.)
3. Sealer (1052917)

Oil pan installation—1989 2.8L V6 engine

1. 20–30 N·m (15–22 ft. lbs.)
   All 8–12 N·m (6–9 ft. lbs.)

Oil pan installation—1987–88 2.8L V6 engine

1. Nut 8 N·m (71 lb. in.)
2. Bolt 8 N·m (71 lb. in.)
3. Oil pan
4. Bolt 25 N·m (18 lb. ft.)
5. Apply sealer
6. Stud 8 N·m (71 lb. in.)

Oil pan installation—1990–92 3.1L V6 engine

Oil Pump

REMOVAL AND INSTALLATION

1.8L, 2.0L and 2.2L OHV Engines

1. Remove the engine oil pan.
2. Remove the pump to rear bearing cap bolt and remove the pump and extension shaft.
3. Remove the extension shaft and retainer.

To install:

4. Heat the retainer in hot water prior to assembling the extension shaft.
5. Install the extension to the oil pump, being careful not to crack the retainer.
6. Install pump to rear bearing cap bolt and torque is 26–38 ft. lbs.
7. Install the oil pan.

1.8L and 2.0L OHC Engines

1. Remove the crankshaft sprocket.
2. Remove the timing belt rear covers.
3. Disconnect the oil pressure switch wires.
4. Remove the oil pan.
5. Remove the oil filter.
6. Unbolt and remove the oil pick-up tube.
7. Unbolt and remove the oil pump.
8. On the 2.0L engine, pry out the front oil seal.
9. Installation is the reverse of removal. Use new gaskets in all instances. On the 2.0L engine, install a new front seal using tool J33083 Seal Installer. Torque the oil pump bolts to 60 inch lbs. Install the bolts to the oil pan with Loctite® on the threads. Torque the pan bolts to 48 inch lbs., and the oil pickup tube bolts to 60 inch lbs.

2.8L and 3.1L OHV V6 Engines

1. Remove the oil pan as described earlier.
2. Unbolt and remove the oil pump and pickup.
3. Installation is the reverse of removal. Torque to 30 ft. lbs.

Timing Belt/Chain Front Cover

REMOVAL AND INSTALLATION

1.8L, 2.0L and 2.2L OHV Engines

NOTE: *The following procedure requires the use of a special tool.*

1. Remove the engine drive belts (1982–86) or the serpentine belt and tensioner (1987–92).
2. Although not absolutely necessary, removal of the right front inner fender splash shield will facilitate access to the front cover.
3. Unscrew the center bolt from the crankshaft pulley and slide the pulley and hub from the crankshaft.
4. On some models, if necessary, remove the alternator lower bracket.
5. Remove the oil pan-to-front cover bolts.

6. Remove the front cover-to-block bolts and then remove the front cover. If the front cover is difficult to remove, use a plastic mallet.

To install:

7. The surfaces of the block and front cover must be clean and free of oil. on 1982–86 models, apply a ⅛ in. (3mm) wide bead of RTV sealant to the cover. The sealant must be wet to the touch when the bolts are torqued down. On 1987–92 models a gasket is used. Torque the bolts to 6–9 ft. lbs.

NOTE: *When applying RTV sealant to the front cover, be sure to keep it out of the bolt holes.*

8. Position the front cover on the block using a centering tool (J-23042) and tighten the screws.
9. Installation of the remaining components is in the reverse order of removal.

1.8L OHC Engine

1. Disconnect the negative battery cable. Remove the generator pivot bolts.

Front cover on the 2.0L and 2.2L OHV engines

COVER SEAL

CENTERING TOOL

When installing the front cover a centering tool can aid in positioning on the OHV 4 cylinder engines

2. Remove the power steering belt.

3. Remove the two upper timing belt cover bolts.

4. Disconnect the canister purge hose.

5. Raise the car and support it safely.

6. Remove the right front wheel.

7. Remove the splash shield.

8. Remove the two lower timing cover bolts.

9. Lower the car and remove the timing belt cover.

10. Reverse the above procedure to install.

2.0L OHC Engine

1. Disconnect the negative battery cable. Remove the belt, tensioner bolt and tensioner.

2. Unsnap the cover (upper first).

Front cover installation on the 1.8L OHC engine

Front cover installation on the 1987–88 2.0L OHC engine

1. Grommet
2. Sleeve
3. Bolt 10 N·m (89 lb. in.)
4. Camshaft sprocket
5. Washer
6. Bolt 45 N·m (33 lb. ft.)
7. Timing belt
8. Front cover
9. Bolt 9 N·m (80 lb. in.)
10. Bolt 155 N·m (114 lb. ft.)
11. Washer
12. Cranshaft sprocket
13. Washer
14. Rear cover
15. Keyway
16. Stud 48 N·m (35 lb. ft.)
17. Bolt 48 N·m (35 lb. ft.)
18. Tensioner
19. Engine
20. Camshaft

Front cover installation on the 1989–92 2.0L OHC engine

3. To install, snap the cover (lower first).

4. Install the tensioner and bolt then the serpentine belt. Torque the timing belt cover bolts and nuts to 89 inch lbs. (54 Nm).

2.8L and 3.1L V6 Engines

1. Disconnect the battery ground cable.

2. Drain the cooling system.

CAUTION: *When draining the coolant, keep in mind that cats and dogs are attracted by the ethylene glycol antifreeze, and are quite likely to drink any that is left in an uncovered container or in puddles on the ground. This will prove fatal in sufficient quantity. Always drain the coolant into a sealable container. Coolant should be reused unless it is contaminated or several years old.*

3. On 1985–86 models, disconnect the MAP sensor and the EGR solenoid.

4. On 1985–86 models, remove the coolant recovery tank.

5. Remove the serpentine belt adjustment pulley.

6. Remove the alternator and disconnect the electrical wires.

7. Remove the power steering pump bracket.

8. Disconnect the heater pipe at the P/S bracket.

9. Jack up the car and support it safely.

10. Remove the inner splash shield.

11. Remove the air conditioning compressor belt.

12. Remove the flywheel cover at the transaxle.

13. Remove the harmonic balancer with tool J-23523-1 or equivalent.

WARNING: *The outer ring (weight) of the harmonic balancer is bonded to the hub with rubber. Breakage may occur if the balancer is hammered back onto the crankshaft. A press or special installation tool is necessary.*

14. Remove the serpentine belt idler pulley.

15. Remove the pan to front cover bolts.

16. Remove the lower cover bolts.

17. Lower the vehicle.

18. Disconnect the radiator hose at the water pump.

19. Remove the heater pipe at the goose neck.

20. Disconnect the bypass and overflow hoses.

21. Disconnect the canister purge hose.

22. Remove the upper front cover bolts and remove the front cover.

To install

23. Clean all the gasket mounting surfaces on the front cover and block and place a new gasket to the front cover sealing surface. Apply a

Front cover sealant placement—1985–86 2.8L V6 engine

1. Front cover
2. Gasket
3. 27 N·m (20 lb. ft.)
4. 38 N·m (28 lb. ft.)
5. Sealer

Front cover installation—1987–92 2.8L and 3.1L V6 engine

continuous ⅛ in. (3mm) wide bead of sealer (1052357 or equivalent) to the oil pan sealing surface of the front cover.

24. Place the front cover on the engine and install the upper front cover bolts.

25. Raise the vehicle and support it safely.

26. Install the lower cover bolts.

27. Install the oil pan to cover screws.

28. Install the serpentine belt idler pulley.

29. Install the harmonic balancer. (See the Harmonic Balancer Removal and Installation procedure.)

30. Install the flywheel cover on the transaxle.

31. Install the air conditioning compressor belt.

32. Install the inner splash shield.

33. Lower the vehicle and install the remainder of the parts in the reverse order of removal.

Timing Cover Oil Seal

REPLACEMENT

1.8L, 2.0L and 2.2L OHV Engines
2.8L and 3.1L V6 Engines

The oil seal can be replaced with the cover either on or off the engine. If the cover is on the engine, remove the crankshaft pulley and hub first. Pry out the seal using a suiable prying tool, being careful not to distort the seal mating surface. Install the new seal so that the open side or lip side is towards the engine. Press it into place with a seal driver made for the purpose. GM recommends a tool, J-35468 Seal Centering Tool. Install the hub if removed.

Timing Chain and Sprockets

REMOVAL AND INSTALLATION

1.8L and 2.0L and 2.2L OHV Engines

1. Remove the front cover as previously detailed.

2. Place the No. 1 piston at TDC of the compression stroke so that the marks on the camshaft and crankshaft sprockets are in alignment (see illustration).

3. Loosen the timing chain tensioner nut as far as possible without actually removing it.

4. Remove the camshaft sprocket bolts and remove the sprocket and chain together. If the sprocket does not slide from the camshaft easily, a light blow with a soft mallet at the lower edge of the sprocket will dislodge it.

5. Use a gear puller (J-2288-8-20) and remove the crankshaft sprocket.

To install:

6. Press the crankshaft sprocket back onto the crankshaft.

7. Install the timing chain over the camshaft sprocket and then around the crankshaft sprocket. Make sure that the marks on the two sprockets are in alignment (see illustration). Lubricate the thrust surface with Molykote® or its equivalent.

8. Align the dowel in the camshaft with the dowel hole in the sprocket and then install the sprocket onto the camshaft. Use the mounting bolts to draw the sprocket onto the camshaft and then tighten to 66–68 ft. lbs.

9. Lubricate the timing chain with clean engine oil. Tighten the chain tensioner.

10. Installation of the remaining components is in the reverse order of removal.

2.8L and 3.1L Engines

1. Remove the front cover.

2. Place the No. 1 piston at TDC and the stamped timing marks on both sprockets are closest to one another and in line between the shaft centers (No. 4 firing position).

3. Take out the three bolts that hold the camshaft sprocket to the camshaft. This sprocket is a light press fit on the camshaft and will come off readily. If the sprocket does not come off easily, a light blow on the lower edge of the sprocket with a plastic mallet should dislodge the sprocket. The chain comes off with the camshaft sprocket. A gear puller will be required to remove the crankshaft sprocket.

Timing chain and sprockets—1982–86 1.8L and 2.0L OHV engine

1. 90–120 N·m (66–88 ft. lbs.)
2. Tensioner
3. Camshaft sprocket
4. Crankshaft sprocket

NOTE—ALIGN TABS ON TENSIONER WITH MARKS ON CAMSHAFT & CRANKSHAFT SPROCKETS.

#1 CYLINDER TDC

#4 CYLINDER TDC

Timing chain and sprockets—1987–92 2.0L and 2.2L OHV engine

DIRECTION OF TENSION TO BE APPLIED

A INSERT PIN AFTER TENSION HAS BEEN APPLIED

B TABS, USED FOR CAMSHAFT AND CRANKSHAFT ALIGNMENT

Timing chain tensioner—1.8L and 2.0L OHV engine

To install:

4. Without disturbing the position of the engine, mount the new crank sprocket on the shaft, then mount the chain over the camshaft sprocket. Arrange the camshaft sprocket in such a way that the timing marks will line up between the shaft centers and the camshaft locating dowel will enter the dowel hole in the cam sprocket.

5. Place the cam sprocket, with its chain mounted over it, in position on the front of the camshaft and pull up with the three bolts that hold it to the camshaft. Torque the bolts to 18 ft. lbs. (25 Nm).

6. Lubricate the timing chain with oil.

7. After the sprockets are in place, turn the engine two full revolutions to make certain that the timing marks are in correct alignment between the shaft centers.

Timing Belt

REMOVAL AND INSTALLATION
1.8L and 2.0L OHC Engine
1983–88

NOTE: *The following procedure requires the use of a special adjustment tool J33039 and*

Timing chain and sprockets—1985–86 2.8L V6 engine

ALIGNMENT MARKS

NOTE—ALIGN TIMING MARKS ON CAM & CRANK SPROCKETS USING ALIGNMENT MARKS ON DAMPER STAMPING OR CAST ALIGNMENT MARKS ON CYL & CASE

1. Timing chain
2. Crank sprocket
3. Camshaft sprocket
4. Damper
5. 28 N·m (21 lb. ft.)
6. 21 N·m (15 lb. ft.)

Timing chain and sprockets—1987–92 2.8L and 3.1L V6 engine

Timing sprocket alignment—2.8L and 3.1L V6 engine

on the 1.8L engine. The timing mark on the crankshaft pulley should line up at 10° BTDC on the indicator scale.

WARNING: *Do not turn the camshaft. Use only the crankshaft nut to turn. Turning the nut on the camshaft directly can damage the camshaft bearings.*

12. Rotate the water pump clockwise using Tool J-33039 until all slack is removed from the belt. Slightly tighten the water pump retaining bolts.

13. Install Tool J-26486 between the water

Belt adjustment tool J26486—A dial reading—1983–88 1.8L and 2.0L OHC engines

tension gauge J26486–A or their equivalents.
1. Remove the timing belt front cover.
2. Raise and support the vehicle safely.
3. Remove the crankshaft pulley as previously described.
4. Check that the camshaft sprocket lines up with mark on the camshaft carrier on the 1.8L engine and the mark on the camshaft sprocket must line up with the mark on the rear timing belt cover on the 2.0L engine. The timing mark on the crankshaft pulley should line up with the 10° BTDC mark on the indicator scale.
5. Lower the vehicle.
6. Remove timing probe holder.
7. Loosen the water pump retaining bolts and rotate the water pump to loosen the timing belt.
8. Remove the timing belt.
To install:
9. Install timing belt on sprockets.
10. Install the crankshaft pulley.
11. Check if the mark on the camshaft sprocket lines up with mark on the camshaft carrier,

Modified tool J33039—1.8L and 2.0L OHC engines

1. Tension gauge J·26486
2. Adjustment tool J·33039

Timing belt adjustment—1.8L and 2.0L OHC engines

Belt Size	19mm
INITIAL ADJUSTMENT	
New Belt	22 lbs.
Used Belt	18 lbs.
CHECKING VALUE	
New Belt	18–27 lbs.
Used Belt	13–22 lbs.

pump and camshaft sprockets so that the pointer is midway between the sprockets.

14. If the tension is incorrect, loosen the water pump and rotate it using Tool J-33039 until the proper tension is obtained.

15. Fully torque the water pump retaining bolts to 18 ft. lbs. taking care not to further rotate the water pump.

16. Install timing probe holder. Torque nuts to 19 ft. lbs.

17. Install the timing belt front cover and torque the attaching bolts to 5 ft. lbs.

18. Install and adjust the generator and power steering belt. Refill the cooling system, if necessary.

1989–92

1. Disconnect the negative battery cable.

2. Remove the serpentine belt and timing belt cover.

3. Loosen the water pump bolts and release tension with tool J-33039 or equivalent.

4. Raise and support the vehicle safely.

5. Remove the crankshaft pulley.

6. Lower the vehicle and remove the timing belt.

To install:

7. Turn the crankshaft and the camshaft gears clockwise to align the timing marks on the gears with the timing marks on the rear cover.

8. Install the timing belt, making sure the portion between the camshaft gear and crankcase gear is in tension.

9. Using tool J–33039 or equivalent, turn the water pump eccentric clockwise until the tensioner contacts the high torque stop. Tighten the water pump screws slightly.

10. Turn the engine by the crankshaft gear bolt 720° to fully seat the belt into the gear teeth.

11. Turn the water pump eccentric counterclockwise until the hole in the tensioner arm is aligned with the hole in the base.

12. Torque the water pump screws to 18 ft. lbs. while checking that the tensioner holes remain as adjusted in the prior step.

13. Install the crankshaft pulley, timing belt cover and the serpentine drive belt.

Timing Belt Rear Cover

REMOVAL AND INSTALLATION

1.8L and 2.0L OHC Engines

1. Remove the timing belt from the crankshaft sprocket as outlined in this Chapter.

2. Remove the timing belt rear cover attaching bolts and the rear cover.

3. Install the rear cover and torque the attaching bolts to 19 ft. lbs. 25 Nm on the 1.8L engine, 54 inch lbs. (6 Nm) on the 1987–88 2.0L engine and 89 inch lbs. (10 Nm) on the 1989–92 2.0L engine.

4. Install the timing belt and adjust as previously outlined.

Camshaft

REMOVAL AND INSTALLATION

1.8L, 2.0L and 2.2L OHV Engine

1. Remove the engine.

2. Remove the cylinder head cover, pivot the rocker arms to the sides, and remove the pushrods, keeping them in order. Remove the valve lifters, keeping them in order. There are special tools which make lifter removal easier.

3. Remove the front cover.

4. Remove the distributor, if so equipped.

5. Remove the fuel pump and its pushrod.

6. Remove the timing chain and sprocket as described earlier in this Chapter.

1. Tensioner arm   2. Hole in base   3. High torque stop

Timing belt tensioner positions—1989–92 2.0L OHC engines

7. Carefully pull the camshaft from the block, being sure that the camshaft lobes do not contact the bearings.

To install:

8. To install, lubricate the camshaft journals with clean engine oil. Lubricate the lobes with Molykote® or the equivalent.

9. Install the camshaft into the engine, being extremely careful not to contact the bearings with the cam lobes.

10. Install the timing chain and sprocket. Install the fuel pump and pushrod. Install the timing cover. Install the distributor.

11. Install the valve lifters. If a new camshaft has been installed, new lifters should be used to ensure durability of the cam lobes.

12. Install the pushrods and rocker arms and the intake manifold. Adjust the valve lash after installing the engine. Install the cylinder head cover.

1.8L and 2.0L OHC Engines

NOTE: *The following procedure requires the use of a special tool.*

1. Remove camshaft carrier cover.

2. Using valve train compressing Fixture J-33302, which holds the valves in place, compress valve springs and remove rocker arms.

3. Remove timing belt front cover.

4. Remove timing belt as previously outlined.

5. Remove camshaft sprocket as previously outlined.

6. Remove distributor.

7. Remove camshaft thrust plate from rear of camshaft carrier.

8. Slide camshaft rearward and remove it from the carrier.

To install:

9. Install a new camshaft carrier front oil seal using Tool J-33085.

10. Place camshaft in the carrier.

WARNING: *Take care not to damage the carrier front oil seal when installing the camshaft.*

11. Install camshaft thrust plate retaining bolts. Torque bolts to 70 inch lbs.

12. Check camshaft end play, which should be within 0.016-0.064mm.

13. Install distributor.

14. Install camshaft sprocket as previously described.

15. Install timing belt as previously described.

16. Install timing belt front cover.

17. Using valve train compressing fixture J-33302, compress valve springs and replace rocker arms.

18. Install camshaft carrier cover as previously described.

2.8L and 3.1L V6 Engines

1. Remove the engine assembly as outlined earlier.

2. Remove intake manifold, valve lifters and timing chain cover as described in this Chapter. If the car is equipped with air conditioning, unbolt the condenser and move it aside without disconnecting any lines.

3. Remove fuel pump and pump pushrod.

4. Remove camshaft sprocket bolts, sprocket and timing chain. A light blow to the lower edge of a tight sprocket should free it (use a plastic mallet).

5. Install two bolts in cam bolt holes and pull cam from block.

To install:

6. Lubricate the camshaft journals with engine oil and reverse removal procedure aligning the sprocket timing marks.

NOTE: *If a new camshaft is being installed, coat the camshaft lobes with GM Engine Oil Supplement (E.O.S.), or equivalent.*

1	BACK-UP NUT	**5**	2 PIECE PULLER SCREW
2	EXPANDING COLLET	**6**	PULLING PLATE
3	BEARING	**7**	THRUST BEARING
4	EXPANDING MANDREL	**8**	PULLING NUT

Removing/installing camshaft bearings

Camshaft Bearings

REMOVAL AND INSTALLATION

1. Remove the camshaft assembly – refer to the necessary service procedures.

2. To remove the camshaft bearings use a special tool (refer to the illustrations) select the proper pilot, nut and thrust washer.

3. Pull out camshaft bearings.

4. To install the camshaft bearings place the bearing onto the tool and index the oil holes of the bearing with the oil passages in the cylinder block. Pull bearing into proper place.

NOTE: *Proper alignment of the oil holes is critical. Restriction of the oil flow will cause severe engine damage.*

Camshaft Carrier

REMOVAL AND INSTALLATION

1.8L and 2.0L OHC Engines

NOTE: *Whenever the camshaft carrier bolts are loosened, it is necessary to replace the cylinder head gasket. To do this, see the previous instructions under Cylinder Head Removal and Installation.*

1. Disconnect the positive crankcase ventilation hose from the camshaft carrier.

2. Remove the distributor.

3. Remove the camshaft sprocket as previously outlined.

4. Loosen the camshaft carrier and cylinder head attaching bolts a little at a time in the sequence shown in the "Cylinder Head Removal and Installation" procedure.

NOTE: *Camshaft carrier and cylinder head bolts should be loosened only when the engine is cold.*

5. Remove the camshaft carrier.

6. Remove the camshaft thrust plate from the rear of the camshaft carrier.

7. Slide the camshaft rearward and remove it from the carrier.

8. Remove the carrier front oil seal.

To install:

9. Install a new carrier front oil seal using Tool J-33085.

10. Place the camshaft in the carrier.

WARNING: *Take care not to damage the carrier front oil seal when installing the camshaft.*

11. Install the camshaft thrust plate and the retaining bolts. Torque the bolts to 70 inch lbs.

12. Check camshaft end-play which should be within 0.04-0.16mm.

13. Clean the sealing surfaces on cylinder head and carrier. Apply a continuous 3mm bead of RTV sealer.

14. Install the camshaft carrier on the cylinder head.

15. Install the camshaft carrier and cylinder head attaching bolts.

16. Torque the bolts a little at a time in the proper sequence, to 18 ft. lbs. Then turn each bolt 60° clockwise in the proper sequence for three times until a 180° rotation is obtained, or equivalent to ½ turn. After remainder of installation is completed (with the exception of brackets that attach to carrier), start engine and let it run until thermostat opens. Torque all bolts an additional 30° to 50° in the proper sequence.

17. Install the camshaft sprocket as outlined below.

18. Install the distributor.

19. Connect the positive crankcase ventilation hose to the camshaft carrier.

Camshaft Sprocket

REMOVAL AND INSTALLATION

1.8L and 2.0L OHC Engines

1. Remove the timing belt front cover.

2. Align the mark on camshaft sprocket with mark on or camshaft carrier or rear timing belt cover.

3. Remove timing probe holder.

4. Loosen the water pump retaining bolts and remove the timing belt from the camshaft sprocket.

5. Remove the camshaft carrier cover as previously outlined.

6. Hold the camshaft with a open-end wrench. For this purpose a hexagonal is provided in the camshaft. Remove the camshaft sprocket retaining bolt and washer and then the sprocket.

To install:

7. Install the camshaft sprocket and align marks on camshaft sprocket and camshaft carrier.

8. Hold the camshaft with a hexagonal open-end wrench. Install the sprocket washer and retaining bolt. Torque to 34 ft. lbs.

9. Install the camshaft carrier cover as previously outlined.

10. Install the timing belt on sprockets and adjust as previously outlined.

11. Install timing probe holder, if so equipped, and torque the nuts to 19 ft. lbs.

12. Install timing belt front cover.

Crankshaft Sprocket

REMOVAL AND INSTALLATION

1.8L and 2.0L OHC Engines

1. Remove the timing belt from the crankshaft sprocket as previously described.

2. Remove the crankshaft sprocket to crankshaft attaching bolt and the thrust washer.

3. Remove the sprocket.

Camshaft sprocket removal—1.8L and 2.0L OHC engines

To install:

4. Position the sprocket over the key on end of crankshaft.

5. Install the thrust washer and the attaching bolt. Torque to 115 ft. lbs. (through 1983), 107 ft. lbs. plus a 45° rotation (1984-87), 96 ft. lbs. plus a 45° rotation (1988) and 114 ft. lbs. (1989–92).

6. Install the timing belt and adjust as previously described.

Pistons and Connecting Rod

REMOVAL

1. Remove the engine assembly from the car, see Engine Removal and Installation service procedures.

2. Remove the intake manifold, cylinder head or heads.

3. Remove the oil pan.

4. Remove the oil pump assembly.

5. Stamp the cylinder number on the machined surfaces of the bolt bosses of the connecting rod and cap for identification when reinstalling. If the pistons are to be removed from the connecting rod, mark the cylinder number on the piston with a silver pencil or quick drying paint for proper cylinder identification and cap to rod location. The 2.8L and 3.1L V6 engines are numbered 1-3-5 on the right bank, 2-4-6 on the left bank.

6. Examine the cylinder bore above the ring travel. If a ridge exists, remove the ridge with a ridge reamer before attempting to remove the piston and rod assembly.

7. Remove the rod bearing cap and bearing.

8. Install a guide hose over threads of rod bolts. This is to prevent damage to bearing journal and rod bolt threads.

9. Remove the rod and piston assembly through the top of the cylinder bore.

10. Remove any other rod and piston assemblies in the same manner.

CLEANING AND INSPECTION

Connecting Rods

Wash connecting rods in cleaning solvent and dry with compressed air. Check for twisted or bent rods and inspect for nicks or cracks. Replace connecting rods that are damaged.

Pistons

Clean varnish from piston skirts and pins with a cleaning solvent. DO NOT WIRE BRUSH ANY PART OF THE PISTON. Clean the ring grooves with a groove cleaner and make sure oil ring holes and slots are clean.

Inspect the piston for cracked ring lands, skirts or pin bosses, wavy or worn ring lands, scuffed or damaged skirts, eroded areas at top of the piston. Replace pistons that are damaged or show signs of excessive wear.

Inspect the grooves for nicks or burrs that might cause the rings to hang up.

Measure piston skirt (across center line of piston pin) and check piston clearance.

PISTON PIN REMOVAL AND INSTALLATION

Use care at all times when handling and servicing connecting rods and pistons. To prevent possible damage to these units, do not clamp rod or piston in vise since they may become distorted. Do not allow pistons to strike against one another, against hard objects or bench surfaces, since distortion of piston contour or nicks in the soft aluminum material may result.

1. Remove piston rings using suitable piston ring remover.

2. Install guide bushing of piston pin removing and installing tool.

3. Install piston and connecting rod assembly on support and place assembly in an arbor press. Press pin out of connecting rod, using the appropriate piston pin tool.

MEASURING THE OLD PISTONS

Check used piston to cylinder bore clearance as follows:

1. Measure the cylinder bore diameter with a telescope gauge.

2. Measure the piston diameter. When measuring piston for size or taper, measurement must be made with the piston pin removed.

3. Subtract piston diameter from cylinder bore diameter to determine piston-to-bore clearance.

4. Compare piston-to-bore clearance obtained with those clearances recommended. Determine if piston-to-bore clearance is in acceptable range.

5. When measuring taper, the largest reading must be at the bottom of the skirt.

1. Ring, piston
2. Piston, w pin
3. Bolt, connecting rod
4. Bearing, connecting rod
5. Pin, cylinder head dowel
6. Plug, cylinder water jacket hole
7. Pin, clutch housing
8. Cord, engine block heater
9. Heater, engine block
10. Retainer
11. Cap, oil fil & gage
12. Bolt
13. Tube, oil fil
14. Seal, oil fil tube
15. Bolt
16. Plug
17. Cover, camshaft rear
18. Bolt
19. Plug
20. Clamp
21. Hose, coolant inlet
22. Bolt
23. Inlet, coolant
24. Gasket, coolant inlet
25. Plug
26. Engine, partial
27. Nut, connecting rod
28. Bearing, crankshaft
29. Seal, crankshaft rear oil
30. Bolt, flywheel
31. Retainer, flywheel
32. Flywheel, crankshaft
33. Bolt, clutch cover & pressure plate
34. Washer, spring lock
35. Cover, plate, clutch pressure
36. Plate, clutch driven
37. Sealant
38. Bolt, crankshaft bearing cap
39. Cap, crankshaft bearing
40. Sealer
41. Bolt
42. Drive, oil pump
43. Shaft, distributor to oil pump
44. Retainer
45. Pump, w screen
46. Bolt, oil pump & screen
47. Stud
48. Seal, oil pan rear
49. Pan, oil
50. Nut
51. Bolt
52. Gasket, oil pan drain screw
53. Screw, oil pan drain
54. Shim, starter motor
55. Motor, starter
56. Bolt, starter motor outboard
57. Bolt, starter motor inboard
58. Bolt
59. Nut
60. Washer, flat
61. Bracket, starter motor
62. Hub, crankshaft pulley
63. Washer
64. Pulley, crankshaft
65. Seal, crankshaft front oil
66. Screw, hex

67. Cover, crankcase front end
68. Chain, camshaft timing
69. Sprocket, crankshaft
70. Key
71. Crankshaft, engine
72. Gasket, water pump
73. Pump, coolant
74. Pulley, water pump
75. Bolt
76. Bolt
77. Bolt, tensioner timing chain
78. Tensioner, timing chain

79. Bolt, hex
80. Washer, camshaft sprocket
81. Sprocket, camshaft
82. Screw, camshaft thrust plate
83. Plate, camshaft thrust
84. Pin
85. Bearing, camshaft
86. Camshaft, engine
87. Switch, fuel pump
88. Valve, oil filter by-pass
89. Filter, oil (PF52)
90. Connector, oil filter adapter

91. Adapter, oil filter
92. Gasket, oil filter adapter
93. Lifter, hydraulic valve
94. Rod, push
95. Coil, w module ignition
96. Bolt
97. Stud, ignition coil
98. Sensor, crankshaft
99. Gasket
100. Bolt, crankshaft pulley hub
101. Bolt, crankshaft pulley
102. Connecting rod

Exploded view of the cylinder block—1987–91 2.0L and 2.2L OHV engine

1. Cord, engine block heater
2. Ring kit, piston
3. Piston, with pin
4. Rod, connecting
5. Screw
6. Bearing, conn
7. Nut
8. Bracket, start mtr
9. Washer
10. Bolt
11. Motor, starter
12. Bolt
13. Stud
14. Bracket, cr/case vent tube
15. Indicator, eng oil level
16. Clamp
17. Hose
18. Flange
19. Bolt
20. Seal
21. Plug
22. Block, cyl
23. Connector, oil pump to filter

24. Bolt, flywheel
25. Gear, flywheel & ring
26. Bolt
27. Washer
28. Seal, crank shaft rear bearing
29. Crankshaft, engine
30. Bearings, crankshaft
31. Cap, cr/shf brg (part of 22)
32. Bolt, cr/shf cap (part of 22)
33. Cover, pressure plate
34. Plate, clutch
35. Gasket, oil pan
36. Scraper, oil pan
37. Pan, oil
38. Bolt
39. Bolt, oil pan drain
40. Ring, oil pan drain bolt
41. Bolt
42. Bolt
43. Pipe, o/pump suction
44. Ring, seal
45. Bracket, suction pipe oil pump
46. Washer
47. Gear, crank shaft timing
48. Washer
49. Bolt
50. Pulley, crank shaft
51. Bolt
52. Bolt

53. Filter, oil (PF40)
54. Plug
55. Sealant, RTV
56. Pump, oil
57. Gasket, body oil pump
58. Key
59. Bolt, conn rod
60. Pulley, drive belt idler
61. Nut
62. Tensioner, drive belt
63. Nut
66. Pump, coolant
67. Seal, coolant pump
68. Stud
69. Seal, engine block heater
70. Heater, engine block
71. Ring, oil pump seal

Exploded view of the lower engine—1989–91 2.0L OHC engine

1. Distributor assembly
2. Oil filter
3. Distributor hold down
4. Dipstick
5. Cam sprocket
6. Thrust plate
7. Camshaft and bearings
8. Cylinder block
9. Engine lift hook
10. Water pump pulley
11. Water pump and gasket
12. Water inlet and gasket
13. Tensioner
14. Piston rings
15. Piston
16. Starter
17. Accessory drive pulley
18. Hub
19. Seal
20. Front cover
21. Timing chain
22. Cranksprocket

23. Main bearings
24. Connecting rod bearing cap
25. Main bearings
26. Crankshaft
27. Main thrust bearing
28. Rear main seal
29. Main bearing caps
30. Flywheel and clutch disc
31. Oil pump
32. Oil pan
33. Seal

Exploded view of the cylinder block—1982–86 1.8L and 2.0L OHV engine

SELECTING NEW PISTONS

1. If the used piston is not acceptable, check service piston sizes and determine if a new piston can be selected. Service pistons are available in standard, high limit and standard 0.254mm oversize.

2. If the cylinder bore must be reconditioned, measure the new piston diameter, then hone cylinder bore to obtain preferable clearance.

3. Select new piston and mark piston to identify the cylinder for which it was fitted. On some cars oversize pistons may be found. These pistons will be 0.254mm oversize.

CYLINDER HONING

1. When cylinders are being honed, follow the manufacturer's recommendations for the use of the hone.

2. Occasionally during the honing operation, the cylinder bore should be thoroughly cleaned and the selected piston checked for correct fit.

3. When finish honing a cylinder bore, the hone should be moved up and down at a sufficient speed to obtain very fine uniform surface finish marks in a cross hatch pattern of approximately 45–65° included angle. The finish marks should be clean but not sharp, free from imbedded particles and torn or folded metal.

4. Permanently mark the piston for the cylinder to which it has been fitted and proceed to hone the remaining cylinders.

WARNING: *Handle pistons with care. Do not attempt to force pistons through cylinders until the cylinders have been honed to correct size. Pistons can be distorted through careless handling.*

5. Thoroughly clean the bores with hot water and detergent. Scrub well with a stiff bristle brush and rinse thoroughly with hot water. It is extremely essential that a good cleaning operation be performed. If any of the abrasive material is allowed to remain in the cylinder bores, it will rapidly wear the new rings and cylinder bores. The bores should be swabbed several times with light engine oil and a clean cloth and then wiped with a clean dry cloth. CYLINDERS SHOULD NOT BE CLEANED WITH KEROSENE OR GASOLINE! Clean the remainder of the cylinder block to remove the excess material spread during the honing operation.

CHECKING CYLINDER BORE

Cylinder bore size can be measured with inside micrometers or a cylinder gauge. The most wear will occur at the top of the ring travel.

Reconditioned cylinder bores should be held to not more than 0.025mm out-of-round and 0.025mm taper.

If the cylinder bores are smooth, the cylinder walls should not be deglazed. If the cylinder walls are scored, the walls may have to be honed before installing new rings. It is important that reconditioned cylinder bores be thoroughly washed with a soap and water solution to remove all traces of abrasive material to eliminate premature wear.

Piston Rings

The pistons have three rings (two compression rings and one oil ring). The oil ring consists of two rails and an expander. Pistons do not have oil drain holes behind the rings.

RING TOLERANCES

When installing new rings, ring gap and side clearance should be check as as follows:

PISTON RING AND RAIL GAP

Each ring and rail gap must be measured with the ring or rail positioned squarely and at the bottom of the ring-travel area of the bore.

Check the ring end gap with the ring installed in the cylinder

Checking the ring side clearance

1. Piston
2. Upper compression ring gap
3. Lower compression ring gap
4. Oil ring asm, gap

FRONT OF ENGINE

Piston ring gap locations—1991 2.2L OHV engine

ENGINE LEFT   ENGINE FRONT   ENGINE RIGHT

"B"

"C"   "A" "D"

"B"

"A" OIL RING SPACER GAP
(Tang in Hole or Slot within Arc)

"B" OIL RING RAIL GAPS

"C" 2ND COMPRESSION RING GAP

"D" TOP COMPRESSION RING GAP

Piston ring gap locations—except 1991 2.2L OHV engine

SIDE CLEARANCE

Each ring must be checked for side clearance in its respective piston groove by inserting a feeler gauge between the ring and its upper land. The piston grooves must be cleaned before checking ring for side clearance. See PISTON RING CLEARANCE CHART in this Chapter for ring side clearance specifications. To check oil ring side clearance, the oil rings must be installed on the piston.

RING INSTALLATION

For service ring specifications and detailed installation productions, refer to the instructions furnished with the parts package.

CONNECTING ROD BEARINGS

Removal, Inspection, Installation

If you have already removed the connecting rod and piston assemblies from the engine, follow only steps 3-7 of the following procedure.

The connecting rod bearings are designed to have a slight projection above the rod and cap faces to insure a positive contact. The bearings can be replaced with removing the rod and piston assembly from the engine.

1. Remove the oil pan, see Oil Pan. It may be necessary to remove the oil pump to provide access to rear connecting rod bearings.

2. With the connecting rod journal at the bottom, stamp the cylinder number on the machined surfaces of connecting rod and cap for identification when reinstalling, then remove caps.

3. Inspect journals for roughness and wear. Slight roughness may be removed with a fine grit polishing cloth saturated with engine oil. Burrs may be removed with a fine oil stone by moving the stone on the journal circumference.
WARNING: *Do not move the stone back and forth across the journal. If the journals are scored or ridged, the crankshaft must be replaced.*

4. The connecting rod journals should be checked for out-of-round and correct size with a micrometer.
NOTE: *Crankshaft rod journals will normally be standard size. If any undersized crankshafts are used, all will be 0.254mm undersize and 0.254mm will be stamped on the number 4 counterweight.*

If plastic gauging material is to be used:

5. Clean oil from the journal bearing cap, connecting rod and outer and inner surface of the bearing inserts. Position insert so that tang is properly aligned with notch in rod and cap.

6. Place a piece of plastic gauging material in the center of lower bearing shell.

7. Remove bearing cap and determine bearing clearances by comparing the width of the flattened plastic gauging material at its widest point with the graduation on the container. The number within the graduation on the envelope indicates the clearance in thousandths of an inch or millimeters. If this clearance is excessive, replace the bearing and recheck clearance with plastic gauging material. Lubricate bear-

ing with engine oil before installation. Repeat Steps 2 through 7 on remaining connecting rod bearings. All rods must be connected to their journals when rotating the crankshaft to prevent engine damage.

PISTON AND CONNECTING ROD

Assembly And Installation

1. Install connecting rod bolt guide hose over rod bolt threads.

2. Apply engine oil to the rings and piston, then install piston ring compressing tool on the piston.

3. Install the assembly in its respective cylinder bore (arrow of the piston towards the front of the engine).

NOTE: *On the OHC engine, code M, the piston must be marked during disassembly.*

4. Lubricate the crankshaft journal with engine oil and install connecting rod bearing and cap, with bearing index tang in rod and cap on same side. On the OHC engines the identification numbers must be on the same side and facing the water pump.

NOTE: *When more than one rod and piston assembly is being installed, the connecting rod cap attaching nuts should only be tightened enough to keep each rod in position until all have been installed. This will aid installation of remaining piston assemblies.*

5. Torque rod bolt nuts to specifications — refer to the "Torque Specifications Chart".

6. Install all other removed parts.

7. Install the engine in the car, see Engine Removal and Installation.

Crankshaft

REMOVAL

1. Remove the engine assembly as previously outlined.

Measuring connecting rod side clearance—double rod journal

Measuring bearing clearance

1. Use a short piece of 3/8″ hose as a guide

Typical connecting rod protector

2. Remove the engine front cover.
3. Remove the timing chain and sprockets.
4. Remove the oil pan.
5. Remove the oil pump.

Measuring connecting rod side clearance—single rod journal

Measuring crankshaft endplay

6. Stamp the cylinder number on the machined surfaces of the bolt bosses of the connecting rods and caps for identification when reinstalling. If the pistons are to be removed from the connecting rod, mark cylinder number on piston with a silver pencil or quick-drying paint for proper cylinder identification and cap to rod location.

7. Remove the connecting rod caps and install thread protectors.

8. Mark the main bearing caps so that they can be installed in their original positions.

9. Remove all the main bearing caps.

10. Note position of keyway in crankshaft so it can be installed in the same position.

11. Lift crankshaft out of block. Rods will pivot to the center of the engine when the crankshaft is removed.

12. Remove both halves of the rear main oil seal.

INSTALLATION

1. Measure the crankshaft journals with a micrometer to determine the correct size rod and main bearings to be used. Whenever a new or reconditioned crankshaft is installed, new connecting rod bearings and main bearings should be installed. See Main Bearings and Rod Bearings.

2. Clean all oil passages in the block (and crankshaft if it is being reused).

NOTE: *A new rear main seal should be installed anytime the crankshaft is removed or replaced.*

3. Install sufficient oil pan bolts in the block to align with the connecting rod bolts. Use rubber bands between the bolts to position the connecting rods as required. Connecting rod position can be adjusted by increasing the tension on the rubber bands with additional turns around the pan bolts or thread protectors.

4. Position the upper half of main bearings in the block and lubricate with engine oil.

5. Position crankshaft keyway in the same position as removed and lower into block. The connecting rods will follow the crank pins into the correct position as the crankshaft is lowered.

6. Lubricate the thrust flanges with 1050169 Lubricant or equivalent. Install caps with lower half of bearings lubricated with engine oil. Lubricate cap bolts with engine oil and install, but do not tighten.

7. With a block of wood, bump shaft in each direction to align thrust flanges of main bearing. After bumping shaft in each direction, wedge the shaft to the front and hold it while torquing the thrust bearing cap bolts.

WARNING: *In order to prevent the possibility of cylinder block and/or main bearing cap damage, the main bearing caps are to be tapped into their cylinder block cavity using a brass or leather mallet before attaching bolts are installed. Do not use attaching bolts to pull main bearing caps into their seats. Failure to observe this information may damage the cylinder block or a bearing cap.*

8. Torque all main bearing caps to specifications – refer to the Torque Specification Chart.

9. Remove the connecting rod bolt thread protectors and lubricate the connecting rod bearings with engine oil.

10. Install the connecting rod bearing caps in their original position. Torque the nuts to specification – refer to the Torque Specifications Chart.

11. Complete the installation by reversing the removal steps.

Main Bearings
CHECKING BEARING CLEARANCE

1. Remove bearing cap and wipe oil from crankshaft journal and outer and inner surfaces of bearing shell.

2. Place a piece of plastic gauging material in the center of bearing.

3. Use a floor jack or other means to hold crankshaft against upper bearing shell. This is necessary to obtain accurate clearance readings when using plastic gauging material.

4. Reinstall bearing cap and bearing. Place engine oil on cap bolts and install Torque bolts to specification.

5. Remove bearing cap and determine bearing clearance by comparing the width of the flattened plastic gauging material at its widest point with graduations on the gauging material container. The number within the graduation on the envelope indicates the clearance in milli-

meters or thousandths of an inch. If the clearance is greater than allowed, REPLACE BOTH BEARING SHELLS AS A SET. Recheck clearance after replacing shells. Refer to Main Bearing Replacement.

REPLACEMENT

Main bearing clearances must be corrected by the use of selective upper and lower shells. UNDER NO CIRCUMSTANCES should the use of shims behind the shells to compensate for wear be attempted. To install main bearing shells, proceed as follows:

1. Remove the oil pan as outlined elsewhere in this Chapter. On some models, the oil pump may also have to be removed.
2. Loosen all main bearing caps.
3. Remove bearing cap and remove lower shell.
4. Insert a flattened cotter pin or roll out pin in the oil passage hole in the crankshaft, then rotate the crankshaft in the direction opposite to cranking rotation. The pin will contact the upper shell and roll it out.
5. The main bearing journals should be checked for roughness and wear. Slight roughness may be removed with a fine grit polishing cloth saturated with engine oil. Burrs may be removed with a fine oil stone. If the journals are scored or ridged, the crankshaft must be replaced.

The journals can be measured for out-of-round with the crankshaft installed by using a crankshaft caliper and inside micrometer or a main bearing micrometer. The upper bearing shell must be removed when measuring the crankshaft journals. Maximum out-of-round of the crankshaft journals must not exceed 0.037mm.

6. Clean crankshaft journals and bearing caps thoroughly before installing new main bearings.
7. Apply special lubricant, No. 1050169 or equivalent, to the thrust flanges of bearing shells.
8. Place new upper shell on crankshaft journal with locating tang in correct position and rotate shaft to turn it into place using cotter pin or roll out pin as during removal.
9. Place new bearing shell in bearing cap.
10. Install a new oil seal in the rear main bearing cap and block.
11. Lubricate the removed or replaced main bearings with engine oil. Lubricate the thrust surface with lubricant 1050169 or equivalent.
12. Lubricate the main bearing cap bolts with engine oil.
NOTE: *In order to prevent the possibility of cylinder block and/or main bearing cap damage, the main bearing caps are to be tapped* *into their cylinder block cavity using a brass or leather mallet before attaching bolts are installed. Do not use attaching bolts to pull main bearing caps into their seats. Failure to observe this information may damage the cylinder block or a bearing cap.*

13. Torque the main bearing cap bolts to the specifications noted in the Torque Chart.

Rear Main Oil Seal

REMOVAL AND INSTALLATION

OHV Engines

1982-84
TWO PIECE SEAL

1. Remove the oil pan and pump.
2. Remove the rear main bearing cap.
3. Gently pack the upper seal into the groove approximately ¼ in. (6mm) on each side.
4. Measure the amount the seal was driven in on one side and add ¹⁄₁₆ in. (0.8mm). Cut this length from the old lower cap seal. Be sure to get a sharp cut. Repeat for the other side.
5. Place the piece of cut seal into the groove and pack the seal into the block. Do this for each side.
6. Install a piece of Plastigage® or the equivalent on the bearing journal. Install the rear cap and tighten to 75 ft. lbs. Remove the cap and check the gauge for bearing clearance. If out of specification, the ends of the seal may be frayed or not flush, preventing the cap from proper seating. Correct as required.
7. Clean the journal, and apply a thin film of sealer to the mating surfaces of the cap and tighten to 70 ft. lbs. Install the pan and pump.
NOTE: *Some 1982 1.8L engines (Code G), experience a rear main seal oil leak. To correct this condition a new crankshaft part No. 14086053 and a one piece rear main seal kit part No. 14081761 has been released for service. The one piece seal kit contains an installation tool, rear main seal, and an instruction sheet.*

COATED AREA INDICATED WITH #1052357 SEALER OR EQUIVALENT.

SEALER

Apply sealer to the rear cap

CUT OFF SECTION OF
OLD ROPE SEAL

USE BEARING CAP
AS HOLDING FIXTURE

Use the bearing cap to hold the old lower seal while you cut it

SPRING SIDE   DUST LIP SIDE

J-34686

SEAL BORE TO SEAL SURFACE
TO BE LUBRICATED
WITH ENGINE OIL BEFORE
ASSEMBLY

1985-92
ONE PIECE SEAL

1. Jack up the engine and support it safely.
2. Remove the transmission as outlined in Chapter 7.
3. Remove the flywheel.

NOTE: *Now is the time to confirm that the rear seal is leaking.*

4. Insert a suitable pry tool in through the dust lip and pry out the seal by moving the tool around the seal until it is removed.

NOTE: *Use care not to damage the crankshaft seal surface with a pry tool.*

5. Before installing, lubricate the seal bore to seal surface with engine oil.
6. Install the new seal using tool J-34686.
7. Slide the new seal over the mandrel until the dust lip bottoms squarely against the tool collar.
8. Align the dowel pin of the tool with the dowel pin hole in the crankshaft and attach the tool to the crankshaft. Tighten the attaching screws to 2-5 ft. lbs.

DUST LIP

Removing the old one piece seal—1985-92 OHV engines

Installation of the one piece seal—1985-92 OHV engines

9. Tighten the T-handle of the tool to push the seal into the bore. Continue until the tool collar is flush against the block.
10. Loosen the T-handle completely. Remove the attaching screws and the tool.

NOTE: *Check to see that the seal is squarely seated in the bore.*

11. Install the flywheel and transmission.
12. Start the engine and check for leaks.

1.8L and 2.0 OHC Engines

NOTE: *The rear main bearing oil seal is a one piece unit and can be replaced without removing the oil pan or the crankshaft.*

1. Remove the transaxle assembly as outlined in Chapter 7.
2. Remove the flywheel retaining bolts and remove the flywheel.
3. If equipped with manual transaxle, remove the pressure plate and disc.
4. Pry out the rear main seal.
5. Clean the block and crankcase to seal mating surfaces.
6. Position the rear main seal to the block and press evenly into place using tool J33084 (1983–86) or tool J–36227 (1987–92). Lubricate the outside of the seal to aid assembly.
7. Use new bolts and install the flywheel and torque the bolts to 44 ft. lbs. (1983–86) or 48 ft. lbs. plus a 30° turn (1987–92).
8. On automatic transaxle models, install the flexplate and torque to 48 ft. lbs.
9. Install the pressure plate and disc, if equipped with manual transaxle.
10. Install the transaxle assembly as outlined in Chapter 7.

2.8L and 3.1L V6 Engines
1985-92

1. Support the engine with J-28467 engine support or equivalent.

Installation of the one piece seal—1983–86 OHC engines

2. Remove the transmission as outlined in Chapter 7.

3. Remove the flywheel.

NOTE: *Now is the time to confirm that the rear seal is leaking.*

4. Insert a suitable pry tool in through the dust lip and pry out the seal by moving the tool around the seal until it is removed.

WARNING: *Use care not to damage the crankshaft seal surface with a pry tool.*

5. Before installing, lubricate the seal bore to seal surface with engine oil.

6. Install the new seal using tool J-34686.

7. Slide the new seal over the mandrel until the dust lip bottoms squarely against the tool collar.

8. Align the dowel pin of the tool with the dowel pin hole in the crankshaft and attach the tool to the crankshaft. Tighten the attaching screws to 2-5 ft. lbs.

9. Tighten the T-handle of the tool to push the seal into the bore. Continue until the tool collar is flush against the block.

10. Loosen the T-handle completely. Remove the attaching screws and the tool.

NOTE: *Check to see that the seal is squarely seated in the bore.*

11. Install the flywheel and transmission.

12. Start the engine and check for leaks.

EXHAUST SYSTEM

Safety Precautions

For a number of reasons, exhaust system work can be the most dangerous type of work you can do on your car. Always observe the following precautions:

• Support the car extra securely. Not only will you often be working directly under it, but you'll frequently be using a lot of force, say, heavy hammer blows, to dislodge rusted parts. This can cause a car that's improperly supported to shift and possibly fall.

• Wear goggles. Exhaust system parts are always rusty. Metal chips can be dislodged, even when you're only turning rusted bolts. Attempting to pry pipes apart with a chisel makes the chips fly even more frequently.

• If you're using a cutting torch, keep it a great distance from either the fuel tank or lines. Stop what you're doing and feel the temperature of the fuel bearing pipes on the tank frequently. Even slight heat can expand and/or vaporize fuel, resulting in accumulated vapor, or even a liquid leak, near your torch.

• Watch where your hammer blows fall and make sure you hit squarely. You could easily tap a brake or fuel line when you hit an exhaust system part with a glancing blow. Inspect all lines and hoses in the area where you've been working.

CAUTION: *Be very careful when working on or near the catalytic converter. External temperatures can reach 1,500°F (816°C) and more, causing severe burns. Removal or installation should be performed only on a cold exhaust system.*

1.	STUD - 25 N·M (18 LBS. FT.)
2.	EXHAUST SEAL
3.	SPRING
4.	NUT - 35 N·M (26 LBS. FT.)

Manifold attachment—2.2L (VIN 4) engine code

1. SEAL
2. STUD — 25 N·m (18 LBS. FT.)
3. SPRING
4. NUT — 35 N·m (26 LBS. FT.)
5. EXHAUST PIPE

Manifold attachment—3.1L (VIN T) engine code

1. CROSSOVER PIPE
2. NUT — 25 N·m (18 LBS. FT.)
3. EXHAUST MANIFOLD

Exhaust crossover pipe—3.1 (VIN T) engine code

1. SEAL
2. BOLT - 29 N.m (21 LBS. FT.)
3. EXHAUST INTERMEDIATE PIPE
4. CATALYTIC CONVERTER

Converter attachment with flange

1. CATALYTIC CONVERTER
2. GUILLOTINE CLAMP - 35 N.m (26 LBS. FT.)
3. FRONT EXHAUST PIPE
4. INTERMEDIATE PIPE

Converter attachment without flange

1. MUFFLER HEAT SHIELD
2. SCREW — FULLY DRIVEN, SEATED AND NOT STRIPPED

Muffler heat shield

1.	CONVERTER SHIELD	7.	42 MM TO 54 MM (1-11/16" TO 2-3/16")
2.	UNDERBODY	8.	18 MM MIN. (3/4")
3.	18 MM TO 35 MM (3/4" TO 1-9/16")	9.	15 MM TO 35 MM (5/8" TO 1-9/16")
4.	CONVERTER	10.	30 MM MIN. (1-7/32)
5.	11 MM MIN. (7/16")	11.	FUEL TANK
6.	INTERMEDIATE EXHAUST PIPE		

Exhaust system to body clearance—1992 Cavalier

1. MUFFLER STRAP
2. BOLT - 16 N.M (12 LEG. FT.)
3. MUFFLER BRACKET

Muffler assembly attachment

Special Tools

A number of special exhaust system tools can be rented from auto supply houses or local stores that rent special equipment. A common one is a tail pipe expander, designed to enable you to join pipes of identical diameter.

It may also be quite helpful to use solvents designed to loosen rusted bolts or flanges. Soaking rusted parts the night before you do the job can speed the work of freeing rusted parts considerably. Remember that these solvents are often flammable. Apply only to parts after they are cool!

COMPONENT REPLACEMENT

System components may be welded or clamped together. The system consists of a head pipe, catalytic converter, intermediate pipe, muffler and tail pipe, in that order from the engine to the back of the car.

The head pipe is bolted to the exhaust manifold, except on turbocharged engines, in which case it is bolted to the turbocharger outlet elbow. Various hangers suspend the system from the floor pan. When assembling exhaust system parts, the relative clearances around all system parts is extremely critical. Observe all clearances during assembly. In the event that the system is welded, the various parts will have to be cut apart for removal. In these cases, the cut parts may not be reused. To cut the parts, a hacksaw is the best choice. An oxy-acetylene cutting torch may be faster but the sparks are DANGEROUS near the fuel tank, and, at the very least, accidents could happen, resulting in damage to other under-car parts, not to mention yourself!

The following replacement steps relate to clamped parts:

1. Raise and support the car on jackstands. It's much easier on you if you can get the car up on 4 stands. Some pipes need lots of clearance for removal and installation. If the system has been in the car for a long time, spray the clamped joints with a rust dissolving solutions such as WD-40(RG) or Liquid Wrench (RG), and let it set according to the instructions on the can.

2. Remove the nuts from the U-bolts; don't be surprised if the U-bolts break while removing the nuts. Age and rust account for this. Besides, you shouldn't reuse old U-bolts. When unbolting the headpipe from the exhaust manifold, make sure that the bolts are free before trying to remove them. If you snap a stud in the exhaust manifold, the stud will have to be removed with a bolt extractor, which often necessitates the removal of the manifold itself. On these cars, the headpipe uses a necked collar for sealing purposes at the manifold, eliminating the need for a gasket. On turbocharged engines, however, a gasket is used at the joint between the headpipe and the turbocharger outlet.

3. After the clamps are removed from the joints, first twist the parts at the joints to break loose rust and scale, then pull the components apart with a twisting motion. If the parts twist freely but won't pull apart, check the joint. The clamp may have been installed so tightly that it has caused a slight crushing of the joint. In this event, the best thing to do is secure a chisel designed for the purpose and, using the chisel and a hammer, peel back the female pipe end until the parts are freed.

4. Once the parts are freed, check the condition of the pipes which you had intended keeping. If their condition is at all in doubt, replace them too. You went to a lot of work to get one or more components out. You don't want to have to go through that again in the near future. If you are retaining a pipe, check the pipe end. If it was crushed by a clamp, it can be restored to its original diameter using a pipe expander, which

can be rented at most good auto parts stores. Check, also, the condition of the exhaust system hangers. If ANY deterioration is noted, replace them. Oh, and one note about parts: use only parts designed for your car. Don't use fits-all parts or flex pipes. The fits-all parts never fit and the flex pipes don't last very long.

5. When installing the new parts, coat the pipe ends with exhaust system lubricant. It makes fitting the parts much easier. It's also a good idea to assemble all the parts in position before clamping them. This will ensure a good fit, detect any problems and allow you to check all clearances between the parts and surrounding frame and floor members.

6. When you are satisfied with all fits and clearances, install the clamps. The headpipe-to-manifold nuts should be torqued to 20 ft. lbs. If the studs were rusty, wire-brush them clean and spray them with WD-40® or Liquid Wrench®. This will ensure a proper torque reading. Position the clamps on the slip points as illustrated. The slits in the female pipe ends should be under the U-bolts, not under the clamp end. Tighten the U-bolt nuts securely, without crushing the pipe. The pipe fit should be tight, so that you can't swivel the pipe by hand. Don't forget: always use new clamps. When the system is tight, recheck all clearances. Start the engine and check the joints for leaks. A leak can be felt by hand. MAKE CERTAIN THAT THE CAR IS SECURE ON THE JACKSTANDS BEFORE GETTING UNDER IT WITH THE ENGINE RUNNING!! If any leaks are detected, tighten the clamp until the leak stops. If the pipe starts to deform before the leak stops, reposition the clamp and tighten it. If that still doesn't stop the leak, it may be that you don't have enough overlap on the pipe fit. Shut off the engine and try pushing the pipe together further. Be careful; the pipe gets hot quickly.

7. When everything is tight and secure, lower the car and take it for a road test. Make sure there are no unusual sounds or vibration. Most new pipes are coated with a preservative, so the system will be pretty smelly for a day or two while the coating burns off.

Emission Controls

EMISSION CONTROLS

There are three sources of automotive pollutants: crankcase fumes, exhaust gases, and gasoline evaporation. The pollutants formed from these substances fall into three categories: unburnt hydrocarbons (HC), carbon monoxide (CO), and oxides of nitrogen (NOx). The equipment that is used to limit these pollutants is commonly called emission control equipment.

Positive Crankcase Ventilation System

All vehicles are equipped with a positive crankcase ventilation (PCV) system to control crankcase blow-by vapors. The system functions as follows:

When the engine is running, a small portion of the gases which are formed in the combustion chamber leak by the piston rings and enter the crankcase. Since these gases are under pressure, they tend to escape from the crankcase and enter the atmosphere. If these gases are allowed to remain in the crankcase for any period of time, they contaminate the engine oil and cause sludge to build up in the crankcase. If the gases are allowed to escape into the atmosphere, they pollute the air with unburned hydrocarbons. The job of the crankcase emission control equipment is to recycle these gases back into the engine combustion chamber where they are reburned.

The crankcase (blow-by gases are recycled in the following way: as the engine is running, clean, filtered air is drawn through the air filter and into the crankcase. As the air passes through the crankcase, it picks up the combustion gases and carries them out of the crankcase, through the oil separator, through the PCV valve, and into the induction system. As they enter the intake manifold, they are drawn into the combustion chamber where they are reburned.

The most critical component in the system is the PCV valve. This valve controls the amount of gases which are recycled into the combustion chamber. At low engine speeds, the valve is partially closed, limiting the flow of gases into the intake manifold. As engine speed increases, the valve opens to admit greater quantities of gases into the intake manifold. If the valve should become blocked or plugged, the gases will be prevented from escaping from the crankcase by the normal route. Since these gases are under pressure, they will find their own way out of the crankcase. This alternate route is usually a weak oil seal or gasket in the engine. As the gas escapes by the gasket, it also creates an oil leak. Besides causing oil leaks, a clogged PCV valve also allows these gases to remain in the crankcase for an extended period of time, promoting the formation of sludge in the engine.

SERVICE

Inspect the PCV system hose and connections at each tune-up and replace any deteriorated hoses. Check the PCV valve at every tune-up and replace it at 30,000 mile intervals. Replacement procedures are in Chapter 1.

Always replace the PCV valve instead of try-

CHECK VALVE

Cross section of a PCV valve

1	HOSE
2	INSTALL HOSE SO THAT ARROW IS POINTING TOWARD COVER
3	COVER - TORQUE TO 10 N·m (89 lb. ft.)
4	SEALS - (O-RINGS)
5	CRANKCASE VENT VALVE (PCV)
6	PUSH AIR INTAKE DUCT (NOT SHOWN) ON TO FITTING UNTIL FULLY SEATED

PCV system—2.2L (VIN 4)

1	PCV VALVE HOSE
2	PCV VALVE
3	ROCKER COVER
4	PLENUM
5	INLET MANIFOLD

PCV system—3.1L (VIN T)

ing to clean the PCV valve. On later models, replace the seals as necessary.

Evaporative Emission Control System

The basic Evaporative Emission Control System (EEC) used on all vehicles is the carbon canister storage method. The system is used to reduce emissions of fuel vapors from the car's fuel system. Evaporated fuel vapors are stored for burning during combustion rather than being vented into the atmosphere when the engine is not running. To accomplish this, the fuel tank and the carburetor float bowl, on those models so equipped, are vented through a vapor canister containing activated charcoal. The canister absorbs these vapors in a bed of activated charcoal and retains them until the canister is purged or cleared by air drawn through the filter at its bottom. The absorbing occurs when the car is not running, while the purging or cleaning occurs when the car is running. The amount of vapor being drawn into the engine at any given time is too small to have an effect on either fuel economy or engine performance.

1.8L OHV Engine

On vehicles equipped with the 1.8L engine (Carbruetor), the ECM controls the vacuum to the purge valve in the charcoal canister with a solenoid valve. When the system is in the Open Loop mode, the solenoid valve is energized and blocks all vacuum to the canister purge valve. When the system is in the Closed Loop mode, the solenoid valve is de-energized and vacuum is then supplied to operate the purge valve. This releases the fuel vapors, collected in the canister, into the intake manifold.

1.8L OHC Engine
2.0L OHC (Code K) Engine
2.0L and 2.2L OHV Engines

The system on these engines uses a 2 tube canister. The fuel vapors vent from the fuel tank to the tank tube of the canister. The canister purge is controlled by a ported vacuum source. The vapors are purged when the engine is running above idle speed.

2.0L OHC (Code M) Engine

On these engines the purge valve is an integral part of the canister. When the engine is running, manifold vacuum is is supplied to the top of the purge valve (control vacuum signal), which lifts the valve diaphragm and opens the valve. The lower tube on the purge valve (PCV) tube is connected to ported vacuum above the throttle valve. The rate of purge is controlled through this port by throttle position.

2.8L Engine

On vehicles equipped with the 2.8L engine (Port Fuel Injection), the Electronic Control Module (ECM) controls the vacuum to the canister purge valve by using an electrically operated solenoid valve. When the system is in the Open Loop mode, the solenoid valve is energized and blocks all vacuum to the canister purge valve. When the system is in the Closed Loop mode, the solenoid valve is de-energized and vacuum is then supplied to operate the purge valve. This releases the fuel vapors, collected in the canister, into the induction system.

The fuel tank pressure control valve located in the engine compartment, is a spring biased diaphragm valve, which is normally closed. When the vapor in the fuel tank exceeds 6.0 kPa, the valve will open alowing the vapors to vent to the canister and then be purged. When the tank pressure drops sufficiently the tank pressure control valve will close, thus keeping the vapors in the fuel tank. The control vacuum tube of the control valve is connected into the canister line to prevent contamination from entering the valve.

If the solenoid is open or not recieving power, the canister can purge to the intake manifold at all times. This can allow extra fuel at idle or during warm-up, which can cause rough or unstable idle, or too rich operation during warm-up.

3.1L Engine

On vehicles equipped with the 3.1L engine (Port Fuel Injection), the Electronic Control Module (ECM) opens a normally opened pulse width modulated solenoid valve which controls vacuum to the purge valve in the charcoal canister. Under cold engine or idle conditions the solenoid is turned **ON** by the ECM, which closes the solenoid and blocks vacuum to the canister purge valve. The ECM turns **OFF** the solenoid valve and allows purge during the following:
- Engine is warm
- After the engine has been running a specified time
- Above a specified road speed
- Above a specified throttle opening

The fuel tank pressure control valve located in the top of the fuel tank, is a spring biased diaphragm valve, which is normally closed. When the vapor in the fuel tank exceeds 6.0 kPa, the valve will open alowing the vapors to vent to the canister and then be purged. When the tank pressure drops sufficiently the tank pressure control valve will close, thus keeping the vapors in the fuel tank. The control vacuum tube of the control valve is connected into the canister line to prevent contamination from entering the valve.

If the solenoid is open or not recieving power, the canister can purge to the intake manifold at all times. This can allow extra fuel at idle or during warm-up, which can cause rough or unstable idle, or too rich operation during warm-up.

RESULTS OF INCORRECT OPERATION

1. Poor idling, stalling and poor drivability can be caused by the following:
• Damaged canister
• Hoses split, cracked and/or not connected to the proper tubes
2. Evidence of fuel loss or vapor odor can be caused by the following:
• Liquid fuel leaking from the fuel lines or TBI unit
• Cracked or damaged vapor canister
• Disconnected, misrouted, kinked, deteriorated or damaged vapor pipe or canister hoses
• Air cleaner or air cleaner gasket improperly seated

VAPOR CANISTER REMOVAL AND INSTALLATION

1. On some models it may be necessary to remove the right side fender fascia and filler panels to gain access to the canister.
2. Loosen the screw holding the canister retaining bracket.
3. If equipped with air conditioning, loosen the attachments holding the accumulator and pipe assembly.
4. Rotate the canister retaining bracket and remove the canister.

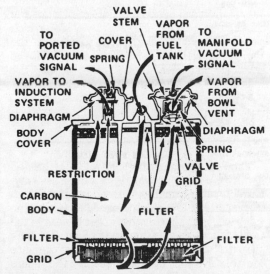

Cross section of a typical vapor canister

5. Tag and disconnect the hoses leading from the canister.
6. Installation is in the reverse order of removal. Always replace any vapor hose thats shows signs of wear.

FILTER REPLACEMENT

NOTE: *On most 1982–87 4 cylinder engines it is possible to replace the filter at the bottom of the canister. Check for new filter availabilty before removing.*
1. Remove the vapor canister.
2. Pull the filter out from the bottom of the canister.
3. Install a new filter and then replace the canister.

Exhaust Emission Controls

Exhaust emission control systems constitute the largest body of emission control devices installed on these vehicles. Included in this category are: Thermostatic Air Cleaner (THERMAC); Air Management System; Early Fuel Evaporation System (EFE); Exhaust Gas Recirculation (EGR); Computer Command Control System (CCC); Deceleration Valve; Mixture Control Solenoid (M/C); Throttle Position Sensor (TPS); Idle Speed Control (ISC); Electronic Spark Timing (EST); Transmission Converter Clutch (TCC); Catalytic Converter and the Oxygen Sensor System. A brief description of each system and any applicable service procedures follows.

Thermostatic Air Cleaner (THERMAC)

All 4 cylinder engines, through 1986, use the THERMAC system except those equipped with ported fuel injection. This system is designed to warm the air entering the carburetor when underhood temperatures are low, and to maintain a controlled air temperature into the carburetor at all times. By allowing preheated air to enter the carburetor, the amount of time the choke is on is reduced, resulting in better fuel economy and lower emissions. Engine warm-up time is also reduced.

The THERMAC system is composed of the air cleaner body, a filter, sensor unit, vacuum diaphragm, damper door, and associated hoses and connections. Heat radiating from the exhaust manifold is trapped by a heat stove and is ducted to the air cleaner to supply heated air to the carburetor. A movable door in the air cleaner case snorkel allows air to be drawn in from the heat stove (cold operation). The door position is controlled by the vacuum motor, which receives intake manifold vacuum as modulated by the temperature sensor.

THERMAC AIR CLEANER ASSEMBLY

TEMPERATURE SENSOR

VACUUM DIAPHRAGM MOTOR

LINKAGE

AIR BLEED VALVE

SNORKEL

DAMPER DOOR

HOT AIR DUCT

VACUUM HOSE TO INTAKE MANIFOLD TEE

Typical THERMAC air cleaner

SYSTEM CHECKS

1. Check the vacuum hoses for leaks, kinks, breaks, or improper connections and correct any defects.

2. With the engine off, check the position of the damper door within the snorkel. A mirror can be used to make this job easier. The damper door should be open to admit outside air.

3. Apply at least 7 in.Hg of vacuum to the damper diaphragm unit. The door should close. If it doesn't, check the diaphragm linkage for binding and correct hookup.

A

HOT AIR DELIVERY MODE

TEMPERATURE SENSOR

VACUUM DIAPHRAGM MOTOR

DIAPHRAGM SPRING

AIR BLEED VALVE CLOSED

SNORKEL

INLET

VACUUM HOSES

DIAPHRAGM

DAMPER DOOR

HOT AIR

HOT AIR DUCT

B

REGULATING MODE

VACUUM DIAPHRAGM MOTOR

TEMPERATURE SENSOR

DIAPHRAGM SPRING

AIR BLEED VALVE PARTIALLY OPEN

SNORKEL

INLET

VACUUM HOSES

DIAPHRAGM

DAMPER DOOR

HOT AIR DUCT

C

COLD AIR DELIVERY MODE

TEMPERATURE SENSOR

VACUUM DIAPHRAGM MOTOR

AIR BLEED VALVE FULLY OPEN

DIAPHRAGM SPRING

SNORKEL

INLET

VACUUM HOSES

DIAPHRAGM

DAMPER DOOR

HOT AIR DUCT

Schematic of the vacuum motor operation

4. With the vacuum still applied and the door closed, clamp the tube to trap the vacuum. If the door doesn't remain closed, there is a leak in the diaphragm assembly.

Air Management System

1982–84

The AIR management system, is used to provide additional oxygen to continue the combustion process after the exhaust gases leave the combustion chamber. Air is injected into either the exhaust port(s), the exhaust manifold(s) or the catalytic converter by an engine driven air pump. The system is in operation at all times and will bypass air only momentarily during deceleration and at high speeds. The bypass function is performed by the Air Management Valve, while the check valve protects the air pump by preventing any backflow of exhaust gases.

The AIR management system helps reduce HC and CO content in the exhaust gases by injecting air into the exhaust ports during cold engine operation. This air injection also helps the catalytic converter to reach the proper temperature quicker during warmup. When the engine is warm (Closed Loop), the AIR system injects air into the beds of a three-way converter to lower the HC and the CO content in the exhaust.

The Air Management system utilizes the following components:

1. An engine driven AIR pump
2. AIR management valves (Air Control, Air Switching)
3. Air flow and control hoses
4. Check valves

5. A dual-bed, three-way catalytic converter

The belt driven, vane-type air pump is located at the front of the engine and supplies clean air to the AIR system for purposes already stated. When the engine is cold, the Electronic Control Module (ECM) energizes an AIR control solenoid. This allows air to flow to the AIR switching valve. The AIR switching valve is then energized to direct air to the exhaust ports.

When the engine is warm, the ECM de-energizes the AIR switching valve, thus directing the air between the beds of the catalytic converter. This provides additional oxygen for the oxidizing catalyst in the second bed to decrease HC and CO, while at the same time keeping oxygen levels low in the first bed, enabling the reducing catalyst to effectively decrease the levels of NOx.

If the AIR control valve detects a rapid increase in manifold vacuum (deceleration), certain operating modes (wide open throttle, etc.) or if the ECM self-diagnostic system detects any problem in the system, air is diverted to the air cleaner or directly into the atmosphere.

The primary purpose of the ECM's divert mode is to prevent backfiring. Throttle closure at the beginning of deceleration will temporarily create air/fuel mixtures which are too rich to burn completely. These mixtures become burnable when they reach the exhaust if combined with the injection air. The next firing of the engine will ignite this mixture causing an exhaust backfire. Momentary diverting of the injection air from the exhaust prevents this.

The AIR management system check valves and hoses should be checked periodically for any leaks, cracks or deterioration.

Air management system operation—warm engine

Air management system operation—cold engine

REMOVAL AND INSTALLATION

Air Pump

1. Remove the AIR management valves and/or adapter at the pump.

2. Loosen the air pump adjustment bolt and remove the drive belt.

3. Unscrew the pump mounting bolts and then remove the pump pulley.

4. Unscrew the pump mounting bolts and then remove the pump.

5. Installation is in the reverse order of removal. Be sure to adjust the drive belt tension after installing it.

Check Valve

1. Release the clamp and disconnect the air hoses from the valve.

2. Unscrew the check valve from the air injection pipe.

Upper check valve and hoses

Air pump mounting details

Lower check valve and hoses

3. Installation is in the reverse order of removal.

Air Management Valve

1. Disconnect the negative battery cable.
2. Remove the air cleaner.
3. Tag and disconnect the vacuum hose from the valve.
4. Tag and disconnect the air outlet hoses from the valve.
5. Bend back the lock tabs and then remove the bolts holding the elbow to the valve.
6. Tag and disconnect any electrical connections at the valve and then remove the valve from the elbow.
7. Installation is in the reverse order of removal.

Early Fuel Evaporation (EFE)

All carbureted models are equipped with this system to reduce engine warm-up time, improve driveability and reduce emissions. The system is electric and uses a ceramic heater grid located underneath the primary bore of the carburetor as part of the carburetor insulator/gasket. When the ignition switch is turned on and the engine coolant temperature is low, voltage is applied to the EFE relay by the ECM. The EFE relay in turn energizes the heater grid. When the coolant temperature increases, the ECM de-energizes the relay which will then shut off the EFE heater.

REMOVAL AND INSTALLATION

1. Remove the air cleaner and disconnect the negative battery cable.
2. Disconnect all electrical, vacuum and fuel connections from the carburetor.
3. Disconnect the EFE heater electrical lead.
4. Remove the carburetor — refer to Chapter 5 for service procedures.
5. Lift off the EFE heater grid.
6. Installation is in the reverse order of re-

EFE heater grid

moval. Always replace any fuel line clamp or gas hose as necessary.

EFE HEATER RELAY REPLACEMENT

1. Disconnect the negative battery cable.
2. Remove the retaining bracket on the right fender skirt.
3. Tag and disconnect all electrical connections.
4. Unscrew the retaining bolts and remove the relay.
5. Installation is in the reverse order of removal.

Exhaust Gas Recirculation (EGR)

DESCRIPTION

All models are equipped with this system, which is used to lower the NOx (oxides of nitro-

Heater relay installation details

1. Diaphragm
2. Pintle position sensor
3. Vacuum connection

1. EGR valve
2. Exhaust gas
3. Intake air
4. Vacuum port
5. Diaphragm
6. Air bleed hole
7. Small spring
8. Large spring

Exhuast gas modulated EGR valve

Integrated electronic EGR valve

gen) emission levels caused by high combustion temperature.

It does this by introducing exhaust gas, which containes very little oxygen, into the intake manifold. The exhaust gas will not support combustion, but does occupy volume, reducing the total amount of air/fuel mixture which burns in the cylinder. This reduces combustion temperatures.

There are 4 types of EGR valves used; The negative backpressure EGR valve, Ported EGR valve, Integrated Electronic EGR valve and the Digital EGR valve. The principle of all systems is the same; the only difference is in the method used to control how far the EGR valve opens.

RESULTS OF INCORRECT OPERATION

1. Too much EGR flow (at idle, cruise, or cold operation) may result in any of the following conditions:
- Engine stops after cold start
- Engine stops at idle after deceleration
- Car surges during cruise
- Rough idle

2. Too little or no EGR flow allows combustion temperatures to get too high during acceleration and load conditions. This could cause the following:
- Spark knock (detonation)
- Engine overheating
- Emission test failure

Negative backpressure valve

1. Solenoid & mounting plate assembly
2. EGR base plate
3. EGR base gasket
4. Insulator gasket
5. EGR base
6. Armature assembly
7. Screw assembly

Digital EGR valve

1. EGR valve
2. Gasket
3. Stud 25 N·m (19 lb. ft.)
4. Nut 25 N·m (19 lb. ft.)

Negative back pressure EGR valve to manifold mounting on the 1987–92 2.0L OHV engine

REMOVAL AND INSTALLATION

EGR Valve

1. Disconnect the negative battery cable.
2. Remove the air cleaner assembly, as necessary, for access to the EGR valve.
3. Disconnect the EGR vacuum hose or solenoid wire, as required the valve.
4. Remove the EGR valve retaining bolts and remove the EGR valve from the manifold.

To install:

5. If reinstalling the old valve inspect the EGR valve passages for excessive build-up of deposits, and clean as necessary.

NOTE: *Loose particles should be completely removed to prevent them from being ingested into the engine.*

6. With a wire wheel buff the deposits from the mounting surfaces.
7. Install the EGR valve to the intake manifold using a NEW gasket and tighten the bolts EVENLY.

1. EGR valve
2. Valve gasket
3. Tube gasket
4. Nut (3) 25 N·m (19 lb. ft.)
5. Bolt (2) 25 N·m (19 lb. ft.)
6. EGR tube
7. Tube nut 25 N·m (19 lb. ft.)

Integrated electronic EGR valve manifold mounting—1985–89 2.8L engine

1. EGR valve
2. EGR valve tube

Negative back pressure EGR valve to manifold mounting on the 1984–86 1.8L OHC and 2.0L OHV engine

1. EGR valve
2. Bolt (2) 22 N·m (16 lb. ft.)
3. Gasket

Negative back pressure EGR valve to manifold mounting on the 1987–92 2.0L OHC Non turbocharged engine

1. EGR valve asm
2. Gasket

Negative back pressure EGR valve to manifold mounting on the 1987–91 2.0L OHC turbocharged engine

8. Install the vacuum hose or solenoid wire connector.

9. Install the air cleaner assembly, if removed.

10. Connect the negative battery cable.

Computer Command Control System (CCC)

The Computer Command Control System (CCC) is an electronically controlled exhaust emission system that can monitor and control a large number of interrelated emission control systems. It can monitor up to 15 various engine/vehicle operating conditions and then use this information to control as many as 9 engine related systems. The system is thereby making constant adjustments to maintain good vehicle performance under all normal driving conditions while at the same time allowing the catalytic converter to effectively control the emissions of HC, CO and NOx.

In addition, the system has a built in diagnostic system that recognizes and identifies possible operational problems and alerts the driver through a "Check Engine" light in the instrument panel. The light will remain on until the problem is corrected. The system also has built in back-up systems that in most cases of an operational problem will allow for the continued operation of the vehicle in a near normal manner until the repairs can be made.

BASIC TROUBLESHOOTING

NOTE: *The following explains how to activate the Trouble Code signal light in the instrument cluster. This is not a full fledged CCC system troubleshooting and isolation procedure.*

Before suspecting the CCC system, or any of its components as being faulty, check the ignition system (distributor, timing, spark plugs and wires). Check the engine compression, the air cleaner and any of the emission control components that are not controlled by the ECM. Also check the intake manifold, the vacuum

hoses and hose connectors for any leaks. Check the carburetor or throttle body and mounting bolts for tightness.

The following symptoms could indicate a possible problem area with the CCC system:
1. Detonation
2. Stalling or rough idling when the engine is cold
3. Stalling or rough idling when the engine is hot
4. Missing
5. Hesitation
6. Surging
7. Poor gasoline mileage
8. Sluggish or spongy performance
9. Hard starting when engine is cold
10. Hard starting when the engine is hot
11. Objectionable exhaust odors
12. Engine cuts out
13. Improper idle speed

As a bulb and system check, the "Check Engine" light will come on when the ignition switch is turned to the **ON** position but the engine is not started.

The "Check Engine" light will also produce the trouble code/codes by a series of flashes which translate as follows: When the diagnostic test terminal under the instrument panel is grounded, with the ignition in the **ON** position and the engine not running, the "Check Engine" light will flash once, pause, and then flash twice in rapid succession. This is a Code 12, which indicates that the diagnostic system is working. After a long pause, the Code 12 will repeat itself two more times. This whole cycle will then repeat itself until the engine is started or the ignition switch is turned **OFF**.

NOTE: *Remove the ground from the test terminal before starting the engine.*

When the engine is started, the "Check Engine" light will remain on for a few seconds and then turn off. If the "Check Engine" light remains on, the self-diagnostic system has detected a problem. If the test terminal is then grounded, the trouble code will flash (3) three times. If more than one problem is found to be in existence, each trouble code will flash (3) three times and then change to the next one. Trouble codes will flash in numerical order (lowest code number to highest). The trouble code series will repeat themselves for as long as the test terminal remains grounded.

A trouble code indicates a problem with a given circuit. For example, trouble code 14 indicates a problem in the cooling sensor circuit. This includes the coolant sensor, its electrical harness and the Electronic Control Module (ECM).

Since the self-diagnostic system cannot diagnose every possible fault in the system, the absence of a trouble code does not necessarily mean that the system is trouble-free. To determine whether or not a problem with the system exists that does not activate a trouble code, a system performance check must be made.

In the case of an intermittent fault in the system, the "Check Engine" light will go out when the fault goes away, but the trouble code will remain in the memory of the ECM. Therefore, if a trouble code can be obtained even though the "Check Engine" light is not on, it must still be evaluated. It must be determined if the fault is intermittent or if the engine must be operating under certain conditions (acceleration, deceleration, etc.) before the "Check Engine" light will come on. In some cases, certain trouble codes will not be recorded in the ECM until the engine has been operated at part throttle for at least 5 to 18 minutes.

On the computer system, depending on how the vehicle is equipped, a trouble code will be stored until the ECM harness connector pigtail or inline fuse has been disconnected from the battery with the key OFF **for at least 10–30 seconds or by removing the ECM fuse.**

WARNING: *To prevent ECM damage, the key must be OFF when disconnecting or reconnecting ECM power.*

Test terminal B ground terminal A location—1982

ACTIVATING THE TROUBLE CODE

On 1982 models, a 5 terminal connector, located on the right side of the fues panel, is used to activate the trouble code system in the ECM. This same connector is use at assembly and known as the Assembly Line Diagnostic Link (ALDL) or Assembly Line Communication Link (ALCL). A trouble code test terminal **D** is located in the 5 terminal connector and a ground terminal **E**, is located next to this terminal. With the ignition **ON**, car not running, jump the test terminal to ground.

On 1983–92 models, the ALDL connector, located under the dash, and sometimes covered

TROUBLE CODE IDENTIFICATION CHART

NOTE: Always ground the test terminal AFTER the engine is running.

Trouble Code	Refers To:
12	No reference pulses to the ECM. This is not stored in the memory and will only flash when the fault is present (not to be confused with the Code 12 discussed earlier).
13	Oxygen sensor circiut. The engine must run for at least 5 min. before this code will set.
14	Shortened coolant circuit. The engine must run at least 2 min. before this code will set.
15	Open coolant sensor circuit. The engine must run at least 5 min. before this code will set.
21	Throttle position sensor circuit. The engine must run up to 25 sec., below 800 rpm, before this code will set.
22	Throttle position sensor (signal voltage low)
23	Intake air temp. sensor (high)
23	Open or grounded carburetor solenoid circuit. (1982)
24	Vehicle Speed Sensor (VSS) circuit. The engine must run for at least 5 min. at road speed for this code to set.
25	Intake air temp. sensor (low)
32	EGR system (1990–91)
32	Altitude Compensator circuit.
33	MAP sensor
34	Vacuum sensor circuit. The engine must run for at least 5 min., below 800 rpm, before this code will set.
35	Idle speed control switch circuit shorted. Over 1/2 throttle for at least 2 sec.
41	No distributor reference pulses to the ECM at specified engine vacuum. This code will store in memory.
42	Electronic Spark Timing (EST) bypass circuit grounded.
44	Lean oxygen sensor indication. The engine must run at least 5 min., in closed loop, at part throttle and road load for this code to set.
45	Rich system indication. The engine must run at least 5 min., in closed loop, at part throttle and road load for this code to set.
44 & 45	(at same time) Faulty oxygen sensor circuit.
51	Faulty calibration until (PROM) or installation. It takes 30 sec. for this code to set.
54	Shorted M/C solenoid circuit and/or faulty ECM.
55	Grounded Vref (terminal 21), faulty oxygen sensor or ECM.

'J' SERIES   RPO: LH8   VIN CODE: O   1.8L L4 TBI

□ COMPUTER HARNESS

C1 Electronic Control Module (ECM)
C2 ALCL diagnostic connector
C3 "SERVICE ENGINE SOON" light
C4 ECM power
C5 ECM harness ground
C6 Fuse panel
C8 Fuel pump test connector

NOT ECM CONNECTED

N1 Crankcase vent valve (PCV)
N9 Exhaust Gas Recirculation valve
N17 Fuel vapor canister

□ CONTROLLED DEVICES

1   Fuel injector solenoid
2   Idle air control valve
3   Fuel pump relay
5   Trans. Conv. Clutch connector
8   Engine fan relay
13 A/C compressor relay
14 A/C fan relay

⬡ Exhaust Gas Recirculation valve

○ INFORMATION SENSORS

A   Manifold pressure (M.A.P.)
B   Exhaust oxygen
C   Throttle position
D   Coolant temperature
F   Vehicle speed
M   P/N switch/neutral start
S   P/S pressure switch

Component locations—1.8L TBI (VIN 0)

'J' SERIES   RPO: LT2   VIN CODE: K   2.0L L4 TBI

COMPUTER HARNESS
C1 Electronic Control Module (ECM)
C2 ALDL diagnostic connector
C3 "SERVICE ENGINE SOON" light
C4 ECM power
C5 ECM harness grounds
C6 Fuse panel
C8 Fuel pump test connector

NOT ECM CONNECTED
N1 Crankcase vent valve (PCV)
N17 Fuel vapor canister

Exhaust Gas Recirculation valve

CONTROLLED DEVICES
1 Fuel injector solenoid
2 Idle air control valve
3 Fuel pump relay
5 Trans. Conv. Clutch connector
8 Engine fan relay
13 A/C compressor relay

INFORMATION SENSORS
A Manifold pressure (M.A.P.)
   (Mounted On Air Cleaner)
B Exhaust oxygen
C Throttle position
D Coolant temperature
F Vehicle speed
M P/N switch/neutral start
S P/S pressure switch
T Manifold Air Temperature
   (Mounted On Air Cleaner)

Component locations—2.0L OHC (VIN K)

'J' SERIES   RPO: **LT3**   VIN CODE: **M**   **2.0L L4** PFI

COMPUTER HARNESS

- **C1** Electronic Control Module (ECM)
- **C2** ALDL diagnostic connector
- **C3** "SERVICE ENGINE SOON" light
- **C4** ECM power (2)
- **C5** ECM harness grounds
- **C6** Fuse panel
- **C8** Fuel pump test connector

NOT ECM CONNECTED

- **N1** Crankcase vent valve (PCV) (inside PCV hose)
- **N17** Fuel vapor canister

CONTROLLED DEVICES

- **1** Fuel injectors
- **2** Idle air control valve
- **3** Fuel pump relay
- **5** Trans. Converter Clutch connector
- **8** Low speed cooling fan relay
- **8a** High Speed cooling fan relay
- **13** A/C compressor relay
- **16** Wastegate solenoid
- **17** EGR Relay (Below Manifold)

INFORMATION SENSORS

- **A** Manifold pressure (M.A.P.)
- **B** Exhaust oxygen
- **C** Throttle position
- **D** Coolant temperature
- **F** PM Generator
- **J** ESC knock (Below Manifold)
- **M** P/N switch/park neutral
- **S** Power Steering Pressure Switch
- **T** Manifold Air Temperature

Component locations—2.0L TURBO (VIN M)

'J' SERIES   RPO: LL8   VIN CODE: 1   2.0L L4 TBI

COMPUTER HARNESS

C1	Electronic Control Module (ECM)
C2	ALDL Diagnostic Connector
C3	"Service Engine Soon" light
C4	ECM Power Fuse
C5	ECM Harness Grounds
C6	Fuse Panel
C8	Fuel Pump Test Connector

NOT ECM CONNECTED

N1	Crankcase Vent Valve (PCV)
N17	Fuel Vapor Canister
⬡	Exhaust Gas Recirculation valve

CONTROLLED DEVICES

1	Fuel Injector Solenoid
2	Idle Air Control Valve
3	Fuel Pump Relay
5	TCC Solenoid Connector
8	Cooling Fan Relay
13	A/C Compressor Relay
14	Direct Ignition System Assembly

INFORMATION SENSORS

A	Manifold Pressure (MAP)
B	Exhaust Oxygen
C	Throttle Position
D	Coolant Temperature
F	Vehicle Speed
M	P/N Switch
S	P/S Pressure Switch
T	MAT Sensor

Component locations—2.0L TBI (VIN 1)

'J' SERIES   RPO: LB6   VIN CODE: W   2.8L V6 PFI

COMPUTER HARNESS

C1 Electronic Control Module (ECM)
C2 ALDL diagnostic connector
C3 "SERVICE ENGINE SOON" light
C5 ECM harness ground
C6 Fuse panel
C8 Fuel pump test connector
C9 Fuel pump / ECM fuse

NOT ECM CONNECTED

N1 Crankcase vent valve (PCV)
N4 Engine temp. switch (telltale)
N5 Engine temp. sensor (gage)
N6 Oil press. switch (telltale)
N7 Oil press. sensor (gage)
N12 Fuel pressure connector

CONTROLLED DEVICES

1   Fuel injector
2   Idle air control motor
3   Fuel pump relay
5   Trans. Converter Clutch connector
6   Direct Ignition System (DIS)
8   Engine fan relay
9. Air Control Solenoid (M/T only)
12 Exh. Gas Recirc. valve
13 A/C compressor relay
15 Fuel vapor canister solenoid

INFORMATION SENSORS

A   Manifold Pressure (MAP)
B   Exhaust oxygen
C   Throttle position
D   Coolant temperature
E   Crank Shaft Sensor
F   Vehicle speed
J   Knock (ESC)
K   MAT
M   P/N switch
S   P/S pressure switch
U   A/C pressure fan switch
V   A/C Low Press. switch (mounted in compressor)
W   A/C Hi Press. cut-out sw.

Component locations—2.8L PFI (VIN W)

"J" CARLINE   RPO: LM3   (VIN G)   2.2L L4 TBI

☐ COMPUTER HARNESS

C1	Electronic Control Module (ECM)
C2	ALDL Diagnostic Connector
C3	"Service Engine Soon" light
C4	ECM Power Fuse
C5	ECM Harness Grounds
C6	Fuse Panel
C8	Fuel Pump Test Connector

⋯ NOT ECM CONNECTED

N1	Crankcase Vent Valve (PCV)
N17	Fuel Vapor Canister

⬡ Exhaust Gas Recirculation (EGR) Valve

☐ CONTROLLED DEVICES

1	Fuel Injector Solenoid
2	Idle Air Control (IAC) Valve
3	Fuel Pump Relay
5	Torque Converter Clutch (TCC) Solenoid Connector
8	Cooling Fan Relay
13	A/C Compressor Relay
14	Direct Ignition System (DIS) Assembly

◯ INFORMATION SENSORS

A	Manifold Absolute Pressure (MAP)
B	Oxygen (O_2) Sensor
C	Throttle Position Sensor (TPS)
D	Coolant Temperature Sensor (CTS)
F	Vehicle Speed Sensor (VSS)
M	Park/Neutral (P/N) Switch
T	Intake Air Temperature (IAT) Sensor (In Air Cleaner Assembly)

Component locations—2.2L TBI (VIN G)

"J" CARLINE   RPO: LE4   VIN CODE: H   2.0L L4 PORT

COMPUTER HARNESS		CONTROLLED DEVICES		INFORMATION SENSORS	
C1	Electronic Control Module (ECM)	1	Fuel Injector	A	Manifold Absolute Pressure (MAP) Sensor
C2	ALDL Diagnostic Connector	2	Idle Air Control (IAC) Valve	B	Oxygen (O$_2$) Sensor
C3	"Check Engine" light	3	Fuel Pump Relay*	C	Throttle Position Sensor (TPS)
C4	Power Feed Connector	5	TCC Solenoid	D	Coolant Temperature Sensor (CTS)
C5	ECM Harness Grounds	8	Cooling Fan Relay	F$_1$	Vehicle Speed (Auto Trans.)
C6	Fuse Panel	13	A/C Compressor Relay*	F$_2$	Vehicle Speed (Manual Trans.)
C8	Fuel Pump Test Connector	14	Direct Ignition System (DIS) Coil Assy. (Under Intake Plenum)	M	Park/Neutral (P/N) Switch
		16	Computer Controlled Purge (CCP) Solenoid	T	Intake Air Temperature (IAT) Sensor (In Air Cleaner Assy.)
NOT ECM CONNECTED		17	Exhaust Gas Recirculation (EGR) Solenoid	U	A/C Pressure Sensor
N1	Crankcase Vent Valve (PCV)		Exhaust Gas Recirculation (EGR) Valve	Z	Crankshaft Position Sensor
N17	Fuel Vapor Canister				

* Actual location may vary.

Component locations—2.0L PFI (VIN H)

"J" CARLINE   RPO: LN2   VIN CODE: 4   2.2L L4 PORT

Component locations—2.2L PFI (VIN 4)

☐ COMPUTER HARNESS
- **C1** Electronic Control Module (ECM)
- **C2** ALDL Diagnostic Connector
- **C3** "Check Engine" Light
- **C4** Power Feed Connector
- **C5** ECM Harness Grounds
- **C6** Fuse Panel
- **C8** Fuel Pump Test Connector

☐ NOT ECM CONNECTED
- **N1** Crankcase Vent Valve (PCV)
- **N17** Fuel Vapor Canister

*   Actual location may vary

☐ CONTROLLED DEVICES
- **1** Fuel Injector
- **2** Idle Air Control (IAC) Valve
- **3** Fuel Pump Relay*
- **5** Torque Converter Clutch (TCC) Solenoid
- **8** Cooling Fan Relay
- **13** A/C Compressor Relay*
- **14** Direct Ignition System (DIS) Assembly (under intake manifold)
- **17** Exhaust Gas Recirculation (EGR) Solenoid

◎ Exhaust Gas Recirculation (EGR) Valve

○ INFORMATION SENSORS
- **A** Manifold Absolute Pressure (MAP) Sensor
- **B** Oxygen (O_2) Sensor
- **C** Throttle Position Sensor (TPS)
- **D** Coolant Temperature Sensor (CTS)
- **F_1** Vehicle Speed (Auto Trans.)
- **F_2** Vehicle Speed (Manual Trans.)
- **M** Park/Neutral (P/N) Switch
- **T** Intake Air Temperature (IAT) Sensor (On Air Cleaner Assembly)
- **U** A/C Pressure Sensor

"J" CARLINE   RPO: LH0   VIN CODE: T   3.1L V6 PFI

Component locations—3.1L PFI (VIN T)

▢ COMPUTER HARNESS

- **C1** Electronic Control Module (ECM)
- **C2** ALDL diagnostic connector
- **C3** "SERVICE ENGINE SOON" light
- **C5** ECM harness ground
- **C6** Fuse panel
- **C8** Fuel pump test connector
- **C9** Fuel pump/ECM fuse
- **C10** ECM Power Feed

⬚ NOT ECM CONNECTED

- **N1** Positive Crankcase Ventilation (PCV) valve
- **N4** Engine temperature sensor gage and (telltale)
- **N6** Fuel pump/oil pressure sensor gage and (telltale)
- **N12** Fuel pressure connector

▢ CONTROLLED DEVICES

- **1** Fuel injector
- **2** Idle Air Control (IAC) motor
- **3** Fuel pump relay
- **5** Trans. Converter Clutch connector
- **6** Direct Ignition System (DIS)
- **8** Cooling fan relay
- **12** Exh. Gas Recirc. valve
- **13** A/C compressor relay
- **15** Fuel vapor canister solenoid

◯ INFORMATION SENSORS

- **A** Manifold Air Pressure (MAP)
- **B** Exhaust oxygen (O_2)
- **C** Throttle Position Sensor (TPS)
- **D** Coolant Temperature Sensor (CTS)
- **E** Crank Shaft Sensor
- **F** Vehicle Speed Sensor (VSS)
- **J** Electronic Spark Control (ESC)
- **K** Intake Air Temperature (IAT)
- **M** P/N switch
- **S** P/S pressure switch
- **U** A/C pressure sensor

with a plastic cover labeled "DIAGNOSTIC CONNECTOR", can be activated by grounding test terminal **B**. The terminal is most easily grounded by connecting it to terminal **A** (internal ECM ground), the terminal to the right of terminal **B** on the top row of the ALDL connector. Once terminals **A** and **B** have been connected, the ignition switch must be moved to the **ON** position with the engine not running.

Oxygen Sensor

An oxygen sensor is used on all models. The sensor protrudes into the exhaust stream and monitors the oxygen content of the exhaust gases. The difference between the oxygen content of the exhaust gases and that of the outside air generates a voltage signal to the ECM. The ECM monitors this voltage and, depending upon the value of the signal received, issues a command to adjust for a rich or a lean condition.

No attempt should ever be made to measure the voltage output of the sensor. The current drain of any conventional voltmeter would be such that it would permanently damage the sensor. No jumpers, test leads or any other electrical connections should ever be made to the sensor. Use these tools ONLY on the ECM side of the wiring harness connector AFTER disconnecting it from the sensor.

REMOVAL AND INSTALLATION

The oxygen sensor must be replaced every 30,000 miles (48,000 km.). The sensor may be difficult to remove when the engine temperature is below 120°F (49°C). Excessive removal force may damage the threads in the exhaust manifold or pipe; follow the removal procedure carefully.

1. Locate the oxygen sensor. It protrudes from the center of the exhaust manifold at the front of the engine compartment (it looks somewhat like a spark plug).

2. Disconnect the electrical connector from the oxygen sensor.

3. Spray a commercial heat riser solvent

TERMINAL IDENTIFICATION

A	GROUND	E	SERIAL DATA
B	DIAGNOSTIC TERMINAL	F	TCC (IF USED)
C	A.I.R. (IF USED)	G	FUEL PUMP (IF USED)
D	SERVICE ENGINE SOON LIGHT (IF USED)	M	SERIAL DATA (IF USED)

Terminal location—1983–92

Oxygen sensor installation—1987–92 2.0L OHV engine

1. Oxygen (O_2) sensor

Oxygen sensor installation—1987–92 2.8L and 3.1L V6 engine

onto the sensor threads and allow it to soak in for at least five minutes.

4. Carefully unscrew and remove the sensor.

To install:

5. First coat the new sensor's threads with G.M. anti-seize compound No. 5613695 or the equivalent. This is not a conventional anti-seize paste. The use of a regular compound may electrically insulate the sensor, rendering it inoperative. You must coat the threads with an electrically conductive anti-seize compound.

6. Installation torque is 30 ft. lbs. (42 Nm.). Do not overtighten.

7. Reconnect the electrical connector. Be careful not to damage the electrical pigtail. Check the sensor boot for proper fit and installation.

Fuel System

CARBURETED FUEL SYSTEM COMPONENTS

Mechanical Fuel Pump

A mechanical fuel pump is used on the 1982 carbureted engines. It is of the diaphragm-type and because of the design is serviced by replacement only. No adjustments or repairs are possible. The pump is operated by an eccentric on the camshaft.

TESTING THE FUEL PUMP

To determine if the fuel pump is in good condition, tests for both volume and pressure should be performed. The tests are made with the pump installed, and the engine at normal operating temperature and idle speed. Never replace a fuel pump without first performing these simple tests.

Be sure that the fuel filter has been changed at the specified interval, If in doubt, install a new filter then test the system.

1. Disconnect the fuel line at the carburetor and connect a fuel pump pressure gauge. Fill the carburetor float bowl with gasoline.

2. Start the engine and check the pressure with the engine at idle. If the pump has a vapor return hose, squeeze it off so that an accurate reading can be obtained. Pressure should not be below 4.5 psi.

3. If the pressure is incorrect, replace the pump. If it is ok, go on to the volume test.

Volume Test

4. Disconnect the pressure gauge. Run the fuel line into a graduated container.

5. Run the engine at idle until one pint of gasoline has been pumped. One pint should be delivered in 30 seconds or less. There is normally enough fuel in the carburetor float bowl to perform this test, but refill it if necessary.

6. If the delivery rate is below the minimum, check the lines for restrictions or leaks, then replace the pump.

REMOVAL AND INSTALLATION

The fuel pump is located at the center rear of the engine.

1. Disconnect the negative cable at the battery. Raise and support the car.

2. Disconnect the inlet hose from the pump. Disconnect the vapor return hose, if equipped.

3. Loosen the fuel line at the carburetor, then disconnect the outlet pipe from the pump.

4. Remove the two mounting bolts and remove the pump from the engine.

To install:

5. Place a new gasket on the pump and install the pump on the engine. Tighten the two mounting bolts ALTERNATELY and EVENLY. Refer to the illustration.

6. Install the pump outlet pipe. This is easier if the pipe is disconnected from the carburetor. Tighten the fitting while backing up the pump nut with another wrench. Install the pipe at the carburetor.

7. Install the inlet and vapor hoses. Lower the car, connect the negative battery cable, start the engine, and check for fuel leaks.

TO CARBURETOR
(20-30 N•m)
15-22 FT-LBS

(20-30 N•m)
15-22 FT-LBS

NUT
(18-30 N•m)
15-22 FT-LBS

GASKET

Fuel pump installation—carbureted engines

CARBURETED FUEL SYSTEM

Carburetor

The Rochester E2SE is used on all 1982 models. It is a two barrel, two stage carburetor of downdraft design used in conjunction with the Computer Command Control system of fuel control. The carburetor has special design features for optimum air/fuel mixture control during all ranges of engine operation.

MODEL IDENTIFICATION

General Motors Rochester carburetors are identified by their model code. The first number indicates the number of barrels, while one of the last letters indicates the type of choke used. These are V for the manifold mounted choke coil, C for the choke coil mounted in the carburetor body, and E for electric choke, also mounted on the carburetor. Model codes ending in A indicate an altitude-compensation carburetor.

REMOVAL AND INSTALLATION

1. Disconnect the negative battery cable. Remove the air cleaner and gasket.
2. Disconnect the fuel pipe and all vacuum lines.
3. Tag and disconnect all electrical connections.
4. Disconnect the downshift cable.
5. If equipped with cruise control, disconnect the linkage.
6. Unscrew the carburetor mounting bolts and remove the carburetor.

To install:

7. Before installing the carburetor, fill the float bowl with gasoline to reduce the battery strain and the possibility of backfiring when the engine is started again.

Rochester E2SE carburetor

Carburetor replacement

The carburetor identification number is stamped on the fuel bowl

Fuel filter assembly

8. Inspect the EFE heater for damage. Be sure that the throttle body and EFE mating surfaces are clean.

9. Install the carburetor and tighten the nuts alternately to the proper specifications. Refer to the section below.

10. Installation of the remaining components is in the reverse order of removal.

CARBURETOR MOUNTING TORQUE

When torquing carburetor after removal, overhaul or replacement or when installing a new EFE heater, torque mounting bolts, in clockwise direction to 13 ft. lbs. evenly.

OVERHAUL

General Information

Efficient carburetion depends greatly on careful cleaning and inspection during overhaul, since dirt, gum, water, or varnish in or on the carburetor parts are often responsible for poor performance.

Overhaul your carburetor in a clean, dust-free area. Carefully disassemble the carburetor, referring often to the exploded views and directions packaged with the rebuilding kit. Keep all similar and look-alike parts segregated during disassembly and cleaning to avoid accidental interchange during assembly. Make a note of all jet sizes.

When the carburetor is disassembled, wash all parts (except diaphragms, electric choke units, pump plunger, and any other plastic, leather, fiber, or rubber parts) in clean carburetor solvent. Do not leave parts in the solvent any longer than is necessary to sufficiently loosen the deposits. Excessive cleaning may remove the special finish from the float bowl and choke valve bodies, leaving these parts unfit for service. Rinse all parts in clean solvent and blow them dry with compressed air or allow them to air dry. Wipe clean all cork, plastic, leather, and fiber parts with a clean, lint-free cloth.

Blow out all passages and jets with compressed air and be sure that there are no restrictions or blockages. Never use wire or similar tools to clean jets, fuel passages, or air bleeds. Clean all jets and valves separately to avoid accidental interchange.

Check all parts for wear or damage. If wear or damage is found, replace the defective parts. Especially check the following:

1. Check the float needle and seat for wear. If wear is found, replace the complete assembly.

2. Check the float hinge pin for wear and the float(s) for dents or distortion. Replace the float if fuel has leaked into it.

3. Check the throttle and choke shaft bores for wear or an out-of-round condition. Damage or wear to the throttle arm, shaft, or shaft bore will often require replacement of the throttle body. These parts require a close tolerance of fit; wear may allow air leakage, which could affect starting and idling.

NOTE: *Throttle shafts and bushings are not included in overhaul kits. They can be purchased separately.*

4. Inspect the idle mixture adjusting needles for burrs or grooves. Any such condition requires replacement of the needle, since you will not be able to obtain a satisfactory idle.

5. Test the accelerator pump check valves. They should pass air one way but not the other. Test for proper seating by blowing and sucking on the valve. Replace the valve check ball and spring as necessary. If the valve is satisfactory, wash the valve parts again to remove breath moisture.

6. Check the bowl cover for warped surfaces with a straightedge.

7. Closely inspect the accelerator pump plunger for wear and damage, replacing as necessary.

8. After the carburetor is assembled, check the choke valve for freedom of operation.

Carburetor overhaul kits are recommended for each overhaul. These kits contain all gaskets and new parts to replace those which deteriorate most rapidly. Failure to replace all parts supplied with the kit (especially gaskets) can result in poor performance later.

Some carburetor manufacturers supply overhaul kits for three basic types: minor repair; major repair; and gasket kits. Basically, the contain the following:

Minor Repair Kits:
- All gaskets
- Float needle valve
- All diagrams
- Spring for the pump diaphragm

Major Repair Kits:
- All jets and gaskets
- All diaphragms
- Float needle valve
- Pump ball valve
- Float
- Complete intermediate rod

• Intermediate pump lever
• Some cover hold-down screws and washers

Gasket Kits:

• All gaskets

After cleaning and checking all components, reassemble the carburetor, using new parts and referring to the exploded view. When reassembling, make sure that all screws and jets are tight in their seats, but do not overtighten as the tips will be distorted. Tighten all screws gradually, in rotation. Do not tighten needle valves into their seats; uneven jetting will result. Always use new gaskets. Be sure to adjust the float level when reassembling.

PRELIMINARY CHECKS

The following should be observed before attempting any adjustments.

1. Thoroughly warm the engine. If the engine is cold, be sure that it reaches operating temperature.

2. Check the torque of all carburetor mounting nuts and assembly screws. Also check the intake manifold-to-cylinder head bolts. If air is leaking at any of these points, any attempts at adjustment will inevitably lead to frustration.

3. Check the manifold heat control valve (if used) to be sure that it is free.

4. Check and adjust the choke as necessary.

5. Adjust the idle speed and mixture. If the mixture screws are capped, don't adjust them unless all other causes of rough idle have been eliminated. If any adjustments are performed that might possibly change the idle speed or mixture, adjust the idle and mixture again when you are finished.

Before you make any carburetor adjustments make sure that the engine is in tune. Many problems which are thought to be carburetor-related can be traced to an engine which is simply out-of-tune. Any trouble in these areas will have symptoms like those of carburetor problems.

ADJUSTMENTS

Float Adjustment

1. Remove the air horn from the throttle body.

2. Use your fingers to hold the retainer in place, and to push the float down into light contact with the needle.

3. Measure the distance from the toe of the float (furthest from the hinge) to the top of the carburetor (gasket removed).

4. To adjust, remove the float and gently bend the arm to specification. After adjustment, check the float alignment in the chamber.

Pump Adjustment

E2SE carburetors have a non-adjustable pump lever. No adjustments are either necessary or possible.

Fast Idle Adjustment

1. Set the ignition timing and curb idle speed, and disconnect and plug hoses as directed on the emission control decal.

2. Place the fast idle screw on the highest step of the cam.

3. Start the engine and adjust the engine speed to specification with the fast idle screw.

Choke Coil Lever Adjustment

1. Remove the three retaining screws and remove the choke cover and coil. On models with

① HOLD RETAINER FIRMLY IN PLACE

(INSET)

③ GAUGE AT LARGE TOE OF FLOAT AT POINT FURTHEST AWAY FROM FLOAT HINGE PIN (SEE INSET)

④ REMOVE FLOAT AND BEND FLOAT ARM UP OR DOWN TO ADJUST

② PUSH FLOAT DOWN LIGHTLY AGAINST NEEDLE

⑤ VISUALLY CHECK FLOAT ALIGNMENT AFTER ADJUSTING

Float adjustment

① PLACE FAST IDLE SCREW
ON HIGHEST STEP OF
FAST IDLE CAM.

② TURN FAST IDLE SCREW
IN OR OUT TO JUST CONTACT
CAM, THEN TURN SCREW IN
SPECIFIED NUMBER OF TURNS.

Fast idle adjustment

a riveted choke cover, drill out the three rivets
and remove the cover and choke coil.

NOTE: *A choke stat cover retainer kit is required for reassembly.*

2. Place the fast idle screw on the high step
of the cam.

3. Close the choke by pushing in on the intermediate choke lever.

4. Insert a drill or gauge of the specified size
into the hole in the choke housing. The choke
lever in the housing should be up against the
side of the gauge.

5. If the lever does not just touch the gauge,
bend the intermediate choke rod to adjust.

Fast Idle Cam (Choke Rod) Adjustment

NOTE: *A special angle gauge should be
used. If it is not available, a linear measurement can be made.*

1. Adjust the choke coil lever and fast idle
first.

2. Rotate the degree scale until it is zeroed.

3. Close the choke and install the degree
scale onto the choke plate. Center the leveling
bubble.

4. Rotate the scale so that the specified degree is opposite the scale pointer.

5. Place the fast idle screw on the second step
of the cam (against the high step). Close the
choke by pushing in the intermediate lever.

6. Bend the fast idle cam rod at the U to adjust the angle to specifications.

Air Valve Rod Adjustment

1. Seat the vacuum diaphragm with an outside vacuum source. Tape over the purge bleed
hole if present.

2. Close the air valve.

3. Insert the specified gauge between the rod
and the end of the slot in the plunger.

4. Bend the rod to adjust the clearance.

Primary Side Vacuum Break Adjustment

1. Follow Steps 1-4 of the Fast Idle Cam
Adjustment.

2. Seat the choke vacuum diaphragm with
an outside vacuum source.

3. Push in on the intermediate choke lever to

① REMOVE RIVETS AND CHOKE
COVER AND COIL ASSEMBLY
FOLLOWING INSTRUCTIONS
IN CHOKE STAT COVER
RETAINER KIT (SEE NOTE).

NOTE: DO NOT REMOVE
RIVETS AND RETAINERS
HOLDING CHOKE COVER AND
COIL ASSEMBLY IN PLACE
UNLESS NECESSARY TO
CHECK THE CHOKE COIL
LEVER ADJUSTMENT. IF
RIVETS AND COVER ARE
REMOVED, A CHOKE STAT
COVER RETAINER KIT IS
REQUIRED FOR
REASSEMBLY.

⑥ BEND INTERMEDIATE CHOKE
ROD TO ADJUST

② PLACE FAST IDLE
SCREW ON HIGH STEP
OF FAST IDLE CAM

③ PUSH ON INTER-
MEDIATE CHOKE
LEVER UNTIL CHOKE
VALVE IS CLOSED

④ INSERT SPECIFIED
PLUG GAUGE INTO
HOLE PROVIDED

⑤ EDGE OF LEVER SHOULD
JUST CONTACT SIDE OF
PLUG GAUGE AS SHOWN

FIG. 6 Choke coil lever adjustment

Choke coil lever adjustment

⑤ SPECIFIED ANGLE (SEE SPECS.)

⑧ BEND ROD TO ADJUST

① DEGREE SCALE

④ LEVELING BUBBLE (CENTERED)

② POINTER

③ CHOKE VALVE CLOSED

MAGNET

FIGURE 1

FAST IDLE CAM

⑥ PLACE FAST IDLE SCREW ON SECOND STEP OF CAM AGAINST RISE OF HIGH STEP

⑦ HOLD CHOKE VALVE TOWARD CLOSED POSITION BY LIGHTLY PUSHING ON INTER- MEDIATE CHOKE LEVER.

FIGURE 2

⑨ REMOVE GAUGE

Fast idle cam (choke rod) adjustment

⑤ SPECIFIED ANGLE (SEE SPECS.)

⑦ ROTATE AIR VALVE IN THE DIRECTION OF OPEN AIR VALVE BY APPLYING A LIGHT PRESSURE TO THE AIR VALVE SHAFT.

① DEGREE SCALE

④ LEVELING BUBBLE (CENTERED)

③ POINTER

MAGNET

FIGURE 1

② AIR VALVE CLOSED

⑥ SEAT VACUUM DIAPHRAGM USING OUTSIDE VACUUM SOURCE

⑧ TO ADJUST, BEND AIR VALVE ROD UNTIL BUBBLE IS CENTERED.

FIGURE 2

Air valve rod adjustment

NOTE: PRIOR TO ADJUSTMENT, REMOVE VACUUM BREAK FROM CARBURETOR. PLACE BRACKET IN VICE AND, USING SAFETY PRECAUTIONS, GRIND OFF ADJUSTMENT SCREW CAP. REINSTALL VACUUM BREAK.

① DEGREE SCALE

④ LEVELING BUBBLE (CENTERED)

<u>FIGURE 1</u>

MAGNET

② POINTER

③ CHOKE VALVE CLOSED (FAST IDLE SCREW MUST BE ON HIGH STEP OF FAST IDLE CAM).

⑤ SPECIFIED ANGLE (SEE SPECS.)

⑥ SEAT DIAPHRAGM USING VACUUM SOURCE (OVER 5" Hg VACUUM AND AIR VALVE ROD NOT RESTRICTING).

⑦ DURING READING OF ANGLE GAUGE, HOLD CHOKE VALVE TOWARD CLOSED POSITION BY LIGHTLY PUSHING ON INTERMEDIATE CHOKE LEVER.

<u>FIGURE 2</u>

⑧ TO ADJUST, USING 1/8" HEX WRENCH, TURN SCREW IN REAR COVER UNTIL BUBBLE IS CENTERED APPLY SEALER (SUCH AS SILICONE SEALANT RTV RUBBER OR EQUIVALENT) OVER SCREW HEAD TO SEAL SETTING.

Primary side vacuum break adjustment

close the choke valve, and hold closed during adjustment.

4. Adjust by using a 1/8 in. (3mm) hex wrench to turn the screw in the rear cover until the bubble is centered.

5. After adjusting, apply RTV silicone sealant over the screw to seal the setting.

Secondary Vacuum Break Adjustment

1. Follow Steps 1-4 of the Fast Idle Cam Adjustment.

2. Seat the choke vacuum diaphragm with an outside vacuum source.

3. Push in on the intermediate choke lever to close the choke valve, and hold closed during

① ADJUSTMENT SCREW ACCESS (CAP REMOVED)

<u>FIGURE 1</u>

⑧ DURING READING OF ANGLE GAUGE, HOLD CHOKE VALVE TOWARD CLOSED POSITION BY LIGHTLY PUSHING ON INTERMEDIATE CHOKE LEVER. MAKE SURE VACUUM DIAPHRAGM IS SEATED (OVER 5" Hg APPLIED TO VACUUM BREAK).

⑨ TO ADJUST, USING 1/8" HEX WRENCH, TURN SCREW IN REAR COVER UNTIL BUBBLE IS CENTERED.

AFTER ADJUSTMENT, APPLY SEALER (SUCH AS SILICONE SEALANT RTV RUBBER OR EQUIVALENT) OVER SCREW HEAD TO SEAL SETTING.

⑥ SPECIFIED ANGLE (SEE SPECS.)

NOTE: PRIOR TO ADJUSTMENT, REMOVE VACUUM BREAK FROM CARBURETOR. PLACE BRACKET IN VICE AND, USING SAFETY PRECAUTIONS, GRIND OFF ADJUSTMENT SCREW CAP. REINSTALL VACUUM BREAK.

⑤ LEVELING BUBBLE (CENTERED)

② DEGREE SCALE

MAGNET

<u>FIGURE 2</u>

③ POINTER

④ CHOKE VALVE CLOSED (FAST IDLE SCREW MUST BE ON HIGH STEP OF FAST IDLE CAM).

⑦ SEAT DIAPHRAGM USING VACUUM SOURCE.

Secondary side vacuum break adjustment

Choke unloader adjustment

adjustment. Make sure the plunger spring is compressed and seated, if present.

4. Adjust by using a ⅛ in. (3mm) hex wrench to turn the screw in the rear cover until the bubble is centered.

5. After adjusting, apply RTV silicone sealant over the screw to seal the setting.

Choke Unloader Adjustment

1. Follow Steps 1-4 of the Fast Idle Cam Adjustment.
2. Hold the primary throttle wide open.
3. If the engine is warm, close the choke valve by pushing in on the intermediate choke lever.

4. Bend the unloader tang until the bubble is centered.

Secondary Lockout Adjustment

1. Pull the choke wide open by pushing out on the intermediate choke lever.
2. Open the throttle until the end of the secondary actuating lever is opposite the toe of the lockout lever.
3. Gauge clearance between the lockout lever and secondary lever should be as specified.
4. To adjust, bend the lockout lever where it contacts the fast idle cam.

E2SE Carburetor Specifications

Year	Carburetor Identification	Float Level (In.)	Fast Idle (rpm)	Choke Coil Lever (In.)	Fast Idle Cam (deg.)	Air Valve Rod (deg.)	Primary Vacuum Break (deg/In.)	Choke Setting (notches)	Secondary Vacuum Break (deg/In.)	Choke Unloader (deg/In.)	Secondary Lockout (In.)
1982	17081600	5/16	①	.085	24	1	20/.110	①	27/.157	35/.220	.012
	17081601	5/16	①	.085	24	1	20/.110	①	27/.157	35/.220	.012
	17081607	5/16	①	.085	24	1	20/.110	①	27/.157	35/.220	.012
	17081700	5/16	①	.085	24	1	20/.110	①	27/.157	35/.220	.012
	17081701	5/16	①	.085	24	1	20/.110	①	27/.157	35/.220	.012

① See underhood emissions sticker

① HOLD CHOKE VALVE WIDE OPEN BY PUSHING COUNTER-CLOCKWISE ON INTERMEDIATE CHOKE LEVER.

④ IF NECESSARY TO ADJUST, BEND LOCKOUT LEVER TANG CONTACTING FAST IDLE CAM.

③ GAUGE CLEARANCE - DIMENSION SHOULD BE AS SPECIFIED.

② OPEN THROTTLE LEVER UNTIL END OF SECONDARY ACTUATING LEVER IS OPPOSITE TOE OF LOCKOUT LEVER.

Secondary lockout adjustment

GM MODEL 300 AND 500 THROTTLE BODY (TBI) INJECTION SYSTEMS

FUEL PRESSURE RELEASE

CAUTION: *To reduce the risk of fire or personal injury, it is necessary to relieve the fuel system pressure before servicing the fuel system.*

1983-86 1.8L and 2.0L (OHC)
1983-84 2.0L (OHV)

1. Remove the fuel pump fuse from the fuse block.
2. Crank the engine. The engine will run until it runs out of fuel. Crank the engine again for 3 seconds making sure it is out of fuel.
3. Turn the ignition off and replace the fuse.

1985-86 2.0L (OHV)

The TBI injection systems used on the 1985-86 engines contain a constant bleed feature in the pressure regulator that relieves pressure any time the engine is turned off. Therefore, no special relieve procedure is required, however, a small amount of fuel may be released when the fuel line is disconnected.

CAUTION: *To reduce the chance of personal injury, cover the fuel line with cloth to collect the fuel and then place the cloth in an approved container.*

FUEL SYSTEM PRESSURE TEST

CAUTION: *To reduce the risk of fire and personal injury, it is necessary to relieve the fuel system pressure before servicing fuel system components (Refer to the appropriate procedure above).*

1.8L and 2.0L OHV Engines

1. Remove the air cleaner. Plug the thermal vacuum port on the throttle body.
2. Remove the fuel line between the throttle body and filter.
3. Install a fuel pressure gauge between the throttle body and fuel filter. The gauge should be able to register at least 15 psi.
4. Start the car. The pressure reading should be 9-13 psi.
5. Depressurize the system and remove the gauge.
6. Assemble the system.

1.8L, 2.0L OHC Engines

1. Release the fuel system pressure.
CAUTION: *To reduce the risk of fire or personal injury, it is necessary to relieve the fuel system pressure before servicing the fuel system. Refer to Fuel System Pressure Release in the appropriate fuel injection system in this Chapter.*
2. Obtain two sections of ⅜ in. steel tubing.

Each should be about 10 in. (254mm) long. Double flare one end of each section.

3. Install a flare nut on each section. Connect each of the above sections of tubing into the flare nut to flre nut adapters that are included in J-29658 gauge.

4. Attach the pipe and the adapter assemblies to the J-29658 gauge.

5. Jack up the car and support it safely.

6. Disconnect the front fuel feed hose from the fuel pipe on the body.

7. Install a 10 in. (254mm) length of ⅜ in. fuel hose on the fuel pipe on the body. Attach the other end of the hose onto one of the sections of the pipe mentioned in Step 2. Secure the hose connections with clamps.

8. Start the engine and check for leaks.

9. Observe the fuel pressure reading. It should be 9-13 psi.

10. Depressurize the fuel system and remove the gauge with adapters. Reconnect the fuel feed hose to the pipe and torque the clamp to 15 inch lbs.

11. Lower the car, start the engine and check for fuel leaks.

Fuel Pump

REMOVAL AND INSTALLATION

1. Release the fuel system pressure.

CAUTION: *To reduce the risk of fire or personal injury, it is necessary to relieve the fuel system pressure before servicing the fuel system. Refer to Fuel System Pressure Release procedure above.*

2. Disconnect the negative battery cable.

3. Jack up the car and support it safely.

4. Remove the fuel tank — refer to the necessary service procedures.

5. Remove the fuel lever sending unit and pump assembly by turning the cam lock ring counterclockwise. Lift the assembly from the fuel tank and remove the fuel pump from the fuel level sending unit.

6. Pull the fuel pump up into the attaching hose or pulsator while pulling outward away from the bottom support. After the pump is clear of the bottom support, pull the pump assembly out of the rubber connector or pulsator for removal.

To install:

7. Position and push the pump into the attaching hose.

8. Install the fuel level sending unit and pump assembly into the tank assembly. Use new O-ring during reassembly.

WARNING: *Be careful not to fold over or twist the strainer when installing the sending unit as it will restrict fuel flow. Also, be care-*

ful the strainer does not block full travel of the float arm.

9. Install the cam lock over the assembly and lock by turning clockwise.

10. Install the fuel tank. Check system for proper operation.

TOOLS

The system does not require special tools for diagnosis. A tachometer, test light, ohmmeter, digital voltmeter with 10 megohms impedance, vacuum pump, vacuum gauge and jumper wires are required for diagnosis. A test light or voltmeter must be used when specified in the procedures.

Idle Air Control Assembly

REMOVAL AND INSTALLATION

1. Remove the air cleaner.

2. Disconnect the electrical connection from the idle air control assembly.

3. Using a 1¼ in. (31.75mm) wrench or a special tool, remove the idle air control assembly from the throttle body.

WARNING: *Before installing a new assembly, measure the distance that the conical valve is extended. This measurement should be made from motor housing to end of cone. It should be greater than 1⅛ in. (28.6mm). If the cone is extended too far damage to the motor may result.*

There are two different types of IAC assemblies that could be used on your car. Identify the replacement IAC assembly as either being type I (having a collar at the electric terminal) or Type II (without a collar). If the meassured demension is greater than 1⅛ in. (28.6mm), the distance must be reduced as follows:

TYPE I: Insert firm pressure on the conical valve to extract it. A slight side to side movement may be helpfull.

TYPE II: Compress the retaining spring from the conical valve inward with a clockwise motion. Return the spring to the original position

Idle air control valve installation—Model 300 and 500

with the straight portion of the spring end aligned with the flat portion of the valve.

4. Install the new idle air control valve to the throttle body with a new gasket and tighten to 13 ft. lbs.

5. Install the electrical connection to the valve.

6. Install the air cleaner.

NOTE: *When the vehicle is operated at normal engine temperature at approximately 30 MPH, the ECM causes the valve pintle to seat in the throttle body.*

Fuel Pressure Regulator Compensator

REMOVAL AND INSTALLATION

CAUTION: *To reduce the risk of fire and personal injury, it is necessary to relieve the fuel system pressure before servicing fuel system components (Refer to the appropriate procedure above).*

1. Remove air cleaner.

2. Disconnect electrical connector to injector by squeezing on two tabs and pulling straight up.

3. Remove five screws securing fuel meter cover to fuel meter body. Notice location of two short screws during removal.

CAUTION: *Do not remove the four screws securing the pressure regulator to the fuel meter cover. The fuel pressure regulator includes a large spring under heavy tension which, if accidentally released, could cause personal injury. The fuel meter cover is only serviced as a complete assembly and includes the fuel pressure regulator preset and plugged at the factory.*

WARNING: *DO NOT immerse the fuel meter cover (with pressure regulator) in any type of cleaner. Immersion in cleaner will damage the internal fuel pressure regulator diaphragms and gaskets.*

4. Installation is the reverse of removal procedure.

Throttle Position Sensor

CHECK

Model 300

1. Remove air cleaner.

2. Disconnect T.P.S. harness from T.P.S.

3. Using three jumper wires connect T.P.S. harness to T.P.S.

4. With ignition **ON**, engine stopped, use a digital voltmeter to measure voltage between terminals B and C.

5. Voltage should read 0.450-1.250 volts.

NOTE: *The TPS on this model is not adjustable.*

Model 500

Throttle position sensor adjustment should be checked after minimum air adjustment is completed.

1. Remove air cleaner.

2. Disconnect T.P.S. harness from T.P.S.

3. Using three jumper wires connect T.P.S. harness to T.P.S.

4. With ignition **ON**, engine stopped, use a digital voltmeter to measure voltage between terminals B and C.

5. Voltage should read 0.525volts ± 0.075 volts.

6. Adjust T.P.S. if required.

7. With ignition **OFF**, remove jumpers and connect T.P.S. harness to T.P.S.

8. Install air cleaner.

Throttle Position Sensor

ADJUSTMENT

Model 500

1. After installing TPS to throttle body, install throttle body unit to engine.

2. Remove EGR valve and heat shield from engine.

3. Using three 6 in. (152mm) jumpers, connect TPS harness to TPS.

4. With ignition **ON**, engine stopped, use a digital voltmeter to measure voltage between TPS terminals B and C.

5. Loosen two TPS attaching screws and rotate throttle position sensor to obtain a voltage reading of 0.525 volts ± 0.075 volts.

6. With ignition **OFF**, remove jumpers and reconnect TPS harness to TPS.

7. Install EGR valve and heat shield to engine, using new gasket as necessary.

8. Install air cleaner gasket and air cleaner to throttle body unit.

REMOVAL AND INSTALLATION

The throttle position sensor (TPS) is an electrical unit and must not be immersed in any type of liquid solvent or cleaner. The TPS is factory adjusted and the retaining screws are spot welded in place to retain the critical setting. With these considerations, it is possible to clean the throttle body assembly without removing the TPS if care is used. Should TPS replacement be required however, proceed using the following steps:

1. Invert throttle body and place on a clean, flat surface.

2. Using a 5/16 in. (8mm) drill bit, drill completely through two (2) TPS screw access holes

in base of throttle body to be sure of removing the spot welds holding TPS screws in place.

3. Remove the two TPS attaching screws, lockwashers, and retainers. Then, remove TPS sensor from throttle body. DISCARD SCREWS. New screws are supplied in service kits.

4. If necessary, remove screw holding Throttle Position Sensor actuator lever to end of throttle shaft.

5. Remove the Idle Air Control assembly and gasket from the throttle body.

WARNING: *DO NOT immerse the idle air control motor in any type of cleaner and it should always be removed before throttle body cleaning. Immersion in cleaner will damage the IAC assembly. It is replaced only as a complete assembly.*

Further disassembly of the throttle body is not required for cleaning purposes. The throttle valve screws are permanently staked in place and should not be removed. The throttle body is serviced as a complete assembly.

ASSEMBLY

1. Place throttle body assembly on holding fixture to avoid damaging throttle valve.

2. Using a new sealing gasket, install idle air control motor in throttle body. Tighten motor securely.

WARNING: *DO NOT overtighten to prevent damage to valve.*

3. If removed, install throttle position sensor actuator lever by aligning flats on lever with flats on end of shaft. Install retaining screw and tighten securely.

NOTE: *Install throttle position sensor after completion of assembly of the throttle body unit. Use thread locking compound supplied in service kit on attaching screws.*

Fuel Injector
REMOVAL AND INSTALLATION

1. Remove the air cleaner.

2. Disconnect injector electrical connector by squeezing two tabs together and pulling straight up.

WARNING: *Use care in removing to prevent damage to the electrical connector pins on top of the injector, injector fuel filter and nozzle. The fuel injector is only serviced as a complete assembly. Do not immerse it in any type of cleaner.*

3. Remove the fuel meter cover.

4. Using a small awl, gently pry up on the injector evenly and carefully remove it.

5. Installation is the reverse of removal, with the following recommendations.

Use Dexron®II transmission fluid to lubri-

cate all O-rings. Install the steel backup washer in the recess of the fuel meter body. Then, install the O-ring directly above backup washer, pressing the O-ring into the recess.

WARNING: *Do not attempt to reverse this procedure and install backup washer and O-ring after injector is located in the cavity. To do so will prevent seating of the O-ring in the recess.*

Fuel Meter Cover
REMOVAL AND INSTALLATION

1. Remove the five fuel meter cover screws and lockwashers holding the cover on the fuel meter body.

2. Lift off fuel meter cover (with fuel pressure regulator assembly).

3. Remove the fuel meter cover gaskets.

CAUTION: *Do not remove the four screws securing the pressure regulator to the fuel meter cover. The fuel pressure regulator includes a large spring under heavy tension which, if accidentally released, could cause personal injury. The fuel meter cover is only serviced as a complete assembly and includes the fuel pressure regulator preset and plugged at the factory.*

WARNING: *Do not immerse the fuel meter cover (with pressure regulator) in any type of cleaner. Immersion in cleaner will damage the internal fuel pressure regulator diaphragms and gaskets.*

4. Remove the sealing ring (dust seal from the fuel meter body).

5. Installation is the reverse of removal.

Removing the fuel meter body assembly—Model 300 and 500

Fuel Meter Body
REMOVAL AND INSTALLATION

1. Remove the fuel inlet and outlet nuts and gaskets from fuel meter body.

2. Remove three screws and lockwashers. Remove fuel meter body from throttle body assembly.

NOTE: *The air cleaner stud must have been removed previously.*

3. Remove fuel meter body insulator gasket.

4. Installation is the reverse of removal procedure.

Throttle Body
REMOVAL AND INSTALLATION

1. Disconnect the battery cables at the battery.

2. Remove the air cleaner assembly, noting the connection points of the vacuum lines.

3. Disconnect the electrical connectors at the injector, idle air control motor, and throttle position sensor.

4. Disconnect the vacuum lines from the TBI unit, noting the connection points. During installation, refer to the underhood emission control information decal for vacuum line routing information.

5. Disconnect the throttle and cruise control (if so equipped) cables at the TBI unit.

6. Disconnect the fuel return line.

7. Disconnect the fuel feed line.

8. Unbolt and remove the TBI unit.

9. Installation is the reverse of the previous steps. Torque the TBI retaining bolts alternately and evenly to the following specifications:

- 1983–85 with 2.0L OHV engine – 26 ft. lbs.
- 1986 with 2.0L OHV engine – 17 ft. lbs.
- 1983–86 with 1.8L OHC engine – 17 ft. lbs.

GM MODEL 700 THROTTLE BODY (TBI) INJECTION SYSTEM

The Model 700 throttle body system is used on the 1987-91 2.0L OHC (non-turbo) and the 1987-91 2.0L and 2.2L OHV engines.

FUEL SYSTEM PRESSURE RELEASE

CAUTION: *The fuel delivery pipe is under high pressure even after the engine is stopped. Direct removal of the fuel line, may result in dangerous fuel spray. Make sure to release the fuel pressure according to the following procedures:*

2.0L and 2.2L OHV Engines
1987

1. Release the fuel vapor pressure in the fuel tank by removing the fuel tank cap and reinstalling it.

2. Disconnect the fuel pump at the rear body connector and wait until the engine stops.

3. Start the engine and allow it to run a few seconds until it runs out of fuel.

4. Once the engine is stopped, crank it a few times with the starter for about 3 seconds to dissipate the fuel in the lines.

1988–91

1. Disconnect the negative battery cable.

2. Release the fuel vapor pressure in the fuel tank by removing the fuel tank cap and reinstalling it.

3. The internal constant bleed feature of the TBI Models 700, relieves the fuel pump system pressure when the engine is turned **OFF** and no further pressure relive procedure is required.

2.0L OHC Engine
1987–90

1. Release the fuel vapor pressure in the fuel tank by removing the fuel tank cap and reinstalling it.

2. Remove the fuel pump fuse from the fuse block.

3. Start the engine and allow it to run a few seconds until it runs out of fuel.

4. Once the engine is stopped, crank it a few times with the starter for about 3 seconds to dissipate the fuel in the lines.

5. If the fuel pressure can't be released in the above manner because the engine failed to run, disconnect the negative battery cable, cover the union bolt of the fuel line with an absorbant rag and loosen the union bolt slowly to release the fuel pressure gradually.

1991

1. Disconnect the negative battery cable.

2. Release the fuel vapor pressure in the fuel tank by removing the fuel tank cap and reinstalling it.

3. The internal constant bleed feature of this Model 700 TBI unit relieves the fuel pump system pressure when the engine is turned **OFF** and no further pressure relive procedure is required.

FUEL PRESSURE TESTING
1987–91

1. Turn the ignition to the **OFF** position.

2. Make sure the fuel tank quanity is sufficient.

3. Install pressure gauge J 29658–B or BT-8205 or equivalent to the fuel line as illustrated.

4. Apply battery voltage to the fuel pump test connector using a 10 amp fused jumper wire.

5. Note the fuel pressure which should be 9–13 psi.

Fuel Pump
REMOVAL AND INSTALLATION

1. Release the fuel system pressure.
CAUTION: *To reduce the risk of fire or personal injury, it is necessary to relieve the fuel system pressure before servicing the fuel system. Refer to Fuel System Pressure Release procedure above.*
2. Disconnect the negative battery cable.
3. Jack up the car and support it safely.
4. Remove the fuel tank.
5. Remove the fuel lever sending unit and pump assembly by turning the cam lock ring counterclockwise. Lift the assembly from the fuel tank and remove the fuel pump from the fuel level sending unit.
6. Pull the fuel pump up into the attaching hose or pulsator while pulling outward away from the bottom support. After the pump is clear of the bottom support, pull the pump assembly out of the rubber connector or pulsator for removal.
To install:
7. Position and push the pump into the attaching hose.
8. Install the fuel level sending unit and pump assembly into the tank assembly. Use new O-ring during reassembly.
WARNING: *Be careful not to fold over or twist the strainer when installing the sending unit as it will restrict fuel flow. Also, be careful the strainer does not block full travel of the float arm.*
9. Install the cam lock over the assembly and lock by turning clockwise.
10. Install the fuel tank. Check system for proper operation.

Throttle Body
REMOVAL AND INSTALLATION

1. Disconnect the battery cables at the battery.
2. Remove the air cleaner assembly, noting the connection points of the vacuum lines.
3. Disconnect the electrical connectors at the injector, idle air control motor, and throttle position sensor.
4. Disconnect the vacuum lines from the TBI unit, noting the connection points. During installation, refer to the underhood emission control information decal for vacuum line routing information.
5. Disconnect the throttle and cruise control (if so equipped) cables at the TBI unit.

6. Disconnect the fuel return line.
7. Disconnect the fuel feed line.
8. Unbolt and remove the TBI unit.
9. Installation is the reverse of the previous steps. Torque the TBI retaining bolts alternately and evenly to the following specifications:
- 1987–88 – 17 ft. lbs.
- 1989–91 – 18 ft. lbs.

Injector
REPLACEMENT

WARNING: *When removing the injectors, be careful not to damage the electrical connector pins (on top of the injector), the injector fuel filter and the nozzle. The fuel injector is serviced as a complete assembly ONLY. The injector is an electrical component and should not be immersed in any kind of cleaner.*
1. Remove the air cleaner.
CAUTION: *To reduce the risk of fire and personal injury, it is necessary to relieve the fuel system pressure before servicing fuel system components (Refer to the appropriate procedure above).*
2. Disconnect the electrical connector to the fuel injector.
3. Remove the injector retainer screw and retainer.
4. Using a fulcrum, place a suitable tool under the ridge opposite the connector end and carefully pry the injector out.
5. Remove the upper and lower O-rings from the injector and in the fuel injector cavity and discard.
WARNING: *Be sure to replace the injector with an identical part. Injectors from other models can fit in the Model 700, but are calibrated for different flow rates. There is a part number located on the top of the injector*
6. Inspect the filter for evidence of contamination.
7. Lubricate the new upper and lower O-rings with automatic transmission fluid and place them on the injector. Make sur the upper O-ring is in the groove and the lower one is flush up against the filter.
8. Install the injector assembly by pushing it straight into the fuel injector cavity.
NOTE: *Make sure the electrical connector end on the injector is facing in the general direction to the cut-out in the fuel meter body for the wire grommet.*
9. Install the injector retainer, using appropriate thread locking compound on the retainer attaching screw. Tighten to 27 inch lbs.
10. With the engine off and the ignition on, check for fuel leaks

1. Gasket—air filter
2. Gasket—flange
3. Fuel meter assembly
4. Screw & washer assembly—fuel meter body attaching
5. Gasket—fuel meter body to throttle body
6. Screw—injector retainer
7. Retainer—injector
8. Fuel injector
9. O-ring—fuel injector—upper
10. O-ring—fuel injector—lower
11. Filter—injector
12. Pressure regulator cover assembly
13. Screw—pressure regulator attaching
14. Seat—spring
15. Spring—pressure regulator
16. Pressure regulator diaphragm assembly
17. Nut—fuel inlet
18. Seal—fuel nut
19. Nut—fuel outlet
20. Throttle body assembly
21. Plug—idle stop screw
22. Screw & washer assembly—idle stop
23. Spring—idle stop screw
24. Sensor—throttle position (TPS)
25. Screw & washer assembly—TPS attaching
26. Screw—TPS
27. Idle air control valve (IACV)
28. Screw—IACV attaching
29. O-ring—IACV
30. Tube module assembly
31. Screw—manifold assembly
32. Gasket—tubes manifold

Exploded view of the Model 700 throttle body injection unit

Pressure Regulator Assembly

REPLACEMENT

WARNING: *To prevent leaks, the pressure regulator diaphragm assembly must be replaced whenever the cover is removed.*

CAUTION: *To reduce the risk of fire and personal injury, it is necessary to relieve the fuel system pressure before servicing fuel system components (Refer to the appropriate procedure above).*

1. Remove the air cleaner and gasket and discard the gasket.

2. Remove the four pressure regulator attaching screws, while keeping the pressure regulator compressed.

CAUTION: *The pressure regulator contains a large spring under heavy compression. Use care when removing the screws to prevent personal injury.*

3. Remove the pressure regulator cover assembly.

4. Remove the spring seat.

5. Remove the pressure regulator diaphragm assembly.

6. Install the pressure regulator diaphragm assembly, making sure it is seated in the groove in the fuel meter body.

7. Install the regulator spring seat and spring into the cover assembly.

8. Install the cover assembly over the diaphragm, while aligning the mounting holes.

9. While maintaining pressure on the regulator spring, install the four screw assemblies that have been coated with appropriate thread locking compound. Tighten the screws to 22 inch lbs.

10. With the engine off and the ignition on, check for fuel leaks.

11. Install the air cleaner and a new gasket.

Idle Air Control Valve

REPLACEMENT

1. Remove the air cleaner.

2. Disconnect the electrical connector from the idle air control valve.

3. Remove the retaining screws and remove the IAC valve.

WARNING: *Before installing a new idle air control valve, measure the distance that the valve extends (from the tip of the valve pintle and the flange mounting surface. The distance should be no greater than 1 1/8 in. (28mm). If it extends too far, damage will occur to the valve when it is installed.*

4. To adjust, exert firm pressure, with slight side to side movement, on the pintle to retract it.

5. To complete the installation, use a new gasket and reverse the removal procedures. Start the engine and allow it to reach operating temperature.

NOTE: *The ECM will reset the idle speed when the vehicle is driven at 30 mph.*

Throttle Position Sensor (TPS)

REPLACEMENT

1. Disconnect the negative battery cable.

2. Remove the air cleaner and gasket and discard the gasket.

3. Disconnect the rear alternator braacket and the metal PCV tube.

4. Remove the two TPS attaching screws and remove the TPS from the throttle body.

5. When installing, make sure the throttle body is closed and install the TPS on the shaft. Rotate counterclockwise to align the mounting holes.

6. Install the two TPS attaching screws and tighten to 18 inch lbs.

7. Install the metal PCV tube and the rear alternator bracket.

8. Install the air cleaner and new gasket.

9. Reconnect the negative battery cable.

BOTTOM FEED PORT (BFP) INJECTION SYSTEM

The Bottom Feed Port (BFP) injection system is used on the 2.2L OHV (VIN 4) engine in 1992.

FUEL SYSTEM PRESSURE RELEASE

1. Loosen the full filler cap to relieve the tank vapor pressure. Leave the cap loose at this time.

2. Raise and support the vehicle safely.

3. Disconnect the fuel pump electrical connector.

4. Lower the vehicle.

5. Start the engine and run until the fuel supply remaining in the fuel pipes is consumed. Engage the starter for 3 seconds to assure relief of any remaining pressure.

6. Raise and support the vehicle safely.

7. Connect the fuel pump electrical connector.

8. Lower the vehicle.

9. Tighten the fuel filler cap.

10. Disconnect the negative battery cable terminal to avoid possible fuel discharge if an accidental attempt is made to start the engine.

| 1 | THROTTLE POSITION SENSOR (TPS) (NONADJUSTABLE) |
| 2 | TPS ATTACHING SCREW ASSEMBLY |

Throttle Position Sensor (TPS)

Throttle Position Sensor (TPS)
REMOVAL AND INSTALLATION
1. Disconnect the negative battery cable.
2. Disconnect the electrical connector from the TPS.
3. Remove the 2 TPS attaching screws and remove the TPS from the throttle body.
To install:
5. When installing, make sure the throttle body is closed, position the TPS on the shaft and align the mounting holes.
6. Install the 2 TPS attaching screws and tighten to 18 inch lbs. (2.0 Nm).
7. Install the electrical connector.
8. Reconnect the negative battery cable.

Idle Air Control (IAC) Valve
REMOVAL AND INSTALLATION
1. Disconnect the negative battery cable.
2. Disconnect the electrical connector from the IAC valve.

1	IAC VALVE O-RING
2	IAC VALVE ATTACHING SCREW ASSEMBLY
A	DISTANCE OF PINTLE EXTENSION
B	DIAMETER OF PINTLE

Idle air control (IAC) valve

3. Remove the IAC valve.
To install:
WARNING: *Before installing a NEW idle air control valve, measure the distance that the valve extends (from the tip of the valve pintle and the flange mounting surface. The distance should be no greater than 1⅛ in. (28mm). If it extends too far, damage will occur to the valve when it is installed.*
4. To adjust, exert firm pressure, with slight side to side movement, on the pintle to retract it.
5. Lubricate the IAC valve O-ring with clean engine oil.
6. Install the IAC valve assembly, coat the screws with the appropriate thread locking material and tighten the retaining screws to 27 inch lbs. (3.0 Nm).
7. Connect the electrical connector.
8. Reset the IAC pintle position as follows:
   a. Disconnect the negative battery cable for at least 10 seconds to clear the ECM memory, if not disconnected in Step 1.
   b. Reconnect the negative battery cable.
   c. Start the engine and check for proper idle operation.

Upper Manifold Assembly
REMOVAL AND INSTALLATION
1. Disconnect the negative battery cable.
2. Remove the air intake duct.
3. Remove the accelerator cable splash shield from the accelerator cable bracket.
4. Disconnect the accelerator, cruise and transmission control cables.
5. Disconnect the vacuum harness from the top of the air inlet.
6. Disconnect the PCV and power brake vacuum hoses from the vacuum tubes on the upper manifold.
7. Disconnect the electrical connectors at the MAP sensor, TPS and IAC valve.
8. Remove the bolts/nuts attaching the throttle cable bracket.
9. Position the EGR and injector wiring out of the way.
10. Remove the upper manifold and gasket and discard the gasket.
To install:
11. Position the EGR valve injector so that the port faces directly towards the throttle bore.
12. Reposition the upper manifold assembly using a new gasket.
13. Reposition the EGR and injector wiring harness.
14. Install the upper manifold bolts/studs (in correct sequence — refer to the illustration) to 22 ft. lbs. (30 Nm).

UPPER MANIFOLD FASTENER
TIGHTENING SEQUENCE

1	BOLT
2	STUD
3	UPPER MANIFOLD ASSEMBLY
4	GASKET
5	LOWER MANIFOLD ASSEMBLY
6	EGR VALVE INJECTOR

Upper manifold assembly—2.2L (VIN 4)

15. Install the accelerator cable bracket with the attaching bolts/nuts finger tight at this time.

WARNING: *The accelerator bracket must be aligned with the accelerator cam to prevent cable wear, which could result in cable breakage.*

16. Align the accelerator bracket as follows:

   a. Place a steel rule across the bore of the throttle body, with one end in contact with the accelerator bracket.

   b. Adjust the accelerator bracket to obtain a $\frac{25}{64}$ in. (9–11mm) gap between the bracket and the throttle body.

   c. Tighten the top bolt first and tighten all bolts/nuts to 18 ft. lbs. (25 Nm).

17. Install the accelerator, cruise and transmission control cables.

18. Install the accelerator cable splash shield from the accelerator cable bracket.

19. Connect the electrical connectors at the MAP sensor, TPS, IAC valve and EGR vacuum solenoid.

AFTER ADJUSTMENT,
TIGHTEN TOP BOLT FIRST

WITHOUT CROSS BRACE:
ADJUST BRACKET TO PROVIDE
10mm ± 1mm (25/64" ± 1/32")
CLEARANCE BETWEEN ACCELERATOR
BRACKET AND THROTTLE BODY

CROSS BRACE

WITH CROSS BRACE:
NO ADJUSTMENT REQUIRED

Accelerator bracket adjustment—2.2L (VIN 4)

20. Connect the vacuum harness to the top of the air inlet.

21. Connect the PCV and power brake vacuum hoses to the vacuum tubes on the upper manifold.

22. Connect the negative battery cable and turn the ignition **ON** for 2 seconds, **OFF** for 10 seconds, then **ON** and check for fuel leaks.

23. Install the air intake duct.

Lower Manifold Assembly

REMOVAL AND INSTALLATION

1. Disconnect the negative battery cable.

2. Release the fuel system pressure.

3. Remove the upper manifold assembly.

4. Disconnect the quick connect fittings at the engine compartment fuel feed and return lines as follows:

   a. Grasp both ends of one fuel line connection and twist ¼ turn in each direction to loosen any dirt in the quick connect fitting. Repeat for each fitting.

   b. If compressed air is available, blow out the dirt from all quick connect fittings before removing.

   c. Insert the correct size tool from J 37088–A tool set, into the female connector, then push inward to release the male connector.

   d. Repeat for the other fitting.

5. Plug the fuel lines as required.

6. Remove the power steering pump brace.

7. Remove the engine fuel inlet pipe retainer nuts and retainers and disconnect the pipe and seal.

8. Remove the nut attaching the transmission fill tube on, automatic transaxles only.

Remove the lower manifold attaching nuts and remove the lower manifold. Discard the gasket.

To install:

9. Transfer components to the replacement manifold as necessary.

10. Clean the gasket material from the sealing surfaces.

WARNING: *Use care when cleaning the machined aluminum surfaces. Sharp tools could damage the sealing surfaces.*

11. Apply pipe sealant to the threaded ends of the EGR transfer pipe. Tighten the EGR transfer nuts to 20 ft.lbs. (27 Nm).

12. Position the EGR valve injector so that the port faces directly toward the throttle bore.

13. Position the lower manifold on the studs, install the nuts and tighten to 22 ft. lbs. (30 Nm) in the sequence shown in the illustration.

14. Install the nut attaching the transmission fill tube, on automatic transaxles.

15. Install a new fuel inlet pipe O-ring seal.

16. Install the inlet pipe nut and finger tighten only.

17. Install the support nut on the bottom of the lower manifold and finger tighten only.

18. Tighten the fuel inlet pipe retaining nut to 22 ft. lbs. (30 Nm). and the fuel pipe support nut to 89 inch lbs. (10 Nm).

19. Install the power steering pump brace with the attaching bolts.

20. Unplug the fuel feed and return lines.

21. Install the fuel feed and return line quick connect fittings.

1	STUD
2	GASKET
3	LOWER MANIFOLD ASSEMBLY
4	NUT
5	CLIP

LOWER MANIFOLD NUT TIGHTENING SEQUENCE

Lower manifold assembly—2.2L (VIN 4)

22. Apply a few drops of clean engine oil to the male tube ends of the engine fuel feed and return pipes.

CAUTION: *During normal operation, O-rings, located in the female connector will swell and may prevent proper reconnection if not lubricated. This will prevent a possible fuel leak.*

23. Push the connectors together to cause the retaining the retaining tabs/fingers to snap into place. Pull on both ends of each connection to make sure they are secure. Repeat for the other fitting.

24. Install the upper manifold assembly as outlined earlier in this Chapter.

25. Tighten the fuel filler cap.

26. Connect the negative battery cable.

Pressure Regulator Assembly

REMOVAL AND INSTALLATION

1. Relieve the fuel system pressure as outlined earlier.

2. Disconnect the negative battery cable.

3. Remove the vacuum hose from the regulator.

4. Place a rag under the connection and remove the fuel return pipe clamp.

5. Remove the fuel return pipe and O-ring from the regulator. Discard the O-ring.

6. Remove the pressure regulator bracket attaching screw.

7. Remove the pressure regulator assembly and O-ring. Discard the O-ring.

To install:

8. Lubricate a new pressure regulator O-ring with clean engine oil, then install on the pressure regulator.

9. Install the pressure regulator assembly onto the manifold.

10. Install the pressure regulator bracket attaching screw coated with the appropriate thread locking material and tighten to 31 inch lbs. (3.5 Nm).

11. Install the vacuum hose to the regulator.

12. Lubricate a new fuel return pipe O-ring with clean engine oil, then install on the end of the pipe.

13. Install the fuel return pipe to the pressure regulator and tighten the attaching nut to 22 inch lbs. (30 Nm).

14. Install the fuel return pipe clamp attaching nut to the lower manifold assembly.

15. Tighten the fuel filler cap.

16. Connect the negative battery cable and turn the ignition **ON** for 2 seconds, **OFF** for 10 seconds, then **ON** and check for fuel leaks.

Bottom Feed Port Fuel Injectors

REMOVAL AND INSTALLATION

WARNING: *Any time the injectors are removed for service, always remove the fuel pressure regulator to drain excess fuel, and prevent fuel from entering the engine cylinders. Flooded cylinders could result in engine damage.*

1. Relieve the fuel system pressure as outlined earlier.

2. Disconnect the negative battery cable.

3. Remove the upper manifold assembly, as outlined earlier in this Chapter.

CAUTION: *To reduce the chance of personal injury, cover the fuel line connections with a shop towel, when disconnecting.*

4. Disconnect the fuel return line retaining bracket nut and move the return line away from the regulator.

5. Remove the pressure regulator assembly.

WARNING: *Do not try to remove the injectors by lifting up on the injector retaining bracket while the injectors are still installed in the in the bracket slots or damage to the bracket and/or injectors could result.*

Do not attempt to remove the bracket without first removing the pressure regulator.

6. Remove the injector retainer bracket attaching screws and carefully slide the bracket off to clear the injector slots and regulator.

7. Disconnect the injector electrical connectors.

8. Remove the fuel injector(s) and discard the O-ring seals.

CAUTION: *To reduce the risk fire and personal injury, make sure that the lower (small) O-ring of each injector does not remain in the lower manifold. If the O-ring is not removed with the injector, the replacement injector, with new O-rings, will not seat properly in the injector socket and could cause a fuel leak.*

9. Cover the injector sockets to prevent dirt from entering the opening.

NOTE: *Each injector is calibrated with a different flow rate. Replace with the identical part numbers.*

To install:

10. Lubricate the new injector O-ring seals with clean engine oil and install on the injector assembly.

11. Install the injector assembly into the lower manifold injector socket, with the electrical connectors facing inward.

12. Carefully position the injector retainer bracket so that the injector retaining slots and regulator are aligned with the bracket slots.

13. Install the injector electrical connectors.

14. Install the pressure regulator assembly.

15. Install the injector retainer bracket retaining screws, coated with thread locking material and tighten to 31 inch lbs. (3.5 Nm).

16. Install the accelerator cable bracket with the attaching bolts/nuts finger tight at this time.

WARNING: *The accelerator bracket must be aligned with the accelerator cam to prevent cable wear, which could result in cable breakage.*

17. Align the accelerator bracket as follows:

a. Place a steel rule across the bore of the throttle body, with one end in contact with the accelerator bracket.

b. Adjust the accelerator bracket to obtain a $\frac{25}{64}$ in. (9–11mm) gap between the bracket and the throttle body.

c. Tighten the top bolt first and tighten all bolts/nuts to 18 ft. lbs. (25 Nm).

18. Tighten the fuel filer cap.

19. Connect the negative battery cable and turn the ignition ON for 2 seconds, OFF for 10 seconds, then ON and check for fuel leaks.

20. Install the air intake duct.

GENERAL MOTORS MULTI-PORT (MFI) & SEQUENTIAL (SFI) FUEL INJECTION SYSTEMS

General Information

On 1985–92 2.8 and 3.1L V6 engines, multi-port fuel injection (MFI) system is available.

FUEL PRESSURE RELEASE

To reduce the risk of fire or personal injury, it is necessary to relieve the fuel system pressure before servicing the fuel system.

1.8L and 2.0L OHC Engines

1983–84

1. Remove the fuel pump fuse from the fuse block.

2. Crank the engine. The engine will run until it runs out of fuel. Crank the engine again for 3 seconds making sure it is out of fuel.

3. Turn the ignition OFF and replace the fuse.

1985–90

1. Disconnect the negative battery cable.

2. Disconnect the fuel filler cap.

3. Connect gauge J–34730–1 or equivalent, to the fuel pressure connection. Wrap a cloth around the fitting to absorb any fuel leakage.

4. Install the bleed hose into an approved container and open the valve to bleed system pressure.

1992 (VIN H)

1. Remove the fuel pump fuse from the fuse block.

2. Crank the engine. The engine will run until it runs out of fuel. Crank the engine again for 3 seconds making sure it is out of fuel.

3. Turn the ignition OFF and replace the fuse.

2.8L and 3.1L V6 Engines

1987–92

1. Disconnect the negative battery cable.

2. Disconnect the fuel filler cap.

3. Connect gauge J–34730–1 or equivalent, to the fuel pressure connection. Wrap a cloth around the fitting to absorb any fuel leakage.

4. Install the bleed hose into an approved container and open the valve to bleed system pressure.

FUEL SYSTEM PRESSURE TEST

1.8L and 2.0L OHC Engine

1984–85

1. Connect pressure gauge J–34370–1, or equivalent, to fuel pressure test point on the fuel rail. Wrap a rag around the pressure tap to absorb any leakage that may occur when installing the gauge.

2. Turn the ignition OFF for 10 seconds and the A/C OFF.

3. Turn the ignition ON and the fuel pump should run for about 2 seconds.

4. Note the fuel pressure after the pump stops. The pressure should be 30–40 psi and hold steady.

1986

1. Connect pressure gauge J–34370–1, or equivalent, to fuel pressure test point on the fuel rail. Wrap a rag around the pressure tap to absorb any leakage that may occur when installing the gauge.

2. Using a fused jumper, run the fuel pump by applying 12 volts to the fuel pump test terminal for several seconds.

3. Note the fuel pressure after the pump stops. The pressure should be 30–40 psi and hold steady.

1987–90

1. Connect pressure gauge J–34370–1, or equivalent, to fuel pressure test point on the fuel rail. Wrap a rag around the pressure tap to absorb any leakage that may occur when installing the gauge.

2. Disconnect the vacuum hose from the pressure regualtor.

3. Turn the ignition OFF for 10 seconds and the A/C OFF.

4. Turn the ignition **ON** and the fuel pump should run for about 2 seconds.

5. Note the fuel pressure after the pump stops. The pressure should be 35–38 psi and hold steady.

2.8L and 3.1L Engine

1. Connect pressure gauge J-34370-1, or equivalent, to fuel pressure test point on the fuel rail. Wrap a rag around the pressure tap to absorb any leakage that may occur when installing the gauge.

2. Turn the ignition **OFF** for 10 seconds and the A/C **OFF**.

3. Turn the ignition **ON** and the fuel pump should run for about 2 seconds.

4. Note the fuel pressure after the pump stops. The pressure should be 40.5–47 psi and hold steady.

Fuel Pump
REMOVAL AND INSTALLATION

1. Release the fuel system pressure.
CAUTION: *To reduce the risk of fire or personal injury, it is necessary to relieve the fuel system pressure before servicing the fuel system. Refer to Fuel System Pressure Release procedure above.*

2. Disconnect the negative battery cable.

3. Jack up the car and support it safely.

4. Remove the fuel tank.

5. Remove the fuel lever sending unit and pump assembly by turning the cam lock ring counterclockwise. Lift the assembly from the fuel tank and remove the fuel pump from the fuel level sending unit.

6. Pull the fuel pump up into the attaching hose or pulsator while pulling outward away from the bottom support. After the pump is

clear of the bottom support, pull the pump assembly out of the rubber connector or pulsator for removal.

To install:

7. Position and push the pump into the attaching hose.

8. Install the fuel level sending unit and pump assembly into the tank assembly. Use new O-ring during reassembly.

WARNING: *Be careful not to fold over or twist the strainer when installing the sending unit as it will restrict fuel flow. Also, be careful the strainer does not block full travel of the float arm.*

9. Install the cam lock over the assembly and lock by turning clockwise.

10. Install the fuel tank.

Fuel Injectors
REMOVAL AND INSTALLATION

1.8L, 2.0L OHC Engines

WARNING: *Use care in removing the fuel injectors to prevent damage to the electrical connector pins on the injector and the nozzle. The fuel injector is serviced as a complete assembly only and should not be immersed in any kind of cleaner.*

1. Relieve fuel system pressure.

2. Remove the injector electrical connections.

3. Remove the fuel rail.

4. Separate the injector from the fuel rail.

5. Installation is the reverse of removal. Replace the O-rings when installing injectors into intake manifold.

1. Fuel rail assembly
2. Injector
3. Intake manifold
4. Injector housing assembly
5. Injector retaining clip
6. Injector retaining groove
7. Injector cup flange
8. Injector control harness
9. Pressure regulator
10. Fuel pressure test point

Exploded view of the fuel rail and injector assembly—1983–87 1.8L and 2.0L OHC engine

2.8L V6 Engines

1985-86

Each port injector is located and held in position by a retainer clip that must be rotated to release and/or lock the injector in place.

1. Rotate the injector retaining clip(s) the the unlocked position.
2. Remove the port injectors.
3. Install new O-ring seals and lubricate with engine oil.
4. Position the injectors to the fuel rail and pressure regulator assembly.
5. Rotate the injector retaining clips to the locking position.

1987-92

1. Remove and support the fuel rail.
2. Remove the injector retaining clip by spreading the open end of the clip slightly and removing from the rail.
3. Remove the injector(s).
4. Remove the O-rings from both ends of the injectors.
5. Install new O-ring seals and lubricate with engine oil.
6. Place new injector retaining clips on the injector assembly. Position the open end of the clip so it is facing the injector electrical connector.

1. Fuel rail assembly
2. Injector
3. Intake manifold
4. Pressure regulator asm.
5. Fuel pressure gage test point
6. Bolt/screw (20–27 N·m)

VIEW A

VIEW B

VIEW C

VIEW D

GEN SUPPORT
BRACKET

BRACKET

BRACKET

Exploded view of the fuel rail and injectors—1988–90 2.0L OHC engine

7. Install the injector assembly(ies) into the fuel rail socket(s). Push in far enough to engage the retainer clip with machined slots on the socket.

Fuel Pressure Regulator
REMOVAL AND INSTALLATION
1.8L, 2.0L OHC Engines

CAUTION: *To reduce the risk of fire or personal injury, it is necessary to relieve the fuel system pressure before servicing the fuel system.*

1. Relieve fuel system pressure.
2. Remove pressure regulator from fuel rail. Place a rag around the base of the regulator to catch any spilled fuel.
3. Installation is the reverse of removal procedure.

2.8L V6 engine
1985-86

The pressure regulator is factory adjusted and is not serviceable. Do not attempt to remove the regulator from the fuel rail.

1987-92

1. Remove and support the fuel rail.
2. Remove the fuel inlet and outlet fittings and gaskets.
3. Remove the pressure regulator bracket attaching screws and mounting bracket.
4. Remove the right and left hand fuel rail assemblies from the pressure regulator assembly.
5. Remove the base to rail connectors from the regulator or rails.
6. Disassemble connector O-rings from the base to rail connectors.
7. Remove the fuel return O-ring from the fuel rails.

To install:

8. Lubricate new fuel return O-rings with engine oil and install on the fuel rails.
9. Lubricate new connector O-rings with engine oil and install to the base to rail connectors.
10. Install the base to rail connectors in the regulator assembly.
11. Install the right and left hand fuel rail assemblies to the pressure regulator assembly.
12. Install the pressure regulator mounting bracket with the attaching screws. Tighten the screws to 28 inch lbs.
13. Install new fuel inlet and outlet fitting gaskets and tighten the fittings to 20 inch lbs.

Fuel Rail Assembly
REMOVAL AND INSTALLATION
1.8L, 2.0L OHC Engines

Refer to the illustration for fuel rail removal on these models.

2.8L V6 Engine
1985-86

1. Disconnect the negative battery cable.
CAUTION: *To reduce the risk of fire or personal injury, it is necessary to relieve the fuel system pressure before servicing the fuel system.*
2. Relieve fuel system pressure. Refer to the procedure above.
3. Remove the intake manifold plenum.
   a. Disconnect the vacuum lines.
   b. Remove the EGR-to-plenum nuts.
   c. Remove the two throttle body bolts.
   d. Remove the throttle cable to bracket bolts.
   e. Remove the plenum bolts and remove the plenum and gasket.
4. Remove the cold start valve and tube assembly.
5. Remove the retaining nut from the stud for the fuel lines at the head.
6. Disconnect the fuel lines at the rail.
7. Disconnect the vacuum line at the regulator.
8. Remove the rail retaining bolts.
9. Disconnect the injector electrical connectors.
10. Remove the fuel rail assembly.
11. To install use new injector O-rings and lubricate with engine oil.
12. Reverse the removal procedure.

1987-92

1. Disconnect the negative battery cable.
CAUTION: *To reduce the risk of fire or personal injury, it is necessary to relieve the fuel system pressure before servicing the fuel system.*
2. Relieve fuel system pressure. Refer to the procedure above.
3. Remove the intake manifold plenum.
   a. Disconnect the vacuum lines.
   b. Remove the EGR-to-plenum nuts.
   c. Remove the two throttle body bolts.
   d. Remove the throttle cable to bracket bolts.
   e. Remove the ignition wire plastic shield bolts.
   f. Remove the plenum bolts and remove the plenum and gasket.
4. Remove the fuel line bracket bolt.
5. Disconnect the fuel lines at the rail.
CAUTION: *Wrap a cloth around the fuel*

1. O-ring—fuel inlet line
2. O-ring—fuel return line
3. Fuel rail and pressure regulator assembly
4. Fuel pressure connection assembly
5. Seal—fuel pressure connection assembly
6. Cap—fuel pressure connection
7. Fuel block
8. Seal—fuel block
9. Screw assembly—fuel block attaching
10. Injector—port
11. Seal—O-ring—injector
12. Clip—injector retainer
13. Valve—cold start
14. Tube and body assembly
15. O-ring seal—valve
16. O-ring seal—body
17. O-ring seal—tube
18. Fitting—cold start

Exploded view of the fuel rail assembly—1985–86 2.8L V6 engine

1. O-ring—fuel inlet line
2. O-ring—fuel return line
3. Fuel pressure connection assembly
4. Seal—fuel pressure connection
5. Cap—fuel pressure connection
6. Fitting—fuel inlet
7. Fitting—fuel outlet
8. Gasket—fuel fitting
9. MPFI multec injector assembly
10. Seal—o-ring-injector
11. Clip—injector retainer
12. Fuel rail & plug assembly—left hand
13. Fuel rail & plug assembly—right hand
14. Pressure regulator assembly
15. Connector—base to rail
16. Seal-o-ring-connector
17. O-ring-fuel return

18. Bracket—pressure regulator mounting
19. Screw assembly—pressure regulator bracket attaching
20. Bracket—rail mounting
21. Screw assembly—bracket attaching

Exploded view of the fuel rail assembly—1987–92 2.8L and 3.1L V6 engine

1. Throttle body assembly
2. Idle stop screw plug
3. Idle stop screw assembly
4. Idle stop screw spring
5. Throttle position sensor (TPS)
6. TPS attaching screw
7. TPS attaching screw retainer
8. Coolant cavity cover
9. Coolant cover attaching screw
10. O-ring
11. Idle air/vacuum signal housing assembly
12. Idle air/vacuum signal screw assembly
13. Idle air/vacuum signal screw assembly
14. Idle air/vacuum signal gasket assembly
15. Idle air control valve assembly (IAC)
16. Idle air control valve gasket

Exploded view of the throttle body assembly—1985–86 2.8L V6 engine

1. Gasket—flange
2. Throttle body assembly
3. Plug—idle stop screw
4. Screw assembly—idle stop
5. Spring—idle stop screw assembly
6. Sensor—throttle position (TPS)
7. Screw assembly—TPS attaching

8. Retainer—TPS attaching screw
9. Cover—coolant cavity
10. Screw assembly—coolant cover attaching
11. O-ring—coolant cover to throttle body
12. Idle air/vacuum signal housing assembly
13. Screw assembly—idle air/vacuum signal assembly
14. Gasket—idle air/vacuum signal assembly
15. Valve assembly—idle air control (IAC)
16. O-ring—idle air control valve
17. Screw assembly—idle air control valve attaching

Exploded view of the throttle body assembly—1987–92 2.8L and 3.1L V6 engine

lines to collect fuel, then place the fuel in an approved container.

6. Remove the fuel line O-rings.

7. Disconnect the vacuum line at the pressure regulator.

8. Remove the four rail retaining bolts.

9. Disconnect the injector electrical connectors.

10. Remove the fuel rail assembly.

11. Remove the O-ring seal from each of the spray tip end of the injector.

To install:

12. Lubricate new the O-ring seals and install to each of the spray tip ends of the injector.

13. Install the fuel rail assembly in the intake manifold and tilt the rail assembly and install the injectors.

14. Install the fuel rail attaching bolts and tighten to 19 ft. lbs.

15. Install the injector electrical connectors.

16. Install the vacuum line at the pressure regulator.

17. Install new O-rings on the inlet and return fuel lines.

18. Use a back-up wrench and install the fuel inlet and outlet fittings.

19. Connect the negative battery cable.

Idle Air Control Valve

REMOVAL AND INSTALLATION

1985–86 2.8L V6 engine
1983–90 2.0L OHC engine
1992 (VIN H)

1. Remove electrical connector from idle air control valve.

2. Remove the idle air control valve using a suitable wrench.

3. Installation is the reverse of removal. Before installing the idle air control valve, measure the distance that the valve is extended. Measurement should be made from the motor housing to the end of the cone. The distance should not exceed 1⅛ in. (28mm), or damage to the valve may occur when installed. Use a new gasket and turn the ignition on then off again to allow the ECM to reset the idle air control valve.

Identify replacement IAC valve as being either Type 1 (with collar at electric terminal end) or Type 2 (without collar). If measuring distance is greater than specified above, proceed as follows:

TYPE 1

Press on valve firmly to retract it.

25 N·m (18 FT. LBS.)

25 N·m (18 FT. LBS.)

1. Intake manifold
2. Fuel rail assembly
3. Gasket
4. Plenum

Fuel rail, injectors and manifold—1985–86 2.8L V6 engine

1. Plenum
2. Bolt (9) 21 N·m (16 ft lbs)
3. Fuel rail asm
4. Gasket
5. Bolt (4) 25 N·m (19 ft lbs)

Fuel rail, injectors and manifold—1987–92 2.8L and 3.1L V6 engine

1. Idle air control valve
2. Less than 1⅛ inch (28 mm)
3. Type 1 (with collar)
4. Type 2 (without collar)
5. Gasket

Idle air control valves used on the 1985–86 2.8L and 1983–90 2.0L OHC engine

TYPE 2

Compress retaining spring from valve while turning valve in with a clockwise motion. Return spring to original position with straight portion of spring end aligned with flat surface of valve.

1987-92 2.8L and 3.1L V6 Engine

1. Disconnect the electrical connector from the idle air control valve.
3. Remove the retaining screws and remove the IAC valve.

WARNING: *Before installing a new idle air control valve, measure the distance that the valve extends (from the tip of the valve pintle and the flange mounting surface.The distance should be no greater than 28mm. If it extends too far, damage will occur to the valve when it is installed.*

4. To adjust, exert firm pressure, with slight side to side movement, on the pintle to retract it.

5. To complete the installation, use a new seal lubricated with engine oil and install the IAC assembly. Tighten the screws to 30 inch lbs. Install the electrical connector. Start the engine and allow it to reach operating temperature.

NOTE: *The ECM will reset whenever the engine is started and then shut off.*

FUEL TANK

REMOVAL AND INSTALLATION

1. Disconnect the negative cable at the battery. Raise and support the car.

2. Drain the tank. There is no drain plug; remaining fuel in the tank must be siphoned through the fuel feed line (the line to the fuel pump), because of the restrictor in the filler neck.

3. Disconnect the hose and the vapor return hose from the level sending unit fittings.

4. Remove the ground wire screw.

5. Unplug the level sending unit electrical connector.

6. Disconnect the vent hose.

7. Unbolt the support straps, and lower and remove the tank. Installation is the reverse of removal.

MODULAR FUEL SENDER ASSEMBLY REPLACEMENT

NOTE: *Always replace fuel sender assembly O-ring when reinstalling the fuel sender assembly*

Fuel tank mounting—1982–87

A. Distance of pintle extension
B. Diameter of pintle
C. IACV O-ring
D. IACV attaching screw assembly

Idle air control valve used on the 1987–92 2.8L and 3.1L V6 engine

1. Supports, underbody
2. Nut
3. Body asm.
4. Bolt—33 N·m (25 lbs. ft.)
5. Tank asm., fuel
6. Nut—12 N·m (106 lbs. in.)
7. Strap asm., left
8. Bolt
9. Strap asm., right

Fuel tank mounting—1988–92

1. Pipes, fuel sender
2. Tank, fuel
3. Harness, fuel tank wiring
4. Insulator, fuel pipe
5. Retainer
6. Connector, body asm.
7. Connector, fuel tank
wiring harness connector

Fuel tank wiring—1988–92

1. Filter, fuel
2. Hose, return
3. Clamp asm.
4. Clamp—1.5 N·m (13 lbs. in.)
5. Insulator
6. Hose, vapor
7. Tank, fuel
8. Pipe, fuel feed
9. Hose, fuel feed
10. Pipe, rear cross-over
11. Back-up wrench required at this location
12. Seal O-ring
13. Fitting—27 N·m (20 lbs. ft.)

Fuel tank unit hoses—1988–92

1. Disconnect the negative battery cable.
2. Relieve fuel system pressure — refer to the necessary service procedures.
3. Drain fuel from the fuel tank assembly.
4. While holding down the fuel sender assembly, remove the snap ring located slots in the retainer.

To install:

5. Install new O-ring on fuel sender to tank assembly.

6. Align tab on front of sender with the slot on front of the retainer snapring.
7. Slowly apply pressure to top of the spring loaded sender until sender aligns flush with retainer on tank assembly.
8. Install snapring into correct position. Be sure that the snapring is fully seated in the retainer.
9. Install fuel tank, lower vehicle and refill the gas tank. Check system for proper operation.

1 Snap Ring
2 Cover - Tab
3 Modular Unit
4 Wire Harness - Above Cover
5 Fuel Tank
6 Tank Isolation Strips (3)
7 Rubber Isolator

Modular fuel sender assembly

HEATER

Blower Motor
REMOVAL AND INSTALLATION

1982-91

1. Disconnect the negative battery cable.
2. Disconnect the electrical connections at the blower motor and blower resistor.
NOTE: *On the 3.1L engine remove the tower to tower brace assembly.*
3. On models through 1989, remove the plastic water shield from the right side of the cowl.
4. Remove the blower motor retaining screws and then pull the blower motor and cage out.
5. Hold the blower motor cage and remove the cage retaining nut from the blower motor shaft.
6. Remove the blower motor and cage.
To install:
7. Install the cage on the new motor.
8. Check that the retaining nut is on tight, the motor rotates and the fan cage is not interferring with the motor.
9. Install the motor in the heater assembly (install tower to tower brace assembly if neceesary) connect the wiring and check the motor operation in all speeds.

1992
2.0L AND 2.2L ENGINES

1. Disconnect the negative battery cable.
2. Mark and remove the electrical connections at blower motor.

1. Heater case air inlet asm.
2. Stud dash panel
3. Locating studs dash panel
4. Heater core
5. Heater module asm.
6. Module cover

Heater module and air inlet assembly—1982–87 without air conditioning

1. Heater & evaporator
2. Drain tube
3. Blower assembly

NOTICE: WHEN REMOVING THE HEATER & EVAPORATOR ASSEMBLY, PULL ASSEMBLY STRAIGHT TOWARD INTERIOR OF CAR UNTIL PLASTIC DRAIN TUBE CLEARS COWL. IF ASSEMBLY IS TILTED IN ANY DIRECTION BEFORE THE TUBE CLEARS THE COWL, THE TUBE MAY BREAK.

Heater evaporator assembly, blower assembly and air inlet installation—1982–87 with air conditioning

1. Heater module assembly
2. Inlet and blower assembly
3. 2.5 N·m (22 lbs. in.)
4. Seal
5. 3.4 N·m (30 lbs. in.)
6. Heater outlet
7. 1.4 N·m (12.5 lbs. in.)

VIEW A

Heater/evaporator module, blower and air inlet installation—1988–89 with or without air conditioning

1. Dash panel asm.
2. Module asm.
3. Gasket
4. Screw—2 N·m (20 lbs. in.)
   A. Install first
   B. Install second
   C. Install last (no sequence)
5. Nut—3 N·m (27 lbs. ft.)
6. Blower asm.
7. Gasket—air inlet

Blower case, air inlet and module assembly installation—1990–92 with or without air conditioning

3. Remove the blower motor cooling tube.

4. Remove the blower motor retaining screws. Remove the blower motor fan.

NOTE: *The blower motor and fan are serviced as an assembly.*

To install:

5. Install the blower motor and fan assembly in the correct position.

6. Install and tighten evenly the fan assembly retaining screws.

7. Install blower motor cooling tube.

8. Connect the electrical connections and reconnect the negative battery cable. Check the blower motor operation in all speeds.

3.1L ENGINE

1. Disconnect the negative battery cable.

2. Remove the tower to tower brace. Mark and remove the electrical connections at blower motor.

3. Remove the blower motor cooling tube.

4. Remove the alternator assembly-refer to the necessary service procedures.

5. Remove the blower motor retaining screws. Remove the blower motor assembly.

NOTE: *The blower motor and fan are serviced as an assembly.*

To install:

5. Install the blower motor and fan assembly in the correct position.

6. Install and tighten evenly the fan assembly retaining screws.

7. Install the alternator assembly. Adjust the drive belt.

8. Install blower motor cooling tube.

9. Connect the electrical connections and install the tower to tower brace.

10. Reconnect the negative battery cable. Check the blower motor operation in all speeds.

Heater Core

REMOVAL AND INSTALLATION

CAUTION: *When draining the coolant, keep in mind that cats and dogs are attracted by the ethylene glycol antifreeze, and are quite likely to drink any that is left in an uncovered container or in puddles on the ground. This will prove fatal in sufficient quantity. Always drain the coolant into a sealable container. Coolant should be reused unless it is contaminated or several years old.*

Cars Without Air Conditioning

1982–87

1. Disconnect the negative battery cable and drain the cooling system.

2. Remove the heater inlet and outlet hoses from the heater core.

3. Remove the heater outlet deflector.

4. Remove the retaining screws and then remove the heater core cover.

5. Remove the heater core retaining straps and then remove the heater core.

6. Installation is the reverse of removal. Refill the cooling system. Check heater system for proper operation.

1988–92

1. Disconnect the negative battery cable and drain the cooling system.

2. Raise and support the vehicle safely.

3. Disconnect the rear lateral transaxle strut mount, if equipped.

4. Disconnect the drain tube from the heater case.

5. Disconnect the heater hoses from the heater core.

6. Lower the vehicle.

7. Remove the right and left sound insulators.

8. Remove the steering column opening filler. Disconnect the heater outlet deflector (floor air outlet duct).

9. Remove the heater core cover.

10. Remove the heater core retaining straps (clamps) and remove the heater core.

To install:

11. Install the heater core and retaining straps (clamps).

12. Install the heater core cover.

13. Reconnect the heater outlet deflector (floor air outlet duct).

14. Install the right and left sound insulators. Install the steering column opening filler.

15. Raise and support the vehicle safely.

16. Connect the heater hoses (use new heater hose clamps if necessary) to the heater core.

17. Connect the drain tube to heater case.

18. Connect the rear lateral transaxle strut mount, if equipped.

19. Lower the vehicle.

20. Fill the cooling system and check for leaks. Check heater system for proper operation.

Cars With Air Conditioning

1982–87

1. Disconnect the negative battery cable and drain the cooling system.

2. Raise and support the front of the vehicle.

3. Disconnect the drain tube from the heater case.

4. Remove the heater hoses from the heater core.

5. Lower the car. Remove the right and left hush panels, the steering column trim cover, the heater outlet duct and the glove box.

6. Remove the heater core cover. Be sure to

pull the cover straight to the rear so as not to damage the drain tube.

7. Remove the heater core clamps and then remove the core.

8. Reverse the above procedure to install, charge the A/C system (refer to Chapter 1), and fill the cooling system.

1988-92

1. Disconnect the negative battery cable and drain the cooling system.

2. Raise and support the vehicle safely.

3. Disconnect the rear lateral transaxle strut mount, if equipped.

4. Disconnect the drain tube from the heater-A/C module.

5. Disconnect the heater hoses from the heater core.

6. Lower the vehicle.

7. Remove the right and left sound insulators, steering column trim cover and the heater (floor) outlet duct.

8. Remove the heater core cover and pull straight rearward.

9. Remove the heater core clamps and remove the core.

To install:

10. Install the heater core and clamps.

11. Install the heater core cover.

12. Install the heater (floor) outlet duct, steering column trim cover and the right and left sound insulators.

13. Raise and support the vehicle safely.

14. Connect the heater hoses to the heater core.

15. Connect the drain tube to the heater-A/C module.

16. Connect the rear lateral transaxle strut mount, if equipped.

17. Lower the vehicle.

18. Connect the negative battery cable.

19. Refill the cooling system. Check system for proper operation.

Control Panel

REMOVAL AND INSTALLATION

1. Disconnect the battery ground cable.

2. Remove the instrument panel trim plate.

3. Remove the control assembly retaining screws and pull the control assembly away from the instrument panel.

4. Disconnect the electrical and vacuum connectors.

5. Disconnect the temperature control cable from the control assembly and remove assembly.

6. Installation is the reverse of the removal procedure. Check system for proper operation.

1 INSTRUMENT PANEL ASM.

2 HEATER AND A/C CONTROL

3 RETAINER (PUSH IN)

Control assembly mounting

1. CLIP
2. PLIERS
3. TEMPERATURE CABLE

CORRECT CLIP GRIP FOR ADJUSTMENT

1. CLIP
2. PLIERS
3. TEMPERATURE CABLE

INCORRECT CLIP GRIP FOR ADJUSTMENT
Temperature control cable clip adjustment

Blower Switch

REMOVAL AND INSTALLATION

1. Disconnect the battery ground cable.

2. Remove the instrument panel (I/P) trim plate.

3. Remove the control assembly retaining screws and pull the control assembly away from the instrument panel.

4. Remove the blower switch knob.

5. Disconnect the electrical connector.

6. Remove the blower switch retaining screws and remove the switch.

7. Installation is the reverse of the removal procedure. Check system for proper operation.

3 BLUE - DEFROST

4 YELLOW - VENT MODE

5 RED - HEATER MODE

6 COWL

7 HEATER CONTROL ASSEMBLY

1 VIOLET - INPUT SOURCE

2 ORANGE (TAPED BACK - NOT USED)

8 CONNECTOR

Vacuum schematic Heater control assembly

1 TEMPERATURE CONTROL CABLE

2 CABLE RETAINER

3 HEATER CONTROL

4 MODE SLAVE LEVER

5 MODULE ASSEMBLY

6 DEFROST VACUUM ACTUATOR

Temperature Control cable

AIR CONDITIONER

CAUTION: *Refer to SECTION 1. Have the A/C system professionally discharged; follow all safety precautions carefully!*

Compressor

REMOVAL AND INSTALLATION

1. Disconnect the battery ground cable.
2. Drain the system of all refrigerant using an approved Recovery/Recycling system (refer to Chapter 1).
3. Remove the compressor drive belt.
4. Raise and safely support vehicle on jack stands.
5. Remove the right air deflector and splash shield.
6. Disconnect the electrical connectors at the compressor switches.
7. Disconnect the compressor/condenser

1	BRACKET
2	BRACE ASSY.
3	COMPRESSOR ASSY
4	10 N·m (88 LBS. IN.)
5	47 N·m (35 LBS. IN.)
6	82 N·m (60 LBS. FT.)
7	6 N·m (53 LBS. IN.)

Compressor mounting 3.1L V6

1	BOLT - 93 N.m (69 LBS. FT.)
2	BOLT - 31 N.m (23 LBS. FT.)
3	A/C COMPRESSOR ASSEMBLY
4	A/C COMPRESSOR BRACE
5	BOLTS - 93 N.m (69 LBS. FT.)

Compressor mounting 2.0L L4

1	STAT-O-SEAL
2	A/C COMPRESSOR - CONDENSER HOSE ASSEMBLY
3	A/C COMPRESSOR

A/C Compressor sealing washer placement

hose assembly at the rear of the compressor and discard the seals.

8. Remove the compressor attaching bolts and remove the compressor.

NOTE: *Drain the compressor oil into a measuring cup this is the amount of new compres-* *sor oil to be put into compressor upon installation.*

9. Disconnect the expansion tube. Inspect the tube for contamination or metal cuttings, clean and or replace as necessary.

To install:

10. Ensure that the compressor (new or used) is completely drained of oil. Refill the compressor with new oil the same amount that was drained.

11. Position the compressor and install the attaching bolts.

12. Connect the condensor/compressor hose assembly at the rear of compressor using new sealing washers that don't need to be lubricated.

13. Connect the electrical connectors to the compressor clutch.

14. Install the drive belt and adjust as necessary.

15. Install the right air deflector and splash shield.

16. Lower the vehicle and connect the battery ground cable.

17. Evacuate, charge and leak test the A/C system (refer to Chapter 1).

Condenser

REMOVAL AND INSTALLATION

NOTE: *On some vehicles some steps can be omitted due different body styles and or vehicle options-modify the service procedure steps as necessary. Review the complete service procedure before starting this repair.*

1. Disconnect the battery ground cable.

2. Drain the system of all refrigerant using an approved Recovery/Recycling system (refer to Chapter 1).

NOTE: *On models so equipped, manually open headlamp doors (make sure negative battery cable is disconnected) by turning headlamp door actuator knob. Remove the 4 retaining bolts from the headlamp door actuators and pull actuator assemblies forward as far as possible. Remove the hood latch release cable and front end panel center brace.*

3. Remove the right and left headlight trim.

4. Remove the center grille assembly.

5. Remove the right and left headlight housing.

6. Remove the hood bracket and latch assembly.

7. Disconnect the refrigerant lines from the condenser and discard the O-ring seals.

8. Remove the condenser air deflector shield if so equipped.

9. Remove the condenser mounting brackets and remove the condenser.

To install:

10. Position the condenser in vehicle and install the mounting brackets.

11. Install the condenser air deflector shield if so equipped.

12. Connect the refrigerant lines to the condenser using new O-ring seals.

NOTE: *If necessary, install headlight actuator assemblies. Install the front end panel center brace and the hood latch release cable.*

13. Install the hood latch and bracket assembly.

14. Install the headlight housings, center grille assembly, and headlight trim.

15. Connect the battery ground cable.

16. Evacuate and charge the A/C system (refer to Chapter 1).

Evaporator Core

REMOVAL AND INSTALLATION

CAUTION: *When draining the coolant, keep in mind that cats and dogs are attracted by the ethylene glycol antifreeze, and are quite likely to drink any that is left in an uncovered container or in puddles on the ground. This*

1	CONDENSER ASM.
2	BOLT/SCREW - FULLY DRIVEN, SEATED AND NOT STRIPPED
3	BRACKET ASM.
4	RETAINER
5	INSULATOR
6	NUT

VIEW A

Condensor mounting

will prove fatal in sufficient quantity. Always drain the coolant into a sealable container. Coolant should be reused unless it is contaminated or several years old.

1982-87

1. Disconnect the negative battery cable and discharge the A/C system and recycle the refrigerent in an approved container.
2. Jack up the car and support it safely.
3. On the 1987 Sunbird, remove the bolts to the transaxle support (automatic only).
4. On the 1987 Firenza, disconnect the rear lateral transaxle strut mount, if equipped.
5. Disconnect the heater hoses and evaporator lines at the heater core and evaporator core.
6. Remove the drain tube.
7. Remove the right hand and left hand hush panels, steering column trim cover, heater outlet duct and glove box.
8. Remove the heater core cover by pulling straight rearward on the cover to avoid breaking the drain tube.
9. Remove the heater core clamps and remove the heater core.
10. Remove the screws holding the defroster vacuum actuator to the module case.
11. Remove the evaporator cover and remove the evaporator core.
12. To install, reposition the core (if installing new evaporator core--check refrigerant oil in system) and install the cover.
13. Install the screws holding the defroster vacuum actuator to the module case.
14. Install the heater core clamps and cover.
15. Install the right hand and left hand hush panels, steering column trim cover, heater outlet duct and glove box.
16. Install the drain tube.
17. Connect the heater hoses and evaporator lines at the heater core and evaporator core.
18. On the 1987 Firenza, connect the rear lateral transaxle strut mount, if equipped.
19. On the 1987 Sunbird, install the bolts to the transaxle support (automatic only).
20. Lower the car and charge the A/C system and fill the cooling system.

1988-89

1. Disconnect the negative battery cable and discharge the A/C system and recycle the refrigerent in an approved container.
2. Drain the cooling system.
3. Raise and support the vehicle safely.
4. Disconnect the rear lateral transaxle strut mount, if equipped.
5. Disconnect the heater hoses and evaporator lines at the heater core and evaporator core.
6. Disconnect the drain tube.

7. Lower the vehicle.
8. Remove the right and left sound insulators, steering column trim cover, the heater outlet duct and the instrument panel compartment.
9. Remove the heater core cover and pull straight rearward.
10. Remove the heater core clamps and remove the core.
11. Remove the screws holding the defroster vacuum actuator to the module case.
12. Remove the evaporator cover and the evaporator core.
To install:
13. To install, reposition the core (if installing new evaporator core--check refrigerant oil in system) and install the cover.
14. Install the screws holding the defroster vacuum actuator to the module case.
15. Install the heater core clamps and cover.
16. Install the steering column trim cover, glove box, right hand and left hand sound insulators and the heater outlet duct.
17. Install the drain tube.
18. Connect the heater hoses and evaporator lines at the heater core and evaporator core.
19. Connect the rear lateral transaxle strut mount, if equipped.
20. Evacuate and charge the A/C system.
21. Connect the negative battery cable.
22. Fill the cooling system.

1990

1. Disconnect the negative battery cable and discharge and recycle the refrigerent in an approved container.
2. Drain the cooling system.
3. Raise and support the vehicle safely.
4. Disconnect the rear lateral transaxle strut mount, if equipped.
5. Disconnect the heater hoses the heater core.
6. Disconnect the evaporator block fitting from the evaporator and discard the O-ring seals.
7. Disconnect the drain tube from the A/C module.
8. Lower the vehicle.
9. Remove the right and left sound insulators, steering column trim cover and the floor air outlet duct.
10. Remove the heater core cover and pull straight rearward.
11. Remove the heater core clamps and remove the core.
12. Remove the screws holding the defroster vacuum actuator to the module case.
13. Remove the evaporator cover and the evaporator core.

To install:

14. To install, reposition the core (if installing new evaporator core--check refrigerant oil in system) and install the cover.
15. Install the screws holding the defroster vacuum actuator to the module case.
16. Install the heater core clamps and cover.
17. Install the floor air outlet duct, steering column trim cover and the right hand and left hand sound insulators.
18. Raise and support the vehicle safely.
19. Install the drain tube.
20. Connect the heater hoses at the heater core.
21. Connect the evaporator block fitting to the evaporator, using new O-ring seals lubricated in clean 525 refrigerent oil.
22. Connect the rear lateral transaxle strut mount, if equipped.
23. Evacuate and charge the A/C system.
24. Connect the negative battery cable.
25. Fill the cooling system.

1991–92

1. Disconnect the negative battery cable and discharge and recycle the refrigerent in an approved container.
2. Drain the cooling system.
3. Raise and support the vehicle safely.
4. Disconnect the heater hoses the heater core.
5. Disconnect the evaporator block fitting from the evaporator and discard the O-ring seals.
6. Disconnect the drain tube from the heater-A/C module.
7. Lower the vehicle.
8. Remove the right and left sound insulators, steering column trim cover and the floor air outlet duct.
9. Remove the heater core cover and pull straight rearward.
10. Remove the heater core clamps and remove the core.
11. Remove the screws holding the defroster vacuum actuator to the module case.
12. Remove the evaporator cover and the evaporator core.

To install:

13. To install, reposition the core (if installing new evaporator core--check refrigerant oil in system) and install the cover.
14. Install the screws holding the defroster vacuum actuator to the module case.
15. Install the heater core clamps and cover.
16. Install the floor air outlet duct, steering column trim cover and the right hand and left hand sound insulators.
17. Raise and support the vehicle safely.
18. Install the drain tube.

19. Connect the heater hoses at the heater core.
20. Connect the evaporator block fitting to the evaporator, using new O-ring seals lubricated in clean 525 refrigerent oil.
21. Evacuate and charge the A/C system.
22. Connect the negative battery cable.
23. Fill the cooling system.

Control Panel

REMOVAL AND INSTALLATION

1. Disconnect the battery ground cable.
2. Remove the steering column opening filler panel.
3. Remove the cigar lighter and control assembly trim plate.
4. Remove the control assembly retaining screws and pull the control assembly rearward.
5. Disconnect the electrical and vacuum connectors. Disconnect the temperature control cable from the control assembly and remove assembly.
6. Installation is the reverse of the removal procedure. Check heater-A/C system for proper operation.

Blower Switch

REMOVAL AND INSTALLATION

1. Disconnect the battery ground cable.
2. Remove the instrument panel (I/P) trim plate.
3. Remove the control assembly retaining screws and pull the control assembly away from the instrument panel.
4. Remove the blower switch knob.
5. Disconnect the electrical connector.
6. Remove the blower switch retaining screws and remove the switch.
7. Installation is the reverse of the removal procedure. Check system for proper operation.

RADIO

Radio Assembly

REMOVAL AND INSTALLATION

1982–87

WARNING: *Do not operate the radio with the speaker leads disconnected. Operating the radio without an electrical load will damage the output transistors.*

1. Disconnect the negative battery cable.
2. Remove the instrument panel trim plate.
3. Check the right side of the radio to determine whether a nut or a stud is used for side retention.
4. If a nut is used, remove the hush panel

1. Radio
2. Screw on side of radio fits here
3. Retainer
4. Grille
5. Speaker
6. Frt speaker assembly
7. Frt speaker assembly
8. Rear speaker wire
9. Antenna
10. Rear speakers
11. Front speakers
12. I.P. harness
13. Receiver asm.
14. I.P. harness

Radio installation details—1982–87

and then loosen the nut from below on cars without air conditioning. On cars with air conditioning, remove the hush panel, the A/C duct and the A/C control head for access to the nut. Do not remove the nut; loosen it just enough to pull the radio out. If a rubber stud is used, go on to Step 5.

5. Remove the two radio bracket-to-instrument panel attaching screws. Pull the radio forward far enough to disconnect the wiring and antenna and then remove the radio.

6. Installation is the reverse of removal.

1988–92 Except
1989–92 Sunbird

1. Disconnect the negative battery cable.
2. Remove the instrument panel cluster or console trim plate.

1. Radio
2. Screw on side of radio fits here
3. Retainer
4. Grille
5. Speaker
6. Frt speaker assembly
7. Frt speaker assembly
8. Rear speaker wire
9. Antenna
10. Rear speakers
11. Front speakers
12. I.P. harness
13. Receiver asm.
14. I.P. harness

Radio installation—1988–90 Cavalier except Z24 and RS models

1. Instrument panel
2. Nut—2.8 N·m (25 lbs. in.)
3. Bolt
4. Radio asm.
5. Retainer—2.8 N·m (25 lbs. in.)
6. Bracket, I.P. accessory

Radio installation—1988–90 Cavalier Z24 and RS models

1. Retainer
2. Console asm.
3. AM—FM radio/cassette tape deck or compact disk player
4. Radio to console bracket
5. Screw—1.4 N·m (12 lbs. in.)
6. Nut—3 N·m (27 lbs. in.)
7. Threaded clip-on stud

Radio installation—1991–92 Cavalier

3. Remove the radio to instrument panel attaching screws or nuts.

4. Pull the radio out far enough to disconnect the wiring harness and antenna and remove the radio.

To install:

5. Reposition the radio and connect the wiring harness and antenna.

6. Install the radio retaining screws or nuts.

7. Install the instrument panel cluster or console trim plate.

8. Connect the negative battery cable.

Radio Reciever

REMOVAL AND INSTALLATION

1989–92 Sunbird

1. Disconnect the negative battery cable.

2. Remove the right instrument panel sound insulator.

3. Remove the nut from the bottom of the reciever securing the reciever to the duct.

4. Disconnect the electrical connector and remove the reciever.

To install:

5. Reposition the reciever and install the nut to the bottom.

6. Install the electrical connector.

7. Install the right instrument panel sound insulator.

8. Connect the negative battery cable.

Radio Control Assembly

REMOVAL AND INSTALLATION

1989–92 Sunbird

1. Disconnect the negative battery cable.

2. Remove the steering column closeout.

3. Remove the right instrument panel trim plate.

4. Remove the 2 screws from the top of the radio control assembly and pull rearward to remove.

5. Disconnect the electrical connector and remove the radio control assembly.

To install:

6. Connect the electrical connector.

7. Install the control assembly into the instrument panel and install the 2 screws.

8. Install the right instrument panel trim plate.

9. Install the steering column closeout.

10. Connect the negative battery cable.

1. Instrument panel asm.
2. Radio control asm.
3. To receiver asm.
4. Air distributor asm.
5. Retainer
6. Stud
7. Radio receiver
8. Nut—9 N·m (6 lbs. ft.)
9. Compact disk lead
10. Lead from compact disk player or cassette player
11. To radio control asm.
12. Tape player/compact disk player wiring harness

Radio receiver mounting—1988–92 Sunbird

1. Instrument panel asm.
2. Screw—fully driven, seated and not stripped
3. Radio control asm.

Radio control mounting—1988–92 Sunbird

1	SPEAKER
2	RETAINING TABS
3	COVER RETAINING SCREW (2)
4	SPEAKER COVER
5	SPEAKER MOUNT BRACKET
6	SPRING HOOK

Rear deck speaker assembly

1	SPEAKER
2	RETAINING TABS
5	SPEAKER MOUNT BRACKET
6	SPRING HOOK
7	RETAINING SLOTS
8	SPRING HOOK RETAINER
9	REAR SPEAKER WIRE HARNESS CONNECTOR

Rear deck speaker mounting

Speakers

REMOVAL AND INSTALLATION

Front Mounted

1. Pry gently upwards on the speaker grille with a screwdriver and remove the grille.

2. Remove the two screws retaining the speaker to instrument panel and pull speaker out.

3. Disconnect the wiring connector.

4. Installation is the reverse of the removal procedure, ensuring that the speaker grille cover snaps snugly into place.

Rear Mounted 2- and 4-Door Models

1. Open deck lid.

2. Remove the speaker cover retaing screws and remove the cover.

3. Disconnect the wiring harness connector.

4. Disconnect the spring hook from the spring retainer.

5. Disconnect the speaker retaining tabs from the retaining slots and remove the speaker.

6. Installation is the reverse of the removal procedure.

1	SPEAKER WIRE HARNESS CONNECTOR	3	RETAINING SCREWS (8)
2	SPEAKER GASKET (2)	4	SPEAKER (2)

Rear gate speakers (station wagon)

Rear Mounted Station Wagon

1. Remove the lift gate trim finishing panel.
2. Remove the speaker retaining screws.
3. Disconnect the wiring harness connector.
4. Remove the speakers.
5. Installation is the reverse of the removal procedure.

WINDSHIELD WIPERS

Blade and Arm

REPLACEMENT

Wiper blade refill replacement procedures are detailed in Chapter 1.

NOTE: *Removal of the wiper arms requires the use of a special tool, G.M. J8966 or its equivalent. Versions of this tool are generally available in auto parts stores.*

1. Insert the tool under the wiper arm and lever the arm off the shaft.
2. Disconnect the washer hose from the arm (if so equipped). Remove the arm.
3. Installation is the reverse of removal.

The proper park position is at the top of the blackout line on the glass. If the wiper arms and blades were in the proper position prior to removal, adjustment should not be required.

ADJUSTMENT

The only adjustment for the wiper arms is to remove an arm from the transmission shaft, rotate the arm the required distance and direction and then install the arm back in position so it is in line with the blackout line on the glass. The wiper motor must be in the park position.

The correct blade-out wipe position on the driver's side is 28mm from the tip of the blade to the left windshield pillar moulding. The correct blade-down wipe position on the passenger side of the car is in line with the blackout line at the bottom of the glass.

Remove the wiper arm with the special tool

Windshield wiper arm installation details

Linkage

REMOVAL AND INSTALLATION

1. Remove the wiper arms.
2. Remove the shroud top vent grille.
3. Loosen (but do not remove) the drive link-to-crank arm attaching nuts.
4. Unscrew the linkage-to-cowl panel retaining screws and remove the linkage.
5. Installation is the reverse of removal. Torque the attaching screws and nuts to 64 inch lbs. (7 Nm).

Wiper Motor

REMOVAL AND INSTALLATION

1. Remove the wiper arm and blade assemblies. Remove the shroud top vent grille. Loosen (but do not remove) the drive link-to-crank arm attaching nuts and detach the drive link from the motor crank arm.
2. Tag and disconnect all electrical leads from the wiper motor.
3. Unscrew the mounting bolts, rotate the motor up and outward and remove it.
4. Guide the crank arm through the opening in the body and then tighten the mounting bolts to 4-6 ft. lbs.
5. Install the drive link to the crank arm with the motor in the park position.
6. Installation of the remaining components is the reverse of removal.

Rear Window Wiper Motor

REMOVAL AND INSTALLATION

Station Wagon

1. Turn the ignition switch OFF.
2. Pull the wiper arm from the pivot shaft.

Wiper motor and transmission (linkage) assembly

1 WIRING HARNESS

2 WASHER PUMP

3 WASHER HOSES

4 GASKET

5 WASHER RESERVOIR

Washer pump and reservoir (typical)

3. Remove the pivot shaft nut and spacers.

4. Open the tailgate and remove the inner trim panel.

5. Remove the license plate housing.

6. Disconnect the license plate light wiring.

7. Disconnect the wiper motor wiring.

8. Remove the linkage arm locking clip, pry off the arm and remove the linkage.

9. Remove the motor and bracket attaching screws and remove the motor.

10. Installation is the reverse of removal.

Washer Pump

REPLACEMENT

1. Drain washer fluid from the washer reservoir.

2. Remove the electrical connection and washer hoses.

3. Remove the washer reservoir.

4. Remove the washer pump from the washer reservoir.

5. Installation is the reverse of removal. Make sure washer pump is pushed all the way into the washer reservoir gasket.

INSTRUMENTS AND SWITCHES

Instrument Cluster

REMOVAL AND INSTALLATION

Cavalier

1982-90

1. Disconnect the negative battery cable.

2. Remove the speedometer cluster trim plate.

3. Remove the speedometer cluster attaching screws.

1. Inst. pnl. carrier
2. I.P. cluster

Base instrument panel and cluster installation—1982–88 Cavalier shown, other models similar

ELECTRONIC
INSTRUMENT
CLUSTER

Electronic instrument panel cluster installation—1985–90 Cavalier shown

4. Lower the steering column. Pull the cluster away from the instrument panel and disconnect the speedometer cable.

5. Disconnect the vehicle speed sensor connector from the cluster. Disconnect all other electrical connectors as required.

6. Remove the cluster housing from the vehicle.

7. Installation is the reverse of the removal procedure.

1991–92

1. Disconnect the negative battery cable.

2. Remove the 4 screws from the steering column opening filler and remove the steering column opening filler.

3. Pull down slightly on the steering column collar to gain access and remove the 2 screws from the bottom of the cluster extension and remove the extension.

4. Disconnect the electrical connectors from the instrument panel dimmer and interior lamp control switches.

5. Remove the 2 screws from the top of the cluster and pull the cluster rearward to remove.
To install:

6. Reposition the cluster and install the 2 screws to the top of the cluster.

7. Connect the electrical connectors to the

1. Socket
2. Bulb
3. Cluster asm.
4. Trim plate
5. Bracket
6. Screw
7. Lens

Disassembled view of the gage instrument panel cluster—1988–90 Cavalier

1. Instrument panel
2. Cluster, instrument
3. Screw—1.4 N·m (12 lbs. in.)

Base instrument panel cluster installation—1989–90 Cavalier

Instrument panel gage cluster installation—1989–90 Cavalier

instrument panel dimmer and interior lamp control switches.

8. Reposition the cluster extension and install the 2 screws to the bottom of the cluster extension.

9. Reposition the steering column opening filler and install the 4 retaining screws.

10. Connect the negative battery cable.

1. Instrument panel
2. Screw—2 N·m (19 lbs. in.)
3. I.P. cluster asm.

Instrument panel cluster installation—1991–92 Cavalier

Cimarron
1982-88

1. Disconnect the negative battery cable.
2. Remove the speedometer cluster trim plate.
3. Remove the speedometer cluster attaching screws.
4. Lower the steering column. Pull the cluster away from the instrument panel and disconnect the speedometer cable.
5. Disconnect the vehicle speed sensor connector from the cluster. Disconnect all other electrical connectors as required.
6. Remove the cluster housing from the vehicle.
7. Installation is the reverse of the removal procedure.

Sunbird
1982-88

1. Disconnect the negative battery cable.
2. Remove the speedometer cluster trim plate.
3. Remove the speedometer cluster attaching screws.
4. Lower the steering column. Pull the cluster away from the instrument panel and disconnect the speedometer cable.
5. Disconnect the vehicle speed sensor connector from the cluster. Disconnect all other electrical connectors as required.
6. Remove the cluster housing from the vehicle.
7. Installation is the reverse of the removal procedure.

1989-92

1. Disconnect the negative battery cable.
2. Remove the speedometer cluster trim plate.
3. Remove the 4 speedometer cluster attaching screws.
4. Remove the steering column opening filler cover which is retained by spring clips.

1. Instrument panel
2. Cluster trim plate
3. Interior lamp switch connector
4. Screw 2 N·m (19 lbs. in.)
5. I.P. lamp dimmer switch connector

Instrument panel cluster extension installation—1991–92 Cavalier

1. Instrument panel asm.
2. Cluster asm., I.P.
3. Screw—1.4 N·m (12 lbs. in.)

Instrument panel cluster installation—1989–92 Sunbird

5. Pull the cluster away from the instrument panel and disconnect the speedometer cable.

6. Disconnect all other electrical connectors as required.

7. Remove the instrument cluster from the vehicle.

8. Installation is the reverse of the removal procedure.

Skyhawk and Firenza

1. Disconnect the negative battery cable.

2. Remove the steering column trim cover. Remove the left and right hand trim cover.

3. Remove the cluster trim cover.

4. Remove the screws attaching the lens and bezel to the cluster carrier.

5. Lower the steering wheel column by removing the 2 upper steering column attaching bolts.

6. Remove the screws attaching the cluster housing to the cluster carrier. Pull the cluster out slightly from the instrument panel and disconnect the speedometer cable. Disconnect all others connectors.

7. Remove the cluster housing from the vehicle.

8. Installation is the reverse of the removal procedure.

NOTE: *Some 1987–88 Firenza vehicles, equipped with manual control air conditioning, may exhibit metallic rattle or buzzing noise coming from the center of the instrument panel. Under certain road or engine load conditions, with the air conditioning ON, the metal defroster valve in the air conditioning module assembly may vibrate against the case causing the noise. The noise may be heard in all modes except defrost.*

Wiper Switch

REMOVAL AND INSTALLATION

**All Models Except
1989–92 Sunbird
1991–92 Cavalier And
Dash Mounted Type Switch**

STANDARD STEERING COLUMNS

Remove the ignition and dimmer switch as outlined in Chapter 8 and remove the parts as shown in the illustration to remove the wiper switch.

1. Switch, wash/wipe
2. Screw, switch
3. Cover, strg col., upper
4. Nut, hexagon
5. Ring, retaining
6. Cam, orientation plate
7. Cam asm, turn signal cancelling
8. Spring, upper strg shaft
9. Washer, thrust
10. Screw, hex hd tapping
11. Ring, retaining
12. Bearing asm
13. Bolt, shear
14. Washer, shear bolt
15. Housing, steering column
16. Jacket asm, steering column
17. Bushing asm, strg col jacket
18. Switch, turn signal

19. Lock cyl asm, ign switch &
20. Switch asm, ignition
21. Screw, ign switch
22. Screw, pan head 6-lobed
23. Nut, spring (U-type)
24. Cover, strg col, lower
25. Shaft asm, steering column
26. Screw, pan head 6-lobed

Disassembled view of the standard steering column, showing the wipe/wash switch installation—1991–92 Cavalier

1. Switch, wash/wipe
2. Screw, switch
3. Cover, strg col, upper
4. Nut, hexagon
5. Ring, retaining
6. Cam, orientation plate
7. Cam asm, turn signal cancelling
8. Spring, upper bearing
9. Seat, inner race

10. Race, inner
11. Bolt, shear
12. Washer, shear bolt
13. Housing asm, steering column
14. Pin, pivot
15. Lock cyl asm, ign switch &
16. Switch asm, ignition
17. Screw, ign switch
18. Switch, wire support

19. Support, wire
20. Lever, tilt
21. Spring, wheel tilt
22. Retainer, spring
23. Switch, turn signal
24. Screw, pan head 6-lobed
25. Nut, spring (U-type)
26. Cover, strg col, lower
27. Screw, pan head 6-lobed

Disassembled view of the tilt steering column, showing the wipe/wash switch installation—1991–92 Cavalier

1. Instrument panel assembly
2. Screw—fully driven, seated and not stripped
3. Switch, windshield wiper
4. Housing, windshield wiper switch
5. Rear window defogger/convertible top switch

Wiper switch installation—1989–92 Sunbird

ADJUSTABLE STEERING COLUMNS

The wiper switch is located inside the steering column cover. To gain access to the switch the steering wheel, turn signal switch and ignition lock will have to be removed. (Refer to Chapter 8 for these procedures). Remove the parts in the illustration, drive out the pivot pin with a punch and remove the switch.

1989–92 Sunbird

1. Disconnect the negative battery cable.
2. Remove the right side trim plate from the instrument panel.
3. Remove the windshield wiper switch housing attaching screw.
4. Disconnect the switch wiring harness connector and remove the switch.

Front and rear windshield wiper/washer and defogger switch

To install:

5. Connect the switch wiring harness connector.

6. Reposition the switch to the to the instrument panel and install the attaching screw.

7. Install the right side trim plate to the instrument panel.

8. Connect the negative battery cable.

1991–92 Cavalier

1. Disconnect the negative battery cable.

2. Remove the pad and horn lead, retainer and nut and remove the steering wheel from the column, using a suitable puller.

3. Remove the 2 lower column cover retaining screws.

4. Remove the 3 bottom retaining screws from lower column cover.

5. Separate the rose bud fastener (integral to wire harness) from the jacket assembly.

6. Remove the wipe/wash switch retaining screws.

7. Depress the locking tab and remove the wire harness connector from the switch and remove the wipe/wash switch.

8. Installation is the reverse of removal. Torque the cover and switch retaining screws to 49 inch lbs. (5.5 Nm) and the steering wheel retaining nut to 30 ft. lbs. (41 Nm).

Dash Mounted Type Switch

1. Disconnect the negative battery cable.

2. Pull out the right pad trim plate.

3. Remove the 2 screws securing the switch to the trim plate.

4. Disconnect the switch electrical connection and remove the switch.

To install:

5. Connect the switch electrical connector.

6. Install the 2 screws securing the switch to the trim plate.

7. Install the right pad trim plate.

8. Connect the negative battery cable.

Wiper switch and related parts, adjustable steering column—except 1989–92 Sunbird and 1991–92 Cavalier

Wiper switch and related parts, standard steering column—except 1989–92 Sunbird and 1991–92 Cavalier

Headlight Switch

REMOVAL AND INSTALLATION

1982–90 All Cavalier except
1985–87 Cavalier Type 10
1988 RS and Z24
1989–90 Z24

1. Disconnect the negative battery cable.
2. Pull the knob out fully, remove the knob from the rod by depressing the retaining clip from the underside the knob.
3. Remove the trimplate.
4. Remove the switch by removing the nut, rotating the switch 180°, then tilting forward and and pulling out. Disconnect the wire harness.
5. Reverse the above to install.

1985–87 Cavalier Type 10
1988 RS and Z24
1989–90 Z24

1. Disconnect the negative battery cable.
2. Pull out the left pad trim plate.

1. Instrument panel
2. Retainer (part of switch asm.)
3. Switch panel asm., headlamp

Headlamp switch installation—1985–87 Cavalier Type 10, 1988 RS and Z24 and 1989–90 Z24

3. Remove the 2 screws securing the switch to the trim plate.
4. Disconnect the switch electrical connection and remove the switch.

To install:

5. Connect the switch electrical connector.
6. Install the 2 screws securing the switch to the trim plate.
7. Install the left pad trim plate.
8. Connect the negative battery cable.

1991–92 Cavalier

NOTE: *On these models the headlamp/parking lamp switch is a rotating switch, located on the left steering column lever, along with the cruise control and turn signal. Please refer to the Turn Signal Switch removal procedure in Chapter 8.*

1. Switch assembly, headlamp
2. Nut
3. Knob assembly

Headlamp switch installation—1982–90 Cavalier with base instrument panel

1. Instrument panel asm.
2. Bolt/screw—fully driven, seated and not stripped
3. Headlamp/foglamp switch asm.
4. Screw—fully driven, seated and not stripped
5. Headlamp switch panel housing

Headlamp switch installation—1989–92 Sunbird

Headlamp switch installation—1982–85 Firenza and Skyhawk

1. Plate
2. Headlamp switch
3. Dimmer switch
4. Fully driven, seated and not stripped

Headlamp switch installation—1986–89 Firenza and Skyhawk

1982–88 J2000, 2000 and Sunbird
1982–88 Cimarron
1982–87 Skyhawk

1. Disconnect the negative battery cable.
2. Pull the knob out fully, remove the knob from the rod by depressing the retaining clip from the underside the knob.
3. Remove the trimplate.
4. Remove the switch by removing the nut, rotating the switch 180°, then tilting forward and and pulling out. Disconnect the wire harness.
5. Reverse the above to install.

1982–89 Firenza
1982–89 Skyhawk
1989–92 Sunbird

1. Disconnect the negative battery cable.
2. Pull out the left pad trim plate.
3. Remove the screws securing the switch to the trim plate.
4. Disconnect the switch electrical connection and remove the switch.
To install:
5. Connect the switch electrical connector.
6. Install the screws securing the switch to the trim plate.

7. Install the left pad trim plate.
8. Connect the negative battery cable.

Clock

REMOVAL AND INSTALLATION

The clock is part of the radio. If the clock is found to be defective the radio will have to be removed and sent to an authorized facility for clock repair.

Speedometer Cable

REPLACEMENT

1. Reach behind the instrument cluster and push the speedometer cable casing toward the speedometer while depressing the retaining spring on the back of the instrument cluster case. Once the retaining spring has released, hold it in while pulling outward on the casing to disconnect the casing from the speedometer.
NOTE: *Removal of the steering column trim plate and/or the speedometer cluster may provide better access to the cable.*
2. Remove the cable casing sealing plug from the dash panel. Then, pull the casing down from behind the dash and remove the cable.
3. If the cable is broken and cannot be entirely removed from the top, support the car securely, and then unscrew the cable casing connector at the transaxle. Pull the bottom part of the cable out, and then screw the connector back onto the transaxle.
4. Lubricate the new cable. Insert it into the casing until it bottoms. Push inward while rotating it until the square portion at the bottom engages with the coupling in the transaxle, permitting the cable to move in another inch or so. Then, reconnect the cable casing to the speedometer and install the sealing plug into the dash panel.

LIGHTING

Headlights

REMOVAL AND INSTALLATION

1982–87

EXCEPT COMPOSITE HALOGEN HEADLIGHTS

1. Disconnect the negative battery cable.
2. Remove the headlamp trim panel (grille panel) attaching screws.
NOTE: *The trim panel retaining screws on the Cavalier are under the hood, on top of the front support (see illustration).*
3. Remove the four headlamp bulb retaining screws. These are the screws which hold the re-

1. Dash panel
2. Cluster asm.
3. Trans
4. Dash panel
5. Cluster asm.
6. Transducer
7. Transmission

FRT

EXCEPT CRUISE CONTROL

WITH CRUISE CONTROL

FRT

Speedometer cable disengagement at the speedometer

FERRULE-PILOTS AND SPEEDO NECK AND PROTECTS TIP

BRAID LINER AND CASING

RETAINING SPRING PUSH TO DISENGAGE

TIP

Speedometer cable disengagement at the speedometer

taining ring for the bulb to the front of the car. Do not touch the two headlamp aiming screws, at the top and side of the retaining ring, or the headlamp aim will have to be readjusted.

4. Pull the bulb and ring forward and separate them. Unplug the electrical connector from the rear of the bulb.

5. Plug the new bulb into the electrical connector. Install the bulb into the retaining ring and install the ring and bulb. Install the trim panel.

1987–92

WITH COMPOSITE HALOGEN HEADLIGHTS

CAUTION: *Halogen bulbs contain gas under pressure. Improper handling of the bulb could cause personal injury. Please note the following:*

● Turn off the lamp switch and allow the bulb to cool before changing bulbs. Leave the lamp switch **OFF** until bulb replacement.

● Wear eye protection.
● Handle the bulb by the base and avoid touching the glass.
● Keep dirt and moisture off of the bulb.
● Carefully place the old bulb in the new bulb's carton and dispose of properly.
● Keep halogen bulbs out of reach of children.

1. Open the hood.
2. Disconnect the negative battery cable.
3. Remove the socket by turning counterclockwise and pulling out.
4. Pull the bulb rearward with a vertical rocking motion.
5. With one hand, grip the wiring harness connector (not the wires). With the other hand, grip the base of the bulb (not the glass) and carefully pull the bulb base apart from the wiring harness connector.

VERTICAL ADJ. SCREW

HORIZONTAL ADJ. SCREW

Headlight aiming screw location—1982–87 without composite halogen lights

To install:

6. Carefully install the bulb socket to the lamp harness connector. Make sure the low beam connector is to the low beam lamp and the high beam connector is to the high beam lamp.

7. Align the bulb flange notch with the lamp housing keyway and insert the bulb into the lamp housing.

8. Install the socket into the housing and turn clockwise.

Signal and Marker Lights
REMOVAL AND INSTALLATION
Front Turn Signal and Parking Lights

Bulbs at the front of the car can normally be replaced from beneath the car or from under the hood. Some bulbs may require removal of the outer lens. Remove the socket from the lamp housing by twisting, then replace the bulb and reinstall the socket.

Rear Stop and turn Signal Lamps

Varoius methods are employed to remove and install the components of the tail lamp assemblies. Tail lamp bulbs can be replaced by removing the screws which retain the lamp assemblies to the rear end panel and then removing the lamp assemblies. On some models it will be necessary to remove the wing nut inside the rear compartment which retains the tail lamp to the body.

Side Marker Lights

The rear quarter or front fender side marker lamp operates in conjuction with the tail lamp circuit. Some models use a wrap around front parking or tail lamp assembly which doubles as a side marker lamp.

On some models the side marker lamp is installed from the inside of the rear compartment or front fender but is retained with screws which are installed from outside the fender or quarter panel. The bulbs on these models can be replaced by reaching behind the front fender or opening the rear compartment and turning the socket to release it from the housing and pulling the bulb out from the socket.

High Mount Stop Light
(4-Door W/O Luggage Rack)

1. Remove the two mounting screws.
2. Disconnect the electrical connector.
3. Remove the two cover screws and remove the bulb.
4. Installation is the reverse of the removal procedure.

High Mount Stop Light
(Station Wagon)

1. Remove the four mounting screws.
2. Disconnect the electrical connector.
3. Remove the two cover screws and remove the bulb.
4. Installation is the reverse of the removal procedure.

High Mount Stop Light
(With Luggage Rack or Aero Wing)

1. Remove the two cover screws and remove the bulb.

1 STOP LAMP ASSEMBLY
2 ATTACHING SCREW
3 MOUNTING BRACKET
4 WIRE HARNESS

CUTOUT IN SHELF TRIM

SHELF PANEL TRIM

High mountr stop lamp W/O luggage rack (4 door)

112   CENTER STOP LAMP
113   RETAINING SCREWS (4)
114   WIRE HARNESS CONNECTOR

115   LAMP MOUNT BRACKET
116   RETAINING SCREWS (2)

High mount stop lamp (station wagon)

1   RAIL, LUGGAGE RACK
2   HOUSING, CHMSL
3   LENS, CHMSL
4   SCREW - FULLY DRIVEN, SEATED AND NOT STRIPPED
5   BULB

High mount stop lamp bulb replacement (luggage rack)

1   REAR AERO EXTENSION
2   BULB
3   LENS
4   SCREW - FULLY DRIVEN, SEATED AND NOT STRIPPED

High mount stop lamp bulb replacement (aero wing)

1 SEAT TO BACK WINDOW
   TRIM PANEL
13 CENTER STOP LAMP
35 STOP LAMP COVER
36 RETAINING NUTS (2)
37 WIRE HARNESS CONNECTORS

High mount stop lamp W/O luggage rack (2 door)

2. Installation is the reverse of the removal procedure.

Fog Lamps

REMOVAL AND INSTALLATION

1. Remove the two screws from the lens retainers.
2. Remove the two lens retainers.
3. Remove the lens/bulb housing.
4. Disconnect the bulb retainer clip.
5. Disconnect the electrical connector and remove the bulb.
6. Installation is the reverse of the removal procedure.

TRAILER WIRING

Wiring the car for towing is fairly easy. There are a number of good wiring kits available and these should be used, rather than trying to design your own. All trailers will need brake lights and turn signals as well as tail lights and side marker lights. Most states require extra marker lights for overly wide trailers. Also, most states have recently required back-up lights for trailers, and most trailer manufacturers have been building trailers with back-up lights for several years.

Additionally, some Class I, most Class II and just about all Class III trailers will have electric brakes.

Add to this number an accessories wire, to operate trailer internal equipment or to charge the trailer's battery, and you can have as many as seven wires in the harness.

Determine the equipment on your trailer and buy the wiring kit necessary. The kit will contain all the wires needed, plus a plug adapter set which included the female plug, mounted on the bumper or hitch, and the male plug, wired into, or plugged into the trailer harness.

When installing the kit, follow the manufac-

turer's instructions. The color coding of the wires is standard throughout the industry.

One point to note, some domestic vehicles, and most imported vehicles, have separate turn signals. On most domestic vehicles, the brake lights and rear turn signals operate with the same bulb. For those vehicles with separate turn signals, you can purchase an isolation unit so that the brake lights won't blink whenever the turn signals are operated, or, you can go to your local electronics supply house and buy four diodes to wire in series with the brake and turn signal bulbs. Diodes will isolate the brake and turn signals. The choice is yours. The isolation units are simple and quick to install, but far more expensive than the diodes. The diodes, however, require more work to install properly, since they require the cutting of each bulb's wire and soldering in place of the diode.

One final point, the best kits are those with a spring loaded cover on the vehicle mounted socket. This cover prevents dirt and moisture from corroding the terminals. Never let the vehicle socket hang loosely. Always mount it securely to the bumper or hitch.

NOTE: *For more information on towing a trailer please refer to Chapter 1.*

CIRCUIT PROTECTION

Fuses

Fuses protect all the major electrical systems in the car. In case of an electrical overload, the fuse melts, breaking the circuit and stopping the flow of electricity.

If a fuse blows, the cause should be investigated and corrected before the installation of a new fuse. This, however, is easier to say than to do. Because each fuse protects a limited number of components, your job is narrowed down somewhat. Begin your investigation by looking for obvious fraying, loose connections, breaks in insulation, etc. Use the techniques outlined at the beginning of this Chapter. Electrical problems are almost always a real headache to solve, but if you are patient and persistent, and approach the problem logically (that is, don't start replacing electrical components randomly), you will eventually find the solution.

The amperage of each fuse and the circuit it protects are marked on the fusebox, which is located under the left side (driver's side) of the instrument panel.

Fusible Links

A fusible link is a protective device used in an electrical circuit. When the current increases beyond a certain amperage, the fusible metal of the wire link melts, thus breaking the electrical circuit and preventing further damage to other components and wiring. Whenever a fusible link is melted because of a short circuit, correct the cause before installing a new one.

To replace a fusible link, cut off the burned

Fusible links before and after a short circuit

Original fusible links with one wire

Original fusible links with two wires

link beyond the original splice. Replace the link with a new one of the same rating. If the splice has two wires, two repair links are required, one for each wire. Connect the new fusible link to the wires, then crimp securely.

WARNING: *Use only replacements of the same electrical capacity as the original, available from your dealer. Replacements of a different electrical value will not provide adequate system protection.*

Circuit Breakers

The headlights are protected by a circuit breaker in the headlamp switch. If the circuit breaker trips, the headlights will either flash on and off, or stay off altogether. The circuit breaker resets automatically after the overload is removed.

The windshield wipers are also protected by a circuit breaker. If the motor overheats, the circuit breaker will trip, remaining off until the motor cools or the overload is removed. One common cause of overheating is operation of the wipers in heavy snow.

Their are also circuit breakers loacted in the fuse block for power windows and an (ACC) Accessory circuit breaker for such options as pow-

A typical convenience center is located on the left side of the kick panel under the dashboard.

er seats, rear defogger, power door locks etc., located in the fuse box.

Flashers

The hazard flasher is located in the convenience center', under the dash, on the left side kick panel. The horn relay and the buzzer assembly may be found here also. The turn signal flasher is installed in a clamp attached to the base of the steering column support inside the car. In all cases, replacement is made by unplugging the old unit and plugging in a new one.

VIEW A

VIEW B

1.	SCREW - 2 N.m (19 LBS. IN.)	7.	I/P HARNESS CONNECTOR
2.	CONVENIENCE CENTER	8.	BOLT - 7 N.m (62 LBS. IN.)
3.	RETAINER	9.	FLASHER ASM. HAZARD
4.	I/P HARNESS	10.	HORN RELAY
5.	BRACKET	11.	MULTI-FUNCTION ALARM
6.	NUT		

Convenience center (late model)

1 TURN SIGNAL FLASHER
2 TURN SIGNAL FLASHER CONNECTOR
3 I.P. GROUND LEAD
4 I.P. LAMP DIMMER MODULE CONNECTOR
5 I.P. REMOTE LAMP DIMMER MODULE

Turn signal flasher and lamp dimmer module

APPLICATION	BULB NO.	QUANTITY	RATING CANDLEPOWER
FRONT LAMPS			
Headlamp – Inner–Std.	4651	2	50 Watts
– Inner–Halogen	H4651	2	50 Watts
– Outer	4652	2	60/40 Watts
Park & Turn Signal	2057	2	32
Sidemarker	194	2	2
REAR LAMPS			
Back-up	1156	2	32
License – Exc. Wagon	194	1	2
– Wagon	194	2	2
Sidemarker	194	2	2
Tail & Stop – Exc. Wagon	2057	2	2/32
Tail, Stop & Turn Signal – Wagon	2057	2	2/32
Turn Signal – Exc. Wagon	1156	2	32
High Mounted Stop – Exc. Conv. and Hatchback	1156	1	32
– Convertible	889	1	–
– Hatchback	906	4	6
INTERIOR ILLUMINATION			
A/C – Heater Control	168	1	3
Ash Tray	168	1	3
Auto Trans	168	1	3
Courtesy Lamp	906	2	6
Dome Lamp Std.	561	1	12
Dome & Reading – Dome	562	1	6
– Reading	90	1	6
Glove Box	194	1	2
Instrument Cluster	194/168	2/4	2/3
Luggage/Cargo – Exc. Wagon	1003	1	15
– Wagon	561	1	12
Radio Dial	194	1	2
Underhood Lamp	93	1	15
WARNING LIGHTS & INDICATORS			
Brake	194	1	2
Service Engine Soon	168	1	3
High Beam	194	1	2
Oil Pressure	194	1	2
Seat Belt	168	1	3
Tailgate Ajar	194	1	2
Door Ajar	194	1	2
Temperature	194	1	2
Turn Signal	194	2	2
Upshift	168	1	3
Volts (Battery)	194	1	2

Bulb usage chart, all models

Drive Train

7

MANUAL TRANSAXLE

Identification

Refer to Chapter 1 for a complete identification of all the types of transaxles used.

Adjustments

LINKAGE

No adjustments are possible on the 1988–92 manual transaxle shifting cables or linkage. If the transaxle is not engaging completely, check for stretched cables or broken shifter components or a faulty transaxle.

4-Speed

1982–87

1. Disconnect the negative battery cable.
2. Place the transaxle in 1st gear, then loosen the shift cable attaching nuts **E** at the transaxle lever **D** and **F**.
3. Remove the console trim plate and remove the shifter boot and retainer.
4. With the shift lever in the 1st gear position (pulled to the left and held against the stop) insert a yoke clip to hold the lever hard against the reverse lockout stop as shown in view **D**. Install a No. 22 ($^5/_{32}$ in.) drill bit into the alignment hole at the side of the shifter assembly as shown in view **C**.

Four speed shift cable adjustment—1982–87

CONTROL ASM

5/32 " DRILL BIT

TRANSAXLE ASM

CABLE A

LEVER G

CABLE B

CONTROL ASM

LOCKING PIN H

1 ST & 2ND

3 RD & 4 TH

3/16" DRILL BIT

5 TH & REV

NUT E

UNDERBODY

NUT E

VIEW B

LEVER F

2ND	N	1ST
4TH	VIEW C	3RD
REV		5TH

VIEW A

Five speed shift cable adjustment—1983–85

5. Remove the lash from the transaxle by rotating the upright select lever (lever D) while tightening the cable attaching pin nut **E**.

6. Tighten nut **E** on letter **F**.

7. Remove the drill bit and yoke at the shifter assembly, install the shifter boot and retainer and connect the negative battery cable.

8. Connect the negative batery cable.

9. Install the shifter boot and trim plate.

10. Road test the vehicle to check for good gate feel during shifting. Fine tune the adjustment as necessary.

5-Speed

1983–85

1. Disconnect the negative battery cable.

2. Place the transaxle in 3rd gear. Remove the lock pin **H** and reinstall with the tapered end down. This will lock the transaxle in 3rd gear.

3. Loosen the shift cable attaching nuts **E** at the transaxle lever **G** and **F**.

4. Remove the console trim plate and remove the shifter boot. Remove the console.

5. Install a No. 22 ($5/32$ in.) drill bit into the alignment hole at the side of the shifter assembly as shown in view **A**.

6. Align the hole in select lever (view B) with the slot in the shifter plate and install a $3/16$ in. drill bit.

7. Tighten nut **E** at levers **G** and **F**.

8. Remove the drill bits from the alignment holes at the shifter. Remove lockpin **H**.

9. Install the console, shifter boot and retainer and connect the negative battery cable.

10. Road test the vehicle to check for good gate feel during shifting. Fine tune the adjustment as necessary.

Clutch Switch

REMOVAL AND INSTALLATION

1988–92

HM–282, ISUZU AND MK7/MT5
5-SPEED

1. Disconnect the negative battery cable.

2. Disconnect the instrument panel harness from the switch.

3. Disconnect the nuts retaining the switch to the harness bracket and remove the switch.

4. Installation is the reverse of removal. Verify proper operation of the switch.

Back-up Light Switch

REMOVAL AND INSTALLATION

1982–87

1. Disconnect the negative battery cable.

2. Remove the console and replace the switch at the side of the shifter.

1. Clutch start switch
2. Nut
3. Retaining bracket
4. Mounting stud
5. Clutch pedal
assembly

Clutch start switch—Model HM-282, 5TM40, Isuzu and MK7/MT5 5-Speed

1. Back-up switch
assembly
2. Transaxle
assembly

Back-up lamp switch installation—Model HM-282 and 5TM40 5-speed

1. Detent plate	7. Transmission control shifter	11. Transmission shifter
2. Tang hole	8. Neutral start and back-up lamp switch	12. Retaining clip
3. Tang slot		13. Back-up lamp switch
4. "Neutral" notch	9. Carrier tang	
5. R	10. Park brake switch	
6. P		

Back-up lamp switch installation—1982–87

HM–282, Isuzu and MK7/MT5 5-Speed

1. Disconnect the negative battery cable.
2. Disconnect the back-up lamp connector.
3. Unscrew the back-up lamp switch assembly.

To install:

4. Install the switch with pipe sealant and tighten to 80–84 inch lbs.

5. Connect the switch electrical connector.
6. Connect the negative battery cable.

Transaxle

REMOVAL AND INSTALLATION

1982–88

NOTE: *On 1982–84 models, whenever the transaxle mount is removed, the alignment*

1. Back-up switch
assembly
2. Transaxle
assembly

Back-up lamp switch installation—Isuzu 5-Speed

Back-up lamp switch installation—MK7/MT5 5-Speed

bolt M6 × 1 × 65 must be installed in the right front engine mount to prevent power train misalignment

1. Disconnect the negative battery cable.

2. Install an engine holding bar so that one end is supported on the cowl tray over the wiper motor and the other end rests on the radiator support. Use padding and be careful not to damage the paint or body work with the bar. Attach a lifting hook to the engine lift ring and to the bar and raise the engine enough to take the pressure off the motor mounts.

NOTE: *If a lifting bar and hook is not available, a chain hoist can be used, however, during the procedure the vehicle must be raised, at which time the chain hoist must be adjusted to keep tension on the engine/transaxle assembly.*

3. Remove the heater hose clamp at the transaxle mount bracket. Disconnect the electrical connector and remove the horn assembly on 4 cyl. models.

4. Remove the transaxle mount attaching bolts. Discard the bolts attaching the mount to the side frame: New bolts must be used at installation.

5. On 1982–84 models, disconnect the clutch cable from the clutch release lever. On 1985–87

J 28467-A

1 THREAD ONTO STRUT ATTACHING BOLTS ABOVE NUTS – 3 PER SIDE

Engine support tool installation—1984–92 all engines

Securing the front engine mount—1982–84

models, disconnect the clutch slave cylinder from the transaxle support bracket and lay aside. Remove the transaxle mount bracket attaching bolts and nuts.

6. On V6 engines remove the following:

a. Remove the air intake duct from the air cleaner.

b. Remove the left fender brace.

c. Disconnect the M.A.T. sensor lead at the air cleaner.

d. Disconnect the mass air flow sensor lead.

e. Remove the PCV pipe retaining clamp from the air intake duct.

f. Remove the clamp retaining the air intake duct to the throttle body.

g. Remove the Mass Air Flow Sensor mounting boltRemove the air cleaner bracket mounting bolts at the battery tray.

h. Remove the air cleaner, mass air flow sensor and air intake duct as an assembly.

i. Remove the heat shield at the crossover pipe and remove the crossover pipe.

7. isconnect the shift cables and retaining clips at the transaxle. Disconnect the ground cables at the transaxle mounting stud.

8. Remove the four upper transaxle-to-engine mounting bolts.

9. Raise the vehicle and support it on stands. Remove the left front wheel.

10. Remove the left front inner splash shield. Remove the transaxle strut and bracket.

11. Remove the clutch housing cover bolts.

12. Disconnect the speedometer cable at the transaxle.

13. Disconnect the stabilizer bar at the left suspension support and control arm.

14. Disconnect the ball joint from the steering knuckle.

15. Remove the left suspension support attaching bolts and remove the support and control arm as an assembly.

16. Install boot protectors and disengage the drive axles at the transaxle. Remove the left side shaft from the transaxle.

17. Position a jack under the transaxle case, remove the lower two transaxle-to-engine mounting bolts and remove the transaxle by sliding it towards the driver's side, away from the engine. Carefully lower the jack, guiding the right shaft out the transaxle.

18. When installing the transaxle, guide the right drive axle into its bore as the transaxle is being raised. The right drive axle CANNOT be readily installed after the transaxle is connected to the engine. Tighten the transaxle-to-engine mounting bolts to 55 ft. lbs. Tighten the suspension support-to-body attaching bolts to 59 ft. Lbs. on 1985–87 models and 65–67 ft. lbs. on all other years. Tighten the clutch housing cover bolts to 10 ft. lbs. Using new bolts, install and tighten the transaxle mount-to-side frame to 40 ft. lbs. When installing the bolts attaching the mount-to-transaxle bracket on the 1982–84 models, check the alignment bolt at the engine mount. If excessive effort is required to remove the alignment bolt, realign the powertrain components and tighten the bolts to 40 ft. lbs., and then remove the alignment bolt.

1989–92

EXCEPT ISUZU TRANSAXLE

1. Disconnect the negative battery cable.

2. Install an engine holding support fixture (bar), J–28467–A or equivalent.

NOTE: *If a lifting bar and hook is not available, a chain hoist can be used, however, during the procedure the vehicle must be raised,*

Transaxle mounting points—1982–85 4-speed

at which time the chain hoist must be adjusted to keep tension on the engine/transaxle assembly.

3. Remove the left sound insulator.

4. Disconnect the clutch master cylinder pushrod from the clutch pedal.

5. Remove the air cleaner and air intake duct assembly.

6. Remove the clutch actuator cylinder from the transaxle support bracket and lay it aside.

7. Remove the transaxle mount through bolt.

8. Raise and support the vehicle safely.

9. Remove the exhaust crossover bolts at the right hand manifold.

10. Lower the vehicle.

11. Disconnect the transaxle mount bracket.

12. Disconnect the shift cables and linkage.

FRONT SUSPENSION SUPPORT
ATTACHING BOLT/SCREW
SEQUENCE

1. INSTALL LOOSELY, THE CENTER SCREW INTO HOLE **A**.

2. INSTALL LOOSELY, THE TIE BAR SCREW INTO THE SMALL SLOTTED OUTBOARD HOLE.

3. INSTALL AND TORQUE BOTH BOLTS IN THE REAR HOLES.

4. INSTALL AND TORQUE 2ND CENTER HOLE **D** BOLT/SCREW.

5. TORQUE CENTER HOLE **A** BOLT.

6. INSTALL OTHER TIE BAR BOLT (FRONT HOLE **E**) AND TORQUE.

7. TORQUE 2ND BOLT/SCREW IN THE (FRONT HOLE **B**).

The front suspension support must be attached in this sequence

13. Remove the transaxle mount tube.

14. Remove the upper transaxle to engine bolts.

15. Raise and support the vehicle safely.

16. Remove the left front tire and wheel.

17. Remove the left front inner splash shield.

18. Disconnect the transaxle strut and bracket.

19. Drain the transaxle.

20. Remove the clutch housing cover bolts.

21. Disconnect the speedometer cable.

22. Disconnect the stabiizer shaft at the left suspension support and control arm.

23. Remove the left suspension support attaching bolts and swing the suspension support aside.

24. Install drive axle boot protector J–34754 or equivalent and remove the left drive axle from the transaxle.

25. Attach the transaxle case to a jack.

26. Remove the ramaining transaxle to engine bolts.

27. Remove the transaxle by sliding it away from the engine and carefully lowering the jack while guiding the intermediate shaft out of the transaxle.

NOTE: *The engine may need to be lowered for transaxle to body clearance.*

To install:

28. Reposition the transaxle and guide the intermediate shaft into the transaxle.

NOTE: *The intermediate shaft cannot be easily installed after the transaxle is connected to the engine.*

29. Install the transaxle to engine mounting bolts to 55 ft. lbs (75 Nm).

30. Install the left drive axle into its bore at the transaxle and seat the driveaxle at the transaxle.

31. Remove the drive axle boot protector.

32. Install the suspension support to body bolts and tighten to 65 ft. lbs. (88 Nm).

33. Install the stabiizer shaft at the left suspension support and control arm.

34. Install the speedometer cable.

35. Install the clutch housing cover bolts and tighten to 115 inch lbs. (13 Nm).

36. Install the strut bracket to the transaxle.

37. Install the strut.

38. Install the inner splash shield.

39. Install the wheel and tighten the wheel nuts to 100 ft. lbs.

40. Lower the vehicle.

41. Install the upper engine to transaxle bolts and tighten to 55 ft. lbs. (75 Nm).

42. Install the transaxle vent tube.

43. Install the shift cables.

44. Install the transaxle mount bracket.

45. Install the left exhaust crossover bolts.

46. Raise and support the vehicle safely.

47. Install the exhaust crossover bolts at the right hand manifold.

48. Lower the vehicle.

49. Install the transaxle mount through bolt.

50. Install the clutch actuator cylinder to the transaxle support bracket.

52. Install the air cleaner and air intake duct assembly.

1	BOLT
2	TRANSAXLE ASSEMBLY
3	STUD
4	ENGINE ASSEMBLY

Transaxle to engine attachment—1989–92 Model 5TM40 and HM-282 5-Speed

53. Remove the engine holding support fixture (bar), J–28467–A or equivalent.

54. Connect the clutch master cylinder pushrod to the clutch pedal.

55. Install the left sound insulator.

56. Check the transaxle fluid level and add as necessary.

55. Connect the negative battery cable.

ISUZU TRANSAXLE

1. Disconnect the negative battery cable.

2. Install an engine holding support fixture (bar), J–28467–A or equivalent and raise the engine enough to take the pressure off the motor mounts.

3. Remove the left sound insulator.

4. Disconnect the clutch master cylinder pushrod from the clutch pedal.

5. Remove the clutch actuator cylinder from the transaxle support bracket and lay it aside.

6. Disconnect the mount harness at the mount bracket.

7. Remove the transaxle mount attaching bolts.

8. Remove the transaxle mount bracket attaching bolts and nuts.

9. Remove the shift cables and retaining clamp at the transaxle.

10. Disconnect the back-up switch connector.

11. Raise and support the vehicle safely.

12. Drain the transaxle.

13. Remove the left front wheel assembly.

14. Remove the left front inner splash shield.

15. Disconnect the transaxle strut and bracket.

16. Remove the clutch housing cover bolts.

17. Disconnect the vehicle speed sensor at the transaxle.

18. Disconnect the stabilizer shaft at the left suspension support and control arm.

19. Remove the left suspension support attaching bolts and swing the suspension support aside.

20. Install drive axle boot protector J–34754 or equivalent, disconnect the drive axles and remove the left shaft from the transaxle.

21. Attach the transaxle case to a jack.

22. Remove the transaxle to engine bolts.

23. Remove the transaxle by sliding it away from the engine and carefully lowering the jack while guiding the right drive axle out of the transaxle.

To install:

24. Reposition the transaxle and guide the right drive axle into its bore as the transaxle is being raised.

NOTE: *The right drive axle cannot be easily installed after the transaxle is connected to the engine.*

25. Install the transaxle to engine mounting bolts to 55 ft. lbs (75 Nm).

26. Install the left drive axle into its bore at the transaxle and seat both drive axles at the transaxle.

27. Remove the drive axle boot protector.

28. Install the suspension support to body bolts and tighten to 65 ft. lbs. (88 Nm).

29. Install the stabilizer shaft at the suspension support and control arm.

FRT

VIEW A

1 | BOLTS
2 | TRANSAXLE ASSEMBLY
3 | STUD
4 | BRACKET
5 | ENGINE ASSEMBLY

Transaxle to engine attachment—1989–92 Model Isuzu 5-Speed

30. Install the vehicle speed sensor at the transaxle.

31. Install the clutch housing cover bolts and tighten to 115 inch lbs. (13 Nm).

32. Install the strut bracket to the transaxle.

33. Install the strut.

34. Install the inner splash shield.

35. Install the wheel and tighten the wheel nuts to 100 ft. lbs.

36. Lower the vehicle.

37. Install the ground cables at the transaxle mounting studs.

FRT

VIEW A

1 | BOLTS
2 | TRANSAXLE ASSEMBLY
3 | STUD
4 | BRACKET
5 | ENGINE ASSEMBLY

Transaxle to engine attachment—Model MK7/MT5 5-Speed

38. Install the back-up switch connector.

39. Install the actuator cylinder to the transaxle bracket aligning the pushrod into the pocket of the clutch release lever and install the retaining nuts and tighten evenly to prevent damage to the cylinder.

40. Install the transaxle mount bracket.

41. Install the transaxle mount to side frame and install the bolts.

42. Install the wiring harness at the transaxle mount bracket.

43. Install the bolt attaching the mount to the transaxle bracket and tigten to 88 ft. lbs. (120 Nm).

44. Remove the engine holding support fixture (bar), J–28467–A or equivalent.

45. Install the shift cables.

46. Check the transaxle fluid level and add as necessary.

47. Connect the negative battery cable.

Drive Axles (Halfshafts)

These vehicles use unequal-length halfshafts. All halfshafts incorporate a male spline; the shafts interlock with the transaxle gears through the use of barrel-type snaprings. Four constant velocity joints are used, two on each shaft. The inner joints are of the double offset design; the outer joints are Rzeppa-type.

REMOVAL AND INSTALLATION

1982–86

1. Remove the hub nut.

2. Raise the front of the car. Remove the wheel and tire.

3. Install an axle shaft boot seal protector, G.M. special tool No. J–28712 or the equivalent, onto the seal.

4. Disconnect the brake hose clip from the MacPherson strut, but do not disconnect the hose from the caliper. Remove the brake caliper from the spindle, and hang the caliper out of the way by a length of wire. Do not allow the caliper to hang by the brake hose.

5. Mark the camber alignment cam bolt for reassembly. Remove the cam bolt and the upper attaching bolt from the strut and spindle.

6. Pull the steering knuckle assembly from the strut bracket.

7. Using G.M. special tool J–28468 or the equivalent, remove the axle shaft from the transaxle.

8. Using G.M. special tool J–28733 or the equivalent spindle remover, remove the axle shaft from the hub and bearing assembly.

9. If a new drive axle is to be installed, a new knuckle seal should be installed first.

10. Loosely install the drive axle into the transaxle and steering knuckle.

11. Loosely attach the steering knuckle to the suspension strut.

12. Install the brake caliper. Tighten the bolts to 30 ft. lbs. (40Nm.).

13. The drive axle is an interference fit in the steering knuckle. Press the axle into place, then install the hub nut. When the shaft begins to turn with the hub, insert a drift through the caliper into one of the cooling slots in the rotor to keep it from turning. Tighten the hub nut to 70 ft. lbs. (100Nm.). to completely seat the shaft.

14. Load the hub assembly by lowering it onto a jackstand. Align the camber cam bolt marks made during removal, install the bolt and tighten to 140 ft. lbs. (190 Nm.). Tighten the upper nut to the same value.

15. Install the axle shaft all the way into the transaxle using a screwdriver inserted into the groove provided on the inner retainer. Tap the screwdriver until the shaft seats in the transaxle.

16. Connect the brake hose clip to the strut. Install the tire and wheel, lower the car, and tighten the hub nut to 185 ft. lbs. (260 Nm).

1987–88

1. Raise the car and suitably support.

2. Remove the wheel assembly.

3. Insert a drift into the into the caliper and rotor to prevent the rotor from turning.

4. Remove the shaft nut and washer.

5. Remove the caliper from the steering knuckle and suspend the caliper assembly with a wire.

6. Remove the rotor from the hub and bearing assembly.

7. Disconnect the stabilizer shaft from the control arm.

8. Remove the ball joint from the steering knuckle.

9. Remove the drive axle from the transaxle. Remove the driveaxle from the hub and bearing assembly using tool J–28733.

To install:

10. Install the drive axle into the hub and bearing assembly and the transaxle.

11. Install the lower ball joint to the steering knuckle.

12. Install the stabilizer shaft to the control arm.

13. Install the rotor to the hub and bearing assembly.

14. Install the caliper to the steering knuckle.

15. Install a washer and a new shaft nut.

16. Insert a drift into the into the caliper and rotor to prevent the rotor from turning and torque drive axle nut to 185 ft. lbs. (260 Nm).

17. Seat the drive axle into the transaxle by

1. Hub nut
2. Washer
3. Knuckle & hub assembly
4. Drive axle—outer joint
5. Drive axle—inner joint

Drive axle removal—1987–88

placing a screwdriver into the groove on the joint housing and tapping until seated.

18. Verify that the drive axle is seated into the transaxle by grasping on the housing and pulling outward.

19. Install the wheel assembly.

20. Lower the car

1989–92

1. Raise the car and suitably support.

2. Remove the wheel assembly.

3. Install drive seal protector J34754 or equivalent, on the outer joint.

4. Insert a drift into the into the caliper and rotor to prevent the rotor from turning.

4. Remove the shaft nut and washer.

5. Remove the lower ball joint cotter pin and nut and loosen the joint using tool J 38892 or equivqlent. If removing the right axle, turn the wheel to the left, if removing the left axle, turn the wheel to the right.

6. Separate the joint, with a pry bar between the suspension support.

7. Disengage the axle from the hub and bearing using J 28733–A or equivalent.

8. Separate the hub and bearing assembly from the drive axle and move the strut and knuckkle assembly rearward.

9. Disconnect the inner joint from the transaxle using tool J–28468 or J–33008 attached to J–29794 and J–2619–01 or from the intermediate shaft (V6 and Turbo engines), if equipped.

To install:

10. Install axle seal protector J–37292–A into the transaxle.

11. Insert the drive axle into the transaxle or intermediate shaft (V6 and Turbo engines), if equipped, by placing a suitable tool into the groove on the joint housing and tapping until seated.

WARNING: *Be careful not to damage the axle seal or dislodge the transaxle seal garter spring when installing the axle.*

12. Verify that the drive axle is seated into the transaxle by grasping on the housing and pulling outward.

13. Install the drive axle into the hub and bearing assembly.

14. Install the lower ball joint to the knuckle. Tighten the ball joint to steering knuckle nut to 41 ft. lbs. (55 Nm) and install the cotter pin.

15. Install the washer and new drive shaft nut.

16. Insert a drift into the caliper and rotor to prevent the rotor from turning and tighten the drive shaft nut to 185 ft. lbs. (260 Nm).

1. Right drive axle
2. Left drive axle
3. J 28468 OR J 33008
4. J 29794
5. J 2619-01

Drive axle removal—1989–92

1. Transaxle
2. Drive axle with male splines

Transaxle seal protector installation—1989–92

17. Remove both J–37292–B and J–34754 seal protectors.
18. Install the tire and wheel assembly.
19. Lower the vehicle and connect the negative battery cable.

Intermediate shaft
REMOVAL AND INSTALLATION
2.8L and 3.1L V6 engine
1987

1. Install engine support bar J–28467.
2. Raise the car and suitably support.

3. Remove the wheel assembly.
4. Drain the transaxle.
5. Install the modified outer seal protector J–34754.
6. Remove the stabilizer shaft from the right control arm.
7. Remove the right ball joint from the knuckle.
8. Disconnect the drive axle from the intermediate axle shaft.
9. Remove the two housing to bracket bolts.
10. Remove the bottom bracket to engine bolt

1. Intermediate shaft assembly
2. Intermediate axle shaft
3. Bracket
4. Axle shaft retaining ring
5. Lip seal
6. Bolt 50 Nm (37 lbs. ft.)
7. Washer
8. Bolt 25 Nm (18 lbs. ft.)
9. Right drive axle
10. "O" ring seal

VIEW A

Intermediate shaft assembly—1987–2.8L V6 engine

and loosen the top bolt, rotate the bracket out of the way.

11. Remove the 3 bolts holding the housing to the transaxle.

12. Carefully disengage the intermediate axle shaft from the transaxle and remove the intermediate shaft assembly.

To install:

13. Place the intermediate shaft into position and lock the intermediate axle shaft into the transaxle.

14. Install the 3 bolts holding the housing to the transaxle and tighten to 18 ft. lbs.

15. Rotate the bracket into position and install the bottom bolt, tighten both bolts to 37 ft. lbs.

16. Install the two housing to bracket bolts and tighten to 37 ft. lbs.

17. Coat the splines with chassis grease.

18. Connect the drive axle to the intermediate axle shaft.

19. Connect the right ball joint to the knuckle.

20. Install the stabilizer shaft to the right control arm.

21. Install the wheel.

22. Lower the car and fill the transaxle with the proper fluid.

1988–92

1. Install engine support bar J–28467.

2. Raise the car and suitably support.

3. Remove the wheel assembly.

4. Drain the transaxle.

5. Install the modified outer seal protector J–34754.

6. Remove the stabilizer shaft from the right control arm.

7. Remove the right ball joint from the knuckle.

8. Disconnect the drive axle from the intermediate axle shaft.

9. Disconnect the rear engine mount.

10. Remove the bolt retaining the intermediate shaft to the engine.

11. Carefully disengage the intermediate axle shaft from the transaxle and remove the intermediate shaft assembly.

To install:

12. Place the intermediate shaft assembly into position and lock the intermediate axle shaft into the transaxle.

13. Install the bolt retaining the intermediate shaft to the engine and tighten to 38 ft. lbs. (52 Nm).

14. Install the rear engine mount.

15. Coat the intermediate axle shaft with chassis grease and install the intermediate axle shaft to the drive axle.

16. Install the right ball joint to the knuckle.

17. Install the stabilizer shaft to the right control arm.

18. Remove the seal protector tool.

19. Install the wheel and lower the vehicle.

1. Intermediate shaft
2. Right axle shaft
3. Engine mount
bracket
4. Bolt 52 Nm (38 lbs. ft.)
5. Bolt 62 Nm (46 lbs. ft.)

Intermediate shaft assembly—1988–90 2.8L and 3.1L V6 engine

1. Engine
2. Bolt 52 Nm (38 lbs. ft.)
3. Intermediate shaft
4. Engine mount
bracket
5. Transaxle

Intermediate shaft assembly—1991–92 3.1L V6 engine

1. Intermediate shaft
2. Right axle shaft
3. Bolt 47 Nm (35 lbs. ft.)

Intermediate shaft assembly—2.0L OHC turbo engine

20. Remove the engine support bar holding fixture.

21. Fill the transaxle with the proper fluid.

2.0L OHC Turbo Engine

1987

1. Install engine support bar J–28467.
2. Raise the car and suitably support.
3. Remove the wheel assembly.
4. Drain the transaxle.
5. Remove the stabilizer shaft from the right control arm.
6. Remove the right ball joint from the knuckle.
7. Disconnect the drive axle from the intermediate axle shaft.
8. Disconnect the detonation sensor and connection.
9. Remove the power steering pump brace.
10. Remove the 3 bolts holding the housing to the transaxle.

To install:

11. To install, place the intermediate shaft into position and lock the intermediate axle shaft into the transaxle.
12. Install the 3 bolts holding the housing to the transaxle and tighten to 18 ft. lbs.
13. Install the power steering pump brace.
14. Connect the detonation sensor.
15. Coat the splines with chassis grease.
16. Connect the drive axle to the intermediate axle shaft.
17. Connect the right ball joint to the knuckle.
18. Install the stabilizer shaft to the right control arm.
19. Install the wheel.

20. Lower the car and fill the transaxle with the proper fluid.

1988–90

1. Install engine support bar J–28467 or equivalent.
2. Raise the car and suitably support.
3. Remove the right wheel assembly.
4. Drain the transaxle.
5. Install the modified outer seal protector J–34754.
6. Remove the stabilizer shaft from the right control arm.
7. Remove the right ball joint from the knuckle.
8. Disconnect the drive axle from the intermediate axle shaft.
9. Remove the bracket to engine bolts and one stud and carefully disengage the intermediate axle shaft from the transaxle and remove the intermediate shaft assembly.

To install:

10. Place the intermediate shaft into position and lock the intermediate axle shaft into the transaxle.
11. Install the bracket to engine bolts and one stud and tighten to 35 ft. lbs. (47 Nm).
12. Coat the splines with chassis grease.
13. Connect the drive axle to the intermediate axle shaft.
14. Connect the right ball joint to the knuckle.
15. Install the stabilizer shaft to the right control arm.
16. Install the wheel.
17. Lower the car and fill the transaxle with the proper fluid.

1. C.V. joint outer race
2. C.V. joint cage
3. C.V. joint inner race
4. Space retaining ring
5. Ball (6)
6. Seal retainer
7. C.V. joint seal
8. Seal retaining clamp
9. Left hand axle shaft
10. Double-offset joint seal
11. Ball retaining ring
12. Ball (6)
13. Double-offset joint inner race
14. Double-offset joint cage
15. Double-offset joint outer race
16. Joint retaining ring
17. Double-offset joint outer race
18. Right hand axle shaft
19. Slinger

AUTOMATIC TRANSAXLE
(LH SIDE ONLY)

Disassembled view of the Double Off-Set design drive axle—1982–84

Outer Joint Assembly

REMOVAL AND INSTALLATION

1. Remove the outer joint seal as outlined earlier.

2. Using a brass drift and a hammer, lightly tap on the inner race cage until it has tilted sufficiently to remove one of the balls. Remove the other balls in the same manner.

3. Pivot the cage 90 degrees and, with the cage ball windows aligned with the outer joint windows, lift out the cage and the inner race.

4. The inner race can be removed from the cage by pivoting it 90° and lifting out. Clean all parts thoroughly and inspect for wear.

To install:

5. To install, put a light coat of the grease provided in the rebuilding kit onto the ball grooves of the inner race and outer joint.

6. Install the parts in the reverse order of removal.

NOTE: *Make sure that the retaining ring side of the inner race faces the axle shaft.*

7. Install the outer seal as outlined earlier.

Cross Groove Joint Seal

REMOVAL AND INSTALLATION

1. Cut the seal retaining clamps with a side cutter.

GENTLY TAP ON CAGE UNTIL TILTED ENOUGH TO REMOVE FIRST BALL. REMOVE OTHER BALLS IN SIMILAR MANNER.

1. Ball
2. CV joint inner race
3. CV joint cage
4. CV joint outer race

CV-joint ball removal—1990–92 Cross Groove and 1991–92 Tri-Pot Type axle

2. Separate the seal from the C/G joint race at the large diameter and slide the seal away from the joint along the axle shaft.

3. Wipe the excess grease from the C/G joint inner race.

4. Spread the ears on the retaining ring with snap ring pliers and remove the C/G joint from the axle shaft.

5. Remove the seal from the axle shaft.

6. Remove the seal from the shaft.

NOTE: *The cross-groove joint design uses precision grinding and selected dimensional component fits for proper assembly and oper-*

ation. *Due to its complexity, disassembly is not recommended.*

7. Flush the grease from the joint prior to installing a new seal.

To install:

8. Install the small retaining clamp on the neck of the new seal, but do not crimp.

9. Slide the seal onto the axle shaft and position the neck of the seal in the seal groove on the axle shaft.

10. Crimp the seal retaining clamp with J 35910 seal clamp tool or equivalent, to 100 ft. lbs. (136 Nm).

11. Place approximately half of the grease provided in the seal kit, inside the seal and repack the C/G joint with the remaining grease.

12. Push the C/G joint onto the axle shaft until the retaining ring is seated in the groove on the axle shaft.

13. Slide the large diameter of the seal over the outside of the C/G joint and locate the lip of the seal in the groove on ball retainer.

WARNING: *The seal must not be dimpled or out of shape in any way. If it is not shaped correctly, equalize pressure in the seal and reshape properly by hand.*

J 8059

1. Axle shaft
2. Race retaining ring

C/G-joint and axle separation—1990–92 Cross Groove axle

BREAKER BAR

11

9

J 35910

TORQUE WRENCH

1. Seal retaining clamp   2. Drive axle inboard seal

Seal retaining clamp installation—1990–92 Cross Groove axle

14. Crimp the seal retaining clamp with J 35910 seal clamp tool or equivalent, to 130 ft. lbs. (176 Nm).

Inner Tri-Pot Seal

REMOVAL AND INSTALLATION

1. Remove the larger seal retaining clamp from the tri-pot joint with a side cutter and discard.

WARNING: *Do not cut through the seal and damage the sealing surface of the tri-pot outer housing and triobal bushing.*

2. Remove the small seal retaining clamp from the axle shaft with a side cutter and discard.

3. Separate the seal from the trilobal tri-pot bushing at the large diameter and slide the seal away from the joint along the axle shaft.

4. Remove the tri-pot housing from the spider and shaft.

5. Spread the spacer ring with snap ring pliers and slide the spacer ring and tri-pot spider back on the axle shaft.

6. Remove the shaft retaining ring from the groove on the axle shaft and slide the spider assembly off of the shaft.

7. Check the tri-pot balls and needle rollers for damage or wear.

PIVOT CAGE AND INNER RACE AT 90° TO CENTER LINE OF OUTER RACE WITH CAGE WINDOWS ALIGNED WITH LANDS OF OUTER RACE. LIFT OUT CAGE AND INNER RACE.

3

LAND

LAND

WINDOWS

2

1. CV joint cage   2. CV joint outer race

Outer race and cage separation—1990–92 Cross Groove and 1991–92 Tri-Pot Type axle

A

1

2

C

B

1. C/V joint inner race
2. C/V joint cage
3. Rotate inner race up and out of cage
4. Cage window
5. Inner race land

Inner race and cage separation—1990–92 Cross Groove and 1991–92 Tri-Pot Type axle

1. C/G joint outer race
2. Axle shaft

C/G-joint to axle installation—1990–92 Cross Groove Type axle

5-1/4"
(133MM)

1. C/G joint outer race
2. Drive axle inboard seal
3. Seal retaining clamp

C/G-joint seal installation measurement—1990–92 Cross Groove Type axle

NOTE *Use care when handling the spider assembly as the tri-pot balls and rollers may separate from the spider trunnions.*

8. Remove the trilobal tri-pot bushing from the tri-pot housing.

9. Remove the spacer ring and seal from the axle shaft.

10. Flush the grease from the tri-pot housing.

To install:

11. Install the small retaining clamp on the neck of the new seal, but do not crimp.

12. Slide the seal onto the axle shaft and position the neck of the seal in the seal groove on the axle shaft.

13. Crimp the seal retaining clamp with J 35910 seal clamp tool or equivalent, to 100 ft. lbs. (136 Nm).

14. Install the spacer ring on the axle shaft and beyond the 2nd groove.

15. Slide the tri-pot spider asembly against the spacer ring on the shaft.

NOTE: *Make sure the counterbored face of the tri-pot spider faces the end of the shaft.*

16. Install the shaft retaining ring in the groove of the axle shaft with the snap ring pliers.

17. Slide the tri-pot spider towards the end of the shaft and reseat the spacer ring in the groove on the shaft.

18. Place approximately half of the grease provided in the seal kit, inside the seal and re-

A SLIDE SPACER RING AND SPIDER ASSEMBLY BACK ON SHAFT. REMOVE RETAINING RING AND SLIDE SPIDER ASSEMBLY OFF OF SHAFT

1. Shaft retaining ring
2. Spider assembly
3. Spacer ring
4. Axle shaft

Spider assembly removal—Tri-Pot type axle

J 35910

1. Spacer ring
2. Spider assembly
3. Axle shaft

Small seal retaining clamp installation—Tri-Pot type axle

J 8059

SLIDE SPACER RING INTO GROOVE ON AXLE SHAFT

1. Torque wrench
2. Breaker bar
3. Seal retaining clamp

Spider assembly installation—Tri-Pot type axle

1. Axle shaft
2. Tri-pot housing assembly

Tri-pot housing installation—Tri-Pot type axle

pack the tri-pot housing with the remaining grease.

19. Install the trilobal tri-pot bushing to the tri-pot housing.

20. Position the larger clamp on the seal.

21. Slide the tri-pot housing over the tri-pot spider.

A 4.9″ (125 MM)   2. Tri-pot joint seal
1. Axle shaft   3. Tri-pot housing assembly

Tri-pot seal installation—Tri-Pot type axle

J 35566

1. Seal retaining clamp

Large seal retaining clamp installation—Tri-Pot type axle

22. Slide the large diameter of the seal, with the larger clamp in place, over the outside of the trilobal bushing and loacet the lip of the seal in the bushing groove.

23. Position the tri-pot assembly at the proper vehicle dimension as shown.

WARNING: *The seal must not be dimpled or out of shape in any way. If it is not shaped correctly, equalize pressure by carefully inserting a thin flat blunt tool (no sharp edges) between the large seal opening and the bushing and reshape properly by hand.*

24. Crimp the seal retaining clamp with J 35566 seal clamp tool or equivalent.

CLUTCH

CAUTION: *The clutch driven disc contains asbestos, which has been determined to be a cancer causing agent. Never clean clutch surfaces with compressed air! Avoid inhaling any dust from any clutch surface! When cleaning clutch surfaces, use a commercially available brake cleaning fluid.*

ADJUSTMENT

All 1982–84 models have a self-adjusting clutch mechanism located on the clutch pedal, eliminating the need for periodic free play adjustments. The self-adjusting mechanism should be inspected periodically as follows:

1. Depress the clutch pedal and look for the pawl on the self-adjusting mechanism to firmly engage the teeth on the ratchet.

2. Release the clutch. The pawl should be lifted off of the teeth by the metal stop on the bracket.

On 1985 and later models, the hydraulic clutch system provides automatic clutch adjustment. No adjustment of clutch linkage or pedal position is required.

Neutral Start Switch

1982–84

A neutral start switch is located on the clutch pedal assembly; the switch prevents the engine from starting unless the clutch is depressed. If the switch is faulty, it can be unbolted and replaced without removing the pedal assembly from the car. No adjustments for the switch are provided.

Neutral Start/Back-Up Light Switch
REPLACEMENT
1985–87

1. Disconnect the negative battery cable.
2. Remove the console.
3. Disconnect the wiring, then replace the switch at the side of the shifter.
4. Installation is the reverse of removal. (See Back-up Switch removal and installation earlier in this Chapter.

Driven Disc and Pressure Plate
REMOVAL AND INSTALLATION

1. Remove the transaxle.
2. Mark the pressure plate assembly and the flywheel so that they can be assembled in the same position. They were balanced as an assembly at the factory.
3. Loosen the attaching bolts one turn at a time until spring tension is relieved.
4. Support the pressure plate and remove the bolts. Remove the pressure plate and clutch disc. Do not disassemble the pressure plate assembly; replace it if defective.
5. Inspect the flywheel, clutch disc, pressure plate, throwout bearing and the clutch fork and pivot shaft assembly for wear. Replace the parts as required. If the flywheel shows any signs of overheating, or if it is badly grooved or scored, it should be refaced or replaced.
6. Clean the pressure plate and flywheel mating surfaces thoroughly. Position the clutch disc and pressure plate into the installed position, and support with a dummy shaft or clutch aligning tool. The clutch plate is assembled with the damper springs offset toward the transaxle. One side of the factory supplied clutch disc is stamped "Flywheel Side".

VIEW A

VIEW C

CABLE
DAMPENER
GASKET
FRT
INSULATOR
WASHER
VIEW C

VIEW B

SHAFT
TRANSAXLE
ASSEMBLY
VIEW A

Clutch cable and bracket assembly—1982–84

VIEW B
SPACER
SPRING
BUMPER
PAWL
BUSHING
VIEW A
FRT
DETENT
BUSHING
SPACER
VIEW A
FRT

NEUTRAL START
SWITCH
VIEW B

Clutch pedal assembly and neutral start switch—1982–84

FLYWHEEL

DRIVEN PLATE ASSEMBLY

PRESSURE PLATE AND
COVER ASSEMBLY

CLUTCH RELEASE BEARING

TRANSAXLE

Clutch components

7. Install the pressure plate-to-flywheel bolts. Tighten them gradually in a criss-cross pattern.

8. Lubricate the outside groove and the inside recess of the release bearing with high temperature grease. Wipe off any excess. Install the release bearing.

9. Install the transaxle.

Clutch Cable
REPLACEMENT
1982–84

1. Press the clutch pedal up against the bumper stop so as to release the pawl from the detent. Disconnect the clutch cable from the release lever at the transaxle assembly. Be careful that the cable does not snap back toward the rear of the car as this could damage the detent in the adjusting mechanism.

2. Remove the hush panel from inside the car.

3. Disconnect the clutch cable from the detent end tangs. Lift the locking pawl away from the detent and then pull the cable forward between the detent and the pawl.

4. Remove the windshield washer bottle.

5. From the engine side of the cowl, pull the clutch cable out to disengage it from the clutch pedal mounting bracket. The insulators, dampener and washers may separate from the cable in the process.

6. Disconnect the cable from the transaxle mounting bracket and remove it.

7. Install the cable into both insulators, damper and washer. Lubricate the rear insulator with tire mounting lube or the like to ease installation into the pedal mounting bracket.

8. From inside the car, attach the end of the cable to the detent. Be sure to route the cable underneath the pawl and into the detent cable groove.

9. Press the clutch pedal up against the bumper stop to release the pawl from the detent. Install the other end of the cable at the release lever and the transaxle mount bracket.

10. Install the hush panel and the windshield washer bottle.

11. Check the clutch operation and adjust as detailed earlier in this Chapter.

Clutch Hydraulic System
REMOVAL AND INSTALLATION

NOTE: *The clutch hydraulic system is used on 1985 and later models and is serviced as a complete unit. It has been bled of air and filled with fluid. Individual components of the system are not available separately.*

2.0L Engine

1. Disconnect the negative battery cable.

2. Remove the hush panel from inside the vehicle.

3. Disconnect the clutch master cylinder push rod from the clutch pedal.

4. Remove the clutch master cylinder retaining nuts at the front of the dash.

Clutch hydraulic system—1985–87

1. Bolt—50 N·m (36 lbs. ft.)
2. Lever
3. Transaxle support
4. Clutch master and actuator cylinder assembly
5. Nut—23 N·m (17 lbs. ft.)
6. Actuator rod
7. Button
   Button end of strap must remain between lever and actuator rod after assembly. The straps will break on first clutch pedal application.
8. Restrictor
   Pedal restrictor should not be removed from replacement system until after slave cylinder has been attached to transaxle support.
9. Nut—22 N·m (16 lbs. ft.)
10. Clutch pedal
11. Master cylinder pushrod—lubricate before installing
12. Nut
13. Bracket

Clutch hydraulic system—1988–89

HM-282 **ISUZU** VIEW A VIEW B

1. Bolt—50 N·m (36 lbs. ft.)
2. Lever
3. Transaxle support
4. Clutch master and actuator cylinder assembly
5. Nut—22 N·m (16 lbs. ft.)
6. Actuator rod
7. Button
Button end of strap must remain between lever and actuator rod after assembly. The straps will break on first clutch pedal application.

8. Restrictor
Pedal restrictor should not be removed from replacement system until after actuator cylinder has been attached to transaxle support.
9. Nut—22 N·m (16 lbs. ft.)
10. Clutch pedal and bracket
11. Master cylinder pushrod—lubricate before installing
12. Nut

Clutch hydraulic system—1990

1. To clutch master cylinder
2. Clutch master and actuator cylinder assembly
3. Nut
4. Pushrod retainer (do not remove)

Clutch hydraulic actuator—1991–92 Model 5TM40 transaxle

5. Remove the slave cylinder (1985–87) or actuator (1988–90) retaining nuts at the transaxle.
6. Remove the hydraulic system as a unit from the vehicle.

To install:

7. Install the new slave cylinder or actuator to the transaxle support bracket aligning the push rod into the pocket on the clutch fork outer lever. Tighten the retaining nuts evenly to prevent damage to the slave cylinder. Tighten to 14–20 ft. lbs.

NOTE: *Do not remove the plastic push rod retainer from the slave or actuator cylinder. The straps will break on the first clutch pedal application.*

8. Position the clutch master cylinder to the front of the dash. Install the retaining nuts and tighten the nuts evenly to prevent damage to the master cylinder. Tighten to 15–25 ft. lbs.

9. Remove the pedal restrictor from the push rod. Lube the push rod bushing on the clutch pedal. Connect the push rod to the clutch pedal and install the retaining clip.

10. If equipped with cruise control, check the switch adjustment at the pedal bracket.

WARNING: *When adjusting the cruise control switch, do not exert an upward force on the clutch pedal pad of more than 20 lbs. or damage to the master cylinder push rod retaining ring can result.*

11. Install the hush panel.
12. Press the clutch pedal down several times. This will break the plastic retaining straps on the slave or actuator cylinder push rod. Do not

1. To clutch master cylinder
2. Clutch master and actuator cylinder assembly
3. Nut
4. Bolt—50 N•m (36 lbs. ft.)
5. Lever
6. Pushrod retainer (do not remove)
7. Nut
8. Transaxle support

Clutch hydraulic actuator—1991–92 Isuzu transaxle

remove the plastic button on the end of the push rod.

13. Connect the negative battery cable.

2.8L and 3.1L V6 Engine

1. Disconnect the negative battery cable.

2. Remove the air cleaner, mass air flow sensor and the air intake duct as an assembly.

3. Disconnect the electrical lead at the washer bottle. Remove the attaching bolts and washer bottle from the vehicle.

4. If equipped with cruise control, remove the mounting bracket retaining nuts from the strut tower.

5. Remove the hush panel from inside the vehicle.

6. Disconnect the clutch master cylinder push rod from the clutch pedal.

7. Remove the clutch master cylinder retaining nuts at the front of the dash.

8. Remove the slave or actuator cylinder retaining nuts at the transaxle.

9. Remove the hydraulic system as a unit from the vehicle.

To install:

10. Install the new slave or actuator cylinder to the transaxle support bracket aligning the push rod into the pocket on the clutch fork outer lever. Tighten the retaining nuts evenly to prevent damage to the slave cylinder. Tighten to 14–20 ft. lbs.

NOTE: *Do not remove the plastic push rod*

A. To transaxle
10. Nut
11. Clutch master and actuator cylinder assembly
12. Pedal restrictor
13. Nut
14. Clutch pedal

Clutch master cylinder and pedal—1991–92

retainer from the slave or actuator cylinder. The straps will break on the first clutch pedal application.

11. Position the clutch master cylinder to the front of the dash. Install the retaining nuts and tighten the nuts evenly to prevent damage to the master cylinder. Tighten to 15–25 ft. lbs.

12. Remove the pedal restrictor from the push rod. Lube the push rod bushing on the clutch pedal. Connect the push rod to the clutch pedal and install the retaining clip.

13. If equipped with cruise control, check the switch adjustment at the pedal bracket.

WARNING: *When adjusting the cruise control switch, do not exert an upward force on the clutch pedal pad of more than 20 lbs. or damage to the master cylinder push rod retaining ring can result.*

14. Install the hush panel.

15. Press the clutch pedal down several times. This will break the plastic retaining straps on the slave or actutator cylinder push rod. Do not remove the plastic button on the end of the push rod.

16. Install the air cleaner, mass air flow sensor and the air intake duct as an assembly.

17. Connect the negative battery cable.

Slave (Actuator) Cylinder

REMOVAL AND INSTALLATION

1990–92 With 2.3 and 3.1L Engines

1. Disconnect the negative terminal from the battery.

2. Remove the air cleaner assembly.

3. Disconnect the slave cylinder nuts at the transaxle.

4. Disconnect the quick connect fitting on the hydraulic line and remove the slave cylinder from the vehicle.

To install:

5. Connect the quick connect fitting on the hydraulic line and install the master cylinder to the vehicle.

6. Install the slave cylinder to the transaxle support bracket, aligning the pushrod into the pocket on the clutch fork lever. Tighten the retaining nuts evenly to 19 ft. lbs. (25 Nm).

7. Depress the clutch pedal several times to break the plastic retaining straps; DO NOT remove the plastic button from the end of the push rod.

8. Install the air cleaner assembly.

9. Connect the negative battery cable.

SYSTEM BLEEDING

1988–89

1. Remove any dirt or grease around the reservoir cap so that dirt cannot enter the system.

2. Fill the reservoir with an approved DOT 3 brake fluid.

3. Loosen, but do not remove, the bleeder screw on the slave cylinder.

4. Fluid will now flow from the master cylinder to the slave cylinder.

NOTE: *It is important that the reservoir remain filled throughout the procedure.*

5. Air bubbles should now appear at the bleeder screw.

6. Continue this procedure until a steady stream of fluid without any air bubbles is present.

7. Tighten the bleeder screw. Check the fluid level in the reservoir and refill to the proper mark.

8. The system is now fully bled. Check the clutch operation by starting the engine, pushing the clutch pedal to the floor and placing the transaxle in reverse.

9. If any grinding of the gears is noted, repeat the entire procedure.

NOTE: *Never under any circumstances reuse fluid that has been in the system. The fluid may be contaminated with dirt and moisture.*

1990–92

1. Disconnect the slave cylinder from the transaxle.

2. Loosen the master cylinder mounting attaching nuts. Do not remove the master cylinder.

3. Remove any dirt or grease around the reservoir cap so dirt cannot enter the system. Fill the reservoir with an approved DOT 3 brake fluid.

4. Depress the hydraulic actuator cylinder pushrod approximately 0.787 in. (20.0mm) into the slave cylinder bore and hold.

5. Install the diaphragm and cap on the reservoir while holding the slave cylinder pushrod.

6. Release the slave cylinder pushrod.

7. Hold the slave cylinder vertically with the pushrod end facing the ground.

NOTE: *The slave cylinder should be lower than the master cylinder.*

8. Press the pushrod into the slave cylinder bore with short 0.390 in. (10.0mm) strokes.

9. Observe the reservoir for air bubbles. Continue until air bubbles no longer enter the reservoir.

10. Connect the slave cylinder to the transaxle.

11. Tighten the master cylinder attaching nuts.

12. Top-up the clutch master cylinder reservoir.

13. To test the system, start the engine and push the clutch pedal to the floor. Wait 10 sec-

onds and select reverse gear. There should be no gear clash. If clash is present, air may still be present in the system. Repeat bleeding procedure.

AUTOMATIC TRANSAXLE

Identification

All of these cars use the Turbo Hydra-Matic 125C automatic transaxle as optional equipment.

On September 1, 1991, Hydra-Matic changed the name designation of the THM 125C automatic transaxle. The new name designation for this transaxle is Hydra-Matic 3T40. Transaxles built between 1989 and 1990 will serve as transitional years in which a dual system, made up of the old designation and the new designation will be in effect.

Fluid Pan and Filter

Pan removal, fluid and filter changes are covered in Chapter 1.

Adjustments

SHIFT CONTROL CABLE ADJUSTMENT

1. Place the shift lever in the **N**.
NOTE: *Neutral can be found by rotating the transaxle selector shaft counterclockwise from P through R to N.*

VIEW A

1. Spacer
2. Bracket
3. Nut—27 N·m (20 lbs. ft.)
4. Bolt—27 N·m (20 lbs. ft.)
5. Transaxle asm.
6. Nut—20 N·m (15 lbs. ft.)
7. Nut—27 N·m (20 lbs. ft.)
8. Lever
9. Cable

Engine compartment shift control

1. Nut—19 Nm (168 lbs. in.)
2. Retainer (clip)
3. Floorshift assembly
A. Lever must be held out of park when torquing nut.
   Impact type tools must not be used.

Floor shift cable routing

Throttle valve cable adjustment

VIEW A

1. Bolt 30 N·m (22 lbs. ft.)
2. Switch asm.
3. Trans. shaft
4. Service adjustment hole
5. 3/32 inch drill bit or 2.34 dia. gage pin

Neutral/back-up switch adjustment—1987–92

2. Loosely attach the cable to the transaxle shift lever with a nut. Assemble the cable to the cable bracket and to shift lever. Tighten the cable to transaxle shift lever nut.

NOTE: *The lever must be held out of P when torquing the nut.*

THROTTLE VALVE (TV) CABLE ADJUSTMENT

Setting of the TV cable must be done by rotating the throttle lever at the carburetor or throttle body. Do not use the accelerator pedal to rotate the throttle lever.

1. With the engine off, depress and hold the reset tab at the engine end of the TV cable.
2. Move the slider until it stops against the fitting.
3. Release the rest tab.
4. Rotate the throttle lever to its full travel.
5. The slider must move (racthet) toward the lever when the lever is rotated to its full travel position.
6. Recheck after the engine is hot and road test the vehicle.

Neutral Start Switch

The automatic transaxle utilizes the neutral safety switch and back-up light switch as a combined unit. This switch is located under the console, next to the shifter on 1982–86 models and on top of the of the transaxle on 1987–91 models.

REMOVAL AND INSTALLATION

1982–86

1. Disconnect the negative battery cable.
2. Remove the console and replace the switch at the side of the shifter.

1987–92

1. Disconnect the negative battery cable and the electrical connector from the switch.
2. Remove the switch-to-transaxle screws and the switch.

1. Neutral notch
2. Park notch
3. Detent plate
4. Tang slot
5. Carrier tang
6. Gage pin

Neutral switch to floor shift mounting—1982–86

1. Neutral start and back-up lamp switch
2. Switch conn.
3. "T" latch

"T" latch wiring connector used on the neutral start/back-up switch—1987–92

To install:

3. Place the transaxle's shift control lever in the N notch in the detent plate.

4. Position the switch onto the transaxle and install the screws loosely.

5. Perform a switch adjustment which follows.

6. Connect the negative battery cable.

7. Start the engine and check the switch operation.

ADJUSTMENT

1. Disconnect the negative battery cable.

2. Loosen the switch attaching screws.

3. Rotate the switch on the shifter assembly to align the service adjustment hole with the carrier tang hole.

4. Using a $3/32$ in. drill bit or gauge pin, insert it into the service adjustment hole to a depth of $5/8$ in. (15mm).

5. Tighten the switch-to-transaxle screws and remove the drill bit or gauge pin.

6. Connect the negative battery cable and test the switch operation.

Transaxle

REMOVAL AND INSTALLATION

1982–86

1. Disconnect the negative battery cable where it attaches to the transaxle.

2. On the 1982–84 models, insert a ¼ in. × 2 in. bolt into the hole in the right front motor mount to prevent any mislocation during the transaxle removal.

3. On 4-cylinder engines, remove the air cleaner.

4. On V6 engines remove the following:

   a. Remove the air intake duct from the air cleaner.

   b. Remove the left fender brace.

   c. Disconnect the M.A.T. sensor lead at the air cleaner.

   d. Disconnect the mass air flow sensor lead.

   e. Remove the PCV pipe retaining clamp from the air intake duct.

   f. Remove the clamp retaining the air intake duct to the throttle body.

   g. Remove the Mass Air Flow Sensor mounting bolt. Remove the air cleaner bracket mounting bolts at the battery tray.

   h. Remove the air cleaner, mass air flow sensor and air intake duct as an assembly.

   i. Remove the heat shield at the crossover pipe and remove the crossover pipe.

5. Disconnect the T.V. cable at the throttle body.

6. Unscrew the bolt securing the T.V. cable to the transaxle. Pull up on the cable cover at the transaxle until the cable can be seen. Disconnect the cable from the transaxle rod.

7. Remove the wiring harness retaining bolt at the top of the transaxle.

8. Remove the hose from the air management valve and then pull the wiring harness up and out of the way.

9. Install an engine support bar as shown in the illustration. Raise the engine just enough to take the pressure off the motor mounts.

CAUTION: *The engine support bar must be located in the center of the cowl and the bolts must be tightened before attempting to support the engine.*

10. Remove the transaxle mount and bracket assembly. It may be necessary to raise the engine slightly to aid in removal.

11. Disconnect the shift control linkage from the transaxle.

12. Remove the top transaxle-to-engine mounting bolts. Loosen, but do not remove, the transaxle-to-engine bolt nearest to the starter.

13. Unlock the steering column. Raise and support the front of the car. Remove the front wheels.

14. Pull out the cotter pin and loosen the castellated ball joint nut until the ball joint separates from the control arm. Repeat on the other side of the car.

15. Disconnect the stabilizer bar from the left lower control arm.

16. Remove the six bolts that secure the left front suspension support assembly.

17. Install drive axle seal protectors and connect an axle shaft removal tool (J–28468) to a slide hammer (J–23907).

18. Position the tool behind the axle shaft cones and then pull the cones out and away from the transaxle. Remove the axle shafts and plug the transaxle bores to reduce fluid leakage.

19. Remove the nut that secures the transaxle control cable bracket to the transaxle, then remove the engine-to-transaxle stud.

20. Disconnect the speedometer cable at the transaxle.

21. Disconnect the transaxle strut (stabilizer) at the transaxle.

22. Remove the four retaining screws and remove the torque converter shield.

23. Scribe a mark for on the flywheel for reassembly and remove the three bolts securing the torque converter to the flex plate.

24. Disconnect and plug the oil cooler lines at the transaxle. Remove the starter.

25. Remove the screws that hold the brake and fuel line brackets to the left side of the underbody. This will allow the lines to be moved slightly for clearance during transaxle removal.

26. Remove the bolt that was loosened in Step 12.

27. Remove the transaxle to the left.

To install:

28. Position the transaxle in the car.

29. Place a small amount of light grease on the torque converter pilot hub.

30. Make sure to properly seat the torque convertor in the oil pump.

31. Guide the right drive axle shaft into its bore as the transaxle is being raised. The right transaxle cannot be installed AFTER the transaxle is connected to the engine.

32. Lower the transaxle to the engine bolts and remove the transaxle jack.

33. Install the transaxle to engine support bracket.

34. Install the transaxle cooler lines.

35. Position the LH axle into the transaxle.

36. Install the torque converter to flywheel bolts torque to 46 ft. lbs. Re-torque the first bolt afetr all three have been tightened.

37. Install the transaxle converter shield.

38. When installing the front suspension support assembly you must follow the tightening sequence shown in the illustration at the end of Chapter 7.

39. The remainder of the installation is the reverse of removal with the following precautions.

    a. Check the suspension alignment.

    b. Check the transaxle fluid level.

1987–92

1. Disconnect the negative terminal from the battery. Remove the air cleaner, bracket, Mass Air Flow (MAF) sensor and air tube as an assembly.

2. Disconnect the exhaust crossover from the right side manifold and remove the left side exhaust manifold, then, raise and support the manifold/crossover assembly.

3. Disconnect the TV cable from the throttle lever and the transaxle.

4. Remove the vent hose and the shift cable from the transaxle.

5. Remove the fluid level indicator and the filler tube.

6. Using the engine support fixture tool J–28467 or equivalent and the adapter tool J–35953 or equivalent, install them on the engine.

7. Remove the wiring harness-to-transaxle nut.

8. Label and disconnect the wires for the speed sensor, TCC connector and the neutral safety/back up light switch.

9. Remove the upper transaxle-to-engine bolts.

10. Remove the transaxle-to-mount through bolt, the transaxle mount bracket and the mount.

11. Raise and safely support the vehicle.

12. Remove the front wheel assemblies.

13. Disconnect the shift cable bracket from the transaxle.

14. Remove the left side splash shield.

15. Using a modified halfshaft seal protector tool J–34754 or equivalent, install one on each halfshaft to protect the seal from damage and the joint from possible failure.

16. Using care not to damage the halfshaft boots, disconnect the halfshafts from the transaxle.

17. Remove the torsional and lateral strut from the transaxle. Remove the left side stabilizer link pin bolt.

18. Remove the left frame support bolts and move it out of the way.

19. Disconnect the speedometer wire from the transaxle.

20. Remove the transaxle converter cover and matchmark the converter to the flywheel for assembly.

21. Disconnect and plug the transaxle cooler pipes.

22. Remove the transaxle-to-engine support.

23. Using a transaxle jack, position and secure it to the transaxle and remove the remaining transaxle-to-engine bolts.

24. Make sure the torque converter does not fall out and remove the transaxle from the vehicle.

NOTE: *The transaxle cooler and lines should be flushed any time the transaxle is removed for overhaul or to replace the pump, case or converter.*

To install:

25. Put a small amount of grease on the pilot hub of the converter and make sure the converter is properly engaged with the pump.

26. Raise the transaxle to the engine while guiding the right-side halfshaft into the transaxle.

27. Install the lower transaxle mounting bolts, tighten to 55 ft. lbs. and remove the jack.

28. Align the converter with the marks made previously on the flywheel and install the bolts hand tight.

29. Torque the converter bolts to 46 ft. lbs.; retorque the first bolt after the others.

30. Install the starter assembly. Install the left side halfshaft.

31. Install the converter cover, oil cooler lines and cover. Install the sub-frame assembly. Install the lower engine mount retaining bolts and the transaxle mount nuts.

32. Install the right and left ball joints. Install the power steering rack, heat shield and cooler lines to the frame.

33. Install the right and left inner fender splash shields. Install the tire assemblies.

34. Lower the vehicle. Connect all electrical

leads. Install the upper transaxle mount bolts, tighten to 55 ft. lbs.

35. Attach the crossover pipe to the exhaust manifold. Connect the EGR tube to the crossover.

36. Connect the TV cable and the shift cable. Install the air cleaner and inlet tube.

37. Remove the engine support tool. Connect the negative battery cable.

Halfshafts

REMOVAL AND INSTALLATION

1982–86

1. Remove the hub nut.
2. Raise the front of the car. Remove the wheel and tire.
3. Install an axle shaft boot seal protector, G.M. special tool No. J–28712 or the equivalent, onto the seal.
4. Disconnect the brake hose clip from the MacPherson strut, but do not disconnect the hose from the caliper. Remove the brake caliper from the spindle, and hang the caliper out of the way by a length of wire. Do not allow the caliper to hang by the brake hose.
5. Mark the camber alignment cam bolt for reassembly. Remove the cam bolt and the upper attaching bolt from the strut and spindle.
6. Pull the steering knuckle assembly from the strut bracket.
7. Using G.M. special tool J–28468 or the equivalent, remove the axle shaft from the transaxle.
8. Using G.M. special tool J–28733 or the equivalent spindle remover, remove the axle shaft from the hub and bearing assembly.
9. If a new drive axle is to be installed, a new knuckle seal should be installed first.
10. Loosely install the drive axle into the transaxle and steering knuckle.
11. Loosely attach the steering knuckle to the suspension strut.
12. Install the brake caliper. Tighten the bolts to 30 ft. lbs. (40Nm.).
13. The drive axle is an interference fit in the steering knuckle. Press the axle into place, then install the hub nut. When the shaft begins to turn with the hub, insert a drift through the caliper into one of the cooling slots in the rotor to keep it from turning. Tighten the hub nut to 70 ft. lbs. (100Nm.). to completely seat the shaft.
14. Load the hub assembly by lowering it onto a jackstand. Align the camber cam bolt marks made during removal, install the bolt and tighten to 140 ft. lbs. (190 Nm.). Tighten the upper nut to the same value.
15. Install the axle shaft all the way into transaxle using a screwdriver inserted into the

groove provided on the inner retainer. Tap the screwdriver until the shaft seats in the transaxle.

16. Connect the brake hose clip to the strut. Install the tire and wheel, lower the car, and tighten the hub nut to 185 ft. lbs. (260 Nm).

1987–88

1. Raise the car and suitably support.
2. Remove the wheel assembly.
3. Insert a drift into the into the caliper and rotor to prevent the rotor from turning.
4. Remove the shaft nut and washer.
5. Remove the caliper from the steering knuckle and suspend the caliper assembly with a wire.
6. Remove the rotor from the hub and bearing assembly.
7. Disconnect the stabilizer shaft from the control arm.
8. Remove the ball joint from the steering knuckle.
9. Remove the drive axle from the transaxle. Remove the driveaxle from the hub and bearing assembly using tool J–28733.
To install:
10. Install the drive axle into the hub and bearing assembly and the transaxle.
11. Install the lower ball joint to the steering knuckle.
12. Install the stabilizer shaft to the control arm.
13. Install the rotor to the hub and bearing assembly.
14. Install the caliper to the steering knuckle.
15. Install a washer and a new shaft nut.
16. Insert a drift into the into the caliper and rotor to prevent the rotor from turning and torque drive axle nut to 185 ft. lbs. (260 Nm).
17. Seat the drive axle into the transaxle by placing a screwdriver into the groove on the joint housing and tapping until seated.
18. Verify that the drive axle is seated into the transaxle by grasping on the housing and pulling outward.
19. Install the wheel assembly.
20. Lower the car

1989–92

1. Raise the car and suitably support.
2. Remove the wheel assembly.
3. Install drive seal protector J34754 or equivalent, on the outer joint.
4. Insert a drift into the into the caliper and rotor to prevent the rotor from turning.
4. Remove the shaft nut and washer.
5. Remove the lower ball joint cotter pin and nut and loosen the joint using tool J 38892 or equivqlent. If removing the right axle, turn the

wheel to the left, if removing the left axle, turn the wheel to the right.

6. Separate the joint, with a pry bar between the suspension support.

7. Disengage the axle from the hub and bearing using J 28733–A or equivalent.

8. Separate the hub and bearing assembly from the drive axle and move the strut and knuckkle assembly rearward.

9. Disconnect the inner joint from the transaxle using tool J–28468 or J–33008 attached to J–29794 and J–2619–01 or from the intermediate shaft (V6 and Turbo engines), if equipped.

To install:

10. Install axle seal protector J–37292–A into the transaxle.

11. Insert the drive axle into the transaxle or intermediate shaft (V6 and Turbo engines), if equipped, by placing a suitable tool into the groove on the joint housing and tapping until seated.

WARNING: *Be careful not to damage the axle seal or dislodge the transaxle seal garter spring when installing the axle.*

12. Verify that the drive axle is seated into the transaxle by grasping on the housing and pulling outward.

13. Install the drive axle into the hub and bearing assembly.

14. Install the lower ball joint to the knuckle. Tighten the ball joint to steering knuckle nut to 41 ft. lbs. (55 Nm) and install the cotter pin.

15. Install the washer and new drive shaft nut.

16. Insert a drift into the caliper and rotor to prevent the rotor from turning and tighten the drive shaft nut to 185 ft. lbs. (260 Nm).

17. Remove both J–37292–B and J–34754 seal protectors.

18. Install the tire and wheel assembly.

19. Lower the vehicle and connect the negative battery cable.

Suspension and Steering

WHEELS

Wheels Front and Rear

REMOVAL AND INSTALLATION

1. Remove the hub cap, if so equipped.
2. Loosen the lug nuts on the wheel to be removed.
3. Raise and safely support vehicle on jack stands.

NOTE: *Always use a suitable floor jack for raising the vehicle to be serviced. Never use the jacking device supplied with the vehicle for vehicle service, that jacking device is designed for emergency use only to change a flat tire.*

4. Remove the wheel lug nuts and remove the wheel assembly.
5. Installation is the reverse of the removal procedure. Tighten the wheel lug nuts to 100 ft. lbs.

INSPECTION

Inspect the tread for abnormal wear, check for nails or other foreign material embedded into the tire. To check for leaks, submerse the wheel assembly into a tub of water and watch for air bubbles.

Wheels must be replaced if they are bent, dented, leak air through welds, have enlongated bolt holes, if wheel nuts won't stay tight, or if the wheels are heavily rusted. Replacement wheels must be equivalent to the original equipment wheels in load capacity, diameter, rim width, offset, and mounting configuration.

A wheel of improper size may affect wheel bearing life, brake cooling, speedometer/odometer calibration, vehicle ground clearance and tire clearance to the body and/or chassis.

NOTE: *Replacement with used wheels is not recommended as their service history may have included severe treatment or very high mileage and they could fail without warning.*

Tire rotation

Wheel Lug Studs

All models use metric wheel nuts and studs. The nut will have the word "metric" stamped on the face and the stud will have the letter "M" into the threaded end.

The thread size of the metric wheel nuts and wheel studs are M12X1.5, this signifies:
- M = Metric
- 12 = Diameter in millimeters
- 1.5 = Millimeters per thread

REPLACEMENT

The hub and bearing assembly must be removed from the vehicle to perform this procedure.

1. Using special tool J6627–A or equivalent, remove the stud to be replaced.

NOTE: *Never try to reuse a wheel stud. Once a wheel stud has been removed, discard it and replace it with a new one.*

2. Install the wheel stud into flange.
3. Place a couple of washers onto the threaded side of wheel stud.
4. Install the wheel stud nut and tighten until the stud is fully seated against the flange.

Five hole wheel, nut tightening sequence

A HUB AND BEARING ASSEMBLY REMOVED FROM VEHICLE

B INSERT WASHERS OVER WHEEL STUD

C TIGHTEN NUT TO DRAW WHEEL STUD INTO CORRECT POSITION

Installation of wheel stud

A HUB AND BEARING ASSEMBLY REMOVED FROM VEHICLE

B WHEEL NUT INSTALLED ON WHEEL STUD

Removal of wheel stud

5. Remove the wheel nut and washers.
6. Install the hub/bearing, and other related parts onto vehicle.

FRONT SUSPENSION

Springs and Shock Absorbers
TESTING

The function of the shock absorber is to dampen harsh spring movement and provide a means of dissipating the motion of the wheels so that the shocks encountered by the wheels are not totally transmitted to the body and, therefore, to you and your passengers. As the wheel moves up and down, the shock absorber shortens and lengthens, thereby imposing a restraint on movement by its hydraulic action.

A good way to see if your shock absorbers are functioning correctly is to push one corner of the car until it is moving up and down for almost the full suspension travel, then release it and watch its recovery. If the car bounces slightly about one more time and then comes to a rest, the shock is alright. If the car continues to bounce excessively, the shocks will probably require replacement.

MacPherson Struts
REMOVAL AND INSTALLATION

The struts retain the springs under tremendous pressure even when removed from the car. For these reasons, several expensive special tools and substantial specialized knowledge are required to safely and effectively work on these parts. We recommend that if spring or shock absorber repair work is required, you remove the strut or struts involved and take them to a repair facility which is fully equipped and familiar with the car.

1. Working under the hood, pry off the shock cover and then unscrew the upper strut-to-body nuts.
2. Loosen the wheel nuts, raise and support the car and allow the suspension to hang free, then remove the wheel and tire.

1. Cover	13. Nut	25. Bolt	37. Support
2. Nut	14. Pin	26. Cover	38. Bolt
3. Nut	15. Seal	27. Bolt	39. Nut
4. Mount	16. Hub	28. Ball joint	40. Bolt
5. Seat	17. Shield	29. Rivet	41. Washer
6. Insulator	18. Bolt	30. Grommet	42. Axle
7. Bumper	19. Washer	31. Washer	43. Spacer
8. Spring	20. Nut	32. Bolt	44. Nut
9. Insulator	21. Washer	33. Arm	45. Shaft
10. Strut	22. Rotor	34. Bushing	46. Nut
11. Nut	23. Knuckle	35. Bolt	47. Insulator
12. Seal	24. Caliper	36. Bolt	48. Clamp

Exploded view of the front suspension—1982–92

Strut assembly removal and installation details— 1982–87

1. Strut assembly
2. Knuckle
3. Bolt
4. Nut—180 N·m (133 lbs. ft.)
5. Suspension support
6. Cover
7. Nut—24 N·m (18 lbs. ft.)

Strut assembly removal and installation details— 1988–92

WARNING: *Use care to prevent damage from over extension of the drive shaft joints. When either end of the shaft is disconnected, over extension of the joint could result in separation of the internal components and possible joint failure. The steering knuckle should be supported and drive axle joint protectors should be used.*

3. Install a drive axle joint protective cover (modified), such as J–34754 or equivalent.

4. Use a two-armed puller and press the tie rod out of the strut bracket.

5. Remove both strut-to-steering knuckle bolts and carefully lift out the strut.

6. Installation is in the reverse order of removal. Observe the following torques:

• Upper strut-to-body nuts: 18–20 ft. lbs. On 1982–87 models, be sure that the flat sides of the strut-to-knuckle bolt heads are horizontal (see illustration) before tightening.

• Tighten the strut-to-knuckle bolts to 140 ft. lbs. (1982) and 133 ft. lbs. (1983–92).

STRUT MODIFICATION

This modification is made only if a camber adjustment is anticipated.

1. Place the strut in a vise. This step is not absolutely necessary; filing can be accom-

BEFORE FILING

AFTER FILING

Modifying the strut mounting holes for camber adjustment

plished by disconnecting the strut from the steering knuckle.

2. File the holes in the outer flanges so as to enlarge the bottom holes until they match the slots already in the inner flanges.

3. Camber adjustment procedures are detailed later in this Chapter.

REMOVAL AND INSTALLATION

CAUTION: *The coil springs are retained under considerable pressure. They can exert enough force to cause serious injury. Exercise extreme caution when disassembling the strut for coil spring removal.*

This procedure requires the use of a spring compressor and several other special tools. It cannot be performed without them. If you do not have access to these tools, DO NOT attempt to disassemble the strut!

1982–84

1. Remove the strut assembly.

2. Clamp the spring compressor J26584 in a vise. Position the strut assembly in the bottom adapter of the compresser and install the special tool J26584–86 (see illustration). Be sure that the adapter captures the strut and that the locating pins are engaged.

3. Rotate the strut assembly so that the top mounting assembly lip aligns with the compressor support notch. Insert two top adapters (J26584–88) between the top mounting assembly and the top spring seat. Position the adapters so that the split lines are in the 3 o'clock and 9 o'clock positions.

4. Using a 1 in. socket, turn the screw on top of the compressor clockwise until the top support flange contacts the adapters. Continue turning the screw until the coil spring is compressed approximately ½ in. (13mm) or 4 complete turns. Never bottom the spring or the strut damper rod.

5. Unscrew the nut from the strut damper shaft and then lift off the top mounting assembly.

6. Turn the compressor adjusting screw counterclockwise until the spring tension has been relieved. Remove the adapters and then remove the coil spring.

To install:

7. Clamp the strut compressor body J 26584 in a vise.

8. Position the strut assembly in the bottom adapter of the compresser and install the special tool J26584–86 (see illustration). Be sure that the adapter captures the strut and that the locating pins are engaged.

9. Position the spring on the strut. Make sure the spring is properly seated on the bottom of the spring plate.

10. Install the spring strut seat assembly on top of the spring.

11. Place BOTH J 26584–88 top adapters over the spring seat assemblies.

12. Turn the compressor forcing the screw until the compressor top support just contacts the top adapters (do not compress the spring at this time).

13. Install long extension with a socket to fit the hex on the damper shaft through the top of

Coil spring removal and installation details—1982–84

SPRING

J-26584-430

STRUT

J-26584-400

Notice: Care must be used not to damage the special coating on the coil springs, or damage could occur to the coils.

Coil spring removal steps—1985–87

the spring seat. Use the extension to guide the components during reassembly.

WARNING: *NEVER place a hard tool such as pliers or screwdriver against the polished surface of the damper shaft. The shaft can be held up with your fingers or an extension in order to prevent it from receding into the strut assembly while the spring is being compressed.*

14. Compress the screw by turning the screw clockwise until approximately 1½ in. (38mm) of damper shaft extends through the top spring plate.

WARNING: *Do not compress the spring until it bottoms.*

15. Remove the extension and socket, position the top mounting assembly over the damper shaft and install the nut. Tighten to 68 ft. lbs.

16. Turn the forcing screw counterclockwise to back off support, remove the top adapters and bottom adapter and remove the strut assembly from the compressor.

1985–87

1. Remove the strut assembly.

2. Mount the strut assembly in spring compressor J–26584, using bottom adapter, special tool J–26584–400. Be sure that the adapter captures the strut and that the locating pins are engaged.

3. Place the top adapter, J–26584–430, on the strut cap. Notice the adapter has holes designating each specific car.

4. Compress the strut approximately ½ its height after initial contact with the top cap.

CAUTION: *Never bottom the spring or damper rod!*

5. Remove the nut from the strut damper shaft and place alignment rod J–34013–27 on top of the damper shaft. Use the rod to guide the damper shaft straight down through the spring cap while decompressing the spring. Remove the components.

To install:

6. Mount the strut assembly in spring compressor J–26584, using bottom adapter, special

Coil spring installation steps—1985–87

Coil spring removal details—1988–92

tool J–26584–400. Be sure that the adapter captures the strut and that the locating pins are engaged.

7. Position the spring on the strut and make sure the spring is properly seated on the spring plate.

8. Install all shields, bumpers and insulators on the spring seat. Install the spring seat on top of the spring.

9. Install the bearing cap on spring seat and make sure they are centered together and aligned properly.

NOTE: *The upper spring seat flat must be aligned ± 10 degrees with the lower strut to knuckle attachment.*

10. Place the top adapter, J–26584–430, on the strut cap. Lower the compressor to capture the cap. Pull up the damper rod to full extension and clamp in place with J–34013–20.

11. Insert alignment rod J–34013–27 throught the bearing and spring caps and position on top of the damper rod. Compress the spring and guide the damper rod through the bearing cap using the alignment rod during compression.

NOTE: *During compression of the spring be sure to use the guide rod to guide the shaft through the exact center of the bearing. If the threads of the damper rod catch on the bearing cap and prevent the rod from passing cleanly through the bearing, stop compressing immediately. Decompress the spring and begin again.*

12. Compress the spring until approximately 1 in. (25mm) of the damper rod protrudes through the bearing cap and not any further.

Install and tighten the nut to 59 ft. lbs. (80 Nm).

13. Remove the damper rod clamp J–34013–20.

14. Back off the spring compressor and remove the strut assembly.

1988–92

1. Remove the strut assembly.

2. Mount the strut compressor J–34013 in holding fixture J–3289–20.

3. Mount the strut assembly into strut compressor. Note that the strut compressor has strut mounting holes drilled for specific car lines.

4. Compress the strut approximately ½ its height after initial contact with the top cap.

CAUTION: *Never bottom the spring or dampener rod!*

5. Remove the nut from the strut dampener shaft and place alignment rod J–34013–27 on top of the dampener shaft. Use the rod to guide the dampener shaft straight down through the spring cap while decompressing the spring. Remove the components.

To install:

6. Install the bearing cap into the strut compressor if previously removed.

Coil spring installation details—1988–92

7. Mount the strut assembly in strut compressor, using bottom locking pin only. Extend the dampener shaft and install clamp J–34013–20 on the dampener shaft.

8. Install the spring over the dampener and swing the assembly up so the upper locking pin can be installed.

9. Install all shields, bumpers and insulators on the spring seat. Install the spring seat on top of the spring. Be sure the flat on the upper spring seat is facing in the proper direction. The spring seat flat should be facing the same direction as the centerline of the strut assembly spindle.

10. Install the guiding rod and turn the forcing screw while the guiding rod centers the assembly. When the threads on the dampener shaft are visable, remove the guiding rod and install the nut. Tighten the nut to 65 ft. lbs. (85 Nm). Use a crowsfoot line wrench while holding the dampener shaft with a socket.

11. Remove the clamp.

Strut Cartridge
REMOVAL AND INSTALLATION

On 1982–87 models only, the internal piston rod, cylinder assembly and fluid can be replaced utilizing a service cartridge and nut. Internal threads are located inside the tube immediately below a cut line groove.

1. Remove the strut and the coil springs. Clamp the strut in a vise. Do not overtighten it as this will cause damage to the strut tube.

2. Locate the cut line groove just below the top edge of the strut tube. It is imperative that the groove be accurately located as any mislocation will cause inner thread damage. Using pipe cutters, cut around the groove until the tube is completely cut through.

3. Remove and discard the end cap, the cylinder and the piston rod assembly. Remove the strut assembly from the vise and pour out the old fluid.

4. Reclamp the strut in the vise. A flaring cup tool is included in the replacement cartridge kit to flare and deburr the edge that was cut on the strut tube. Place the flaring cup on the open edge of the tube and strike it with a mallet until its flat outer surface rests on the top edge of the tube. Remove the cup and discard it.

5. Try the new nut to make sure that it threads properly. If not, use the flaring cup again until it does.

6. Place the new strut cartridge into the tube. Turn the cartridge until it settles into the indentations at the base of the tube. Place the nut over the cartridge.

7. Using tool J–29778–A or equivalent, and a torque wrench, tighten the nut as specified in the kit drirections. Pull the piston rod up and down to check for proper operation.

8. Installation of the remaining components is in the reverse order of removal.

Lower Ball Joint
INSPECTION

1. Raise and support the front of the car and let the suspension hang free.

2. Grasp the wheel at the top and the bottom and shake it in an in-and-out motion. Check for any horizontal movement of the steering knuckle relative to the lower control arm. Replace the ball joint if such movement is noted.

3. If the ball stud is disconnected from the steering knuckle and any looseness is detected, or if the ball stud can be twisted in its socket using finger pressure, replace the ball joint.

REMOVAL AND INSTALLATION

Only one ball joint is used in each lower arm. The MacPherson strut design does not use an upper ball joint.

Replacing the strut cartridge—1982–87

1982–87

1. Loosen the wheel nuts, raise the car, and remove the wheel.

2. Use a ⅛ in. (3mm) drill bit to drill a hole through the center of each of the three ball joint rivets.

3. Use a ½ in. (13mm) drill bit to drill completely through the rivet.

4. Use a hammer and punch to remove the rivets. Drive them out from the bottom.

5. Use the special tool J29330 or a ball joint removal tool to separate the ball joint from the steering knuckle (see illustration). Don't forget to remove the cotter pin.

6. Disconnect the stabilizer bar from the lower control arm. Remove the ball joint.

7. Install the new ball joint into the control arm with the three bolts supplied as shown and torque to 50 ft. lbs. Installation of the remaining components is in the reverse order of removal. Tighten the castellated nut on the ball joint to 55 ft. lbs. and use a new cotter pin. Check the toe setting and adjust as necessary.

1988–92

1. Raise and support the vehicle safely.

2. Place jack stands under the suspension support.

3. Lower the car slightly so the weight of the car rests on the suspension supports and not the control arms.

4. Remove the tire and wheel assembly.

WARNING: *Use care to prevent damage from over extension of the drive shaft joints. When either end of the shaft is disconnected, over extension of the joint could result in separation of the internal components and possible joint failure. The steering knuckle should be supported and drive axle joint protectors should be used.*

5. Install a drive axle joint protective cover (modified), such as J–34754 or equivalent.

6. Remove the cotter pin from the ball joint.

7. Use the special ball joint removal tool, J–29330 or equivalent, to separate the ball joint from the steering knuckle.

8. Use a ⅛ in. (3mm) drill bit to drill a hole through the center of each of the three ball joint rivets.

9. Use a ½ in. (13mm) drill bit to drill completely through the rivet.

10. Loosen the stabilizer shaft bushing assembly nut.

11. Remove the ball joint from the steering knuckle and control arm.

To install:

12. Install the new ball joint into the control arm with the three bolts supplied as shown and torque to specifications given in the kit.

13. Install the ball joint to the knuckle and tighten the nut to a minimum of 37 ft. lbs. (50 Nm) or a maximum of 55 ft. lbs. (75 Nm) torque to install the pin.

14. Tighten the stabilizer insulator clamp nuts to 16 ft. lbs. (22 Nm).

15. Remove the seal protector.

16. Install the tire and wheel assembly.

17. Raise the car slightly to allow removal of the jack stands and lower the car.

Stabilizer Bar (Sway Bar)

REMOVAL AND INSTALLATION

NOTE: *On 1984-86 vehicles, a squawk noise from the front stabilizer bar insulator bushings may be corrected by installing a new Teflon lined bushing. The new bushings are being used on later models.*

1. Safely raise the car and allow the front lower control arms to hang free.

2. Remove the left front wheel and tire.

3. Disconnect the stabilizer shaft from the control arms.

4. Disconnect the stabilizer shaft from the support assemblies.

USING 1/8" DRILL, DRILL A PILOT HOLE COMPLETELY THROUGH THE RIVET.

DRILL PILOT HOLE

USING A 1/2" OR 13mm DRILL, DRILL COMPLETELY THROUGH THE RIVET. REMOVE BALL JOINT. DO NOT USE EXCESSIVE FORCE TO REMOVE BALL JOINT.

DRILL FINAL HOLE

PLACE J 29330 INTO POSITION AS SHOWN. LOOSEN NUT AND BACK OFF UNTIL . . .

J29330   KNUCKLE

. . . THE NUT CONTACTS THE TOOL. CONTINUE BACKING OFF THE NUT UNTIL THE NUT FORCES THE BALL STUD OUT OF THE KNUCKLE.

SEPARATING BALL JOINT FROM KNUCKLE USING J29330

BOLT MUST BE INSTALLED IN DIRECTION SHOWN

INSTALL BALL JOINT TO CONTROL ARM

75 N·m (55 FT. LBS.)

FRT

Ball joint removal and installation details—1982–87

1. Pin
2. Nut—50 N·m (37 lbs. ft.)
minimum torque 75 N·m (55 lbs. ft.)
maximum torque to install pin
3. Ball joint

Ball joint to knuckle installation—1988–92

5. Loosen the front bolts and remove the bolts from the rear and center of the support assemblies.

6. When installing the stabilizer, loosely assemble all components while insuring that the stabilizer is centered, side to side.

Control Arm/Suspension Support

REMOVAL AND INSTALLATION

1. Raise and support the front of the car. Remove the wheel.

NOTE: *Use care to prevent damage from over extension of the drive shaft joints. When either end of the shaft is disconnected, over extension of the joint could result in separation of the internal components and possible joint failure. Drive axle joint (boot) protectors should be used on this type of repair.*

2. Disconnect the stabilizer bar from the control arm and/or support.

3. Separate the ball joint from the steering knuckle as previously detailed.

4. Remove the two control arm-to-support bolts and remove the control arm.

5. If control arm support bar removal is necessary, unscrew the six mounting bolts and remove the support.

1. Service ball joint
2. Ball joint mounting bolts
3. Nut
4. Control arm
5. Steering arm
5. Steering knuckle
6. Nut—50 N·m (37 lbs. ft.) minimum torque 75 N·m (55 lbs. ft.) maximum torque to install pin
7. Pin

Ball joint installation—1988–92

INSTALL STABILIZER SHAFT INSULATOR WITH SLIT TOWARD FRONT OF VEHICLE AS SHOWN.

INSULATOR

SUPPORT

FRT

28 N·m (20 FT. LBS.)

HOLD STABILIZER SHAFT AT APPROX. 55.0mm FROM BOTTOM OF SUPPORT ARM WHEN TIGHTENING STABILIZER SHAFT INSULATORS.

55mm

FRT

SUPPORT

Stabilizer shaft installation—1982–87

1. Stabilizer shaft
2. Clamp
3. Insulator
4. Nut—22 N·m (16 lbs. ft.)
5. Suspension support
6. Bolt
7. Washer
8. Grommet
9. Spacer
10. Nut—17 N·m (13 lbs. ft.)
11. Control arm

Stabilizer shaft installation—1988–92

6. Installation is in the reverse order of removal. Tighten the control arm support rail bolts in the sequence shown. Check the toe and adjust as necessary.

Wheel Bearings

The front wheel bearings are sealed, non-adjustable units which require no periodic attention. They are bolted to the steering knuckle by means of an integral flange.

Front Hub, Knuckle And Bearing

REMOVAL AND INSTALLATION

WARNING: *You will need a special tool to pull the bearing free of the halfshaft (drive axle), G.M. tool no. J-28733 or the equivalent. You should also use a halfshaft boot protector, G.M. tool no. J-28712 or J-34754 or the equivalent, to protect the parts from damage.*

1. Remove the wheel cover, loosen the hub nut, and raise and support the car. Remove the front wheel.

2. Install the drive axle boot cover.

3. Remove and discard the hub nut. Be sure to use a new one on assembly, not the old one.

4. Remove the brake caliper and rotor:

a. Remove the caliper mounting bolts.

b. Remove the caliper from the knuckle and suspend from a length of wire. Do not allow the caliper to hang from the brake hose. Pull the rotor from the knuckle.

5. Remove the three hub and bearing attaching bolts. If the old bearing is to be reused, match mark the bolts and holes for installation. The brake rotor splash shield will have to come off, too.

6. Attach a puller, G.M. part no. J-28733 or the equivalent, and remove the bearing. If corrosion is present, make sure the bearing is loose in the knuckle before using the puller.

1. Control arm
2. Suspension support
3. Bolt—83 N·m (61 lbs. ft.)
4. Washer
5. Nut
6. Bolt—90 N·m (66 lbs. ft.) tighten first
7. Bolt—88 N·m (65 lbs. ft.) tighten second
8. Bolt—88 N·m (65 lbs. ft.) tighten third

Control arm/suspension support installation and tightening sequence—1988–92

FRONT SUSP SUPPORT ASM ATTACHING BOLT/SCREW SEQUENCE

1. LOOSELY INSTALL CENTER BOLT INTO HOLE (A).
2. LOOSELY INSTALL TIE BAR BOLT INTO OUTBOARD HOLE (B).
3. INSTALL BOTH REAR BOLTS INTO HOLES (C) TORQUE REAR BOLTS.
4. INSTALL BOLT INTO CENTER HOLE(D), THEN TORQUE.
5. TORQUE BOLT IN HOLE (A).
6. INSTALL BOLT INTO FRONT HOLE (E), THEN TORQUE.
7. TORQUE BOLT IN HOLE (B).

SUPPORT-TO-BODY BOLTS . . . . . . .90 N·m (63 FT. LBS.)
LCA PIVOT BOLTS . . . . .95 N·m (67 FT. LBS.)

TO REMOVE, INSERT J 29792-1 INTO BUSHING, SUPPORT CONTROL ARM ON J 29792-2, AND PRESS AS SHOWN.

TO INSTALL, SUPPORT CONTROL ARM ON J 29792-3, PLACE BUSHING INTO J 29792-2, AND PRESS BUSING INTO CONTROL ARM USING J 29792-1. LUBRICATE BUSHING.

Control arm/suspension support installation and tightening sequence—1982–87

Exploded view of the hub and bearing assembly

Insert a bolt into the rotor when installing the hub nut

Use a seal driver when installing the new seal into the knuckle

To install:

7. Clean the mating surfaces of all dirt and corrosion. Check the knuckle bore and knuckle seal for damage. If a new bearing is to be installed, remove the old knuckle seal and install a new one. Grease the lips of the new seal before installation; install with a seal driver made for the purpose, G.M. tool no. J–28671 or the equivalent.

8. Push the bearing onto the halfshaft. Install a new washer and hub nut.

9. Tighten the new hub nut on the halfshaft until the bearing is seated. If the rotor and hub start to rotate as the hub nut is tightened, insert a long bolt through the cut-out in the hub assembly to prevent rotation. Do not apply full torque to the hub nut at this time. Just seat the bearing.

10. Install the brake shield and the bearing retaining bolts. Tighten the bolts evenly to 63 ft. lbs. (85 Nm).

11. Install the caliper and rotor. Be sure that the caliper hose isn't twisted. Install the caliper bolts and tighten to 21–38 ft. lbs. (28–51 Nm.).

12. Install the wheel. Lower the car. Tighten the hub nut to 185 ft. lbs. (260 Nm.).

Front End Alignment

The toe setting is the only adjustment normally required on a J-car. However, in special circumstances, such as damage due to road hazard, collision, etc., camber may be adjusted after modifying the strut as detailed earlier in this Chapter. Caster is not adjustable.

CAMBER

Camber is the inward or outward tilt from the vertical, measured in degrees, of the front wheels at the top. An onward tilt gives the wheel positive camber; an inward tilt is called negative camber. Proper camber is critical to assure even tire wear.

1. Modify the suspension strut as detailed earlier.

2. Loosen the strut-to-knuckle bolts just enough to allow movement between the strut and the knuckle.

3. Grasp the top of the tire and move it in or out until the proper specification is obtained.

4. Tighten both bolts just enough to hold the adjustment. Remove the wheels and tighten the bolts to the proper specifications.

5. Replace the wheels.

TOE

Toe is the amount, measured in a fraction of a millimeter, that the wheels are closer together at one end than the other. Toe-in means that the front wheels are closer together at the front than the rear; toe-out means the rear of the front wheels are closer together than the front. J-cars are designed to have a slight amount of toe-out.

Toe is adjusted by turning the tie rods. It must be checked after camber has been adjust-

Wheel alignment: toe (left) and camber (right)

Toe adjustment is made at the tie rods

ed, but it can be adjusted without disturbing the camber setting. You can make this adjustment without special equipment if you make very careful measurements. The wheels must be straight ahead.

1. Toe can be determined by measuring the distance between the centers of the tire treads, at the front of the tire and at the rear. If the tread pattern makes this impossible, you can measure between the edges of the wheel rims, but make sure to move the car forward and measure in a couple of places to avoid errors caused by bent rims or wheel runout.

2. If the measurement is not within specifications, loosen the nuts at the steering knuckle end of the tie rod, and remove the tie rod boot clamps. Rotate the tie rods to align the toe to specifications. Rotate the tie rods evenly, or the steering wheel will be crooked when you're done.

3. When the adjustment is correct, tighten the nuts to 14 ft. lbs. (20 Nm.). Adjust the boots and tighten the clamps.

REAR SUSPENSION

Springs
REMOVAL AND INSTALLATION

CAUTION: *The coil springs are under a considerable amount of tension. Be very careful when removing or installing them; they can exert enough force to cause very serious injuries. Make sure vehicle is safely supported on the proper type equipment.*

1. Raise and support the car on a hoist. Do not use a twin-post hoist. The swing arc of the axle may cause it to slip from the hoist when the bolts are removed. If a suitable hoist is not available, raise and support the car on jackstands, and use a jack under the axle.

2. Support the axle with a jack that can be raised and lowered.

3. Remove the brake hose attaching brackets (right and left), allowing the hoses to hang freely. Do not disconnect the hoses.

WHEEL ALIGNMENT

Year	Model	Caster		Camber		Toe-in (in.)
		Range (deg.)	Preferred Setting (deg.)	Range (deg.)	Preferred Setting (deg.)	
1982	Cavalier	NA	NA	0.10P–1.10P	0.60P	0.125P
	Cimarron	NA	NA	0.10P–1.10P	0.60P	0.125P
	Firenza	NA	NA	0.10P–1.10P	0.60P	0.125P
	Skyhawk	NA	NA	0.10P–1.10P	0.60P	0.125P
	2000	NA	NA	0.10P–1.10P	0.60P	0.125P
1983	Cavalier	NA	NA	0.20P–1.20P	0.70P	0.13N
	Cimarron	NA	NA	0.20P–1.20P	0.70P	0.13N
	Firenza	NA	NA	0.20P–1.20P	0.70P	0.13N
	Skyhawk	NA	NA	0.20P–1.20P	0.70P	0.13N
	2000	NA	NA	0.20P–1.20P	0.70P	0.13N
1984	Cavalier	NA	NA	0.20P–1.20P	0.70P	0.13N
	Cimarron	NA	NA	0.20P–1.20P	0.70P	0.13N
	Firenza	NA	NA	0.20P–1.20P	0.70P	0.13N
	Skyhawk	NA	NA	0.20P–1.20P	0.70P	0.13N
	2000 Sunbird	NA	NA	0.20P–1.20P	0.70P	0.13N
1985	Cavalier	0.70P–2.70P	1.70P	0.20P–1.50P	0.80P	0.13N
	Cimarron	0.70P–2.70P	1.70P	0.20P–1.50P	0.80P	0.13N
	Firenza	0.70P–2.70P	1.70P	0.20P–1.50P	0.80P	0.13N
	Skyhawk	0.70P–2.70P	1.70P	0.20P–1.50P	0.80P	0.13N
	Sunbird	0.70P–2.70P	1.70P	0.20P–1.50P	0.80P	0.13N
1986	Cavalier	0.70P–2.70P	1.70P	0.20P–1.50P	0.80P	0.06N
	Cimarron	0.70P–2.70P	1.70P	0.20P–1.50P	0.80P	0.06N
	Firenza	0.70P–2.70P	1.70P	0.20P–1.50P	0.80P	0.06N
	Skyhawk	0.70P–2.70P	1.70P	0.20P–1.50P	0.80P	0.06N
	Sunbird	0.70P–2.70P	1.70P	0.20P–1.50P	0.80P	0
1987	Cavalier	0.70P–2.70P	1.70P	0.20P–1.50P	0.80P	0 ②
	Cimarron	0.70P–2.70P	1.70P	0.20P–1.50P	0.80P	0
	Firenza	0.70P–2.70P	1.70P	0.20P–1.50P	0.80P	0
	Skyhawk	0.70P–2.70P	1.70P	0.20P–1.50P	0.80P	0
	Sunbird	0.70P–2.70P	1.70P	0.20P–1.50P	0.80P	0
1988	Cavalier	1.70P–4.20P	1.70P	0.20N–1.80P	0.80P ③	0
	Cimarron	1.70P–4.20P	1.70P	0.20N–1.80P	0.80P	0
	Firenza	1.70P–4.20P	1.70P	0.20N–1.80P	0.80P	0
	Skyhawk	1.70P–4.20P	1.70P	0.20N–1.80P	0.80P	0
	Sunbird	1.70P–4.20P	1.70P	0.20N–1.80P	0.80P	0
1989	Cavalier	0.70P–2.70P	1.70P	0.20N–1.80P	0.80P ③	0
	Skyhawk	0.70P–2.70P	1.70P	0.20N–1.80P	0.80P	0
	Sunbird	0.70P–2.70P	1.70P	0.20N–1.80P	0.80P	0
1990	Cavalier	0.70P–2.70P	1.70P	0.20N–1.80P	0.80P ③	0
	Sunbird	0.70P–2.70P	1.70P	0.20N–1.80P	0	0
1991	Cavalier	0.70P–2.70P	1.70P	0.70N–0.70P	0	0
	Sunbird	0.70P–2.70P	1.70P	0.70N–0.70P	0	0
1992	Cavalier	0.70P–2.70P	1.70P	0.70N–0.70P	0	0
	Sunbird	0.70P–2.70P	1.70P	0.70N–0.70P	0	0

① Caster is not adjustable on all models
② Z-24 with option S6 0.13N degrees
③ Z-24 0 degrees

4. Remove both shock absorber lower attaching bolts from the axle.

5. Lower the axle. Remove the coil spring and insulator.

To install:

6. Position the spring and insulator on the axle. The leg on the upper coil of the spring must be parallel to the axle.

NOTE: *Prior to installing springs, it may be necessary to install the upper insulators to the body with adhesive to keep them in position while raising the axle assembly. The ends of the upper coil in the spring must be positioned in the spring seat and within 15mm of the spring stop.*

7. Install the shock absorber bolts. Tighten to 41 ft. lbs. (55 Nm.). Install the brake line brackets. Tighten to 8 ft. lbs. (11 Nm.).

Shock Absorbers

TESTING

Visually inspect the shock absorber. If there is evidence of leakage and the shock absorber is covered with oil, the shock is defective and should be replaced.

If there is no sign of excessive leakage (a small amount of weeping is normal) bounce the car at one corner by pressing down on the fender or bumper and releasing. When you have the car bouncing as much as you can, release the fender or bumper. The car should stop bouncing after the first rebound. If the bouncing continues past the center point of the bounce more than once, the shock absorbers are worn and should be replaced.

REMOVAL AND INSTALLATION

NOTE: *Do not remove both shock absorbers at one time as suspending rear axle at full length could result in damage to the brake lines/hoses.*

1. Open the hatch or trunk lid, remove the trim cover if present, and remove the upper shock absorber nut.

2. Raise and support the car at a convenient working height if you desire. It is not necessary to remove the weight of the car from the shock absorbers, however, so you can leave the car on the ground if you prefer.

3. Remove the lower attaching bolt and remove the shock.

1. 17 N·m (13 ft. lb.)
2. 14 N·m (10 ft. lb.)
3. Shock stud
4. Upper shock absorber mount
5. Underbody
6. 37 N·m (28 ft. lb.)
7. Shock
8. Axle assembly
9. Shock absorber insulator
10. Spring insulator
11. Control arm bushing
12. Brace
13. Spacer must contact brace when spacer and parts are installed

VIEW B
SHOCK TO AXLE R. H. SHOWN

VIEW A

Rear axle and suspension components—1982–87

1. Stabilizer shaft
2. Insulator
3. Clamp
4. Upper spacer
5. Lower spacer
6. Bolt
7. Nut—22 N·m (16 lbs. ft.)
8. Clamp

9. Nut
10. Bolt—18 N·m (13 lbs. ft.)
11. Axle
12. Bumper
13. Spring
14. Insulator
15. Underbody
16. Washer

17. Nut—83 N·m (61 lbs. ft.)
18. Tab nut
19. Bolt—47 N·m (35 lbs. ft.)
20. Shock absorber
21. Mount
22. Retainer
23. Nut—29 N·m (21 lbs. ft.)
24. Nut—17 N·m (13 lbs. ft.)

Rear axle and suspension components—1988–92

To install:

4. If new shock absorbers are being installed, repeatedly compress them while inverted and extend them in their normal upright position. This will purge them of air.

5. Install the shocks in the reverse order of removal. Tighten the lower mount nut and bolt to 55 ft. lbs. (41 Nm.), the upper to 13 ft. lbs. (17 Nm.).

Rear Axle/Control Arm

The control arms and axle are are one unit. The axle structure itself maintains the gometrical relationship of the wheels relative to the body. The axle assembly attaches to the underbody through a rubber bushing located at the front of each control arm. Each control arm bolts to underbody brackets.

REMOVAL AND INSTALLATION

1. Raise the vehicle and support the with jackstands under the control arms.

2. Remove the stabilizer bar from the axle assembly.

3. Remove the wheel and tire assembly and brake drum.

WARNING: *Do not hammer on the brake drum as damage to the bearing could result!*

4. Remove the shock absorber lower attaching bolts and paddle nuts at the axle and disconnect the shocks from the control arm.

5. Disconnect the parking brake cable (and rear ABS wiring connector and clip if so equipped) from the axle assembly.

6. Disconnect the brake line at the brackets from the axle assembly.

7. Lower the rear axle and remove the coil springs and insulators.

8. Remove the control arm bolts from the underbody bracket and lower the axle.

9. Remove the hub attaching bolts and remove the hub, bearing and backing plate assembly.

To install:

10. Install the hub, bearing and backing plate assembly. Hold the nuts and tighten the attaching bolts to 39 ft. lbs.

11. Place the axle assembly on a transmission jack and raise into position. Attach the control arms to the underbody bracket with bolts and nuts. Do not torque the bolts at this time. It will be necessary to torque the bolts of the control arm at standing height.

12. Install the stabilizer bar to the axle assembly.

13. Install the brake line connections to the axle assembly.

14. Attach the brake cable to the rear axle assembly (and rear ABS wiring connector and clip if so equipped).

15. Position the coil springs and insulators in seats and raise the rear axle.

16. The end of the upper coil on the springs must be parallel to the axle assembly and seated in the pocket.

17. Install the shock absorber lower attachment bolts and paddle nuts to the rear axle and torque the bolts to 41 ft. lbs.

18. Install the parking brake cable to the guide hook and adjust as necessary.

19. Install the brake drums and wheel and tire assemblies. Tighten the lug nuts.

20. Bleed the brake system and lower the car.

Stabilizer Bar

REMOVAL AND INSTALLATION

1. Raise the vehicle and support the body with jackstands.

2. Remove the nuts and bolts at both the axle and control arm attachments and remove the control arm and remove the bracket, insulator and stabilizer bar.

3. Install the U-bolts, upper clamp, spacer and insulators in the trailing axle. Position the stabilizer bar in the insulators and loosely install the lower clamp and nuts.

4. Attach the end of the stabilizer bar to the control arms and torque all nuts to 13. ft. lbs.

5. Torque the axle attaching nut to 10 ft. lbs.

6. Lower the vehicle.

Rear Hub and Bearing

REMOVAL AND INSTALLATION

1. Loosen the wheel lug nuts. Raise and support the car and remove the wheel.

2. Remove the brake drum. Removal procedures are covered in the next Chapter, if needed.

WARNING: *Do not hammer on the brake drum to remove; damage to the bearing will result.*

3. Remove the four hub and bearing retaining bolts and remove the assembly from the axle. The top rear attaching bolt will not clear the brake shoe when removing the hub and bearing assembly. Partially remove the hub and bearing assembly prior to removing this bolt.

4. Disconnect the rear ABS wheel speed sensor wire connector.

5. Installation is the reverse. Hub and bearing bolt torque is 39 ft. lbs. (52 Nm.).

Rear hub and bearing assembly

Rear End Alignment

The Rear end alignment is not adjustable. If the Rear wheels appear to be out of alignment, inspect the underbody and rear suspension for damaged and or broken parts.

STEERING

Steering Wheel

REMOVAL AND INSTALLATION

Standard Wheel

1. Disconnect the negative cable at the battery.
2. Pull the pad from the wheel. The horn lead is attached to the pad at one end; the other end of the pad has a wire with a spade connector. The horn lead is disconnected by pushing and turning; the spade connector is simply unplugged.
3. Remove the retainer under the pad (if so equipped).
4. Remove the steering shaft nut.
5. There should be alignment marks already present on the wheel and shaft. If not, matchmark the parts.
6. Remove the wheel with a puller.

To install:

7. Install the wheel on the shaft, aligning the matchmarks. Install the shaft nut and tighten to 30 ft. lbs. (40 Nm.).
8. Install the retainer.
9. Plug in the spade connector, and push and turn the horn lead to connect. Install the pad. Connect the negative battery cable.

Sport Wheel

1. Disconnect the negative cable at the battery.
2. Pry the center cap from the wheel.
3. Remove the retainer (if so equipped).

Sport steering wheel removal—1982–86

1. Steering wheel
2. Cap
3. Retainer
4. Nut—41 N·m (30 lbs. ft.)
5. Emblem
6. Insulator
7. Eyelet
8. Spring

Steering wheel removal—1988–90

Standard steering wheel removal—1982–86

Remove the steering wheel with a puller

1. Nut 41 N·m (30 lbs. ft.)   3. Steering wheel pad
2. Retainer   4. Steering wheel

Steering wheel removal—1991–92

Depress the lock plate and remove the snap ring—1982–92

Remove these parts to get at the turn signal switch—standard column shown, adjustable columns similar—1982–90

4. Remove the shaft nut.

5. If the wheel and shaft do not have factory installed alignment marks, matchmark the parts before removal of the wheel.

6. Install a puller and remove the wheel. A horn spring, eyelet and insulator are underneath; don't lose the parts.

To install:

7. Install the spring, eyelet and insulator into the tower on the column.

8. Align the matchmarks and install the wheel onto the shaft. Install the retaining nut and tighten to 30 ft. lbs. (40 Nm.).

9. Install the retainer. Install the center cap. Connect the negative battery cable.

Turn Signal Switch

REMOVAL AND INSTALLATION

1982–90

1. Remove the steering wheel. Remove the trim cover.

2. Pry the cover from the steering column.

3. Position a U-shaped lockplate compressing tool on the end of the steering shaft and compress the lock plate by turning the shaft nut clockwise. Pry the wire snapring out of the shaft groove.

4. Remove the tool and lift the lockplate off the shaft.

5. Slip the cancelling cam, upper bearing preload spring, and thrust washer off the shaft.

6. Remove the turn signal lever. Remove the hazard flasher button retaining screw and remove the button, spring and knob.

7. Pull the switch connector out of the mast jacket and tape the upper part to facilitate switch removal. Attach a long piece of wire to the turn signal switch connector. When installing the turn signal switch, feed this wire through the column first, and then use this wire to pull the switch connector into position. On tilt wheels, place the turn signal and shifter housing in low position and remove the harness cover.

8. Remove the three switch mounting screws. Remove the switch by pulling it straight up while guiding the wiring harness cover through the column.

To install:

9. Install the replacement switch by working the connector and cover down through the housing and under the bracket. On tilt models, the connector is worked down through the housing, under the bracket, and then the cover is installed on the harness.

10. Install the switch mounting screws and the connector on the mast jacket bracket. Install the column-to-dash trim plate.

Turn signal switch installation details—1982–90

11. Install the flasher knob and the turn signal lever.

12. With the turn signal lever in neutral and the flasher knob out, slide the thrust washer, upper bearing preload spring, and cancelling cam onto the shaft.

13. Position the lock plate on the shaft and press it down until a new snapring can be inserted in the shaft groove. Always use a new snapring when assembling.

14. Install the cover and the steering wheel.

1991–92

1. Disconnect the negative battery cable.

2. Remove the pad and horn lead, retainer and nut and remove the steering wheel from the column, using a suitable puller.

3. Remove the 2 lower column cover retaining screws.

4. Remove the 3 bottom retaining screws from lower column cover.

5. Separate the rose bud fastener (integral to wire harness) from the jacket assembly.

6. Remove the turn signal switch retaining screws.

7. Depress the locking tab and remove the 2 wire harness connector from the switch.

8. Depress the locking tab and remove the cruise connector from the wire harness, if so equipped.

9. Installation is the reverse of removal. Torque the cover and switch retaining screws to 49 inch lbs. (5.5 Nm) and the steering wheel retaining nut to 30 ft. lbs. (41 Nm).

Ignition Switch

REMOVAL AND INSTALLATION

1982–90

The switch is located on the steering column and is completely inaccessible without first lowering the steering column. The switch is actuated by a rod and rack assembly. A gear on the end of the lock cylinder engages the toothed upper end of the rod.

1. Lower the steering column; be sure to properly support it.

2. Put the switch in the **Off-Unlocked** position. With the cylinder removed, the rod is in **Off-Unlocked** position when it is in the next to the uppermost detent.

3. Remove the two switch screws and remove the switch assembly.

4. Before installing, move the new switch slider (standard columns with automatic transmission) to the extreme left position. Move the switch slider (stanadrd columns with manual transmission) to the extreme left position. Move the slider (adjustable columns with automatic transmission) to the extreme right position and then move the slider one detent to the left (off lock). Move the slider (adjustable columns with manual transmission) to the extreme right position.

5. Install the activating rod into the switch and assemble the switch on the column. Tighten the mounting screws. Use only the specified screws, since overlength screws could impair the collapsibility of the column.

6. Reinstall the steering column.

1991–92

1. Disconnect the negative battery cable.

2. Remove the pad and horn lead, retainer and nut and remove the steering wheel from the column, using a suitable puller.

3. Remove the tilt lever, if so equipped.

4. Remove the 2 lower column cover retaining screws.

5. Remove the 3 bottom retaining screws from lower column cover.

6. Depress the locking tabs and remove the 2 wire harness connectors from the ignition switch.

7. Remove the ignition switch screws and remove the ignition switch from the housing.

To install:

8. Connect the ignition switch to the lock cylinder housing. Make sure the tab on the lock cylinder shaft aligns with the slotted opening on the ignition switch. Tighten the ignition switch retaining screws to 21 inch lbs. (2.4 Nm).

9. The remainder of the installation is the reverse of removal. Torque the cover and switch retaining screws to 49 inch lbs. (5.5 Nm) and the steering wheel retaining nut to 30 ft. lbs. (41 Nm).

1. Retainer	25. Rack preload spring
2. Hexagon jam nut	26. Switch actuator rack
3. Shaft lock cover	27. Switch actuator rod
4. Retaining ring	28. Spring thrust washer
5. Steering shaft lock	29. Switch actuator pivot pin
6. Turn signal cancelling cam assy	30. Wave washer
7. Upper bearing spring	31. Key release lever
8. Binding head cross recess screw	32. Key release spring
9. Round washer head screw	33. Wiring protector
10. Switch actuator arm assy	34. Dimmer and ignition switch mounting stud
11. Turn signal switch assy	35. Washer head screw
12. Hex washer head tapping screw	36. Ignition switch assy
13. Thrust washer	37. Floor shift bowl
14. Buzzer switch assy	38. Shift bowl shroud
15. Buzzer switch retaining clip	39. Binding head cross recess screw
16. Lock retaining screw	40. Dimmer switch actuator rod
17. Steering column housing	41. Dimmer switch assy
18. Switch actuator sector assy	42. Hexagon nut
19. Steering column lock cylinder set	43. Steering column jacket assy
20. Bearing assy	44. Retaining ring
21. Bearing retaining bushing	45. Steering shaft assy
22. Upper bearing retainer	46. Hex washer head tapping screw
23. Pivot & switch assy	47. Flat head screw
24. Spring & bolt assy	48. Steering column jacket bushing

Key release standard steering column—1982–90

1. Retainer
2. Hexagon jam nut
3. Shaft lock cover
4. Retaining ring
5. Steering shaft lock
6. Turn signal cancelling cam asm
7. Upper bearing spring
8. Binding head cross recess screw
9. Round washer head screw
10. Switch actuator arm asm
11. Turn signal switch asm
12. Hex washer head tapping screw
13. Thrust washer

14. Buzzer switch asm
15. Buzzer switch retaining clip
16. Lock retaining screw
17. Steering column housing
18. Switch actuator sector
19. Steering column lock cylinder set
20. Bearing asm
21. Bearing retaining bushing
22. Upper bearing retainer
23. Pivot & switch asm
24. Lock bolt
25. Rack preload spring
26. Switch actuator rack

27. Switch actuator rod
28. Spring thrust washer
29. Switch actuator pivot pin
30. Wiring protector
31. Floor shift bowl
32. Binding hd cross recess screw
33. Dimmer switch actuator rod
34. Dimmer switch asm
35. Hexagon nut
36. Steering column jacket asm
37. Adapter & bearing asm
38. Hex washer head tapping screw

39. Bearing retainer
40. Lower bearing seat
41. Lower bearing spring
42. Lower spring retainer
43. Strg. column jacket bushing
44. Retaining ring
45. Steering shaft asm
46. Ign. switch housing asm
47. Washer head screw
48. Pan hd screw
49. Dimr & ign sw mounting stud
50. Ignition switch asm

Park lock standard steering column—1982–90

1. Retainer
2. Hexagon jam nut
3. Shaft lock cover
4. Retaining ring
5. Steering shaft lock
6. Turn signal cancelling cam asm
7. Upper bearing spring
8. Binding head cross recess screw
9. Round washer head screw
10. Signal switch arm asm
11. Turn signal switch asm
12. Upper bearing inner race seat
13. Inner race
14. Pan head cross recess screw
15. Asm buzzer switch
16. Buzzer switch retaining clip

17. Lock retaining screw
18. Lock housing cover
19. Steering column lock cylinder set
20. Dimmer switch rod actuator
21. Bearing asm
22. Lock bolt
23. Lock bolt spring
24. Steering wheel lock shoe
25. Steering wheel lock shoe
26. Drive shaft
27. Dowel pin
28. Pivot pin
29. Shoe spring
30. Release lever spring
31. Release lever pin

32. Shoe release lever
33. Bearing asm
34. Ign switch actuator asm
35. Switch actuator rack
36. Rack preload spring
37. Steering column housing
38. Switch actuator sector
39. Hex washer head screw
40. Spring guide
41. Wheel tilt spring
42. Spring retainer
43. Column housing cover end cap
44. Switch actuator pivot pin
45. Pivot & switch asm
46. Pin preload spring
47. Wiring protector
48. Race & upper shaft asm
49. Centering sphere
50. Joint preload spring
51. Lower steering shaft asm

52. Support screw
53. Dowel pin
54. Steering column housing support
55. Lock plate
56. Steering column housing shroud
57. Steering column jacket asm
58. Dimmer switch actuator rod
59. Dimmer switch asm
60. Hexagon nut
61. Adapter & bearing asm
62. Hex washer head tapping screw
63. Bearing retainer
64. Lower bearing seat
65. Lower bearing spring
66. Lower spring retainer
67. Strg column jacket bushing
68. Washer head screw
69. Dimmer & ignition switch mounting stud
70. Ignition switch asm
71. Pan hd screw
72. Ign switch inhibitor housing asm

Park lock tilt wheel steering column—1982–90

1. Retainer
2. Hexagon jam nut
3. Shaft lock cover
4. Retaining ring
5. Shaft lock
6. Turn signal cancelling cam assy
7. Upper bearing spring
8. Binding head cross recess screw
9. Round washer head screw
10. Signal switch arm assy
11. Turn signal switch assy
12. Upper bearing inner race seat
13. Inner race
14. Pan head cross recess screw
15. Buzzer switch assy
16. Buzzer switch retaining clip
17. Lock retaining screw
18. Lock housing cover

19. Steering column lock cylinder set
20. Dimmer switch rod actuator
21. Tilt lever opening shield
22. Bearing assy
23. Lock bolt
24. Lock bolt spring
25. Steering wheel lock shoe
26. Steering wheel lock shoe
27. Drive shaft
28. Dowel pin
29. Pivot pin

30. Shoe spring
31. Release lever spring
32. Release lever pin
33. Shoe release lever
34. Bearing assy
35. Ignition switch actuator assy
36. Switch actuator rack
37. Rack preload spring
38. Steering column housing
39. Switch actuator sector
40. Hex washer head screw
41. Spring guide
42. Wheel tilt spring
43. Spring retainer
44. Column housing cover end cap
45. Switch actuator pivot pin

46. Pivot & switch assy
47. Pin preload spring
48. Ignition switch assy

49. Dimmer & ignition switch mounting stud
50. Washer head screw
51. Shroud retaining plate
52. Oval head cross recess screw
53. Dowel pin
54. Wiring protector
55. Race & upper shaft assy
56. Centering sphere
57. Joint preload spring
58. Lower steering shaft assy
59. Support screw
60. Steering column housing support
61. Lock plate
62. Release lever finger pad
63. Key release lever
64. Key release spring
65. Steering column housing shroud
66. Dimmer switch rod
67. Dimmer switch assy
68. Hexagon nut
69. Steering column jacket assy.
70. Steering column jacket bushing

Key release tilt wheel steering column—1982–90

1. Switch, wash/wipe
2. Screw, switch
3. Cover, strg col, upper
4. Nut, hexagon
5. Ring, retaining
6. Cam, orientation plate
7. Cam asm, turn signal cancelling
8. Spring, upper strg shaft
9. Washer, thrust
10. Screw, hex hd tapping
11. Ring, retaining
12. Bearing asm
13. Bolt, shear
14. Washer, shear bolt
15. Housing, steering column
16. Jacket asm, steering column
17. Bushing asm, strg col jacket
18. Switch, turn signal
19. Lock cyl asm, ign switch &
20. Switch asm, ignition
21. Screw, ign switch
22. Screw, pan head 6-lobed
23. Nut, spring (U-type)
24. Cover, strg col, lower
25. Shaft asm, steering column
26. Screw, pan head 6-lobed

Disassembled view of the standard steering column—1991–92

1. Switch, wash/wipe
2. Screw, switch
3. Cover, strg col, upper
4. Nut, hexagon
5. Ring, retaining
6. Cam, orientation plate
7. Cam asm, turn signal cancelling
8. Spring, upper bearing
9. Seat, inner race
10. Race, inner
11. Bolt, shear
12. Washer, shear bolt
13. Housing asm, steering column
14. Pin, pivot
15. Lock cyl asm, ign switch &
16. Switch asm, ignition
17. Screw, ign switch
18. Screw, wire support
19. Support, wire
20. Lever, tilt
21. Spring, wheel tilt
22. Retainer, spring
23. Switch, turn signal
24. Screw, pan head 6-lobed
25. Nut, spring (U-type)
26. Cover, strg col, lower
27. Screw, pan head 6-lobed
28. Shaft asm, lower steering
29. Sphere, centering
30. Spring, joint preload
31. Shaft asm, race & upper
32. Shaft asm, steering
33. Screw, hex hd tapping
34. Bumper, tilt
35. Support, strg column housing
36. Jacket asm, steering column
37. Bushing asm, strg col jacket

Disassembled view of the tilt steering column—1991–92

Ignition Lock Cylinder
REMOVAL AND INSTALLATION
1982–90

1. Remove the steering wheel.
2. Turn the lock to the Run position.
3. Remove the lock plate, turn signal switch or combination switch, and the key warning buzzer switch. The warning buzzer switch can be fished out with a bent paper clip.
4. Remove the lock cylinder retaining screw and lock cylinder.

WARNING: *If the screw is dropped on removal, it could fall into the column, requiring complete disassembly to retrieve the screw.*

5. Rotate the cylinder clockwise to align the cylinder key with the keyway in the housing.
6. Push the lock all the way in.
7. Install the screw. Tighten to 15 inch lbs.
8. The rest of installation is the reverse of removal. Turn the lock to Run to install the key warning buzzer switch, which is simply pushed down into place.

Remove the key warning buzzer switch with a paper clip—1982–90

Steering Column
REMOVAL AND INSTALLATION

WARNING: *Once the steering column is removed from the car, the column is extremely susceptible to damage. Dropping the column assembly on its end could collapse the steering shaft or loosen the plastic injections which maintain column rigidity. Leaning on the column assembly could cause the jacket to bend or deform. Under no conditions should the end of the shaft be hammered upon. Any of the above damage could impair the column's collapsible design.*

Lock cylinder installation—1982–90

1. Disconnect the battery ground cable.
2. Remove the left instrument panel sound insulator.
3. Remove the left instrument panel trim pad and steering column trim collar.
4. Remove the horn contact pad, (only if column is to be disassembled).
5. Remove the steering wheel, (only if column is to be disassembled).
6. Disconnect the steering shaft to intermediate shaft connection.
7. Remove the column bracket support bolts and column bracket support nut.
8. Disconnect any electrical connections.
9. Remove the steering column.
10. Insert the steering shaft into the flexible coupling and raise the coupling into position.
11. Loosely install the three steering column attaching bolts.
12. Center the steering shaft within the steering column jacket bushing and tighten the lower attaching bolt. This can be done by moving the steering column jacket jacket assembly up and down or side to side until the steering shaft is centered.
13. Tighten the two upper attaching bolts and torque to 20–22 ft. lbs.
14. Install the flexible coupling pinch bolt and torque to 30–34 ft. lbs.
15. Turn the steering wheel from stop to stop and observe if the steering shaft binds or rubs against the column bushing. Re-center the steering shaft if necessary.
16. Pull the seal assembly up over the end of the column bushing until the seal locks into place.
17. Install the sound insulator.
18. Connect the battery cable.

1. Upper support
2. Bolt—install first—27 N·m (20 lbs. ft.)
3. Bolt—install second—27 N·m (20 lbs. ft.)
4. Bolt—install these bolts last—27 N·m (20 lbs. ft.)
5. Bolt—27 N·m (20 lbs. ft.)
6. Upper pinch bolt—46 N·m (34 lbs. ft.)
7. Seal
8. Coupling
9. Instrument panel bracket
10. Lower pinch bolt—40 N·m (29 lbs. ft.)

Steering column mounting—1982–90

Steering Linkage

REMOVAL AND INSTALLATION

Tie Rod Ends

1. Loosen both pinch bolts at the outer tie rod.

2. Remove the tie rod end from the strut assembly using a suitable removal tool.

3. Unscrew the outer tie rod end from the tie rod adjuster, counting the number of revolutions required before they are disconnected.

To install:

4. Install the new tie rod end, screwing it on the same number of revolutions as counted in Step 3. When the tie rod end is installed, the tie rod adjuster must be centered between the tie rod and the tie rod end, with an equal number of threads exposed on both sides of the adjuster nut. Tighten the pinch bolts to 20 ft. lbs.

5. Install the tie rod end to the strut assembly and tighten to 50 ft. lbs. If the cotter pin cannot be installed, tighten the nut up to $\frac{1}{16}$ in. (1.6mm) further. Never back off the nut to align the holes for the cotter pin.

6. Have the front end alignment checked or adjusted.

1. Upper pinch bolt—40 N·m (29 lbs. ft.)
2. Flange and steering coupling
3. Retainers
4. Steering column
5. Bolt—26 N·m (20 lbs. ft.)
6. Bolt—26 N·m (20 lbs. ft.)
7. Bolt 30 N·m (22 lbs. ft.)
8. Steering column upper support
9. Shims

VIEW A

Steering column mounting—1991–92

The rod end removal and installation details

Rack and Pinion Unit

REMOVAL AND INSTALLATION

1. From the driver's side, remove the sound insulator.

2. From under the instrument panel, pull the seal assembly down from the steering column and remove the upper pinch bolt from the flexible coupling.

3. Remove the air cleaner and the windshield washer jar, if necessary for easier access.

4. On power steering models: disconnect the pressure line from the steering gear and remove the screw securing the pressure line bracket to the cowl. Move the pressure line aside.

5. Raise and support the car on jackstands.

6. Remove both front wheels.

7. Disconnect both tie rods from the struts.

8. Lower the car.

9. Remove the right side rack mounting clamp.

10. Remove the left side rack mounting clamp.

11. Move the gear forward slightly. On power steering models, disconnect the fluid return pipe from the gear.

12. Remove the lower pinch bolt from the flexible coupling and separate the rack from the coupling.

13. Remove the dash seal from the rack assembly.

14. Raise and support the car on jackstands.

15. On some models it may be necessary to remove the splash shield from the inner, left fender.

16. Turn the left knuckle and hub assembly to the full left turn position and remove the rack and pinion assembly through the access hole on the left fender.

17. Installation is the reverse of removal while noting the following points:

   a. If the mounting studs backed out during removal, it will be necessary to re-position them prior to rack installation. Double-nut the stud so that it can be torqued to 15 ft. lbs.

   b. It will be good to have a helper inside the car to guide the flexible coupling onto the stub shaft and onto the steering column.

1. Steering gear assembly
2. L.H. clamp—horizontal slot at top
3. R.H. clamp—horizontal slot at top
4. Nut—30 N·m (22 lbs. ft.)—hand start all nuts. Tighten left side clamp nuts first, then tighten right side nuts.
5. Stud—20 N·m (15 lbs. ft.) after second reuse of stud, thread locking kit no. 1052624 must be used.
6. Nut—50 N·m (35 lbs. ft.)
   75 N·m (50 lbs. ft.) maximum to install cotter pin
7. Cotter pin

Power rack and pinion mounting—1988–92

1. Steering gear asm.
2. L.H. clamp (dark)
3. R.H. clamp (light)
4. Nut—30 N·m (22 lbs. ft.)—hand start all nuts, tighten left side clamp nuts first, then tighten right side nuts.
5. Stud—20 N·m (15 lbs. ft.) after second reuse of stud, thread locking kit no 1052624 must be used.
6. Nut 50 N·m (35 lbs. ft.)
   75 N·m (50 lbs. ft.) maximum to install cotter pin
7. Cotter pin

Manual rack and pinion mounting—1988–92

c. Observe the following torques:
- Coupling-to-stub shaft:
   37 ft. lbs. (1982–86)
   29–30 ft. lbs. (1987–92)
- Coupling-to-column: 30 ft. lbs.
- Mounting clamps:
   28 ft. lb. (1982–86)
   22 ft. lbs. (1987–92)
- Tie rod nuts: 35–37 ft. lbs.

Power Steering Pump

REMOVAL AND INSTALLATION

1. Disconnect the negative battery cable.
2. Disconnect the vent hole at the carburetor if so equipped.
3. Loosen the adjusting bolt and pivot bolt on the pump or release tension on drive belt tensioner assembly; remove the pump's drive belt.
4. Remove the three pump-to-bracket or mounting bolts (through the access hole in the pulley as necessary) and remove the adjusting bolt if so equipped.
5. Remove the high pressure fitting from the pump.
6. Disconnect the reservoir-to-pump hose from the pump.
7. Remove the pump.
8. Installation is in the reverse order of removal. Adjust the belt tension and bleed the system.

VIEW A

1. OUTLET HOSE
2. INLET HOSE
3. INLET PIPE
4. 27 N·m (20 LBS. FT.)
5. CLAMP 1.7 N·m (15 LBS. IN.)
6. RESERVOIR
7. POWER STEERING PUMP
8. IDLE SPEED POWER STEERING PRESSURE SWITCH
9. RETAINER
10. STEERING GEAR
11. SCREW – 8 N·m (71 LBS. IN.)

Power steering line routing 1.8L and 2.0L L4 engines

1. POWER STEERING PUMP
2. PULLEY
3. BOLT — 27 N·m (20 LBS. FT.)

Power steering pump mounting 1.8L and 2.0L L4 engines

1 POWER STEERING PUMP
2 BOLTS - 25 N.m (18 LBS. FT.)
3 PULLEY
4 FRONT COVER ASSEMBLY

Power steering pump mounting 3.1L V6 engines

STANDARD DRIVE BELT ADJUSTMENT

The belt tension on most components is adjusted by moving the component (power steering pump) within the range of the slotted bracket. Check the belt tension every 12 months or 10,000 miles. Push in on the drive belt about midway between the crankshaft pulley and the driven component. If the belt deflects more than $9/16$ in. (14mm) or less than $3/8$ in. (9.5mm), adjustment is required.

1. Loosen the adjustment nut and bolt in the slotted bracket. Slightly loosen the pivot bolt.
2. Pull (don't pry) the component outward to increase tension. Push inward to reduce tension. Tighten the adjusting nut and bolt and the pivot bolt.
3. Recheck the drive belt tension and readjust if necessary.

SERPENTINE BELT BELT ADJUSTMENT

Serpentine belt is tensioned by loosening a bolt and rotating the belt tensioner. The correct belt tension is indicated on the indicator mark of the belt tensioner. If the indicator mark is not within specification, replace the belt or the tensioner.

NOTE: *To remove or install the belt, push and rotate the tensioner. Care should be taken to avoid twisting or bending the tensioner when applying torque.*

SYSTEM BLEEDING

1. Raise the front of the vehicle and support safely. This will minimize steering effort. Fill the power steering pump reservoir with Dexron®II.
2. With the engine off, keep the reservoir full as someone turns the steering wheel from lock to lock several times. Stop with the steering system at one lock.
3. Pull the high tension lead out of the coil. Continue to keep the reservoir full while cranking the engine for 30 seconds at a time (with a one minute rest in between), until fluid level remains constant.
4. Turn the steering wheel to the opposite lock and repeat Step 3.
5. Reconnect the high tension lead, start the engine and allow it to idle. Turn the wheel from lock to lock several times. Note the level of the fluid.
6. Lower the vehicle to the ground. Note the fluid level. Repeat Step 5, stopping with the wheel at the centered position.
7. The fluid level should not have risen more than 0.2 in. (5mm). If it has, repeat Step 6 until the level does not rise appreciably.

Brakes

9

BRAKE SYSTEM

These cars have a diagonally split hydraulic system. This differs from conventional practice in that the left front and right rear brakes are on one hydraulic circuit, and the right front and left rear are on the other.

A diagonally split system necessitates the use of a special master cylinder design. The master cylinder incorporates the functions of a standard tandem master cylinder, plus a warning light switch and proportioning valves. On 1985–86 V6 models the proportioning valve is located on the framne rail. Additionally, the master cylinder is designed with a quick take-up feature which provides a large volume of fluid to the brakes at low pressure when the brakes are initially applied. The low pressure fluid acts to quickly fill the large displacement requirements of the system.

The front disc brakes are single piston sliding caliper units. Fluid pressure acts equally against the piston and the bottom of the piston bore in the caliper. This forces the piston outward until the pad contacts the rotor. The force on the caliper bore forces the caliper to slide over, carrying the other pad into contact with the other side of the rotor. The disc brakes are self-adjusting.

Rear drum brakes are conventional duo-servo units. A dual piston wheel cylinder, mounted to the top of the backing plate, actuates both brake shoes. Wheel cylinder force to the shoes is supplemented by the tendency of the shoes to wrap into the drum (servo action). An actuating link, pivot and lever serve to automatically engage the adjuster as the brakes are applied when the car is moving in reverse. Provisions for manual adjustment are also provided. The rear brakes also serve as the parking brakes; linkage is mechanical.

Vacuum boost is a standard unit. The booster is a conventional tandem vacuum unit.

EXTERNAL CONDITIONS THAT AFFECT BRAKE PERFORMANCE

Tires

Tires having unequal contact and grip on road will cause unequal braking. Tires must be equally inflated, identical in size and the tread pattern of the right and left tires must be approximately equal.

Vehicle Loading

A heavily loaded vehicle requires more braking effort. When a vehicle has unequal loading, the most heavily loaded wheels require more braking power than others.

Wheel Alignment

Misalignment of the wheels, particularly in regard to excessive camber and caster, will cause the brakes to pull to one side.

Trailer Towing

Towing a trailer requires longer braking distances and tends to overheat the brakes sooner.

ADJUSTMENT

Disc Brakes

The front disc brakes are inherently self-adjusting. No adjustments are either necessary or possible.

Drum Brakes

The drum brakes are designed to self-adjust when applied with the car moving in reverse. However, they can also be adjusted manually. This manual adjustment should also be performed whenever the linings are replaced.

1982–86

1. Use a punch to knock out the stamped area on the brake drum. If this is done with the drum installed on the car, the drum must then be removed to clean out all metal pieces. After

adjustments are complete, obtain a hole cover from your dealer (Part no. 4874119 or the equivalent) to prevent entry of dirt and water into the brakes.

2. Use an awl, a screwdriver, or an adjusting tool especially made for the purpose to turn the brake adjusting screw star wheel. Expand the shoes until the drum can just barely be turned by hand.

3. Back off the adjusting screw 12 notches. If the shoes still are dragging lightly, back off the adjusting screw one or two additional notches. If the brakes still drag, the parking brake adjustment is incorrect or the parking brake is applied. Fix and start over.

4. Install the hole cover into the drum.

5. Check the parking brake adjustment.

NOTE: *On some models, no marked area or stamped area is present on the drum. In this case, a hole must be drilled in the backing plate:*

1. All backing plates have two round flat areas in the lower half through which the parking brake cable is installed. Drill a ½ in. (13mm) hole into the round flat area on the backing plate opposite the parking brake cable. This will allow access to the star wheel.

2. After drilling the hole, remove the drum and remove all metal particles. Install a hole plug (Part no. 4874119 or the equivalent) to prevent the entry of water or dirt.

1987–92

1. Raise and support the vehicle safely.

2. Remove the tire and wheel assembly.

3. Mark the relationship of the wheel to the axle flange and remove the brake drum.

4. Measure the drum inside diameter using tool J 2177–A, or equivalent.

5. Turn the star wheel, and adjust the shoe and lining diameter to be 0.050 in. − 1.27mm (1987–90) or 0.030 in. − 0.76mm (1991–92) less than the inside drum diameter for each wheel.

6. Install the drums and wheels aligning the previous marks.

7. Lower the vehicle.

8. Tighten the wheel nuts to 100 ft. lbs.

9. Make several alternate forward and reserve stops applying firm force to the brake pedal until ample pedal reserve is built up.

J 21177-A

1. Setting tool to drum	3. Brake drum
2. Setting brake shoes to tool	4. Brake linings

Measuring the drum and shoe for adjustment

PROPER SPRING INSTALLATION

1. Primary shoe
2. Secondary shoe
3. Adjusting screw spring
4. Socket
5. Pivot nut
6. Adjusting screw
7. Adjusting screw assembly

STAR WHEEL

(L.H. SHOWN)

Adjusting screw assembly

Brake Light Switch

REMOVAL AND INSTALLATION

1. Disconnect the battery ground cable.
2. Remove the drivers side hush panel.
3. Remove the retaining nut from switch.
4. Disconnect the electrical connector, and remove the switch.
5. Installation is the reverse of the removal procedure.

Master Cylinder

REMOVAL AND INSTALLATION

1. Unplug the electrical connector from the master cylinder.
2. Place a number of cloths or a container under the master cylinder to catch the brake fluid. Disconnect the brake tubes from the master cylinder; use a flare nut wrench if one is available. Tape over open ends of the tubes.

Warning: *Brake fluid eats paint. Wipe up any spilled fluid immediately, then flush the area with clear water.*

3. Remove the two nuts attaching the master cylinder to the booster or firewall.
4. Remove the master cylinder.

To install:

5. Attach the master cylinder to the booster with the nuts. Torque to 22–30 ft. lbs. (30–45 Nm.).
6. Remove the tape from the lines and connect to the master cylinder. Torque to 10–15 ft. lbs. (13–20 Nm.). Connect the electrical lead.
7. Bleed the brakes.

OVERHAUL

This is a tedious, time-consuming job. You can save yourself a lot of trouble by buying a new master cylinder from your dealer or parts supply house.

1. BRAKE PEDAL MOUNTING BRACKET
2. CRUISE CONTROL RELEASE VALVE (VACUUM) (MANUAL TRANSAXLE ONLY)
3. TORQUE CONVERTER CLUTCH TERMINALS
4. TCC AND CRUISE CONTROL RELEASE SWITCH/ VALVE (AUTOMATIC TRANSAXLE ONLY)
5. STOPLAMP SWITCH
6. CRUISE CONTROL RELEASE SWITCH TERMINALS
7. STOP LAMP SWITCH TERMINALS
8. BRAKE PEDAL ASM

Stop lamp switch mounting location

1. CLIP NUT
2. BOLT - 32 N.m (24 LBS. FT.)
3. NUT - 21 N.m (15 LBS. FT.)
4. PEDAL COVER
5. BOOSTER PUSH ROD
6. WASHER
7. RETAINER
8. VACUUM BOOSTER
9. BRAKE PEDAL
10. BRACKET

Brake pedal assembly

Vacuum Booster

REMOVAL AND INSTALLATION

1. Remove the master cylinder from the booster. It is not necessary to disconnect the lines from the master cylinder. Just move the cylinder aside.

2. Disconnect the vacuum booster pushrod from the brake pedal inside the car. It is retained by a bolt. A spring washer is under the bolt head, and a flat washer goes on the other side of the pushrod eye, next to the pedal arm.

3. Remove the four attaching nuts from inside the car. Remove the booster.

To install:

4. Install the booster on the firewall. Tighten the mounting nuts to 22–33 ft. lbs. (30–45 Nm.).

5. Connect the pushrod to the brake pedal.

6. Install the master cylinder. Mounting torque is 22–33 ft. lbs. (30–45 Nm).

OVERHAUL

This job is not difficult, but requires a number of special tools which are expensive, especially if they're to be used only once. Generally, it's better to buy a new or rebuilt vacuum booster and install it yourself.

Proportioning Valves and Failure Warning Switch

These parts are installed in the master cylinder body on all models except the 1985–86 V6 engine. On these models the proportioning valve and the brake pressure differential warning switch is located to the left frame rail below the master cylinder.

Brake Hose

REMOVAL AND INSTALLATION

Front

1. Raise and support the car safely.
2. Remove the tire and wheel .
3. Clean the dirt from both hose end fittings.
4. Remove the brake pipe from the hose.

Vacuum booster mounting

5. Remove the brake hose from the caliper and discard the two copper gaskets on either side of the fitting block.

To install:

6. Install the hose using new copper gaskets.

7. Check that the hose doesn't rub in extreme left and right turn conditions.

8. Fill and maintain the brake fluid level in the reservoir and bleed the brake system.

Rear

1. Raise and support the car safely.
2. Clean the dirt from both hose end fittings.
3. With the aid of a backup wrench, disconnect the brake pipe fitting on both ends of the brake hose.
4. Remove the retaining clips from both ends.
5. After installing the hose fill and maintain the brake fluid level in the reservoir and bleed the brake system.

Bleeding

NOTE: *For vehicles equipped with "Anti-Lock Brake System" refer to the service procedure in that section.*

The purpose of bleeding the brakes is to expel air trapped in the hydraulic system. The system must be bled whenever the pedal feels spongy, indicating that compressible air has entered the system. It must also be bled whenever the system has been opened or repaired. You will need a helper for this job.

Always maintain the brake fluid level in the reservoir during the bleeding procedure. Adjust the rear brakes before starting the brake bleeding procedure.

If the master cylinder is know or suspected to have air in the bore (this condition is present when master cylinder assembly is replaced it must be bleed first), then it must be bled BEFORE any wheel cylinder or caliper in the following manner. Connect 2 short pieces of brake line to the outlet fittings, bend them until the free end is below the fluid level in the master cylinder reservoir. Fill the reservoir with fresh brake fluid. Pump the piston slowly until no more air bubbles appear in the reservoirs. Disconnect the 2 short lines, refill the master cylinder and securely install the cylinder caps.

If the master cylinder is on the vehicle, it can still be bled, using a flare nut wrench. Open the brake lines slightly with the flare nut wrench while pressure is applied to the brake pedal by a helper inside the vehicle. Be sure to tighten the line before the brake pedal is released. Repeat the process with both lines until no air bubbles come out.

Bleeding the brakes

CAUTION: *Never reuse brake fluid which has been bled from the brake system.*

1. The sequence for bleeding for 1982-91 vehicles is right rear, left front, left rear and right front. The sequence for bleeding 1992 vehicles is right rear, left rear, right front and left front. If the car has power brakes, remove the vacuum by applying the brakes several times. Do not run the engine while bleeding the brakes.

2. Clean all the bleeder screws. You may want to give each one a shot of penetrating solvent to loosen it up; seizure is a common problem with bleeder screws, which then break off, sometimes requiring replacement of the part to which they are attached.

3. Fill the master cylinder with DOT 3 brake fluid.

WARNING: *Brake fluid absorbs moisture from the air. Don't leave the master cylinder or the fluid container uncovered any longer than necessary. Be careful handling the fluid; it eats paint.*

Check the level of the fluid often when bleeding, and refill the reservoirs as necessary. Don't let them run dry, or you will have to repeat the process.

4. Attach a length of clear vinyl tubing to the bleeder screw on the wheel cylinder. Insert the other end of the tube into a clear, clean jar half filled with brake fluid.

5. Have your assistant slowly depress the brake pedal (rapid pumping of the brake pedal pushes the master cylinder secondary piston down the bore in a way that makes it difficult to bleed the system). As this is done, open the bleeder screw $1/3$–$1/2$ of a turn, and allow the fluid to run through the tube. Then close the bleeder screw before the pedal reaches the end of its travel. Have your assistant slowly release the pedal. Repeat this process until no air bubbles appear in the expelled fluid.

6. Repeat the procedure on the other three brakes, checking the level of fluid in the master cylinder reservoir often.

After you're done, there should be no sponginess in the brake pedal feel. If there is, either there is still air in the line, in which case the process should be repeated, or there is a leak somewhere, which of course must be corrected before the car is moved.

FRONT DISC BRAKES

Pads
INSPECTION

The pad thickness should be inspected every time that the tires are removed for rotation. The outer pad an be checked by looking in at each end, which is the point at which the highest rate of wear occurs. The inner pad can be checked by looking down through the inspection hole in the top of the caliper. If the thickness of the pad is worn to within $1/32$ in. (0.8mm) of the rivet at either end of the pad, all the pads should be replaced. This is the factory recommended measurement; your state's automobile inspection laws may not agree with this.

NOTE: *Always replace all pads on both front wheels at the same time. Failure to do so will result in uneven braking action and premature wear.*

REMOVAL AND INSTALLATION

CAUTION: *Brake shoes contain asbestos, which has been determined to be a cancer causing agent. Never clean the brake surfaces with compressed air! Avoid inhaling any dust from any brake surface! When cleaning brake surfaces, use a commercially available brake cleaning fluid.*

1. Siphon $2/3$ of the brake fluid from the master cylinder reservoir. Loosen the wheel lug nuts and raise the car. Remove the wheel.

2. Position a C-clamp across the caliper so that it presses on the pads and tighten it until the caliper piston bottoms in its bore.

NOTE: *If you haven't removed some brake fluid from the master cylinder, it will overflow when the piston is retracted.*

3. Remove the C-clamp.

4. Remove the allen head caliper mounting bolts. Inspect the bolts for corrosion, and replace as necessary.

5. Remove the caliper from the steering knuckle and suspend it from the body of the car with a length of wire. Do not allow the caliper to hang by its hose.

Install the retaining spring on the inboard pad

1. Inboard shoe and lining
2. Caliper housing
3. Shoe retainer spring

Installing the inboard shoe and lining

1. Outboard shoe and lining
2. Wear sensor
3. Caliper housing

Installing the outboard shoe and lining

6. Remove the pad retaining springs and remove the pads from the caliper.

7. Remove the plastic sleeves and the rubber bushings from the mounting bolt holes.

8. Install new sleeves and bushings. Lubricate the sleeves with a light coating of silicone grease before installation. These parts must al-

ways be replaced when the pads are replaced. The parts are usually included in the pad replacement kits.

NOTE: *On 1987–92 models the mounting bolt and sleeve comes as an assembly. Lubricate in the same manner.*

9. Install the outboard pad into the caliper.

10. Install the retainer spring on the inboard pad. A new spring should be included in the pad replacement.

11. Install the new inboard pad into the caliper. The retention lugs fit into the piston.

12. Install the caliper onto the steering knuckle. Tighten the mounting bolts to 21–35 ft. lbs. (28–47 Nm.).

13. Apply a firm force 3 times to the brake to seat linings.

14. Pry up on the outboard shoe with a LARGE flat blade screwdriver or similar tool, between the outboard shoe and the flange and hat section of the rotor. Keep the tool in place during the following step.

CAUTION: *Use a suitable size prying tool that will not break and cause physical injury.*

15. Hold moderate force of 50 lbs. (222 N) on the brake pedal and cinch the outboard shoe tabs, using a plastic mallet and a ball peen hammer, as shown in the illustration.

1. Large flat-blade screwdriver   2. Caliper housing

First step of cinching the shoe to the caliper

1. Caliper body
2. Outboard shoe tab

Second step of cinching the shoe to the caliper

1. Add silicone grease to inside diameter of bushing
2. Mounting bolt and sleeve assembly
3. Bushing
4. Caliper housing

Lubricating the caliper cavity

Use air pressure to remove the piston from the bore

16. Install the wheel and lower the car. Fill the master cylinder to its proper level with fresh brake fluid meeting DOT 3 specifications. Since the brake hose wasn't disconnected, it isn't really necessary to bleed the brakes, although most mechanics do this as a matter of course.

Brake Caliper

REMOVAL AND INSTALLATION

CAUTION: *Brake shoes contain asbestos, which has been determined to be a cancer causing agent. Never clean the brake surfaces with compressed air! Avoid inhaling any dust from any brake surface! When cleaning brake surfaces, use a commercially available brake cleaning fluid.*

1. Follow Steps 1, 2 and 3 of the pad replacement procedure.
2. Before removing the caliper mounting bolts, remove the bolt holding the brake hose to the caliper.
3. Remove the allen head caliper mounting bolts. Inspect them for corrosion and replace them if necessary.
4. With the pads installed as outlined in pad replacement, install the caliper and mounting bolts and torque to 21–35 ft. lbs. (28–47 Nm.). The brake hose fitting should be tightened to 18–30 ft. lbs. (24–40 Nm.).

OVERHAUL

1. Remove the caliper.
2. Remove the pads.
3. Place some cloths or a slat of wood in front of the piston. Remove the piston by applying compressed air to the fluid inlet fitting. Use just enough air pressure to ease the piston from the bore.

CAUTION: *Do not try to catch the piston with your fingers, which can result in serious injury!*

Remove the piston boot with a screwdriver

4. Remove the piston boot with a screwdriver, working carefully so that the piston bore is not scratched.
5. Remove the bleeder screw.
6. Inspect the piston for scoring, nicks, corrosion, wear, etc., and damaged or worn chrome plating. Replace the piston if any defects are found.
7. Remove the piston seal from the caliper bore groove using a piece of pointed wood or plastic. Do not use a screwdriver, which will damage the bore. Inspect the caliper bore for nicks, corrosion, and so on. Very light wear can be cleaned up with crocus cloth. Use finger pressure to rub the crocus cloth around the circumference of the bore; do not slide it in and out. More extensive wear or corrosion warrants replacement of the part.
8. Clean any parts which are to be reused in denatured alcohol. Dry them with compressed air or allow to air dry. Don't wipe the parts dry with a cloth, which will leave behind bits of lint.
9. Lubricate the new seal, provided in the repair kit, with clean brake fluid. Install the seal in its groove, making sure it is fully seated and not twisted.
10. Install the new dust boot on the piston. Lubricate the bore of the caliper with clean brake fluid and insert the piston into its bore.

Exploded view of the disc brake caliper, 1982—84

1. Mounting bolt
2. Sleeve
3. Bushing
4. Outboard shoe & lining
5. Inboard shoe & lining
6. Wear sensor
7. Shoe retainer spring
8 Boot
9. Piston
10. Piston seal
11. Bleeder valve
12. Caliper housing
22. Boot

Exploded view of the disc brake caliper, 1985—86

* ON SOME MODELS THE RETAINER SPRING IS
ALREADY STAKED TO THE INBOARD SHOE.

1. Mounting bolt and sleeve asembly
3. Bushing
4. Outboard shoe & lining
5. Inboard shoe & lining
6. Wear sensor
7. Shoe retainer spring
8. Boot
9. Piston
10. Piston seal
11. Bleeder valve
12. Caliper housing
22. Boot

Exploded view of the disc brake caliper, 1987–90

1. Mounting bolt and sleeve assembly
2. Bushing
3. Bleeder valve
4. Piston seal
5. Piston
6. Boot
7. Inboard shoe and lining
8. Outboard shoe and lining
9. Wear sensor
10. Caliper housing

Exploded view of the disc brake caliper, 1991–92

Position the boot in the caliper housing and seat with a seal driver of the appropriate size, or G.M. tool no. J-29077 or equivalent.

11. Install the bleeder screw, tightening to 80–140 inch lbs. (9–16 Nm.). Do not overtighten.

12. Install the pads, install the caliper, and bleed the brakes.

Brake Disc (Rotor)

REMOVAL AND INSTALLATION

1. Remove the caliper.
2. Remove the rotor.
3. To install, reposition the rotor and install the caliper and pads as outlined earlier.

INSPECTION

1. Check the rotor surface for wear or scoring. Deep scoring, grooves or rust pitting can be removed by refacing, a job to be referred to your local machine shop or garage. Minimum thickness is stamped on the rotor (21.08 mm). If the rotor will be thinner than this after refinishing, it must be replaced.

2. Check the rotor parallelism; it must vary less thn 0.013 mm measured at four or more points around the circumference. Make all measurements at the same distance in from the edge of the rotor. Refinish the rotor if it fails to meet this specification.

3. Measure the disc runout with a dial indicator. If runout exceeds 0.127 mm, and the wheel bearings are OK (if runout is being measured with the disc on the car), the rotor must be refaced or replaced as necessary.

Check the runout with a dial indicator

REAR DRUM BRAKES

Brake Drums
REMOVAL AND INSTALLATION

CAUTION: *Brake shoes contain asbestos, which has been determined to be a cancer causing agent. Never clean the brake surfaces with compressed air! Avoid inhaling any dust from any brake surface! When cleaning brake surfaces, use a commercially available brake cleaning fluid.*

1. Loosen the wheel lug nuts. Raise and support the car. Mark the relationship of the wheel to the axle and remove the wheel.

2. Mark the relationship of the drum to the axle and remove the drum. If it cannot be slipped off easily, check to see that the parking brake is fully released. If so, the brake shoes are probably locked against the drum. Perform the following to back off the adjuster:

a. Use a punch to knock out the stamped area on the brake drum. If this is done with the drum installed on the car, the drum must then be removed to clean out all metal pieces. After adjustments are complete, obtain a hole cover from your dealer (Part no. 4874119 or the equivalent) to prevent entry of dirt and water into the brakes.

b. Use an awl, a screwdriver, or an adjusting tool especially made for the purpose to turn the brake adjusting screw star wheel.

3. To install, reposition the drum making sure to align the matchmarks made during removal. Lug nut torque is 100 ft. lbs. (140 Nm.).

INSPECTION

1. After removing the brake drum, wipe out the accumulated dust with a damp cloth.

CAUTION: *Do not blow the brake dust out of the drums with compressed air or lungpower. Brake linings contain asbestos, a known cancer causing substance. Dispose of the cloth used to clean the parts after use.*

2. Inspect the drums for cracks, deep grooves, roughness, scoring, or out-of-roundness. Replace any drum which is cracked; do not try to weld it up.

3. Smooth any slight scores by polishing the friction surface with fine emery cloth. Heavy or extensive scoring will cause excessive lining wear and should be removed from the drum through resurfacing, a job to be referred to your local machine shop or garage. The maximum finished diameter of the drums is 200.64mm. The drum must be replaced if the diameter is 201.40mm or greater.

Backing off the adjusting screw

Brake Shoes

CAUTION: *Brake shoes contain asbestos, which has been determined to be a cancer causing agent. Never clean the brake surfaces with compressed air! Avoid inhaling any dust from any brake surface! When cleaning brake surfaces, use a commercially available brake cleaning fluid.*

INSPECTION

After removing the brake drum, inspect the brake shoes. If the lining is worn down to within $\frac{1}{32}$ in. (0.8mm) of a rivet, the shoes must be replaced.

NOTE: *This figure may disagree with your state's automobile inspection laws.*

If the brake lining is soaked with brake fluid or grease, it must be replaced. If this is the case, the brake drum should be sanded with crocus cloth to remove all traces of brake fluid, and the wheel cylinders should be rebuilt. Clean all grit from the friction surface of the drum before replacing it.

Exploded view of the drum brakes, 1982–84

If the lining is chipped, cracked, or otherwise damaged, it must be replaced with a new lining.

NOTE: *Always replace the brake linings in sets of two on both ends of the axle. Never replace just one shoe, or both shoes on one side.*

Check the condition of the shoes, retracting springs, and holddown springs for signs of overheating. If the shoes or springs have a slight blue color, this indicates overheating and replacement of the shoes and springs is recommended. The wheel cylinders should be rebuilt as a precaution against future problems.

REMOVAL AND INSTALLATION

CAUTION: *Brake shoes contain asbestos, which has been determined to be a cancer causing agent. Never clean the brake surfaces with compressed air! Avoid inhaling any dust from any brake surface! When cleaning brake surfaces, use a commercially available brake cleaning fluid.*

1. Loosen the lug nuts on the wheel to be serviced, raise and support the car, and remove the wheel and brake drum.

NOTE: *It is not really necessary to remove the hub and wheel bearing assembly from the axle, but it does make the job easier. If you can work with the hub and bearing assembly in place, skip down to Step 3.*

2. Remove the four hub and bearing assembly retaining bolts and remove the assembly from the axle.

3. Remove the return springs from the shoes with a pair of needle nose pliers. There are also special brake spring pliers for this job.

4. Remove the hold down springs by gripping them with a pair of pliers, then pressing down and turning 90 degrees. There are special tools to grab and turn these parts, but pliers work fairly well.

5. Remove the shoe holddown pins from behind the brake backing plate. They will simply slide out once the holddown spring tension is relieved.

6. Lift up the actuator lever for the self-adjusting mechanism and remove the actuating link. Remove the actuator lever, pivot, and the pivot return spring.

7. Spread the shoes apart to clear the wheel cylinder pistons and remove the parking brake strut and spring.

8. If the hub and bearing assembly is still in place, spread the shoes far enough apart to clear it.

9. Disconnect the parking brake cable from the lever. Remove the shoes, still connected by their adjusting screw spring, from the car.

*LUBRICATE WITH THIN COATING OF 5450032 LUBRICANT (OR EQUIVALENT)

1. Return spring
2. Return spring
3. Hold-down spring
4. Lever pivot
5. Hold-down pin
6. Actuator link
7. Actuator lever
8. Lever return spring
9. Parking brake strut
10. Strut spring
11. Primary shoe & lining
12. Secondary shoe & lining
13. Adjusting screw spring
17. Retaining ring
18. Pin
19. Parking brake lever
27. Backing plate
29. Adjusting screw assembly
30. Shoe retainer
32. Anchor pin
33. Shoe pads (6 places)

Exploded view of the drum brakes, 1985–87

1 RETURN SPRING
2 RETURN SPRING
3 HOLD-DOWN SPRING
4 BEARING SLEEVE
5 HOLD-DOWN PIN
6 ACTUATOR LINK
7 ACTUATOR LEVER
8 LEVER RETURN SPRING
9 PARKING BRAKE STRUT
10 STRUT SPRING

11 PRIMARY SHOE AND LINING
12 SECONDARY SHOE AND LINING
13 ADJUSTING SCREW SPRING
14 SOCKET
15 PIVOT NUT
16 ADJUSTING SCREW
17 RETAINING RING
18 PIN
19 PARKING BRAKE LEVER
20 BLEEDER VALVE

21 BOLT
22 BOOT
23 PISTON
24 SEAL
25 SPRING ASSEMBLY
26 WHEEL CYLINDER
27 BACKING PLATE
30 SHOE RETAINER
32 ANCHOR PIN
33 SHOE PADS (6 PLACES)

*LUBRICATE WITH THIN COATING
OF 1052196 LUBRICANT OR EQUIVALENT

Exploded view of the drum brakes, 1988–92

10. With the shoes removed, note the position of the adjusting spring and remove the spring and adjusting screw.

11. Remove the C-clip from the parking brake lever and remove the lever from the secondary shoe.

12. Use a damp cloth to remove all dirt and dust from the backing plate and brake parts. See the warning about brake dust in the drum removal procedure.

13. Check the wheel cylinders by carefully pulling the lower edges of the wheel cylinder boots away from the cylinders. If there is excessive leakage, the inside of the cylinder will be moist with fluid. If leakage exists, a wheel cylinder overhaul is in order. Do not delay, because brake failure could result.

NOTE: *A small amount of fluid will be present to act as a lubricant for the wheel cylinder pistons. Fluid spilling from the boot center hole, after the piston is removed, indicates cup leakage and the necessity for cylinder overhaul.*

14. Check the backing plate attaching bolts to make sure that they are tight. Use fine emery cloth to clean all rust and dirt from the shoe contact surfaces on the plate.

15. Lubricate the fulcrum end of the parking brake lever with brake grease specially made for the purpose. Install the lever on the secondary shoe and secure with C-clip.

16. Install the adjusting screw and spring on the shoes, connecting them together. The coils of the spring must not be over the star wheel on the adjuster. The left and right hand springs are not interchangeable. Do not mix them up.

17. Lubricate the shoe contact surfaces on the backing plate with the brake grease. Be certain when you are using this stuff that none of it actually gets on the linings or drums. Apply the same grease to the point where the parking brake cable contacts the plate. Use the grease sparingly.

18. Spread the shoe assemblies apart and connect the parking brake cable. Install the shoes on the backing plate, engaging the shoes at the top temporarily with the wheel cylinder pistons. Make sure that the star wheel on the adjuster is lined up with the adjusting hole in the backing plate, if the hole is back there.

19. Spread the shoes apart slightly and install the parking brake strut and spring. Make sure that the end of the strut without the spring engages the parking brake lever. The end with the spring engages the primary shoe (the one with the shorter lining).

20. Install the actuator pivot, lever and return spring. Install the actuating link in the shoe retainer. Lift up the actuator lever and hook the link into the lever.

21. Install the holddown pins through the back of the plate, install the lever pivots and holddown springs. Install the shoe return springs with a pair of pliers. Be very careful not to stretch or otherwise distort these springs.

22. Take a look at everything. Make sure the linings are in the right place, the self-adjusting mechanism is correctly installed, and the parking brake parts are all hooked up. If in doubt, remove the other wheel and take a look at that one for comparison.

23. Measure the width of the linings, then measure the inside width of the drum. Adjust the linings by means of the adjuster so that the drum will fit onto the linings.

24. Install the hub and bearing assembly onto the axle if removed. Tighten the retaining bolts to 35 ft. lbs. (55 Nm.).

25. Install the drum and wheel. Adjust the brakes using the procedure given earlier in this Chapter. Be sure to install a rubber hole cover in the knock-out hole after the adjustment is complete. Adjust the parking brake.

26. Lower the car and check the pedal for any sponginess or lack of a hard feel. Check the braking action and the parking brake. The brakes must not be applied severely immediately after installation. They should be used moderately for the first 200 miles of city driving or 1000 miles of highway driving, to allow the linings to conform to the shape of the drum.

Wheel Cylinders
REMOVAL AND INSTALLATION
1982–87

CAUTION: *Brake shoes contain asbestos, which has been determined to be a cancer causing agent. Never clean the brake surfaces with compressed air! Avoid inhaling any dust from any brake surface! When cleaning brake surfaces, use a commercially available brake cleaning fluid.*

1. Loosen the wheel lug nuts, raise and support the car, and remove the wheel. Remove the drum and brake shoes. Leave the hub and wheel bearing assembly in place.

2. Remove any dirt from around the brake line fitting. Disconnect the brake line.

3. Remove the wheel cylinder retainer by using two awls or punches with a tip diameter of ⅛ in. (3mm) or less. Insert the awls or punches into the access slots between the wheel cylinder pilot and retainer locking tabs. Bend both tabs away simultaneously. Remove the wheel cylinder from the backing plate.

To install:

4. Position the wheel cylinder against the backing plate and hold it in place with a wooden

Remove the wheel cylinder retainer from the backing plate with a pair of awls or punches

Installing a new retainer

block between the wheel cylinder and the hub and bearing assembly.

5. Install a new retainer over the wheel cylinder abutment on the rear of the backing plate by pressing it into place with a 1⅛ in. 12-point socket and an extension.

6. Install a new bleeder screw into the wheel cylinder. Install the brake line and tighten to 10–15 ft. lbs. (13–20 Nm.).

7. The rest of installation is the reverse of removal. After the drum is installed, bleed the brakes using the procedure outlined earlier in this Chapter.

1988–92

1. Raise and support the rear of the vehicle on jackstands. Remove the tire and brake drum.

2. Clean any dirt from around the wheel cylinder.

3. Disconnect and plug the brake line from the wheel cylinder.

4. Remove the wheel cylinder bolts using a #6 Torx socket.

5. Remove the wheel cylinder.

To install:

6. Position the wheel assembly and hold in place with a wooden block between the cylinder and axle flange.

7. Install the wheel cylinder bolts using a # 6 Torx socket and tighten to 15 ft. lbs. (20 Nm).

8. Install the inlet tube nut and torque to 13 ft. lbs. (17 Nm).

9. Bleed the brake system. Inspect the brake operation.

OVERHAUL

As is the case with master cylinders, overhaul kits are available for the wheel cylinders. And, as is the case with master cylinders, it is usually more profitable to simply buy new or rebuilt wheel cylinders rather than rebuilding them.

Exploded view of a wheel cylinder

PARKING BRAKE

ADJUSTMENT

1. Raise and support the car with both rear wheels off the ground.

2. If the vehicle is equipped with a hand parking brake lever, pull the parking brake lever exactly 5 ratchet clicks. If the vehicle is equipped with a foot operated parking brake, pull the parking brake lever exactly 2 ratchet clicks.

3. Loosen the equalizer locknut, then tighten the adjusting nut until the left rear wheel can just be turned backward using two hands, but is locked in forward rotation.

4. Tighten the locknut.

5. Release the parking brake. Rotate the rear wheels; there should be no drag.

6. Lower the car.

Cable

REMOVAL AND INSTALLATION

Front Cable

1. Place the gear selector in Neutral and apply the parking brake.

2. Remove the center console as detailed in Chapter 6.

3. Disconnect the parking brake cable from the lever.

4. Remove the cable retaining nut and the bracket securing the front cable to the floor panel.

5. Raise the car and loosen the equalizer nut.

6. Loosen the catalytic converter shield and then remove the parking brake cable from the body.

7. Disconnect the cable from the equalizer and then remove the cable from the guide and the underbody clips.

To install:

8. Position the cable to the equalizer, guide and underbody clips.

9. Install the parking brake cable to the body and tighten the catalytic converter shield.

10. Tighten the equalizer nut.

11. Install the cable retaining nut and the bracket securing the front cable to the floor panel.

12. Connect the parking brake cable to the lever.

13. Install the center console as detailed in Chapter 6.

14. Adjust the cable.

Right and Left Rear Cables

1. Raise and support the rear of the car.

2. Back off the equalizer nut until the cable tension is eliminated.

3. Remove the tires, wheels and brake drums.

4. Insert a screwdriver between the brake shoe and the top part of the brake adjuster bracket. Push the bracket to the front and then release the top brake adjuster rod.

5. Remove the rear hold down spring. Remove the actuator lever and the lever return spring.

1. Front parking brake cable
2. Right parking brake cable
3. Left parking brake cable
4. Clip
5. Guide
6. Parking brake lever
7. Bolt—25 N·m (18 lbs. ft.)
8. Washer
9. Nut—28 N·m (21 lbs. ft.)
10. Equalizer
11. Adjuster nut

Parking brake cable routing—1987–92

Parking brake cable routing—1982–86

6. Remove the adjuster screw spring.

7. Remove the top rear brake shoe return spring.

8. Unhook the parking brake cable from the parking brake lever.

9. Depress the conduit fitting retaining tangs and then remove the conduit fitting from the backing plate.

10. Remove the cable end button from the connector.

11. Depress the conduit fitting retaining tangs and remove the conduit fitting from the axle bracket.

To install:

12. Install the conduit fitting to the axle bracket.

13. Install the cable end button to the connector.

14. Install the conduit fitting to the backing plate.

15. Hook the parking brake cable to the parking brake lever.

16. Install the top rear brake shoe return spring.

17. Install the adjuster screw spring.

18. Install the rear hold down spring. Install the actuator lever and the lever return spring.

19. Install the top brake adjuster rod.

20. Install the tires, wheels and brake drums.

21. Adjust the cable.

ANTI-LOCK BRAKE SYSTEM

Description and Operation

ABS-VI has been designed to improve the controllability and steerability of a vehicle during braking that would cause one or more wheels to lock. ABS-VI accomplishes this objective by controlling the hydraulic pressure applied to each wheel brake.

Anti-Lock Brake System Service

Precaution

Failure to observe the following precautions may result in system damage.

• Before performing electric arc welding on the vehicle, disconnect the Electronic Brake Control Module (EBCM) and the hydraulic modulator connectors.

• When performing painting work on the vehicle, do not expose the Electronic Brake Control Module (EBCM) to temperatures in excess of 185°F (85°C) for longer than 2 hrs. The system may be exposed to temperatures up to 200°F (95°C) for less than 15 min.

• Never disconnect or connect the Electronic Brake Control Module (EBCM) or hydraulic modulator connectors with the ignition switch ON.

1   **BLEEDER VALVES**

ABS hydraulic modulator assembly bleeder locations

1 FLUID LEVEL SENSOR

Fluid level sensor location

1	BOLT SCREW	4	DASH PANEL
2	ENABLE RELAY	5	EBCM
3	CLENCH NUT		

The Enable relay location

• Never disassemble any component of the Anti-Lock Brake System (ABS) which is designated non-serviceable; the component must be replaced as an assembly.

• When filling the master cylinder, always use Delco Supreme 11 brake fluid or equivalent, which meets DOT-3 specifications; petroleum base fluid will destroy the rubber parts.

Electrical Connectors

Some ABS-VI components are equipped with electrical connectors using a Connector Position Assurance (CPA) lock.

1. Remove the lock before separating the electrical connectors.

2. Be careful not to damage the locking pin during removal.

3. Make sure that the rubber connector seal is in place on the connector before and after connection.

4. Always install the lock after ther connection is made.

ABS Hydraulic Modulator Assembly Bleeder Valves

REMOVAL AND INSTALLATION

1. Remove the bleeder valve or valves.

2. Install the bleeeder valve and tighten to 65 inch lbs. (7 Nm).

Fluid Level Sensor

REMOVAL AND INSTALLATION

1. Disconnect the electrical connection from the fluid level sensor.

2. Remove the fluid level sensor using needle nose pliers to compress the switch locking tabs at the inboard side of the master cylinder.

To install:

3. Insert the fluid level sensor unit until the locking tabs snap in place.

4. Connect the electrical connector to the sensor.

Enable Relay

REMOVAL AND INSTALLATION

1. Disconnect the electrical connection.

2. Release the retainer on the bracket and slide the relay off the bracket.

To install:

3. Slide the relay onto the bracket and make sure the retainer kocks the relay to the bracket.

4. Connect the electrical connection.

1   SOLENOID ELECTRICAL CONNECTOR

2   TORX® HEAD BOLTS

3   SOLENOID ASSEMBLY

4   ABS HYDRAULIC MODULATOR

Brake control solenoid removal

1   EBCM ELECTRICAL CONNECTORS

2   HEX HEAD SCREWS

3   EBCM

ABS-6 Electronic Control Unit removal

1	FRONT SENSOR ELECTRICAL CONNECTOR
2	FRONT SENSOR ATTACHING BOLT
3	FRONT SENSOR
4	KNUCKLE

Front wheel speed sensor removal

1	ENGINE HARNESS CLIPS
2	STEEL RIVETS
3	ENGINE HARNESS

FORWARD

Left front wheel speed sensor harness

1	ENGINE HARNESS CLIP
2	STEEL RIVETS
3	ENGINE HARNESS

FRT

Right front wheel speed sensor harness

FIG. 72 Rear wheel speed sensor/bearing removal

1	REAR SENSOR ELECTRICAL CONNECTOR
2	SENSOR RETAINING BOLTS (4)
3	SENSOR RETAINING NUTS (4)
4	BOLT REMOVAL ACCESS HOLE
5	DRUM BRAKE ASSEMBLY
6	REAR BEARING/SENSOR ASSEMBLY

Rear wheel speed sensor/bearing removal

1   REAR SENSOR ELECTRICAL CONNECTOR (2)   4   REAR SENSOR HARNESS

2   FUEL SENDER/ABS CONNECTOR   5   REAR BEARING/SENSOR ASSEMBLY

3   REAR SENSOR HARNESS RETAINING RIVETS (7)

Rear speed sensor wiring harness removal

1   SOLENOID ELECTRICAL   5   MASTER CYLINDER
    CONNECTORS   ATTACHING NUTS (2)
2   FLUID LEVEL SENSOR   6   HYDRAULIC MODULATOR
    CONNECTOR   AND MASTER CYLINDER
3   MOTOR PACK   ASSEMBLY
    CONNECTORS   7   VACUUM BOOSTER
4   HYDRAULIC BRAKE
    PIPES (4)

ABS Hydraulic Modulator assembly

ABS Lamp Driver Module

REMOVAL AND INSTALLATION

1. Disconnect the negative battery cable.
2. Remove the right side lower sound insulator panel.
3. Slide the glove box all the way out or remove it completely.
4. The lamp driver module is above the cruise control module taped to the instrument panel harness and is light green in color.
5. Open the connector and slide the circuit board out of the connector.

To install:
6. Install the circuit board to the connector.
7. Reposition the connector to the instrument panel harness and make sure it is retaped in place.
8. Slide the glove box back into the dash or reinstall the screws, if removed.
9. Install the right side lower sound insulator panel.
10. Connect the negative battery cable.

ABS Hydraulic Modulator Assembly

REMOVAL AND INSTALLATION

CAUTION: *To avoid personal injury, use the Tech I Scan tool to relieve the gear tension in the hydraulic modulator. This procedure must be performed prior to removal of the brake control and motor assembly.*

1. Disconnect the negative battery cable.
2. Disconnect the 2 solenoid electrical connectors and the fluid level sensor connector.
3. Disconnect the 6-pin and 3-pin motor pack electrical connectors.
4. Wrap a shop towel around the hydraulic brake lines and disconnect the 4 brake lines from the modulator.

NOTE: *Cap the disconnected lines to prevent the loss of fluid and the entry of moisture and contaminants.*

5. Remove the 2 nuts attaching the ABS hydraulic modulator assembly to the vacuum booster.
6. Remove the ABS hydraulic modulator assembly from the vehicle.

To install:
7. Install the ABS hydraulic modulator assembly to the vehicle. Install the 2 attaching nuts and tighten to 20 ft. lbs. (27 Nm).
8. Connect the 4 brake pipes to the modulator assembly. Tighten to 13 ft. lbs. (17 Nm).
9. Connect the 6-pin and 3-pin electrical connectors and the fluid level sensor connector.
10. Properly bleed the system.
11. Connect the negative battery cable.

Hydraulic Modulator Solenoid Assembly

REMOVAL AND INSTALLATION

1. Disconnect the negative battery cable.
2. Disconnect the solenoid electrical connector.
3. Remove the Torx® head bolts.
4. Remove the solenoid assembly.

To install:
5. Lubricate the O-rings on the new solenoid with clean brake fluid.
6. Position the solenoid so the connectors face each other.
7. Press down firmly by hand until the solenoid assembly flange seats on the modulator assembly.
8. Install the Torx® head bolts. Tighten to 39 inch lbs. (5 Nm).
9. Connect the solenoid electrical connector.
10. Properly bleed the brake system.
11. Connect the negative battery cable.

Front Wheel Speed Sensor

REMOVAL AND INSTALLATION

1. Disconnect the negative battery cable.
2. Raise and safely support the vehicle.
3. Disconnect the front sensor electrical connector.
4. Remove the Torx® bolt.
5. Remove the front wheel speed sensor.

To install:
6. Install the front wheel speed sensor on the mounting bracket.

NOTE: *Ensure the front wheel speed sensor is properly aligned and lays flat against the bracket bosses.*

7. Install the Torx® bolt. Tighten to 106 inch lbs. (12 Nm).
8. Connect the front sensor electrical connector.
9. Lower the vehicle.
10. Connect the negative battery cable.

Rear Wheel Bearing And Speed Sensor Assembly

REMOVAL AND INSTALLATION

NOTE: *The rear integral wheel bearing and sensor assembly must be replaced as a unit.*

1. Disconnect the negative battery cable.
2. Raise and safely support the vehicle.
3. Remove the rear wheel.
4. Remove the brake drum.
5. Disconnect the rear sensor electrical connector.
6. Remove the bolts and nuts attaching the rear wheel bearing and speed sensor assembly to the backing plate.

*USED WITH PRESSURE BLEEDING
PROCEDURE ONLY

ABS pressure bleeding procedure

Pressure bleeding of brake pipe connections

NOTE: *With the rear wheel bearing and speed sensor attaching bolts and nuts removed, the drum brake assembly is supported only by the brake line connection. To avoid*

bending or damage to the brake line, do not bump or exert force on the assembly.

7. Remove the rear wheel bearing and speed sensor assembly.

To install:

8. Install the rear wheel bearing and speed sensor assembly by aligning the bolt hoses in the wheel bearing and speed sensor assembly, drum brake assembly and rear suspension bracket. Install the attaching bolts and nuts. Tighten to 38 ft. lbs. (52 Nm).

9. Connect the rear speed sensor electrical connector.

10. Install the brake drum.

11. Install the rear wheel.

12. Lower the vehicle.

13. Connect the negative battery cable.

ABS Manual Bleeding Procedure

Brake Control Assembly

NOTE: *Only use brake fluid from a sealed container which meets DOT 3 specifications.*

1. Clean the area around the master cylinder cap.

2. Check fluid level in master cylinder reservoir and top-up, as necessary. Check fluid level frequently during bleeding procedure.

3. Attach a bleeder hose to the rear bleeder valve on the brake control assembly. Slowly open the bleeder valve.

4. Depress the brake pedal slowly until fluid begins to flow.

5. Close the valve and release the brake pedal.

6. Repeat for the front bleeder valve on the brake control assembly.

NOTE: *When fluid flows from both bleeder valves, the brake control assembly is sufficiently full of fluid. However, it may not be completely purged of air. Bleed the individual wheel calipers/cylinders and return to the control assembly to purge the remaining air.*

Wheel Calipers/Cylinders

NOTE: *Prior to bleeding the rear brakes, the rear displacement cylinder must be returned to the top-most position. This can be accomplished using the Tech I Scan tool or T-100 (CAMS), by entering the manual control function and applying the rear motor.*

If a Tech I or T-100 are unavailable, bleed the front brakes. Ensure the pedal is firm. Carefully drive the vehicle to a speed above 4 mph to cause the ABS system to initialize. This will return the rear displacement cylinder to the top-most position.

1. Clean the area around the master cylinder cap.

2. Check fluid level in master cylinder reservoir and top-up, as necessary. Check fluid level frequently during bleeding procedure.

3. Raise and safely support the vehicle.

4. Attach a bleeder hose to the bleeder valve of the right rear wheel and submerge the opposite hose in a clean container partially filled with brake fluid.

5. Open the bleeder valve.

6. Slowly depress the brake pedal.

7. Close the bleeder valve and release the brake pedal.

8. Wait 5 seconds.

9. Repeat Steps 5–8 until the pedal begins to feel firm and no air bubbles appear in the bleeder hose.

10. Repeat Steps 5–9, until the pedal is firm and no air bubbles appear in the brake hose, for the remaining wheels in the following order:

    a. left rear

    b. right front

    c. left front.

11. Lower the vehicle.

BRAKE SPECIFICATIONS

All measurements in inches unless noted.

Year	Model	Master Cylinder Bore	Brake Disc			Brake Drum Diameter			Minimum Lining Thickness	
			Original Thickness	Minimum Thickness	Maximum Runout	Original Inside Diameter	Max. Wear Limit	Maximum Machine Diameter.	Front	Rear
1982	All	0.94	0.885	0.830 ⑦	0.004	7.879	7.929	7.899	①	①
1983	All	0.94	0.885	0.830 ⑦	0.004	7.879	7.929	7.899	①	①
1984	All	0.94	0.885	0.830 ⑦	0.004	7.879	7.929	7.899	①	①
1985	All	0.94	0.885	0.830 ⑦	0.004	7.879	7.929	7.899	①	①
1986	All	0.94	0.885	0.830 ⑦	0.004	7.879	7.929	7.899	①	①
1987	All	0.94	0.885	0.830 ⑦	0.004	7.879	7.929	7.899	①	①
1988	Cavalier	②	0.885	0.830 ⑦	0.004	7.879	7.929	7.899	①	①
	Sunbird	③	0.885	0.830 ⑦	0.004	7.879	7.929	7.899	①	①
	Firenza	④	0.885	0.830 ⑦	0.004	7.879	7.929	7.899	①	①
	Skyhawk	⑤	0.885	0.830 ⑦	0.004	7.879	7.929	7.899	①	①
	Cimarron	⑥	0.885	0.830 ⑦	0.004	7.879	7.929	7.899	①	①
1989	All	0.874	0.885	0.830 ⑦	0.004	7.879	7.929	7.899	①	①
1990	All ⑧	0.874	0.885	0.830 ⑦	0.004	7.879	7.929	7.899	①	①
1991	All ⑧	0.874	0.885	0.830 ⑦	0.004	7.879	7.929	7.899	①	①
1992	All ⑧	0.874	0.885	0.830 ⑦	0.004	7.879	7.929	7.899	①	①

① Worn to within 0.030 inches of rivet at either end of the shoe.
② Prior to VIN 1G1F11WOJ7109958—0.937 inches
  Prior to VIN 1G1JE1114JJ136414—0.937 inches
  After VIN 1G1JF11WOJ7109957—0.874 inches
  After VIN 1G1JE1114JJ136413—0.874 inches
③ Prior to VIN 1G2JB51K4J7506603—0.937 inches
  After VIN 1G2JB51K4J7506602—0.874 inches
④ Prior to VIN 1G3JC51K7JK304666—0.937 inches
  After VIN 1G3JC51K7JK304665—0.874 inches
⑤ Prior to VIN 1G4JS11KXJK409094—0.937 inches
  After VIN 1G4JS11KXJK409093—0.874 inches
⑥ Prior to VIN 1G6JG51W1JJ502420—0.937 inches
  After VIN 1G6JG51W1JJ502419—0.874 inches
⑦ Discard thickness 0.815 inches
⑧ Cavalier and Sunbird only

Body

10

EXTERIOR

Doors

REMOVAL AND INSTALLATION

1. On doors equipped with power operated components proceed as folllows:

a. Remove the door trim panel, insulator pad (if so equipped), and the inner panel water deflector.

b. Disconnect the wiring components inside the door.

c. Remove the rubber conduit from the door, then remove the wiring harness from the door through the conduit access hole.

2. Tape the area (on the door pillar and body pillar) above the lower hinge with fabric tape.

CAUTION: *Before performing the following step, cover the spring with a towel to prevent the spring from flying out and possibly causing personal injury!*

3. Insert a suitable, long, flat bladed tool under the pivot point of the hold-open link and over top of the spring. The tool should be positioned so as not to apply pressure to the hold-open link. Cover the spring with a shop cloth and lift the tool to disengage the spring. The spring can also be removed by using tool J-28625, or equivalent, door hinge spring compressor tool. The tool is stamped right side and left side. For all the J-cars the tool stamped, "left side" is used to service the right side hinge spring. The tool stamped, "right side" is used to service the left hand hinge spring.

a. Install the two jaws of the tool over the spring. The jaw with the slots slides over spring at the hold-open link. The jaw with the hole fits over the spring at the bubble on the door hinge pillar.

b. Install the bolt to the jaws of the tool and tighten to compress the spring.

c. Remove the tool and spring from the door hinge assembly. Do not remove the spring from the tool.

4. When removing the hinge pin, save the "barrel" clips as follows:

a. Using two, suitable, flat bladed tools, spread the clip enough to move the clip above the recess toward the pointed end of the pin.

b. As the pin is removed, the clip will ride the shank of the pin and fall free.

c. Reinstall the clips onto the pins before installing the door.

5. With the aid of a helper to support the door, remove the lower hinge pin, using a soft headed hammer and locking type pliers. The helper can aid in removing the hinge pin by raising and lowering the rear of the door.

6. Insert the bolt into the hole of the lower hinge to maintain door attachment during upper hinge pin removal.

7. Remove the upper hinge pin in the same manner as the lower. Remove the bolt from the lower hinge and remove the door from the body.

To install:

NOTE: *Before installing the door, replace the hinge pin clips or reuse the old clips as explained in the removal procedure.*

8. With the aid of a helper, position the door and insert a bolt in the lower hinge hole.

9. The upper hinge pin is inserted with the pointed end up. The lower hinge pin is inserted with the pointed end down. With the door in the full open position, install the upper hinge pin using locking-type pliers and a soft headed hammer. Use a drift punch and hammer to complete pin installation.

10. Remove the screw from the lower hinge and install the lower hinge pin. The use of the special tool J-28625 or equivalent is the recommended method for installing the hinge spring.

WARNING: *If the spring is installed before installing the upper hinge pin, damage to the hinge bushings may result!*

Front door hinge system

11. If the spring was removed using a long, flat bladed tool, install the spring as follows:

a. Place the spring in tool J-28625 or equivalent.

b. Place the tool and spring in a bench vise.

c. Compress the tool in a vise and install the bolt until the spring is fully compressed.

d. Remove the tool with the compressed spring from the vise and install in the proper position in the door lower hinge. The slot in the jaw of the tool fits over the hold-open link. The hole in the other jaw fits over the bubble.

e. Remove the bolt from the tool to install the spring.

f. Remove the tool from the door hinge. (The tool will fall out in three pieces). Cycle the door to check spring operation.

12. If tool J-28625 or equivalent was used to remove the spring, follow Steps d, e, and f above to install the spring.

13. Remove the tape from the door and body pillars.

14. On the doors with power operated components, install all previously removed parts.

ADJUSTMENTS

The front door hinges are made of steel and are welded to the door and bolted to the body hinge pillars. No adjustment provisions are used in this type of door system.

Hood

REMOVAL AND INSTALLATION

1. Raise the hood and install protective coverings over the fender areas to prevent damage to the painted surfaces and mouldings.

2. Mark the position of the hinge on the hood to aid alignment during installation.

3. While supporting the hood, preferably with the aid of an assistant, remove the hinge to hood screws on each side of the hood and remove the hood assembly.

4. Install the hood using the alignment marks made when removed.

Hood latch adjustment—1982–87

1 HOOD ASM
2 INSULATOR
3 RETAINER

VIEW A
TYPICAL

Hood assembly—1982–87

1. Primary latch asm
2. Bolt 10 N·m (7 ft. lbs.)
3. "U" nut
4. Upper tie bar
5. Hood latch bolt

Primary latch—1982–87

HOOD ASM

1. Secondary latch
2. Bolt & spring asm 20 N·m (15 ft. lbs.)
3. Bolt 10 N·m (7 ft. lbs.)

Hood secondary latch—1982–87

1. Hood
2. Shim (as required)
3. Hinge assembly

4. Bolt (4). Torque to 27 N·m (20 lbs. ft.)

Hood hinge to hood installation—1988–92

ALIGMMENT

Fore and aft hood adjustment may be made at the hinge to hood attaching screws. Vertical adjustment at the front may be made by adjusting the rubber bumpers up and down.

Trunk Lid

REMOVAL AND INSTALLATION

2- and 4-Door Sedans

The trunk lid hinge is welded to the body and bolts to the lid.

1. Open the trunk lid and place protective coverings over the rear compartment (to protect the paint from damage).

2. Mark the location of the hinge-to-trunk lid bolts and disconnect the electrical connections and wiring from the lid (if equipped).

3. Using an assistant (to support the lid), remove the hinge-to-lid bolts and the lid from the vehicle.

4. To install, reverse the removal procedures. Adjust the position of the trunk lid to the body.

Hatchback Assembly

REMOVAL AND INSTALLATION

1. Prop open the lid and place protective coverings along the edges of the lift window opening (to protect the paint from damage).

2. Where necessary, disconnect the wire harness from the lift window.

3. While a helper supports the lid, use an awl or flat bladed tool to remove the clips on the gas supports and pull the supports off the retainer studs.

4. Close the lift window assembly.

5. Remove the rear upper garnish moulding at the rear of the headlining.

6. Remove the nuts retaining the lift window to the body.

7. With the aid of a helper, remove the lift window assembly from the body.

8. Installation is the reverse of removal.

NOTE: *The gas support assemblies are attached to the lid and the body and are secured by retaining clips and/or bolts.*

Lift Gate
(Station Wagon)

REMOVAL AND INSTALLATION

1. Prop open the lift gate and place protective coverings along the edges of the lift gate opening (to protect the paint from damage).

2. Where necessary, disconnect the wire harness from the lift gate.

3. While a helper supports the lid, use an awl or flat bladed tool to remove the clips on the gas supports and pull the supports off the retainer studs.

4. Use a $^3/_{16}$ in. (5mm) diameter rod to remove the hinge pins from the hinges. Place the end of the rod against the pointed end of the hinge pin; then strike the rod firmly to shear the retaining clip tabs and drive the pin through the hinge. Repeat the same thing on the opposite side hinge and with the aid of a helper remove the lift gate from the body.

REAR COMPARTMENT
LIFT WINDOW
ASSEMBLY

HINGE

SHIMS

RETAINING NUTS

Lift window to body bolts

Lift window gas support

5. To install, reverse the removal procedure. Prior to installing the hinge pins, install new retaining clips in the notches provide in the hinge pins. Position the retaining clips so that the tabs point toward the head of the pin.

NOTE: *The gas support assemblies are attached to the lid and the body and are secured by retaining clips and/or bolts.*

ADJUSTMENTS

Trunk Lid

Fore and aft adjustment of the lid assembly is controlled by the hinge to lid attaching bolts. To adjust the lid, loosen the hinge to lid attaching bolts and shift the lid to the desired position, then tighten the bolts. To increase opening assist, use tool J-211412-1 or equivalent and move the torque rods one step toward the rear of the vehicle. To decrease opening assist, move the torque rods one step toward the front of the vehicle.

Hatchback Assembly

The rear compartment lift window assembly (hatchback) height, fore and aft and side adjustments are controlled at the hinge to body location. This area of the body has oversize hinge attaching holes in addition to the hinge to body shims. Adjustment at the hinge location must be made at the lower panel by adjusting the

Lift gate gas supports—1982–88

rubber bumpers. The retaining bolts holding the hinge to body should be tightened to 15-20 ft. lbs.

1. Compartment lid
2. Hinge pin
3. Retaining ring
4. Rod

Lift gate, hinge pin, right side shown—1982–88

1. Lift gate
2. Support end clip
3. Ball stud (2)
4. Lift gate support
5. Support end clip

Lift gate gas supports—1989–92

1. Lift gate
2. Hinge pin
3. Hinge pin retaining clip

Lift gate hinge pin—1989–92

Typical power mirror parts

Outside Remote Mirrors

With the remote control door outside mirror, the remote control mirror cable must be disengaged from the door trim assembly on the standard trim styles to permit trim panel removal.

On custom trim styles the remote control mirror cable must be disengaged from the upper trim panel and the upper trim panel must be removed to permit lower trim panel removal.

Refer to the illustrations for both custom trim and standard trim.

NOTE: *The mirror glass face may be replaced by placing a piece of tape over the glass then breaking the mirror face. Adhesive back mirror faces are available.*

Remote control mirror cable and bezel attachment, standard trim

REMOVAL AND INSTALLATION

1. Remove the door trim panel as described in this Chapter. On standard trim styles, peel back the insulator and water deflector to gain access to the mirror cable.

2. Detach the cable from any retaining tabs in the door.

3. Remove the attaching nuts and remove the mirror and cable assembly from the door.

4. Install the base gasket and reverse the above to install the mirror.

Antenna

REMOVAL AND INSTALLATION

1. Unscrew the antenna mast, nut and bezel from on top of the fender.

2. Lift the hood and disconnect the antenna cable from the bottom of the antenna base.

3. Remove the two antenna retaining screws from inside the fender.

4. Reverse the above to install. Make sure all connections are tight.

INTERIOR

Instrument Panel

REMOVAL AND INSTALLATION

1982–88

1. Disconnect the battery ground cable.

2. Remove the left side I. P. (instrument panel) hush panel.

3. Remove the lower steering column trim cover and A/C outlet.

4. Remove center A/C duct and right close out panel (2 clips hold the A/C duct in the center). Disconnect the courtesy light.

5. Remove 3 steering column to I.P. bolts and lower steering column.

6. Remove the glove box door and trunk release switch, if so equipped.

7. Remove 2 radio to I.P. screws, disconnect electrical connectors and antenna lead from radio.

8. Remove 4 cluster to I.P. screws, disconnect the speedometer cable and remove 1 screw from speed sensor.

9. Remove 3 heater A/C control to I.P. screws. Remove clip and screw securing bowden cable to heater door.

10. Remove trim plate at right of steering column (spring clip attachment).

11. Disconnect the lighter connector. Remove headlamp switch knob and trimplate at left of steering column. Remove plastic nut at headlamp switch and remove the switch.

12. Remove rear defogger switch, if so equipped. Remove ashtray assembly and ashtray light. Remove hood release cable handle (1 screw and plastic nut).

1. Nut
2. Bezel
3. Cable asm
4. Bolt/screw
5. Front fender asm
6. Stud

NOTE LOCATE STUDS OF ITEM **2** INTO HOLE CUTOUTS IN FENDER AS SHOWN.

Antenna mounting

LEFT SIDE A/C

RIGHT SIDE A/C

LEFT SIDE—HEATER

RIGHT SIDE—HEATER

1 ACCELERATOR ROD	6 A/C HEATER DUCT	11 I.P. PAD
2 DASH MAT	7 ACCELERATOR ROD	12 BRACKET
3 CARPET	8 INSTRUMENT PANEL	13 SUPT I.P. PAD
4 I.P. PAD	9 CARPET	14 ECM
5 ECM BRACKET	10 DASH MAT	15 AIR DISTRIBUTION DUCT

Instrument panel hush panels 1982–88

1. DASH PANEL
2. WELD NUTS
3. CENTER REINF
4. PAD ASM.
5. SNAP-IN CLIPS
6. R.H. LOWER I.P. TRIM PLATE
7. L.H. LOWER I.P. TRIM PLATE
8. I.P. TRIM PLATE
9. TORX SCREW
10. HUSH PANEL
11. STEERING COLUMN TRIM COVER

Instrument panel and trim plates 1982–88

Instrument panel pad mounting 1982–88 Type 10

Instrument panel steering column trim cover 1982–88 Type 10

13. Remove defroster grilles (pry up) and 4 screws at defroster outlets.

14. Remove the conveniece center (1 screw), I.P. harness and bulk head connector (2 nuts, 1 screw). Remove 1 brace to glove box screw.

15. Remove the nuts at either side of I.P. carrier lower back of panel and disconnect the electrical connectors (I.P. duct work must be removed from harness).

16. Remove the carrier and lay on seat. Remove A/C ductwork, screws and clips attaching the wiring harness to carrier.

17. Remove the radio speakers and grilles.

To install:

18. Install the radio speakers and grilles.

19. Install the carrier. Install A/C ductwork, screws and clips attaching the wiring harness to carrier.

20. Install the nuts at either side of I.P. carrier lower back of panel and connect the electrical connectors.

21. Install the convenience center (1 screw), I.P. harness and bulk head connector (2 nuts, 1 screw). Install 1 brace to glove box screw.

22. Install defroster grilles (pry up) and 4 screws at defroster outlets.

23. Install rear defogger switch, if so equipped. Install ashtray assembly and ashtray light. Install hood release cable handle (1 screw and plastic nut).

24. Connect the lighter connector. Install headlamp switch knob and trimplate at left of steering column. Install the switch, Install plastic nut at headlamp switch.

25. Install trim plate at right of steering column (spring clip attachment).

26. Install 3 heater A/C control to I.P. screws. Install clip and screw securing bowden cable to heater door.

27. Connect the speedometer cable and Install 1 screw in speed sensor. Install 4 cluster to I.P. screws.

28. Connect electrical connectors and antenna lead to radio. Install 2 radio to I.P. screws.

29. Install the glove box door and trunk release switch, if so equipped.

30. Raise steering column. Install 3 steering column to I.P. bolts.

31. Install center A/C duct and right close out panel (2 clips hold the A/C duct in the center). Connect the courtesy light.

1. "U" NUT
2. DASH PANEL
3. WELD NUTS
4. BOLT/SCREW – 10 N·m (8 LBS. FT.)
5. CENTER SUPPORT, INSTRUMENT PANEL
6. BOLT/SCREW – 7 N·m (5 LBS. FT.)
7. NUT – 10 N·m (8 LBS. FT.)
8. BOLT/SCREW – 1 N·m (8 LBS. IN.)

Instrument panel 1988–92

32. Install the lower steering column trim cover and A/C outlet.

33. Install the left side I. P. (instrument panel) hush panel.

34. Connect the battery ground cable.

1989–92

1. Disconnect the battery ground cable.

2. Remove The right and left sound insulators, steering column filler, right and left I.P.(instrument panel) trim plates.

3. Remove the console housing and glove box door.

4. Remove the heater and A/C control.

5. Remove the convenience center. Disconnect the forward lamp harness and engine harness from bulkhead.

6. Remove the bulkhead from cowl. Remove the hood release handle (retained by two set screws), and defroster grilles.

7. Remove 4 upper I.P. retaining screws located in defroster duct openings. Remove 2 lower corner I.P. retaining nuts.

8. Remove 1 screw to I.P. brace at left side of I.P. compartment opening.

9. Remove 2 nuts securing wire harness to neutral start switch (manual transmissions only).

10. Remove 3 steering column rertaining bolts, 2 at I.P. pad and 1 at cowl and lower steering column.

11. Pull I.P. assembly out far enough to disconnect ignition switch, headlamp dimmer switch and turn signal switch. Disconnect all other electrical wiring connectors, vacuum lines and radio antenna lead to remove the I.P. assembly.

12. Remove the instrument panel (I.P.) with wiring harness attached.

To install:

13. Position the I.P to cowl and connect all electrical connectors and vacuum hoses.

14. Install 3 steering column retaining bolt. Install screw into I.P. brace at left side of I.P. compartment, tighten to 57 inch lbs.

15. Install 2 lower corner I.P. retaining nuts, tighten to 12 inch lbs. Install 4 screws through defroster ducts into cowl, tighten to 12 inch lbs.

16. Install 2 lower nuts securing wire harness to neutral start switch (manual transmission only).

17. Install defroster grilles, hood release handle, bulkhead and forward lamp and engine harness into bulkhead.

18. Install convenience center, heater A/C control assembly and glove box door.

19. Install console housing, right and left trim plates and steering column filler.

20. Install the left and right sound insulators.

21. Connect the battery ground cable.

Console

REMOVAL AND INSTALLATION

1. Place gear selector in the neutral position and apply the parking brake.Remove front ashtray, then remove 2 screws (some models use Torx®) under ash tray.

2. On automatic trans., gently pry out the emblem in the center of the shift knob, then re-

1	CONSOLE ASM.
2	REAR SEAT ASH TRAY ASSEMBLY
3	ASH TRAY
4	TRIMPLATE ASM.
5	CONSOLE
6	NUT
7	TRIMPLATE
8	LENS
9	FILTER
10	HOUSING
11	CONSOLE
12	TRANSMISSION SHIFTER ASSEMBLY
13	INDICATOR LAMP
14	POINTER

Console automatic transmission 1982–88

AUTOMATIC TRANSMISSION

FRONT

A

VIEW A

1	STRAP TO SHIFTER CABLE
2	HARNESS ROUTES UNDER CARPET
3	TO I.P. HARNESS
4	ASHTRAY LAMP
5	CONSOLE TRIMPLATE
6	SHIFTER
7	TO NEUT. START SW.
8	TO PARK BRAKE SW.
9	GROUND
10	SHIFT INDICATOR LAMP
11	JUMPER WIRE
12	HEATER
13	I.P. HARNESS
14	TO I.P. HARNESS
15	HARNESS ROUTES UNDER CARPET
16	ASH TRAY LAMP
17	TRANS. CONTROL ASM.
18	PARK BRAKE SWITCH
19	GROUND LEAD
20	BACK-UP LAMP SWITCH

MANUAL TRANSMISSION

FRT

Console wiring harness 1982–88

INSTRUMENT PANEL ASM

BRACKET FRONT

FRT

FLOOR PANEL

FRONT MOUNTING BRACKET

SHIFTER ASM

VIEW A

MANUAL

FRT

REAR MOUNTING BRACKET

Console assembly 1982–88 Type 10

Console assembly shift indicator 1982–88 Type 10

Console assembly ash tray 1982–88 Type 10

1. SCREWS - 1.5 N.M (12 LBS. IN.)
2. CONSOLE REAR TRIM PLATE
3. PARKING BRAKE ASM.
4. CONSOLE ASM.
5. REAR CONSOLE BRACKET
6. FLOOR PANEL

Console assembly rear trim plate 1989–92

1	"U" NUT
2	BOLT/SCREW — 7 N•m (5 LBS. FT.)
3	COMPARTMENT, FLOOR CONSOLE ARMREST
4	ARMREST ASM.
5	PARKING BRAKE ASM.
6	FLOOR CONSOLE ASM.
7	REAR BRACKET, FLOOR CONSOLE

Console assembly arm rest 1989–92

move snapring securing knob. Lift trimplate assembly out by pulling front end up first and disconnect wire harness.

3. On manual trans., remove the shift knob by removing the set screw under the knob.

4. On automatic trans., remove 3 screws under the trim plate, then remove rear ashtray and remove screw under ashtray. Lift console off.

5. On manual trans., remove 1 screw under parking brake handle and 2 screws at sides of console in rear. Lift console off.

6. Installation is the reverse of the removal procedure.

Door Panel

REMOVAL AND INSTALLATION

NOTE: *Removing a window crank handle (with a retaining clip inside the handle) without the special tool can be problem. An alternative method is take a clean shop towel and wedge it between the window crank handle and the door panel. Then move it up, while pulling it from left to right, as in a sawing motion working the clean shop towel until the retaining clip comes free. Then remove the window crank handle. Refer to the illustration in this Chapter.*

1. CONSOLE FRONT BRACKET
2. NUT — 24 N·m (18 LBS. FT.)
3. TRANSAXLE CONTROL ASM.
4. BOLT
5. FLOOR PANEL

Console assembly housing bracket 1989–92

1. BRACKET ASM., FLOOR CONSOLE
2. BOLT/SCREW — 2 N·m (17 LBS. IN.)
3. "U" NUT
4. CONSOLE ASM.

Console assembly front bracket 1989–92

1982-87

A one piece trim panel is used on styles with standard trim. The custom trim has an upper metal trim panel. The one piece trim hangs over the door inner panel across the top and is secured by clips down the sides and across the bottom. It is retained by screws located in the areas of the top front of the panel assembly.

1. Remove all door inside handles.

2. Remove the door inside locking rod knob.

3. Remove the screws inserted through the door armrest and pull the handle assembly into the door inner panel or armrest hanger support bracket.

4. On styles with remote control mirrors assemblies, disengage the end of the mirror control cable from the bezel on the standard trim, or from the upper trim panel on the custom trim. On custom trim, remove the upper trim panel.

5. On styles with power window or door lock controls located in the door trim panel, disconnect the wire harnesses at the switch assemblies. On the four door sedan and the two door hatchback, remove the switch cover by pushing down at the switch area and pulling down at the bottom of the cover. The switch and base may be removed from the trim with the cover removed.

6. Remove the remote control handle bezel screws.

7. Remove the screws used to hold the armrest to the inner panel.

8. Remove the screws and plastic retainers from the perimeter of the door trim using tool BT-7323A or equivalent and a screwdriver. To remove the trim panel, push the trim panel upward and outboard to disengage from the door inner panel at the beltline.

9. On styles with an insulator pad fastened to the door inner panel, use tool J-21104 or equivalent to remove the fasteners and the insulator pad.

10. On styles with the water defector held in place by fasteners, use tool BT-7323A or equivalent to remove the fasteners and the water deflector.

11. On styles with the armrest bracket riveted to the inner panel and installed over the water deflector, drill out the armrest bracket rivets using a $3/16$ in. (5mm) drill bit.

12. To install the insulator pad or water deflector, locate the fasteners in the holes in the door inner panel and press in place. Replace all tape which may have been applied to assist in holding insulator pad or water deflector in place. Where necessary, install the armrest support bracket over the water deflector and onto the door inner panel using $3/16$ in. × $11/32$ in.

Front door armrest and pull handle attachment, custom trim—1982–89

(5mm × 9mm) rivets.

13. Before installing the door trim panel, check that all trim retainers are securely installed to the assembly and are not damaged. Replace retainers where required.

14. Connect all electrical components.

15. To install the door trim panel, locate the top of the assembly over the upper flange of the door inner panel, inserting the door handle through the handle slot in the panel and press down on the trim panel to engage the upper retaining clips.

16. Position the trim panel to the door inner panel so the trim retainers are align with the attaching holes in the panel and tap the retainers into the holes with the palm of your hand or a clean rubber mallet.

17. Install all previously removed items.

Front Door Lock
REMOVAL AND INSTALLATION

1. Raise the door window and remove the door trim panel and water deflector.

2. Disengage the following rods at the lock assembly:

    a. Inside locking rod.

Removing the trim clip retained door inside handle

Removing the window crank handle with a clean shop towel

Front door armrest and pull handle attachment, standard trim—1982–89

Window regulator handle installation

ARMREST HANGER PLATE

UPPER TRIM PANEL RETAINER

SECTION B-B

FASTENER

SECTION A-A

POWER DOOR LOCK AND
POWER WINDOW HARNESS

CUSTOM TRIM PANEL

DOOR INNER PANEL

TRIM PANEL

SECTION C-C

Front door trim panel retention

BEZEL
DOOR LOCK
AND REMOTE
CONTROL
HANDLE

VIEW A

LOCKING ROD

LOCKING ROD KNOB

Door lock remote control handle and bezel

b. Inside handle to locking rod.

c. Lock cylinder to locking rod.

3. Remove the lock screws and lower the lock to disengage the outside handle to the lock rod. Remove the lock from the door.

4. To install, first install the the spring clips to the lock assembly, then reverse the removal procedure. Tighten the lock retaining screws to 80-100 inch lbs.

Rear Door Lock

REMOVAL AND INSTALLATION

1. Remove the door trim and water deflector.

2. Remove the door glass assembly and the stationary vent glass assembly.

3. Disconnect the inside handle to lock rod and inside locking knob to lock rod.

4. Disconnect the outside handle to lock rod.

5. Remove the lock screws and remove the lock through the access hole.

6. To install, reverse the removal procedure and tighten the lock retaining screws to 80-100 inch lbs.

Front Door Glass

REMOVAL AND INSTALLATION

Except Convertible

1. Raise the door window to the full up position and remove the door trim panel and water deflector.

2. Remove the bolts holding the front glass retainer to the door inner panel and remove the retainer through the rear access hole. Lower the glass to approximately 3 in. (76mm) above the beltline.

3. Rotate the glass forward to disengage the window regulator roller from the sash channel.

5. Lower the glass into the door to disengage the rear guide (on the glass) from the rear run channel.

6. Using care, raise the glass while tilting forward and remove the glass inboard of the upper frame.

7. To install, tilt the front edge of the glass downward to locate the glass in the door.

8. Apply pressure rearward and snap the glass rear guide into the rear run channel.

9. Lower the glass to about 3 in. (76mm) above the beltline and install the widow regulator roller to sash channel.

10. Run the glass to the full up position.

11. Place the front glass retainer in position and install the bolts.

12. Check the window to make sure it operates correctly, then install the remaining trim parts.

Convertible

1. Remove the door trim panel, sound absorber, armrest bracket and water deflector.

2. Position the glass so that the up stop spanner nut on the glass is visible through the access hole.

3. Using tool J-22055 or equivalent, remove the spanner nut, bushing and stop from the glass.

4. Position the glass so the spanner nuts are visible through the access hole.

5. Remove the spanner nuts and bushings.

6. Loosen the upper stabilizers.

7. Disengage the glass from the studs on the sash where the spanner nuts were removed.

8. Lower the regulator to the full-down position.

9. Grasp the glass and pull the glass up, with the front of the glass tilted down and remove the glass.

10. Installation is the reverse of removal. Before installing trim parts, check the window operation for proper alignment and adjust as needed.

Rear Door Glass

REMOVAL AND INSTALLATION

NOTE: *The stationary vent assembly must be removed with the rear glass assembly as a unit.*

1. Remove the door trim panel and the water deflector.

2. Lower the glass to the full down position.

3. Remove the screws at the top of the division channel.

4. Remove the bolt holding the vent glass support at the belt.

5. Remove the screws at the rear of the door face holding the bottom of the division to the door.

6. Push the stationary vent assembly down and forward to disengage the vent assembly from the run channel. Now that the vent assembly is inboard of the door frame, lift up until the vent assembly is stopped against the door glass.

7. Raise the door glass 6-8 in. (152–203mm) and tilt the whole assembly rearward and disengage the roller from the glass sash channel.

8. To install, place the rear door glass in the vent division channel.

9. Load the rear window and vent assembly by lowering the assemblies through the door belt opening. Rotate the glass forward to engage the regulator roller in the glass sash channel. Reposition the vent glass into the door frame.

10. Replace the screws at the top of the division channel.

1	INSIDE LOCK KNOB ROD	6	ELECTRICAL CONNECTOR	11	ACTUATOR	
2	RIVET	7	BELLCRANK ROD	12	INSIDE LOCK KNOB ROD	
3	ACTUATOR	8	GUIDE CLIP	13	CLIP	
4	BELLCRANK	9	RIVET (3)	14	RIVET (2)	
5	RIVET (2)	10	BELLCRANK			

Front door lock bellcrank and actuator

11. Replace the screws at the rear face of the door holding division and lower support in place.

12. Replace the bolt securing the division channel support at the belt.

13. Replace all previously removed trim.

Front Window Regulator And Motor

NOTE: *The following procedure includes both manual and power window regulator removal and installation. Besides the regulators, window motors and rollers including the washer and pin are serviced separately.*

REMOVAL AND INSTALLATION

Except Convertible

1. Remove the door trim panel and the water deflector.

2. Raise the glass to the full up position and tape the glass to the door frame using fabric tape.

3. Punch out the center pins of the regulator rivets using a ¼ in. (6mm) drill bit. On electric regulators, drill out the rivets supporting the motor to the door inner panel.

4. Move the regulator rearward and disconnect the wiring harness from the motor, if so equipped. Disengage the roller on the regulator lift arm from the glass sash channel.

5. Remove the regulator through the rear access hole.

6. Using a ³⁄₁₆ in. (5mm) drill bit, drill out the motor attaching rivets and remove the motor from the regulator, if so equipped.

To install:

7. If so equipped, attach the motor to the regulator using a rivet tool and ³⁄₁₆ in. (5mm) rivets or ³⁄₁₆ in. (5mm) nuts and bolts.

8. Place the regulator through the rear access hole into the door inner panel. If an electric regulator is being installed, connect the wire connector to the motor prior to installing the regulator in the panel.

9. Locate the lift arm roller into the glass sash channel.

10. Using rivet tool J-29022 or equivalent, rivet the regulator to the inner panel of the

VIEW A

1	HANDLE ASSEMBLY—INSIDE	6	LOCK ASSEMBLY
2	ROD—LOCK REMOTE CONTROL TO LOCK	7	ROD—INSIDE LOCKING TO LOCK
3	ROD—OUTSIDE HANDLE TO LOCK	8	ROD—INSIDE LOCKING TO ACTUATOR
4	HANDLE ASSEMBLY—OUTSIDE	9	ACTUATOR ASSEMBLY—ELECTRIC LOCK
5	LOCK SCREWS (3)	10	KNOB—INSIDE LOCKING

Rear door lock system

1. Front glass run channel
2. Front up stop
3. Catch—front up stop
4. Glass retainer
5. Bushing
6. Cam assembly door glass
7. Front stabilizer
8. Glass assembly
9. Rear stabilizer
10. Guide block
11. Rivets—regulator
12. Rivets—regulator motor
13. Rear up stop block
14. Rivets—rear cam assembly lower
15. Attaching nuts inner panel cam door reinforcement

Front door hardware, convertible

1. Rod—remote control to lock
2. Handle—inside lock remote control
3. Filler—sealing strip—front
4. Knob—inside lock
5. Retainer—glass front run channel
6. Regulator assembly
7. Actuator assembly—door lock
8. Glass down stop
9. Handle—window regulator
10. Shoe—inside locking rods
11. Rod—inside lock to actuator
12. Rod—inside lock knob to lock
13. Rod—outside handle to lock
14. Filler—sealing strip rear
15. Support—vent glass
16. Vent assembly—stationary
17. Bell crank
18. Glass assembly
19. Handle—outside glass
20. Glass guide
21. Glass sash channel
22. Lock assembly

Rear door hardware

door using ¼ in. × ½ in. (6mm × 13mm) aluminum peel type rivets (part no. 9436175 or equivalent). If a rivet tool is not available, use the following nut and bolt method:

  a. Install U-clips on the regulator and motor (if so equipped), at the attaching locations. Be sure to install clips with clinch nuts on the outboard side of the regulator.

  b. Place the regulator through the rear access hole into the door inner panel. If an electric regulator is being installed, connect the wire connector to the motor prior to installing the regulator in the panel.

  c. Locate the lift arm roller into the glass sash channel.

  d. Align the regulator with the clinch nuts to the holes in the inner panel.

  e. Attach the regulator and motor to the door inner panel with ¼ in.–20 × ½ in. screws into ¼ in. nuts with integral washers. Tighten the screws to 90-125 inch lbs.

11. If an electrical window regulator is being installed use a rivet mentioned in step 10 to rivet the regulator motor to the door inner panel.

12. Replace all previously removed parts.

Cavalier Convertible

1. Remove the door trim panel, sound absorber, armrest bracket and water deflector.

2. Using a ¼ in. (6mm) drill bit, drill out the rivets supporting the motor to the door inner panel.

3. Disconnect the electrical connector from the regulator motor.

4. Support the door glass in the full-up position, using rubber wedge door stops.

5. Remove the nuts holding the cam assembly door reinforcement to the inner panel and remove the cam assembly.

6. Remove the bolt holding the upper portion of the rear cam assembly to the inner panel.

7. Using a ³⁄₁₆ in. (5mm) drill bit, drill out the rivets, holding the lower section of the rear cam assembly to the inner panel.

8. Remove the up stop from the rear cam assembly.

9. Remove the rear cam assembly through the access hole.

10. Disengage the regulator from the glass sash channel and remove the regulator through the access hole.

11. If equipped with an electric window regulator and you wish to remove the motor from the regulator proceed as follows:

CAUTION: *When removing the electric motor from the regulator, the sector gear must be locked in position. The regulator lift arm is under tension from the counterbalance spring and could cause personal injury if the sector gear is not locked in position.*

a. Drill a hole through the regulator sector gear and backplate and install a bolt and nut to lock the sector gear in position.

b. Using a $3/16$ in. (5mm) drill bit, drill out the motor attaching rivets and remove the motor from the regulator.

c. To install the motor to the regulator use a rivet tool J-29022 or equivalent and install $3/16$ in. (5mm) rivets or $3/16$ in. (5mm) nuts and bolts. Remove the bolt and nut used to secure the sector gear in position.

To install:

12. Make sure the regulator is in the full up position.

13. Install the regulator arm rollers to the glass sash channel.

14. Install the rear cam assembly using $3/16$ in. (5mm) aluminum peel-type rivets making sure to install the up stop in the cam assembly.

15. Connect the electrical connector to the motor on the regulator.

16. Engage the roller on the regulator lift arm in the cam assembly door reinforcement.

17. Install the cam assembly door reinforcement to the inner panel.

18. Align the attaching holes in the regulator with the holes in the inner panel.

19. Install the regulator to the inner panel, using a rivet gun and $1/4$ in. × $1/2$ in. (6mm × 13mm) aluminum peel type rivets.

Rear Window Regulator

NOTE: *The following procedure includes both manual and power window regulator removal and installation. Besides the regulators, window motors and rollers including the washer and pin are serviced separately.*

REMOVAL AND INSTALLATION

1. Remove the door trim panel and the water deflector.

2. Raise the glass to the full up position and tape the glass to the door frame using fabric tape.

3. Punch out the center pins of the regulator rivets using a $1/4$ in. (6mm) drill bit. On electric regulators, drill out the rivets supporting the motor to the door inner panel.

4. Disconnect the wiring harness from the motor, if so equipped. Disengage the roller on the regulator lift arm from the glass sash channel.

5. Remove the regulator through the rear access hole.

6. Using a $3/16$ in. (5mm) drill bit, drill out the motor attaching rivets and remove the motor from the regulator, if so equipped.

7. To install, if so equipped, attach the motor to the regulator using a rivet tool and $3/16$ in. (5mm) rivets or $3/16$ in. (5mm) nuts and bolts.

8. Place the regulator through the rear access hole into the door inner panel. If an electric regulator is being installed, connect the wire connector to the motor prior to installing the regulator in the panel.

9. Locate the lift arm roller into the glass sash channel.

10. Using rivet tool J-29022 or equivalent, rivet the regulator to the inner panel of the door using $1/4$ in. × $1/2$ in. (6mm × 13mm) aluminum peel type rivets (part no. 9436175 or equivalent). If a rivet tool is not available, use the following nut and bolt method:

a. Install U-clips on the regulator and motor (if so equipped), at the attaching locations. Be sure to install clips with clinch nuts on the outboard side of the regulator.

b. Place the regulator through the rear access hole into the door inner panel. If an electric regulator is being installed, connect the wire connector to the motor prior to installing the regulator in the panel.

c. Locate the lift arm roller into the glass sash channel.

d. Align the regulator with the clinch nuts to the holes in the inner panel.

e. Attach the regulator and motor to the door inner panel with $1/4$ in.–20 × $1/2$ in. screws into $1/4$ in. nuts with integral washers. Tighten the screws to 90-125 inch lbs.

11. If an electrical window regulator is being installed use a rivet mentioned in step 10 to rivet the regulator motor to the door inner panel.

12. Replace all previously removed parts.

Inside Rearview Mirror
REPLACEMENT

The rearview mirror is attached to a support which is secured to the windshield glass. This support is installed by the glass supplier using a plastic-polyvinyl butyl adhesive.

Service replacement windshield glass has the mirror support bonded to the glass assembly.

Service kits are available to replace a detached mirror support or install a new part. Follow the manufacturer's instructions for replacement.

TAB OF ADJUSTER
INSERTED INTO
POCKET OF COVER

VIEW A

ADJUSTER
LEG COVER

FLOOR PAN TO
SEAT ADJUSTER
ATTACHING NUT

PUSH-ON FASTENER

A

ADJUSTER LEG COVER

FRONT SEAT ADJUSTER COVER

Seat to floor pan installation, six way power seat

SEAT ADJUSTER
COVER

SEAT ADJUSTER
COVER

SEAT ADJUSTER COVERS

SEAT ADJUSTER
TO FLOOR PAN NUT

Seat to floor pan installation, manual seat

Removal and installation of the front seat adjuster control arm knob

Installing the rear seat cushion

Front Seat

REMOVAL AND INSTALLATION

1. Operate the seat to the full-forward position. If a six way power seat is operable, move the seat to the full-forward and up positions. To gain access to the adjuster to floor pan retaining nuts, remove the adjuster rear foot covers or carpet retainers.

2. Remove the track covers where necessary, then remove the rear attaching nuts. Remove the front foot covers, then remove the adjuster to floor pan front attaching nuts.

3. On seats with power adjusters, tilt the seat rearward and disconnect the feed wire connector.

4. Remove the seat assembly from the car.

5. To install the seat assembly reverse the removal procedure. Tighten the seat adjuster to floor pan attaching bolts or nuts to 21 ft. lbs.

Rear Seat Cushion

REMOVAL AND INSTALLATION

1. Remove the rear seat cushion attaching bolts, located at the center of the right and left sections of the rear seat cushion.

2. Lift the cushion upward and remove from the vehicle.

3. To install, reverse the removal procedure. Torque the seat cushion attaching bolts to 14-20 ft. lbs.

Power Seat Motors

REMOVAL AND INSTALLATION

1. Remove the front seat assembly and place upside down on a clean surface.

2. Disconnect the motor feed wires from the motor.

3. Remove the nut securing the front of the motor support bracket to the inboard adjuster and withdraw the assembly from the adjuster and the gearnut drives.

4. Disconnect the drive cables from the motor and complete the removal of the support bracket with motors attached.

5. Grind off the peened over ends(s) of the grommet assembly securing the motor to the support and separate the motors from the support, as required.

6. To install, reverse the removal procedure except as noted:

    a. Drill out the top end of the grommet assembly using a $\frac{3}{16}$ in. (5mm) drill.

    b. Install the grommet assembly to the motor support bracket and secure the motor to the grommet using a $\frac{3}{16}$ in. (5mm) rivet.

Mechanic's Data

11

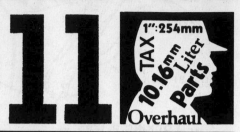

General Conversion Table

Multiply By	To Convert	To	
LENGTH			
2.54	Inches	Centimeters	.3937
25.4	Inches	Millimeters	.03937
30.48	Feet	Centimeters	.0328
.304	Feet	Meters	3.28
.914	Yards	Meters	1.094
1.609	Miles	Kilometers	.621
VOLUME			
.473	Pints	Liters	2.11
.946	Quarts	Liters	1.06
3.785	Gallons	Liters	.264
.016	Cubic inches	Liters	61.02
16.39	Cubic inches	Cubic cms.	.061
28.3	Cubic feet	Liters	.0353
MASS (Weight)			
28.35	Ounces	Grams	.035
.4536	Pounds	Kilograms	2.20
—	To obtain	From	Multiply by

Multiply By	To Convert	To	
AREA			
.645	Square inches	Square cms.	.155
.836	Square yds.	Square meters	1.196
FORCE			
4.448	Pounds	Newtons	.225
.138	Ft./lbs.	Kilogram/meters	7.23
1.36	Ft./lbs.	Newton-meters	.737
.112	In./lbs.	Newton-meters	8.844
PRESSURE			
.068	Psi	Atmospheres	14.7
6.89	Psi	Kilopascals	.145
OTHER			
1.104	Horsepower (DIN)	Horsepower (SAE)	.9861
.746	Horsepower (SAE)	Kilowatts (KW)	1.34
1.60	Mph	Km/h	.625
.425	Mpg	Km/1	2.35
—	To obtain	From	Multiply by

Tap Drill Sizes

National Coarse or U.S.S.

Screw & Tap Size	Threads Per Inch	Use Drill Number
No. 5	40	.39
No. 6	32	.36
No. 8	32	.29
No. 10	24	.25
No. 12	24	.17
1/4	20	8
5/16	18	.F
3/8	16	5/16
7/16	14	.U
1/2	13	27/64
9/16	12	31/64
5/8	11	17/32
3/4	10	21/32
7/8	9	49/64

National Coarse or U.S.S.

Screw & Tap Size	Threads Per Inch	Use Drill Number
1	8	7/8
1 1/8	7	63/64
1 1/4	7	1 7/64
1 1/2	6	1 11/32

National Fine or S.A.E.

Screw & Tap Size	Threads Per Inch	Use Drill Number
No. 5	44	.37
No. 6	40	.33
No. 8	36	.29
No. 10	32	.21

National Fine or S.A.E.

Screw & Tap Size	Threads Per Inch	Use Drill Number
No. 12	28	.15
1/4	28	3
6/16	24	1
3/8	24	.Q
7/16	20	.W
1/2	20	29/64
9/16	18	33/64
5/8	18	37/64
3/4	16	11/16
7/8	14	13/16
1 1/8	12	1 3/64
1 1/4	12	1 11/64
1 1/2	12	1 27/64

Drill Sizes In Decimal Equivalents

Inch	Decimal	Wire	mm
1/64	.0156		.39
	.0157		.4
	.0160	78	
	.0165		.42
	.0173		.44
	.0177		.45
	.0180	77	
	.0181		.46
	.0189		.48
	.0197		.5
	.0200	76	
	.0210	75	
	.0217		.55
	.0225	74	
	.0236		.6
	.0240	73	
	.0250	72	
	.0256		.65
	.0260	71	
	.0276		.7
	.0280	70	
	.0292	69	
	.0295		.75
	.0310	68	
1/32	.0312		.79
	.0315		.8
	.0320	67	
	.0330	66	
	.0335		.85
	.0350	65	
	.0354		.9
	.0360	64	
	.0370	63	
	.0374		.95
	.0380	62	
	.0390	61	
	.0394		1.0
	.0400	60	
	.0410	59	
	.0413		1.05
	.0420	58	
	.0430	57	
	.0433		1.1
	.0453		1.15
3/64	.0465	56	
	.0469		1.19
	.0472		1.2
	.0492		1.25
	.0512		1.3
	.0520	55	
	.0531		1.35
	.0550	54	
	.0551		1.4
	.0571		1.45
	.0591		1.5
	.0595	53	
	.0610		1.55
1/16	.0625		1.59
	.0630		1.6
	.0635	52	
	.0650		1.65
	.0669		1.7
	.0670	51	
	.0689		1.75
	.0700	50	
	.0709		1.8
	.0728		1.85

Inch	Decimal	Wire	mm
	.0730	49	
	.0748		1.9
	.0760	48	
	.0768		1.95
5/64	.0781		1.98
	.0785	47	
	.0787		2.0
	.0807		2.05
	.0810	46	
	.0820	45	
	.0827		2.1
	.0846		2.15
	.0860	44	
	.0866		2.2
	.0886		2.25
	.0890	43	
	.0906		2.3
	.0925		2.35
	.0935	42	
3/32	.0938		2.38
	.0945		2.4
	.0960	41	
	.0965		2.45
	.0980	40	
	.0981		2.5
	.0995	39	
	.1015	38	
	.1024		2.6
	.1040	37	
	.1063		2.7
	.1065	36	
	.1083		2.75
7/64	.1094		2.77
	.1100	35	
	.1102		2.8
	.1110	34	
	.1130	33	
	.1142		2.9
	.1160	32	
	.1181		3.0
	.1200	31	
	.1220		3.1
1/8	.1250		3.17
	.1260		3.2
	.1280		3.25
	.1285	30	
	.1299		3.3
	.1339		3.4
	.1360	29	
	.1378		3.5
	.1405	28	
9/64	.1406		3.57
	.1417		3.6
	.1440	27	
	.1457		3.7
	.1470	26	
	.1476		3.75
	.1495	25	
	.1496		3.8
	.1520	24	
	.1535		3.9
	.1540	23	
5/32	.1562		3.96
	.1570	22	
	.1575		4.0
	.1590	21	
	.1610	20	

Inch	Decimal	Wire & Letter	mm
	.1614		4.1
	.1654		4.2
	.1660	19	
	.1673		4.25
	.1693		4.3
	.1695	18	
11/64	.1719		4.36
	.1730	17	
	.1732		4.4
	.1770	16	
	.1772		4.5
	.1800	15	
	.1811		4.6
	.1820	14	
	.1850	13	
	.1850		4.7
	.1870		4.75
3/16	.1875		4.76
	.1890		4.8
	.1890	12	
	.1910	11	
	.1929		4.9
	.1935	10	
	.1960	9	
	.1969		5.0
	.1990	8	
	.2008		5.1
	.2010	7	
13/64	.2031		5.16
	.2040	6	
	.2047		5.2
	.2055	5	
	.2067		5.25
	.2087		5.3
	.2090	4	
	.2126		5.4
	.2130	3	
	.2165		5.5
7/32	.2188		5.55
	.2205		5.6
	.2210	2	
	.2244		5.7
	.2264		5.75
	.2280	1	
	.2283		5.8
	.2323		5.9
	.2340	A	
15/64	.2344		5.95
	.2362		6.0
	.2380	B	
	.2402		6.1
	.2420	C	
	.2441		6.2
	.2460	D	
	.2461		6.25
	.2480		6.3
1/4	.2500	E	6.35
	.2520		6.
	.2559		6.5
	.2570	F	
	.2598		6.6
	.2610	G	
	.2638		6.7
17/64	.2656		6.74
	.2657		6.75
	.2660	H	
	.2677		6.8

Inch	Decimal	Letter	mm
	.2717		6.9
	.2720	I	
	.2756		7.0
	.2770	J	
	.2795		7.1
	.2810	K	
9/32	.2812		7.14
	.2835		7.2
	.2854		7.25
	.2874		7.3
	.2900	L	
	.2913		7.4
	.2950	M	
	.2953		7.5
19/64	.2969		7.54
	.2992		7.6
	.3020	N	
	.3031		7.7
	.3051		7.75
	.3071		7.8
	.3110		7.9
5/16	.3125		7.93
	.3150		8.0
	.3160	O	
	.3189		8.1
	.3228		8.2
	.3230	P	
	.3248		8.25
	.3268		8.3
21/64	.3281		8.33
	.3307		8.4
	.3320	Q	
	.3346		8.5
	.3386		8.6
	.3390	R	
	.3425		8.7
11/32	.3438		8.73
	.3445		8.75
	.3465		8.8
	.3480	S	
	.3504		8.9
	.3543		9.0
	.3580	T	
	.3583		9.1
23/64	.3594		9.12
	.3622		9.2
	.3642		9.25
	.3661		9.3
	.3680	U	
	.3701		9.4
	.3740		9.5
3/8	.3750		9.52
	.3770	V	
	.3780		9.6
	.3819		9.7
	.3839		9.75
	.3858		9.8
	.3860	W	
	.3898		9.9
25/64	.3906		9.92
	.3937		10.0
	.3970	X	
	.4040	Y	
13/32	.4062		10.31
	.4130	Z	
	.4134		10.5
27/64	.4219		10.71

Inch	Decimal	mm
	.4331	11.0
7/16	.4375	11.11
	.4528	11.5
29/64	.4531	11.51
15/32	.4688	11.90
	.4724	12.0
31/64	.4844	12.30
	.4921	12.5
1/2	.5000	12.70
	.5118	13.0
33/64	.5156	13.09
17/32	.5312	13.49
	.5315	13.5
35/64	.5469	13.89
	.5512	14.0
9/16	.5625	14.28
	.5709	14.5
37/64	.5781	14.68
	.5906	15.0
19/32	.5938	15.08
39/64	.6094	15.47
	.6102	15.5
5/8	.6250	15.87
	.6299	16.0
41/64	.6406	16.27
	.6496	16.5
21/32	.6562	16.66
	.6693	17.0
43/64	.6719	17.06
11/16	.6875	17.46
	.6890	17.5
45/64	.7031	17.85
	.7087	18.0
23/32	.7188	18.25
	.7283	18.5
47/64	.7344	18.65
	.7480	19.0
3/4	.7500	19.05
49/64	.7656	19.44
	.7677	19.5
25/32	.7812	19.84
	.7874	20.0
51/64	.7969	20.24
	.8071	20.5
13/16	.8125	20.63
	.8268	21.0
53/64	.8281	21.03
27/32	.8438	21.43
	.8465	21.5
55/64	.8594	21.82
	.8661	22.0
7/8	.8750	22.22
	.8858	22.5
57/64	.8906	22.62
	.9055	23.0
29/32	.9062	23.01
59/64	.9219	23.41
	.9252	23.5
15/16	.9375	23.81
	.9449	24.0
61/64	.9531	24.2
	.9646	24.5
31/32	.9688	24.6
	.9843	25.0
63/64	.9844	25.0
1	1.0000	25.4

AIR/FUEL RATIO: The ratio of air to gasoline by weight in the fuel mixture drawn into the engine.

AIR INJECTION: One method of reducing harmful exhaust emissions by injecting air into each of the exhaust ports of an engine. The fresh air entering the hot exhaust manifold causes any remaining fuel to be burned before it can exit the tailpipe.

ALTERNATOR: A device used for converting mechanical energy into electrical energy.

AMMETER: An instrument, calibrated in amperes, used to measure the flow of an electrical current in a circuit. Ammeters are always connected in series with the circuit being tested.

AMPERE: The rate of flow of electrical current present when one volt of electrical pressure is applied against one ohm of electrical resistance.

ANALOG COMPUTER: Any microprocessor that uses similar (analogous) electrical signals to make its calculations.

ARMATURE: A laminated, soft iron core wrapped by a wire that converts electrical energy to mechanical energy as in a motor or relay. When rotated in a magnetic field, it changes mechanical energy into electrical energy as in a generator.

ATMOSPHERIC PRESSURE: The pressure on the Earth's surface caused by the weight of the air in the atmosphere. At sea level, this pressure is 14.7 psi at 32°F (101 kPa at 0°C).

ATOMIZATION: The breaking down of a liquid into a fine mist that can be suspended in air.

AXIAL PLAY: Movement parallel to a shaft or bearing bore.

BACKFIRE: The sudden combustion of gases in the intake or exhaust system that results in a loud explosion.

BACKLASH: The clearance or play between two parts, such as meshed gears.

BACKPRESSURE: Restrictions in the exhaust system that slow the exit of exhaust gases from the combustion chamber.

BAKELITE: A heat resistant, plastic insulator material commonly used in printed circuit boards and transistorized components.

BALL BEARING: A bearing made up of hardened inner and outer races between which hardened steel ball roll.

BALLAST RESISTOR: A resistor in the primary ignition circuit that lowers voltage after the engine is started to reduce wear on ignition components.

BEARING: A friction reducing, supportive device usually located between a stationary part and a moving part.

BIMETAL TEMPERATURE SENSOR: Any sensor or switch made of two dissimilar types of metal that bend when heated or cooled due to the different expansion rates of the alloys. These types of sensors usually function as an on/off switch.

BLOWBY: Combustion gases, composed of water vapor and unburned fuel, that leak past the piston rings into the crankcase during normal engine operation. These gases are removed by the PCV system to prevent the buildup of harmful acids in the crankcase.

BRAKE PAD: A brake shoe and lining assembly used with disc brakes.

BRAKE SHOE: The backing for the brake lining. The term is, however, usually applied to the assembly of the brake backing and lining.

BUSHING: A liner, usually removable, for a bearing; an anti-friction liner used in place of a bearing.

BYPASS: System used to bypass ballast resistor during engine cranking to increase voltage supplied to the coil.

CALIPER: A hydraulically activated device in a disc brake system, which is mounted straddling the brake rotor (disc). The caliper contains at least one piston and two brake pads. Hydraulic pressure on the piston(s) forces the pads against the rotor.

CAMSHAFT: A shaft in the engine on which are the lobes (cams) which operate the valves. The camshaft is driven by the crankshaft, via a belt, chain or gears, at one half the crankshaft speed.

CAPACITOR: A device which stores an electrical charge.

CARBON MONOXIDE (CO): a colorless, odorless gas given off as a normal byproduct of combustion. It is poisonous and extremely dangerous in confined areas, building up slowly to toxic levels without warning if adequate ventilation is not available.

CARBURETOR: A device, usually mounted on the intake manifold of an engine, which mixes the air and fuel in the proper proportion to allow even combustion.

CATALYTIC CONVERTER: A device installed in the exhaust system, like a muffler, that converts harmful byproducts of combustion into carbon dioxide and water vapor by means of a heat-producing chemical reaction.

CENTRIFUGAL ADVANCE: A mechanical method of advancing the spark timing by using flyweights in the distributor that react to centrifugal force generated by the distributor shaft rotation.

CHECK VALVE: Any one-way valve installed to permit the flow of air, fuel or vacuum in one direction only.

CHOKE: A device, usually a moveable valve, placed in the intake path of a carburetor to restrict the flow of air.

CIRCUIT: Any unbroken path through which an electrical current can flow. Also used to describe fuel flow in some instances.

CIRCUIT BREAKER: A switch which protects an electrical circuit from overload by opening the circuit when the current flow exceeds a predetermined level. Some circuit breakers must be reset manually, while other reset automatically

COIL (IGNITION): A transformer in the ignition circuit which steps of the voltage provided to the spark plugs.

COMBINATION MANIFOLD: An assembly which includes both the intake and exhaust manifolds in one casting.

COMBINATION VALVE: A device used in some fuel systems that routes fuel vapors to a charcoal storage canister instead of venting

them into the atmosphere. The valve relieves fuel tank pressure and allows fresh air into the tank as fuel level drops to prevent a vapor lock situation.

COMPRESSION RATIO: The comparison of the total volume of the cylinder and combustion chamber with the piston at BDC and the piston at TDC.

CONDENSER: 1. An electrical device which acts to store an electrical charge, preventing voltage surges.
2. A radiator-like device in the air conditioning system in which refrigerant gas condenses into a liquid, giving off heat.

CONDUCTOR: Any material through which an electrical current can be transmitted easily.

CONTINUITY: Continuous or complete circuit. Can be checked with an ohmmeter.

COUNTERSHAFT: An intermediate shaft which is rotated by a mainshaft and transmits, in turn, that rotation to a working part.

CRANKCASE: The lower part of an engine in which the crankshaft and related parts operate.

CRANKSHAFT: The main driving shaft of an engine which receives reciprocating motion from the pistons and converts it to rotary motion.

CYLINDER: In an engine, the round hole in the engine block in which the piston(s) ride.

CYLINDER BLOCK: The main structural member of an engine in which is found the cylinders, crankshaft and other principal parts.

CYLINDER HEAD: The detachable portion of the engine, fastened, usually, to the top of the cylinder block, containing all or most of the combustion chambers. On overhead valve engines, it contains the valves and their operating parts. On overhead cam engines, it contains the camshaft as well.

DEAD CENTER: The extreme top or bottom of the piston stroke.

DETONATION: An unwanted explosion of the air fuel mixture in the combustion chamber caused by excess heat and compression, advanced timing, or an overly lean mixture. Also referred to as "ping".

DIAPHRAGM: A thin, flexible wall separating two cavities, such as in a vacuum advance unit.

DIESELING: A condition in which hot spots in the combustion chamber cause the engine to run on after the key is turned off.

DIFFERENTIAL: A geared assembly which allows the transmission of motion between drive axles, giving one axle the ability to turn faster than the other.

DIODE: An electrical device that will allow current to flow in one direction only.

DISC BRAKE: A hydraulic braking assembly consisting of a brake disc, or rotor, mounted on an axle, and a caliper assembly containing, usually two brake pads which are activated by hydraulic pressure. The pads are forced against the sides of the disc, creating friction which slows the vehicle.

DISTRIBUTOR: A mechanically driven device on an engine which is responsible for electrically firing the spark plug at a predetermined point of the piston stroke.

DOWEL PIN: A pin, inserted in mating holes in two different parts allowing those parts to maintain a fixed relationship.

DRUM BRAKE: A braking system which consists of two brake shoes and one or two wheel cylinders, mounted on a fixed backing plate, and a brake drum, mounted on an axle, which revolves around the assembly. Hydraulic action applied to the wheel cylinders forces the shoes outward against the drum, creating friction and slowing the vehicle.

DWELL: The rate, measured in degrees of shaft rotation, at which an electrical circuit cycles on and off.

ELECTRONIC CONTROL UNIT (ECU): Ignition module, module, amplifier or igniter. See Module for definition.

ELECTRONIC IGNITION: A system in which the timing and firing of the spark plugs is controlled by an electronic control unit, usually called a module. These systems have not points or condenser.

ENDPLAY: The measured amount of axial movement in a shaft.

ENGINE: A device that converts heat into mechanical energy.

EXHAUST MANIFOLD: A set of cast passages or pipes which conduct exhaust gases from the engine.

FEELER GAUGE: A blade, usually metal, of precisely predetermined thickness, used to measure the clearance between two parts. These blades usually are available in sets of assorted thicknesses.

F-Head: An engine configuration in which the intake valves are in the cylinder head, while the camshaft and exhaust valves are located in the cylinder block. The camshaft operates the intake valves via lifters and pushrods, while it operates the exhaust valves directly.

FIRING ORDER: The order in which combustion occurs in the cylinders of an engine. Also the order in which spark is distributed to the plugs by the distributor.

FLATHEAD: An engine configuration in which the camshaft and all the valves are located in the cylinder block.

FLOODING: The presence of too much fuel in the intake manifold and combustion chamber which prevents the air/fuel mixture from firing, thereby causing a no-start situation.

FLYWHEEL: A disc shaped part bolted to the rear end of the crankshaft. Around the outer perimeter is affixed the ring gear. The starter drive engages the ring gear, turning the flywheel, which rotates the crankshaft, imparting the initial starting motion to the engine.

FOOT POUND (ft.lb. or sometimes, ft. lbs.): The amount of energy or work needed to raise an item weighing one pound, a distance of one foot.

FUSE: A protective device in a circuit which prevents circuit overload by breaking the circuit when a specific amperage is present. The device is constructed around a strip or wire of a lower amperage rating than the circuit it is designed to protect. When an amperage higher than that stamped on the fuse is present in the circuit, the strip or wire melts, opening the circuit.

GEAR RATIO: The ratio between the number of teeth on meshing gears.

GENERATOR: A device which converts mechanical energy into electrical energy.

HEAT RANGE: The measure of a spark plug's ability to dissipate heat from its firing end. The higher the heat range, the hotter the plug fires.

HUB: The center part of a wheel or gear.

HYDROCARBON (HC): Any chemical compound made up of hydrogen and carbon. A major pollutant formed by the engine as a byproduct of combustion.

HYDROMETER: An instrument used to measure the specific gravity of a solution.

INCH POUND (in.lb. or sometimes, in. lbs.): One twelfth of a foot pound.

INDUCTION: A means of transferring electrical energy in the form of a magnetic field. Principle used in the ignition coil to increase voltage.

INJECTION PUMP: A device, usually mechanically operated, which meters and delivers fuel under pressure to the fuel injector.

INJECTOR: A device which receives metered fuel under relatively low pressure and is activated to inject the fuel into the engine under relatively high pressure at a predetermined time.

INPUT SHAFT: The shaft to which torque is applied, usually carrying the driving gear or gears.

INTAKE MANIFOLD: A casting of passages or pipes used to conduct air or a fuel/air mixture to the cylinders.

JOURNAL: The bearing surface within which a shaft operates.

KEY: A small block usually fitted in a notch between a shaft and a hub to prevent slippage of the two parts.

MANIFOLD: A casting of passages or set of pipes which connect the cylinders to an inlet or outlet source.

MANIFOLD VACUUM: Low pressure in an engine intake manifold formed just below the throttle plates. Manifold vacuum is highest at idle and drops under acceleration.

MASTER CYLINDER: The primary fluid pressurizing device in a hydraulic system. In automotive use, it is found in brake and hydraulic clutch systems and is pedal activated, either directly or, in a power brake system, through the power booster.

MODULE: Electronic control unit, amplifier or igniter of solid state or integrated design which controls the current flow in the ignition primary circuit based on input from the pickup coil. When the module opens the primary circuit, the high secondary voltage is induced in the coil.

NEEDLE BEARING: A bearing which consists of a number (usually a large number) of long, thin rollers.

OHM: (Ω) The unit used to measure the resistance of conductor to electrical flow. One ohm is the amount of resistance that limits current flow to one ampere in a circuit with one volt of pressure.

OHMMETER: An instrument used for measuring the resistance, in ohms, in an electrical circuit.

OUTPUT SHAFT: The shaft which transmits torque from a device, such as a transmission.

OVERDRIVE: A gear assembly which produces more shaft revolutions than that transmitted to it.

OVERHEAD CAMSHAFT (OHC): An engine configuration in which the camshaft is mounted on top of the cylinder head and operates the valve either directly or by means of rocker arms.

OVERHEAD VALVE (OHV): An engine configuration in which all of the valves are located in the cylinder head and the camshaft is located in the cylinder block. The camshaft operates the valves via lifters and pushrods.

OXIDES OF NITROGEN (NOx): Chemical compounds of nitrogen produced as a byproduct of combustion. They combine with hydrocarbons to produce smog.

OXYGEN SENSOR: Used with the feedback system to sense the presence of oxygen in the exhaust gas and signal the computer which can reference the voltage signal to an air/fuel ratio.

PINION: The smaller of two meshing gears.

PISTON RING: An open ended ring which fits into a groove on the outer diameter of the piston. Its chief function is to form a seal between the piston and cylinder wall. Most automotive pistons have three rings: two for compression sealing; one for oil sealing.

PRELOAD: A predetermined load placed on a bearing during assembly or by adjustment.

PRIMARY CIRCUIT: Is the low voltage side of the ignition system which consists of the ignition switch, ballast resistor or resistance wire, bypass, coil, electronic control unit and pick-up coil as well as the connecting wires and harnesses.

PRESS FIT: The mating of two parts under pressure, due to the inner diameter of one being smaller than the outer diameter of the other, or vice versa; an interference fit.

RACE: The surface on the inner or outer ring of a bearing on which the balls, needles or rollers move.

REGULATOR: A device which maintains the amperage and/or voltage levels of a circuit at predetermined values.

RELAY: A switch which automatically opens and/or closes a circuit.

RESISTANCE: The opposition to the flow of current through a circuit or electrical device, and is measured in ohms. Resistance is equal to the voltage divided by the amperage.

RESISTOR: A device, usually made of wire, which offers a preset amount of resistance in an electrical circuit.

RING GEAR: The name given to a ring-shaped gear attached to a differential case, or affixed to a flywheel or as part a planetary gear set.

ROLLER BEARING: A bearing made up of hardened inner and outer races between which hardened steel rollers move.

ROTOR: 1. The disc-shaped part of a disc brake assembly, upon which the brake pads bear; also called, brake disc.
2. The device mounted atop the distributor shaft, which passes current to the distributor cap tower contacts.

SECONDARY CIRCUIT: The high voltage side of the ignition system, usually above 20,000 volts. The secondary includes the ignition coil, coil wire, distributor cap and rotor, spark plug wires and spark plugs.

SENDING UNIT: A mechanical, electrical, hydraulic or electromagnetic device which transmits information to a gauge.

SENSOR: Any device designed to measure engine operating conditions or ambient pressures and temperatures. Usually electronic in nature and designed to send a voltage signal to an on-board computer, some sensors may operate as a simple on/off switch or they may provide a variable voltage signal (like a potentiometer) as conditions or measured parameters change.

SHIM: Spacers of precise, predetermined thickness used between parts to establish a proper working relationship.

SLAVE CYLINDER: In automotive use, a device in the hydraulic clutch system which is activated by hydraulic force, disengaging the clutch.

SOLENOID: A coil used to produce a magnetic field, the effect of which is produce work.

SPARK PLUG: A device screwed into the combustion chamber of a spark ignition engine. The basic construction is a conductive core inside of a ceramic insulator, mounted in an outer conductive base. An electrical charge from the spark plug wire travels along the conductive core and jumps a preset air gap to a grounding point or points at the end of the conductive base. The resultant spark ignites the fuel/air mixture in the combustion chamber.

SPLINES: Ridges machined or cast onto the outer diameter of a shaft or inner diameter of a bore to enable parts to mate without rotation.

TACHOMETER: A device used to measure the rotary speed of an engine, shaft, gear, etc., usually in rotations per minute.

THERMOSTAT: A valve, located in the cooling system of an engine, which is closed when cold and opens gradually in response to engine heating, controlling the temperature of the coolant and rate of coolant flow.

TOP DEAD CENTER (TDC): The point at which the piston reaches the top of its travel on the compression stroke.

TORQUE: The twisting force applied to an object.

TORQUE CONVERTER: A turbine used to transmit power from a driving member to a driven member via hydraulic action, providing changes in drive ratio and torque. In automotive use, it links the driveplate at the rear of the engine to the automatic transmission.

TRANSDUCER: A device used to change a force into an electrical signal.

TRANSISTOR: A semi-conductor component which can be actuated by a small voltage to perform an electrical switching function.

TUNE-UP: A regular maintenance function, usually associated with the replacement and adjustment of parts and components in the electrical and fuel systems of a vehicle for the purpose of attaining optimum performance.

TURBOCHARGER: An exhaust driven pump which compresses intake air and forces it into the combustion chambers at higher than atmospheric pressures. The increased air pressure allows more fuel to be burned and results in increased horsepower being produced.

VACUUM ADVANCE: A device which advances the ignition timing in response to increased engine vacuum.

VACUUM GAUGE: An instrument used to measure the presence of vacuum in a chamber.

VALVE: A device which control the pressure, direction of flow or rate of flow of a liquid or gas.

VALVE CLEARANCE: The measured gap between the end of the valve stem and the rocker arm, cam lobe or follower that activates the valve.

VISCOSITY: The rating of a liquid's internal resistance to flow.

VOLTMETER: An instrument used for measuring electrical force in units called volts. Voltmeters are always connected parallel with the circuit being tested.

WHEEL CYLINDER: Found in the automotive drum brake assembly, it is a device, actuated by hydraulic pressure, which, through internal pistons, pushes the brake shoes outward against the drums.

ABBREVIATIONS AND SYMBOLS

A: Ampere

AC: Alternating current

A/C: Air conditioning

A-h: Ampere hour

AT: Automatic transmission

ATDC: After top dead center

μA: Microampere

bbl: Barrel

BDC: Bottom dead center

bhp: Brake horsepower

BTDC: Before top dead center

BTU: British thermal unit

C: Celsius (Centigrade)

CCA: Cold cranking amps

cd: Candela

cm^2: Square centimeter

cm^3, cc: Cubic centimeter

CO: Carbon monoxide

CO_2: Carbon dioxide

cu.in., in^3: Cubic inch

CV: Constant velocity

Cyl.: Cylinder

DC: Direct current

ECM: Electronic control module

EFE: Early fuel evaporation

EFI: Electronic fuel injection

EGR: Exhaust gas recirculation

Exh.: Exhaust

F: Fahrenheit

F: Farad

pF: Picofarad

μF: Microfarad

FI: Fuel injection

ft.lb., ft. lb., ft. lbs.: foot pound(s)

gal: Gallon

g: Gram

HC: Hydrocarbon

HEI: High energy ignition

HO: High output

hp: Horsepower

Hyd.: Hydraulic

Hz: Hertz

ID: Inside diameter

in.lb.; in. lb.; in. lbs: inch pound(s)

Int.: Intake

K: Kelvin

kg: Kilogram

kHz: Kilohertz

km: Kilometer

km/h: Kilometers per hour

kΩ: Kilohm

kPa: Kilopascal

kV: Kilovolt

kW: Kilowatt

l: Liter

l/s: Liters per second

m: Meter

mA: Milliampere

mg: Milligram

mHz: Megahertz

mm: Millimeter

mm^2: Square millimeter

m^3: Cubic meter

MΩ: Megohm

m/s: Meters per second

MT: Manual transmission

mV: Millivolt

μm: Micrometer

N: Newton

N-m: Newton meter

NOx: Nitrous oxide

OD: Outside diameter

OHC: Over head camshaft

OHV: Over head valve

Ω: Ohm

PCV: Positive crankcase ventilation

psi: Pounds per square inch

pts: Pints

qts: Quarts

rpm: Rotations per minute

rps: Rotations per second

R-12: A refrigerant gas (Freon)

SAE: Society of Automotive Engineers

SO$_2$: Sulfur dioxide

T: Ton

t: Megagram

TBI: Throttle Body Injection

TPS: Throttle Position Sensor

V: 1. Volt; 2. Venturi

μV: Microvolt

W: Watt

x: Infinity

‹: Less than

›: Greater than

Index